THE LIFE OF
JOSEPH ADDISON

JOSEPH ADDISON IN THE LAST YEARS OF HIS LIFE
from a portrait signed by Kneller

In the possession of the author

THE LIFE OF
JOSEPH ADDISON

PETER SMITHERS

SECOND EDITION

OXFORD
AT THE CLARENDON PRESS
1968

Oxford University Press, Ely House, London W. 1

GLASGOW NEW YORK TORONTO MELBOURNE WELLINGTON
CAPE TOWN SALISBURY IBADAN NAIROBI LUSAKA ADDIS ABABA
BOMBAY CALCUTTA MADRAS KARACHI LAHORE DACCA
KUALA LUMPUR HONG KONG TOKYO

© OXFORD UNIVERSITY PRESS 1968

FIRST EDITION 1954
SECOND EDITION 1968

PRINTED IN GREAT BRITAIN

PREFACE TO THE SECOND EDITION

In this second edition, additions and corrections have been made in the light of work published since the first edition appeared. Several scholars have kindly made suggestions for this purpose and I am grateful to them all. Professor Donald F. Bond has been most generous, and his splendid edition of the *Spectator* (Oxford, 1965) was a valuable source for changes in this revision. Professor Arthur L. Cooke's interesting research into the personality and household of Lady Warwick has prompted several important additions. I am indebted to the late Professor George Sherburn and to Professors Robert M. Schmitz and Richmond P. Bond for many helpful suggestions. Finally I am particularly obliged to Dr. James Leheny, of Washington University, St. Louis, who, at a time when I have had many distractions from scholarly pursuits, has assembled the necessary material for the amendments to this edition and has kindly seen it through the press.

P. S

The Council of Europe
Strasbourg
26 August 1966

PREFACE

THIS book is the first full-length biography of Joseph Addison. Thomas Tickell wrote an authoritative biographical preface to the first edition of Addison's *Works*, published immediately after his death. A Life of Addison containing much detailed information was published by T. Birch in volume i of the *General Dictionary*, 1733, and upon this most later writing was founded. Johnson wrote a forceful account of Addison's life and work for the *Lives of the Poets*, published in 1781. Miss Lucy Aikin published a short 'life' in 1843, in which she printed some of Addison's letters. Her work was criticized in July of the same year by Macaulay in the *Edinburgh Review*, in an 'essay' which is one of his most famous and brilliant compositions. Many other men and women have written about Addison; but in spite of the importance which his personality had acquired in the eighteenth and nineteenth centuries, no attempt was made to supply the need for a full biography. This was because of the difficulty of the subject. Addison abhorred irrelevant self-revelation by authors,[1] and was meticulous in his own avoidance thereof. Partly for this reason and partly because of his reticence in human relationships, a scholar who studied his work only eighty years after his death was forced to admit that:

> Of the manners and habits of the man who filled so large a space in the public eye and who contributed so much to the improvement of our literature and morals, it is to be lamented that little satisfactory can now be told.[2]

In 1941 Professor Walter Graham published a substantial edition of Addison's letters. Before that date the only available text of the correspondence was that of Henry Bohn which appeared in 1854–6. The surviving letters though considerable in number are lacking in material of direct

[1] *Spectator*, No. 562.
[2] N. Drake, *Essays Illustrative of the Tatler, Spectator and Guardian*, 1805, i. 425.

biographical interest. Not a single letter exchanged between Addison and his father, his wife, or his brothers is preserved, and those to friends about personal matters are few. The reticence and self-criticism which were such a remarkable feature of his character have apparently served to conceal from posterity all but the barest details of his daily life, both because he did not readily permit himself to write self-revelatory correspondence, and because he, or his widow or daughter by his instruction, was careful to destroy his papers. If there is any 'black box' containing the key to Addison's private life waiting for discovery, it has so far eluded the search.

Of the *Works* there is no definitive edition, no readily readable modern edition, and no reasonably complete early edition. They were first collected and published by Tickell in 1721, two years after Addison's death, in four volumes quarto. Baskerville produced in 1761 a somewhat similar text in an elegant format. There were many reprints and new editions. In 1854–6 Bohn published one with the letters, containing Addisoniana, notes, and much new and doubtful material. This appeared in six small ugly volumes in the diminutive light-face type of the period. Finally in 1914 A. C. Guthkelch published two volumes of *Miscellaneous Works*, but did not live to complete a larger project. There have been innumerable reprints of single works, editions of periodicals to which Addison was a contributor, and collections and selections of particular material. A tentative bibliography appears in vol. ii of the *Cambridge Bibliography of English Literature*.

The study of Addison has suffered in the past from pre-occupation with his literary work. The circle of wits in the coffee-house, their writings, their friendships, and their quarrels, which made up so large a part of the lives of many of them, are of secondary significance in Addison's career. He was and envisaged himself as an important figure in the administrative and political life of England, and he held posts for which the aristocratic and wealthy competed fiercely. So fully rounded was his view of life that literary output became a by-product, though a very important one, of a life well lived. The present work, therefore, in following as closely as possible the materials available, has laid stress upon Addison's political and administrative career. His literary achievement, by which he will always be remembered, cannot be understood except in the light of his own purposes.

Addison was a reformer in his daily actions, and his purposes are expressed in minute detail in his writings. The internal evidence which they provide, when applied to the framework of dates and facts which can be assembled from official and private documents, is the best material for his biography. It may be thought that such works as the *Spectator* have been given undue weight by the present writer as evidence of Addison's views both before and after the time of their publication. But the striking consistency of his life and the steadfastness with which he adhered to his opinions throughout his career, as well as the freedom with which he used material long by him, justify some latitude in this respect. The limitations of space have made it impossible to do more than sketch in the barest historical background, or to deal exhaustively with Addison's administration in Ireland and as Secretary of State in England. In the last two respects drastic pruning of the manuscript has taken place. For similar reasons all explanatory references to persons have been omitted where they would not be required by those acquainted with the period.

This book was begun in 1938, and since that date the author has received help from many scholars. It would be impossible to thank them all. But to Professor D. Nichol Smith he is deeply grateful for criticism, encouragement, and for innumerable corrections, offered with a kindness and modesty equalled only by their authority. The memory of this generous help will be a lasting source of pleasure. To the late Professor Walter Graham, to Miss Rae Blanchard, to Mr. Willard Connely, and to Professor A. L. Cooke, he must also declare a special obligation. The author also offers his thanks to the authorities of the Public Record Office, the British Museum, the Bodleian, the Quai d'Orsay, and other public collections mentioned in the footnotes for the help which he has received; and he must record a special indebtedness to the Duke of Marlborough for access to the collection of manuscripts at Blenheim.

Looking back over fourteen years during which he has lived with Addison as his constant companion, it is not perhaps irrelevant if the author records his feelings towards his subject. They are those of deep admiration for a man who set himself a noble pattern of life in youth, and who, in spite of defects of character which he mastered, lived and died consistently therein. That such a man was possessed of literary ability of the highest order is the good fortune of posterity. That so many details of his life are apparently lost for ever is our misfortune.

P. S.

House of Commons
23 July 1952

CONTENTS

LIST OF PLATES

A NOTE UPON
REFERENCES TO SOURCES

THE number of references in the original draft of this book proved to be intolerable. Many have been struck out and the following further measures have been taken to disencumber the text, inevitably at some inconvenience to those who may use it:

1. *The Letters of Joseph Addison*, ed. Walter Graham, Oxford, Clarendon Press, 1941. Quotations from and references to this work are so abundant and so easy to locate that no reference is given.

2. *The Correspondence of Richard Steele*, ed. Rae Blanchard, Oxford University Press, 1941. The foregoing principle has been applied to quotations from this source.

3. Quotations from the *Spectator* are taken from Donald F. Bond's edition (Oxford, 1965) and quotations from other periodicals are taken from the original folio sheets. A. C. Guthkelch's *Miscellaneous Works of Joseph Addison* (London, 1914) is the source for all other works except the *Travels*, for which the first edition is used.

4. Quotations stated to be from Johnson or Macaulay and given without reference are from Johnson's 'Life' of Addison in the *Lives of the Poets* and Macaulay's 'Life and Writings of Addison' in the *Edinburgh Review* of July 1843, published in his *Miscellaneous Works*.

5. Information about proceedings in Parliament given without reference is from the *Journals* of the House of Commons or of the Irish House of Commons, or the House of Lords, all of which are printed chronologically with full indexes.

6. In Chapter III quotations without reference, which are not from the Addison correspondence, are from the appropriate portion of Addison's *Remarks upon Several Parts of Italy &c.*, where they are easily located. In Chapters VI and VII quotations without reference from Swift are from the *Journal to Stella*.

ABBREVIATIONS

USED IN REFERENCES

S.P.	State Papers at the Public Record Office.
S.O.	Signet Office Papers at the Public Record Office.
C.O.	Colonial Papers at the Public Record Office.
P.C.	Privy Council Papers at the Public Record Office.
Blanchard	Miss Rae Blanchard's edition of the *Correspondence of Steele*.
B.M.	British Museum.
Sherburn	George Sherburn's edition of the *Correspondence of Alexander Pope*.
Williams	Harold Williams's edition of the *Correspondence of Jonathan Swift*.
D.N.B.	*Dictionary of National Biography*.
Graham	Walter Graham's edition of the *Letters of Addison*.
H.M.C.	Reports of the Historical Manuscripts Commission.
T.	the *Tatler*.
S.	the *Spectator*.
G.	the *Guardian*.
F.	the *Freeholder*.
Bohn	Bohn's edition of Addison's *Works*, 6 vols., 8vo, 1854–6.
Spence	*Anecdotes, Observations and Characters of Books and Men by the Rev. Joseph Spence*, ed. S. W. Singer, 1820.

I

A SON OF THE CHURCH
1672–1687

JOSEPH ADDISON was born in the remote Wiltshire hamlet of Milston, a cluster of houses set about a diminutive
medieval church in the muddy bottom of the upper Avon
valley. It was May Day of the year 1672. Salisbury Plain
rolled inhospitably to east and west, and through the centuries the Wiltshire folk had availed themselves of the shelter
provided by the river valley, a narrow fold in the chalk, to
maintain a string of waterlogged settlements with uncouth
Saxon names: Enford, Longstreet, Fittleton, Netheravon,
Figheldean, Ablington, Brigmerston, Milston, Durrington,
and the small country town of Amesbury. The Avon itself
in these upper reaches was little more than a brook, and in
many places the valley was less than half a mile wide; but
the flat bottom-lands when channelled and drained provided
good water-meadows. Several of the villages were built upon
the nearest firm ground to these meadows, Milston church
standing a stone's throw from reclaimed marsh-land and
hardly four feet above it. Fifty yards behind, on ground
not much higher, stood a substantial thatched cottage dignified with the name of 'Rectory'. Lancelot Addison was
the newly installed rector and here it was that his eldest
son Joseph was born. In the church on the verge of the
water-meadows his father christened him, and this remote
valley was his home during those early years which the
psychologists assure us are of decisive importance in the
life of a man.

The Addison family was not deeply rooted in Wiltshire,
nor was the rector a country parson whose world was
limited to the bucolic affairs of his parish. Lancelot Addison
was a creature of passage, resting and writing in that tran-
quil valley during an interlude in a life spent in the dangerous
places of dangerous times. The family was of Westmorland

stock, and there had been Addisons on record in that county since the reign of King Henry III, as there still are today. Lancelot was a son of the parsonage at Maltismeaburn. He passed from Appleby Grammar School to The Queen's College at Oxford, a foundation traditionally associated with the north country. A man of marked ability at the university, he was chosen in the Commonwealth year 1657 to deliver a speech as *terrae filius*. He made use of this occasion of academic pantomime to display the impetuousness which marred a good brain, warm heart, and courageous character. It was customary for a *terrae filius* to exercise some licence in learned jests at the expense of the authorities of Church, State, and University; but Lancelot was compelled to retract his words publicly in supplicant posture. After leaving Oxford he found employment ministering privately to Royalist families in Sussex while waiting for better times. His brother John had emigrated to Maryland where he married a widow and prospered; but Lancelot had his reward at the Restoration of 1660 when the indiscretions which had sent him into semi-retirement recommended him for promotion.

Joseph Williamson, a distant relative and friend at The Queen's College, was an important official in the restored royal administration, and it was probably at his suggestion that Lancelot Addison was offered the chaplaincy of the British garrison at Dunkirk. Simultaneously he was offered the prospect of a 'living'. It was characteristic of Lancelot that he chose adventure and insecurity at Dunkirk in preference to the broad path of ecclesiastical preferment; and that he did not repent his action. When in the year 1662 the royal government sold the fortress back to France, he accompanied the Earl of Teviot, its governor, to his new command in the remote outpost of Tangier. During his period of residence there Lancelot Addison exercised an observant and humane mind. The customs and faith of Moor and Jew were the objects of his minute study, and garrison life was rendered tolerable and indeed enjoyable to one who was a lover of mankind without regard to differences of race or religion. In the year 1670 the chaplain returned to England on leave. A tradition survives that he was superseded in his post against his will during this absence. But it seems probable that there was a more gratifying reason for Lancelot's failure to return to Barbary; he had become engaged and married, and knew that Tangier was no place to take a bride or in which to raise a family.

Lancelot Addison and Jane Gulston settled down in a 'living' for a spell of pastoral duties. Jane's brother, William Gulston, was a minor figure of promise in the Church, and was amongst those who, like Lancelot, had benefited by the Restoration. In 1663 he had been appointed to the rectory of Milston, a benefice which had perhaps been held in plurality with some other cure, by Frederick Hyde the patron of the 'living'. Amongst the fragments of the Milston registers which are preserved, William Gulston is not now on record as having discharged any pastoral duties. When Lancelot married he was appointed by the same patron to succeed his brother-in-law in the Milston 'living', and was thus provided with a home and an income of about £120 per annum.[1] But the pastoral duties must have been exceptionally light, and a man of scholarly tastes would have opportunities for study.

The new incumbent lost little time in demonstrating his continued interest in national politics and religion. In 1670, soon after taking up his duties, Rector Addison, with memories of Tangier still fresh in his mind, raised a collection in Milston for redeeming 'the English that are Captives in Barbary'.[2] In the following year he published a readable and observant work *West Barbary, or a Short Narrative of the Revolutions of the Kingdoms of Fez and Morocco*. The book was dedicated to Joseph Williamson, Esquire, who was a delegate of the Sheldonian Press, and may have sponsored the publication of his friend's work 'in Oxford at the Theater'. The title-page bore the proud announcement that the author was 'a Chaplain in Ordinary to His Majesty', and thus a man marked for preferment. Along with the first book came the first child, Jane, who was baptised in Milston church on 23 April but died in infancy. The second child was born on 1 May 1672, and was named Joseph at his christening, no

[1] Sir R. C. Hoare, *Hist. of Modern Wiltshire, Vale of Avon*, p. 40.
[2] Milston Parish Registers.

doubt in compliment to the friend who had done much to
forward the family fortunes. Birch, an early authority,
states that Joseph was christened on the day of his birth
because he was expected to die; and a close friend testified
that throughout life his pulse was uneven.[1] The vellum page
of the Milston register which would have borne witness to
the date of the christening had been cut from the book
before Johnson's time. But if the physical portents which
attended young Joseph's entry into the world were menacing, the ecclesiastical ones were certainly propitious. Not
only was his father a clergyman of the Church of England,
but so also were both of his male grandparents. Nor was his
father in any sense an ordinary parson; he was a good
scholar, a prolific writer, an accomplished traveller, and a
courageous and ambitious man of the world with powerful
friends. It might have been assumed in the family circle
that the eldest son would enter the Church.

During the years which followed Joseph's birth, the
rectory at Milston saw an outpouring of books and children
which would have done honour to a more dignified establishment. Gulston Addison was born in 1673, and was
named for his uncle, the previous rector. In 1674 there
followed *A seasonable Discourse of Catechizing*, dedicated by
the author to the bishop of his diocese with the awkward
grace of one not born to be a courtier. In the same year came
a sister, Dorothy. In 1675 Jane Addison enjoyed a respite
from childbirth, but Lancelot published *The Present State of
the Jews, more particularly relating to those in Barbary*, dedicated
to Sir Joseph Williamson, and he proceeded to the degrees
of Bachelor and Doctor of Divinity. He had also become a
prebendary of Salisbury Cathedral, an event which may have
been connected with the dedication of the *Seasonable Discourse* in the year previous. Sister Anne was born in 1676;
and the year ˙677 saw the publication of *A Modest Plea for
the Clergy*, a spirited book which amongst its other merits
quoted 'the excellent Chaucer' whose works were therefore
probably upon the Milston bookshelf. The year following

[1] Tickell, who was close to Addison in later years, in his Preface to
Addison's *Works*. Steele said he never knew this. For Addison's early life
see *A General Dictionary*, 1734, ed. Birch.

produced *The First State of Muhammedanism* and there also began a series of second editions and reprints. Meanwhile Jane's brother had been progressing in the hierarchy and in 1679 was appointed to the bishopric of Bristol. In 1680 the last child of the rectory was born, a boy christened Lancelot. On 25 March of the same year sister Anne died,[1] and in 1681 there appeared *The Moores Baffled, being a Discourse concerning Tangier*, a political tract advocating the appointment of a strong governor and the completion of the fortifications.

Birch states that Joseph began his schooling under the Reverend Thomas Naish at Amesbury and that later he boarded and studied with Mr. Taylor, master of the Grammar School in Castle Street, Salisbury. He was a sensitive and reticent child. Macaulay doubted a story current in the neighbourhood a century later which would hardly be worthy of attention were it not perfectly in harmony with Addison's character in later years. After the commission of some trivial misdeed the child was so overcome with shame that he fled to the countryside and was with difficulty recovered by his parents. The same sensitiveness caused the haunting of Squire Mompesson's house at Tidworth to make so deep an impression upon his mind that it revived as a literary project many years later. Upon such a nature the events of daily life struck forcibly, and something of the rhythm and tranquillity of the yearly cycle in the Avon valley grew into the character of the man who in maturity pondered upon valleys spiritual:

> Where peaceful rivers, soft and slow,
> Amid the verdant landscape flow.[2]

The calamity which put an end to this period of childhood came with dramatic and terrible suddenness, and remained a warning of the frailty of human plans. *The Moores Baffled* was the last publication to come from the little thatched rectory at Milston, for in 1681 it was burned to the ground.

---

[1] T. Harwood, *Lichfield*, pp. 94-99, gives the date as 25 Mar. 1680, and describes a tombstone in the choir of Lichfield Cathedral carrying it and describing her father as dean, a position which he did not then occupy. The stone has disappeared in repaving, and no entry of the burial is to be found.

[2] Paraphrase of the 23rd Psalm; *S.* 441.

The atmosphere prevailing at the rectory had been one of literary output and constant steps towards preferment. It was in the year 1683 that preferment came. Partly in recognition of services to the Government at Dunkirk and at Tangier, partly as solace for losses in the rectory fire, partly to mark real ability and also loyalty to Church and State, and perhaps partly also by the influence of his friend Secretary Williamson, Lancelot Addison was appointed Dean of Lichfield, while continuing to hold the rectory of Milston and to enjoy the small revenues which attached thereto. The royal mandate was dated from Windsor on 25 May 1683;[1] on 8 June the new dean was elected, confirmed, and installed in his cathedral;[2] and he presided at the annual formal chapter on 1 October. Three days later he took the oaths of supremacy and allegiance, and of a Justice of the Peace, thus completing the formalities of his installation.

Such preferment carried the Addison family to the relatively bustling atmosphere of a provincial capital, with an admirable school, which Joseph attended, nine minutes walk from the deanery. Lichfield Grammar School was an ancient foundation under the direction of an eminent headmaster, Robert Shaw. Housed in a handsome new building in St. John Street, it accorded well with the antique splendour of the cathedral, with the relative stateliness of the deanery and with the dignified avenue running in front thereof. From this school there proceeded a number of famous men. Gregory King had been educated there, and, superb trophy for any foundation, Samuel Johnson was to follow. In his own generation Joseph had been preceded there by George Smalridge, destined to fame at Oxford and in the Church, and to be his lifelong friend; but all that is preserved of his school record is a story heard by Johnson when a boy, which credits him with organizing an end-of-term 'rag'.

Joseph cannot have failed to be impressed with his new surroundings. The deanery stood on the north side of the Gothic red sandstone cathedral, facing a splendid perpendicular window, since mutilated, in the transept fifty

<hr/>

[1] *Lichfield Cathedral Acta Capitularia*, vii. 69. I am indebted to Canon J. E. W. Wallis for access to this document.   [2] Ibid., f. 70.

yards away. 'Dean's Walk', a fine avenue of trees, extended to right and left. The deanery boasted a great parlour, a study, a little parlour, six principal 'chambers' besides those of the staff, the usual offices, and a buttery, cellar, brew-house, coach house, and stables.[1] Beside it stood the recently completed and classically elegant Bishop's Palace of fine grey stone. The brilliant contrast of gothic and classical styles, of elaborate fancy and rational severity, impressed itself on young Joseph's mind and upon it he founded a principle of taste which developed throughout life. It must also have been about the age of eleven and upon arriving in these relatively splendid surroundings, that he became aware of the significance of his father's advancement in ecclesiastical dignity and consequently of his own improved prospects. With the deanery went the prebends of Brewood and Adbaston, and in 1684 there was added to Lancelot's benefices the arch-deaconry of Coventry, to be held *in commendam* with Lichfield and Milston. But if these appointments improved the finances of the Addison family, they were still poor and in debt. The household was large, the revenues of Milston had been small, and Lancelot Addison's humane nature was not without its irresponsible side. It appears that he left Wiltshire owing a substantial amount to Mr. Taylor for school fees, and perhaps other debts. There was now an extra burden for dilapidations at Milston. Thus the move to the dignity and increased emoluments of a deanery can have done little to benefit the family for some time to come, except to ease the task of paying off liabilities while the household lived in extremely narrow circumstances. The struggle against poverty by a man of fine intellect, with a long record of service to Church and State, was a lesson not lost upon young Joseph, who from youth included amongst the sterner virtues at his command, an extreme caution in matters of finance.

It was at this time of hard but improving fortune that Jane Addison, Joseph's mother, died,[2] as the family which she had raised was entering upon happier times; and it is likely that a moderating influence was thus removed from

[1] Will of Dr. Lancelot Addison, Birmingham Probate Registry.
[2] 30 June 1684.

the elbow of the impetuous dean. She was buried in the choir of his cathedral where her tombstone recorded that she died 'full of hope'.[1] Little is known of Mrs. Addison, nor are the works of her famous son shot through with recollection of her as with that of her husband. But if her qualities were insufficient to attract the attention of contemporaries, she evidently possessed womanly ability to fill her place in a happy if often anxious family life.

The significance of three years spent at Lichfield lay mainly in the home. Joseph was now able not merely to continue his education at a first-class school in an age when classical learning was a passport to preferment of many kinds, but also to live under the scholarly personal tuition and guidance of his father. The family at the deanery has been described for posterity by one who occasionally shared it:

I remember among all my Acquaintance but one Man whom I thought to live with his Children with Equanimity and a good Grace. He had Three Sons and One Daughter, whom he bred with all the Care imaginable in a liberal and ingenuous Way. I have often heard him say, He had the Weakness to love one much better than the other, but that he took as much Pains to correct that as any other Criminal Passion that could arise in his Mind. His Method was to make it the only Pretension in his Children to his Favour to be kind to each other; and he would tell them, That he who was the best Brother, he would reckon the best Son. This turned their Thoughts into an Emulation for the Superiority in kind and tender Affection towards each other. The Boys behaved themselves very early with a Manly Friendship; and their Sister, instead of the gross Familiarities and impertinent Freedoms in Behaviour, usual in other Houses, was always treated by them with as much complaisance as any other young Lady of their Acquaintance. It was an unspeakable Pleasure to visit or sit at a Meal in that Family. I have often seen the old Man's Heart flow at his Eyes with Joy upon Occasions which would appear indifferent to such as were Strangers to the Turn of his Mind; But a very slight Accident, wherein he saw his Children's Good-Will to one other, created in him the Godlike Pleasure of loving them, because they loved each other. This great Command of himself, in hiding his first Impulse to Partiality, at last im-

[1] T. Harwood, *Lichfield*, pp. 94-95.

proved to a steady Justice towards them; and that which at first was but an Expedient to correct his Weakness, was afterwards the Measure of his Virtue.[1]

It is evident that this disciplined affection was fully returned by the son who in later years and at the height of fame and power, wrote of 'My father . . . whom I must always Name with Honour and Gratitude . . .'.[2] It is safe to conjecture that it was during three critical years of adolescence spent in the deanery that there were confirmed in Addison's mind those singular qualities of character which marked him early amongst his contemporaries as a great man.

Lancelot Addison now held at least four offices in the Church, and he might properly aspire to send his son to the ancient foundation of the Charterhouse in the year 1686 at the age of fourteen. If Lichfield Grammar School was distinguished in a provincial sense, the Charterhouse stood forth as a national institution which received gentleman commoners and poor scholars from all parts of the kingdom. Possibly it was beneath the dignity of the dean to place his son in the latter capacity; yet it must have cost him what he could ill afford to send Joseph to London as a gentleman commoner and to provide his lodgings. But he was probably aware that his son's stay at the Charterhouse would be brief. Joseph had made such good use of his opportunities at Lichfield that he was already learned in classical poetry. The Charterhouse could only supply the extra polish of a great educational foundation, and this Joseph acquired within a year. Though delicate and diffident, he had entered life with a seriousness of purpose which matched the excellence of the opportunities opening before him. He had, it is true, been diverted from one school to another, four in all, in a manner which might have spoiled his progress; but his father had provided an indispensable thread of continuity, and in an age when excellence in the classics was greatly admired, he was able to surprise his contemporaries with critical pronouncements upon the Latin poets, delivered with wit and judgement. Thus it was that at an early age he began to command from other men that loyalty which is only accorded to those who are deeply respected. Amongst

[1] Steele, *T.* 235.   [2] *S.* 261.

Joseph's Charterhouse admirers was Richard Steele, a gifted poor scholar from Ireland, who spent his holidays at the deanery and who won the affection of the dean. Both boys were Oxford bound. Joseph at the age of fifteen was formidably armoured in character and equipped, as Macaulay put it, with 'a classical taste and a stock of learning which would have done honour to a Master of Arts'. He was, in fact, ripe for the university whither his father sent him. From this time onwards he forwarded himself by his own remarkable abilities.

II

AN OXFORD CAREER
1687–1699

LANCELOT ADDISON sent his son to his own Oxford college, The Queen's, where Joseph matriculated on 18 May 1687. If an additional reason for the choice were needed, it was that Sir Joseph Williamson was a principal benefactor of this Foundation. Fifteen was not an unusually tender age at which to proceed to the university, and Joseph had other relatives in college and a family connexion there dating back for many years. The year of his entry was a fateful one. The revolution which was now impending was to deliver the nation and the university from the threat of personal tyranny. Both at Charterhouse and at Magdalen the king carried such a threat into violent effect. He forced upon the former an unwanted inmate, and to the latter he nominated a President in violation of the Founder's statutes, and sent the Fellows who rejected him flying for refuge to the countryside. No young man tasting the realities of the world for the first time could have predicted that from the violent happenings of those years there would spring two centuries of orderly constitutional development. But Joseph was fortunate in his endowment with those qualities of tact and restraint which the age demanded. He came to Oxford determined to perfect his critical appreciation of the Latin poets and to improve his skill in the writing of verse. Versifying in the dead languages could serve him as a harmless scholarly pastime to embellish an ecclesiastical career, or could be made the advertisement for literary ability then much in demand amongst politicians.

The bursar of The Queen's College at this time was Dr. William Lancaster, familiarly known to his undergraduate body as 'smooth-boots':

> Here *Lancaster*, adorned with every grace,
> Stands chief in merit, as the chief in place;

To his lov'd name our earliest lays belong,
The theme at once, and patron of our song:
Long may he o'er his much lov'd *Queen's* preside,
Our arts encourage and our counsels guide.[1]

Thus sang a member of the college when Lancaster later became Provost. At this time he was renowned as one of the best tutors in the university. Like Dean Addison, he was a Westmorland man and a friend of Sir Joseph Williamson, who in 1676 had sent him to study in Paris with the help of a grant from the exchequer. A high churchman and a man of the world, Lancaster earned from the remorseless Hearne the description of 'old hypocritical ambitious drunken sot', an opinion belied by his conduct in refusing a bishopric in order that he might stay at Queen's to earn gratitude as a builder of the college.

The piece which is reputed to have won favourable comment from Dr. Lancaster is Addison's earliest literary production to survive, a dialogue entitled 'Tityrus et Mopsus'. It was printed in a collection of Oxford tributes to the new establishment published in 1689 as *Vota Oxoniensia pro Gulielmo Rege*, and was dated from The Queen's College. Thus early did Addison declare himself a supporter of the Government of King William. In his political opinions he had probably been much influenced by Dr. Burnet at the Charterhouse, who had resisted King James II's will during the last months of Addison's pupilage at that Foundation. The violation of Magdalen by royal tyranny had temporarily discredited the Stuart concept of monarchy in the eyes of the younger generation at Oxford, and the subsequent reinstatement of the President and Fellows under pressure of necessity had also made apparent its weakness.

It is improbable that Addison's lines struck so experienced a tutor as Lancaster with great astonishment, though he doubtless discerned in their author good scholarly abilities and remarkable traits of character.[2] But a prolonged stay at Oxford would be necessary to a young man with his eye upon a fellowship, and this was more than the Dean of

---

[1] Tickell, 'Oxford', 1706.
[2] For a discussion of this point see L. Bradner, 'The Composition and Publication of Addison's Latin Poems', *Modern Philology*, xxxv. 359.

Lichfield could afford for one of three sons. It was therefore in seeking other provision for Joseph, who was as yet unendowed, that Lancaster's support would be decisive. The moment was a fortunate one. The wealth and dignity of Magdalen College were such that her Demies might well pretend to a peculiar distinction; but the troubles of the college at the hands of King James II had both depleted her finances and also reduced the number of Demies upon the Foundation considerably below the customary thirty. In 1689, however, when it was once more possible to collect incomings, the revenues recovered fast; and accordingly it was possible to elect an unusually large number of promising young men in the famous 'Golden Election' of that year. 'Tityrus et Mopsus' was something of a scholarship performance, and the subject would appeal to the restored Fellows of the college. While at Oxford, and almost certainly at an early stage of his career there, he received 'countenance and Encouragement' from the Duke of Ormonde, then Chancellor of the University.[1] The duke had accepted a dedication of a sensational book, *Telluris Theoria Sacra*, by Dr. Burnet, the Master of the Charterhouse, in 1689. This was much admired by Addison, and it is possible that he was recommended by the Master to the duke when he went to Oxford or not long thereafter. Addison succeeded at the election on 30 July, and was admitted to Waynflete's Foundation, repeating *do fidem* upon his knees before that Dr. Hough who had been expelled and then reinstated by King James II.

Several young men destined to distinction as scholars, clerics, or minor poets were elected at the same time. Such were Richard Smallbroke from Trinity, later Bishop of Lichfield and an opponent of Whiston, Hugh Boulter, later Primate of Ireland, and Henry Sacheverell. Also born into a parson's family, Sacheverell was about two years younger than Addison. If the tradition that they shared a room at Magdalen is correct, the two young men must have appeared to be suitable companions in the eyes of the college authorities; and if gossip insinuates that Joseph paid attention to Henry's sister, there is no evidence that this was more than

[1] Graham, p. 343.

the civility which she might expect from her brother's room-mate. Magdalen carried upon the Foundation forty Fellows as well as the thirty Demies. It was the custom after the annual balancing of the college books for any surplus re-maining to be divided up amongst the society. The sur-plus varied in the latter part of the century from £500 to about £1,200, the fluctuations perhaps representing the quality of the crops. The individual shares must have been small, but Fellows and Demies had numerous privileges, such as free lodgings, which stood in lieu of income. There were also several small funds available for distribution. From the time of his entry into the college Addison was awarded part of the Higden scholarship, sharing it with four Fellows and three other Demies. Beyond such small supplements, there remained a source of income in the tuition of the dozen or more relatively well-to-do young gentleman commoners. Thus by one means or another an industrious member of the Foundation could support himself above the level of indigence. Addison might therefore now regard himself as an independent man of the academic world, no longer necessarily calling upon his father's resources which were needed for educating two younger brothers; and although the debt of the Salisbury school fees remained undischarged, Dr. Taylor might think himself rewarded for his labour by the promise of his pupil. But beyond the imme-diate prospect of financial independence, a demyship offered another substantial advantage; it gave good security for the future. A Demy who conducted himself properly and who had fair abilities might reasonably count upon proceeding to a fellowship in order of seniority. Addison could expec to comply with both these conditions.

While his tactful son was thus engaged in establishing himself upon the Foundation at Magdalen, and paying his court to the new political order, Dean Addison was once more propagating his views out of season. He had been talked of in influential circles as a candidate for a bishopric; but he made a display of anti-Revolution principles in the Convocation of 1689, an assembly whose main task was to adjust the position of the Church to the new political dis-pensation. This forthrightness relegated the dean to his deanery for the remainder of his life, and forfeited him the chaplaincy-in-ordinary which he had held under the two preceding sovereigns. Henceforth Dr. Addison spent his time in reprinting his works, in the cares of his office, and particularly in attending to the fabric of his cathedral. The course of events had now placed father and son at opposite ends of the political spectrum, but no estrangement occurred between them, nor have we any hint of friction. Yet the dean's troubles multiplied. In 1692 Bishop Lloyd, one of the seven prelates put upon trial by King James II and subsequently a principal supporter of the Revolution, was translated to Lichfield; and, not surprisingly, there began a series of quarrels between the dean and his chapter in which the bishop and his successor supported the latter, and which lasted until the dean's death. Perhaps it was as well that upon taking up his demyship at Magdalen, Joseph must have been denied that companionship with his father which had been such an important feature of his youth; for the academic year was divided into four terms each of thirteen weeks, and for the period for which records are preserved Joseph was a regular resident even in summer time.

Enough evidence survives for us to be able to form a fairly clear picture of Addison's habits of life in the university. Though conscious of ability, and by no means backward in bringing his attainments to public notice, and though ambition in him became exalted to the Roman virtue of public service, yet he was notorious for his shy and retiring nature:

The Soul, considered abstractedly from its Passions, is of a remiss and sedentary Nature, slow in its Resolves, and languishing in its Executions. The use therefore of the Passions, is to stir it up and put it upon Action. . . . As this is the End of Passions in general, so it is particularly of Ambition. . . .[1]

This later reflection was no doubt a backward glance, and a reproach to his own 'languishing' soul. But the external qualities of great personal charm and a delightfully witty manner in private conversation once the reserves were overcome, made a combination most telling in academic as in other circles. It is, however, doubtful whether even in the flush of youth the physical frame was adequate to the spirit with which it was animated. The young man with the uneven pulse had never been recorded as indulging himself in any robust activity; even as an undergraduate his wit and conversation were tempered with the grave melancholy of a *memento mori*. True, he advocated shadow boxing for scholars:

this opens the Chest, exercises the Limbs, and gives a Man all the Pleasure of Boxing, without the Blows. I could wish that several Learned Men would lay out that Time which they employ in Controversies and Disputes about nothing, in *this method* of fighting with their own Shadows. It might conduce very much to evaporate the Spleen, which makes them uneasy to the Publick as well as to themselves.[1]

But the only physical activity recorded of him at Magdalen is a fondness for strolling beneath the trees in the water walks.

According to college tradition, during part of his residence Addison lived in rooms in the north-east corner of the cloisters. The fabric, since rebuilt, then rose to three stories, and faced across the then much larger grove and down the water walks towards 'Dover Pier'. In later years a fellow Demy, Richard West, who knew Addison particularly well, used to point to his favourite seat in the walks under a large tree; and Addison has recorded for us his own recollection of conversational strolls in these surroundings:

Philander used every morning to take a walk in a neighbouring wood, that stood on the borders of the *Thames*. It was cut through by abundance of beautiful alleys, which terminating on the water, looked like so many painted views in a perspective. The banks of the river and the thickness of the shades drew into them all the birds of the country, that at Sun-rising filled the wood with such a variety of notes as made the prettiest confusion imaginable. I know in descriptions of this nature the scenes are generally supposed to grow out of the author's imagination. . . . For my own part, as I design only to fix the scene of the following Dialogue, I shall not endeavour to give it any other ornaments than those which nature has bestowed upon it. . . . *Philander* was here

[1] *S.* 115.

enjoying the cool of the morning, the dews that lay on every thing about him, and that gave the air such a freshness as is not a little agreeable in the hot part of the year . . . the Sun began to gather strength upon them, and had pierced the shelter of their walks in several places. *Philander* had no sooner done talking, but he grew sensible of the heat himself, and immediately proposed to his friends the retiring to his lodgings, and getting a thicker shade over their heads.[1]

As a Demy Addison was under the supervision of William Cradock, a Fellow of the college of some spirit, who, though elected by special mandate of King Charles II, had been temporarily deprived of his fellowship for refusing to submit to King James's nominee for the Presidency.[2] In later years there was some competition amongst those who claimed the honour of having encouraged Addison's youthful genius, one of the contestants being James Fayrer, about this time bursar of the college. Addison's reading was intensive in poetry and extensive elsewhere, in an age when universal knowledge did not seem beyond the grasp of a deeply studious man. Yet when his books were sold many years later, it was noticed with disappointment that they were but sparsely annotated.[3] Indeed for the minutiae of scholarship Addison had a contempt which sometimes spilled over upon genuine projects of learning, for example upon 'Editors, Commentators, Interpreters, Scholiasts, and Criticks; and in short, all Men of deep Learning without common Sense'.[4] It was for the dignity of a comprehensive culture that he reserved his admiration.[5]

Addison was endowed with the relish of nature which springs from a country childhood, but he was as suspicious

---

[1] *Dialogues upon the Usefulness of Ancient Medals*, Dialogue III.

[2] Cradock was probably an extreme Tory. His father's loyalty had earned the gratitude of King Charles II and his treatment by King James does not seem to have altered his principles. It is related that when in the height of fame Addison, then travelling near Cradock's rectory of Slymbridge in Gloucestershire, sent a message to his old tutor to come to meet him, this received the haughty reply that it was for the pupil to visit the tutor, as a result of which the meeting did not take place. (Carter, *Notes on Slymbridge*, p. 22.) This story, if true, and it appears to be consistent with Cradock's character, would indicate that the relationship between tutor and pupil was not of the affectionate nature which willingly overlooks offence.

[3] Sotheby Sale Cat. 27/5/1799.

[4] *T.* 158.

[5] *T.* 158.

of a devotion to detail in natural science as in scholarship. When carried to any length it outraged his sense of proportion:

> There are some Men whose Heads are so oddly turned . . . that tho they are utter Strangers to the common Occurrences of Life, they are able to discover the Sex of a Cockle, or describe the Generation of a Mite in all its circumstances. . . .[1]

This distrust of abstruse detail extended even to the Royal Society, whose Fellows he classified with 'all contemplative Tradesmen, titular Physitians . . . Templers that are not given to be contentious, and Statesmen that are out of Business'.[2] Yet the Society:

> had . . . a very good Effect, as it turned many of the greatest Genius's of that Age to the Disquisitions of natural Knowledge, who, if they had engaged in Politicks with the same Parts and Application, might have set their Country in a Flame. The Air-Pump, the Barometer, the Quadrant, and the like Inventions, were thrown out to those busy Spirits, as Tubs and Barrels are to a Whale, that he may let the Ship sail on without Disturbance while he diverts himself with those innocent Amusements.[3]

It was not for the refinements of research but for the 'majestic Simplicity of the Ancients' that Addison reserved his wholehearted admiration. He 'dreamed' 'that an old *Greek* or *Latin* Author weighed down a whole Library of Moderns',[4] and when all was said and done,'. . . of all the Diversions of Life there is none so proper . . . as . . . reading . . .'.[5] Therefore 'Of all the Species of Pedants . . . the Book-Pedant is much the most supportable; he has at least an exercised Understanding, and a Head which is full though confused'.[6] In a society which included such people, Addison took his place as a tutor in 1691. His pupils at various times included Sir John Harper, Sir James Rushout of Northwick Park near Evesham, Philip Frowde, and Hugh Parker. His own tutor left the college for the rectory of Slymbridge in 1692.[7]

It would have been surprising if Addison, who, in later

---

[1] *T.* 216.   [2] *S.* 10.   [3] *S.* 262.
[4] *S.* 463.   [5] *S.* 93.   [6] *S.* 105.
[7] Vice-President's Register, 3/11/1692 and 22/12/1692.

time, held such views upon scholarship, had wished to play his part in life wholly within the university. He was remarkably gifted, and his endowments of character matched his considerable intellectual ability; but the picture of him at Oxford is one of overmuch gravity for a very young man. He lacked the physical fibre to exercise his talents exuberantly.

Since President Hough ruled at Magdalen classical studies have ascended to their zenith of popularity and have once more been lost in all but obscurity. The criticism of the intervening period therefore seems harsh to a generation most members of which would be grateful to possess the half of Addison's classical accomplishments. Johnson said that 'his learning was not profound'. But Macaulay points out that although he had but a working knowledge of Greek and although he knew little of Greek literature or even of Latin prose, yet of the Latin poets he was perfect master:

> . . . his proficiency was such as it is hardly possible to overrate. His knowledge . . . was singularly exact and profound. He understood them thoroughly, entered into their spirit, and had the finest and most discriminating perception of all their peculiarities of style and melody; nay, he copied their manner with admirable skill, and surpassed, we think, all their British imitators who had preceded him, Buchanan and Milton alone excepted.

This mastery in what is so small a part of the learning of our own time, bulked large in the restricted academic world of which Addison became a full citizen when, together with West his immediate senior on the Foundation, he took his degree of Bachelor of Arts on 6 May 1691;[1] and it was as a Latin poet that he worked to build up his early Oxford reputation.

Meanwhile his Charterhouse friend Dick Steele had all but spent a brief university career. He entered Christ Church as a commoner and matriculated on 21 December 1689. He then set about searching for an endowment to finance his studies. Steele called upon Dr. Hough to seek his support

---

[1] The Vice-President's Register gives the presentation under an entry made the following day.

for a Christ Church studentship, which he failed to obtain. He then aimed elsewhere and hit the mark, transferring to Merton in August 1691 upon the offer of a 'Postmaster-ship'. The move halved his distance from Addison at Magdalen, but there is no surviving memorial of an Oxford friendship between the two men, and Steele went down from the university in March 1692 without distinction, and without a degree.[1]

Joseph was now reading the philosophers sufficiently to include an impatient glance at Aristotle, a sanguine estimate of the Cartesians, and approval of the mechanical experiments of Boyle and of the scientific spirit. At the Encaenia on 7 July 1693 he and his Magdalen colleagues, Smallbroke and Taylor, delivered Latin orations on the old and the new orders of thought. His speech, 'Nova philosophia veteri praeferenda est', was translated by Rawlinson and published posthumously by Curll in a miscellany volume with an advertisement puff announcing that:

Mr. Addison's speech at Oxford 1692 [sic] in Defence of the New Philosophy, is worth more than the price of the whole volume which is but 6s.[2]

It reads like the superficially confident essay of one who has taken the opinion of older men on trust; and the author evidently did not think highly of this piece in retrospect, for it was not included in his collected works. But when it appeared under his name it was reprinted at least five times in a century, in similar fashion to *A Discourse on Ancient and Modern Learning*, which when posthumously attributed to Addison ran through nine printings in the same period.[3]

Meanwhile he persevered in Latin poetry. In 1690 he had followed his 'Tityrus et Mopsus' with a set of verses addressed to the king on his victorious return from Ireland,

---

[1] Convivial company may not have been entirely excluded from Addison's Oxford career, and a report is preserved that a Mr. Addison was arrested by the Proctors, on 11 May 1691 (B.M. Add. MS. Lansd. 697), for some cause unknown.

[2] Advertised in *A Compleat Key to the Dunciad*, 1728. The translation was first published in *The Altar of Love*. 1727.

[3] *B.M. Catalogue of Printed Books.*

published in a volume from the Sheldonian Press entitled *Academiae Oxoniensis Gratulatio pro exoptato serenissimi Regis Gulielmi ex Hibernia reditu.* In later years Addison was not proud of this poem, and, like its predecessor, it was not republished in his collected works. Besides, such verses were rarefied productions which would not carry fame much beyond university circles, the more erudite of the clergy, and some amateurs of learning. Yet an increasing number of gentlemen and citizens who had little Latin desired to read the classics, and at Oxford in Addison's day publishers were in eager search of competent translators.

On 14 February 1693, when Addison took his Master's degree, Dryden was the dean of this school of literary art as of all English letters. No new writer had arisen who could provide even a foil for his genius. It is therefore not surprising that a young Latin poet at Magdalen, anxious to try his hand at translation, should seek to reach the notice of 'Mr. Bayes'. He began by addressing Dryden in verse:

> How long, great Poet, shall thy sacred Lays
> Provoke our Wonder, and transcend our Praise?
> Can neither injuries of Time, nor Age,
> Damp thy Poetick Heat, and quench thy Rage?

In the lines 'To Mr. Dryden' Addison went on to hint sympathy for the poet's penury and the criticism of high places which such sympathy implied.[1] The poem compliments the elder man upon his translations: indeed a casual reader might gain the impression that it was addressed to one whose principal claim to fame was that of a translator. Dryden's translations, said Addison, heightened Virgil's majesty and would have astonished Horace; they rendered Persius's style smoother and clearer, and sharpened the satire of Juvenal, in fact:

> Thy Copy casts a fairer Light on all,
> And still out-shines the bright Original.

[1] Dryden's second son, John, admitted to Magdalen under pressure from King James II, was removed by the Visitor after the Revolution.

This ecstasy led up to a passage on the translation of Ovid which Dryden then had in hand:

> O mayst thou still the noble Task prolong,
> Nor Age, nor Sickness interrupt thy song:
>
> .   .   .   .   .
>
> Then will thy *Ovid*, thus transform'd, reveal
> A Nobler Change than he himself can tell.

How far Addison's flattery succeeded appeared in the event. The poem 'To Mr. Dryden' dated from Magdalen on 2 June 1693 was printed in *Examen Poeticum*: *being the Third Part of Miscellany Poems*, of which Dryden himself was the editor. With Addison's piece he included a contribution from another of his admirers, John Dennis, fifteen years Addison's senior. Such recognition stamped the contributors with approval, and was a triumph for any young poet. Next year Addison made a serious bid for fame in English verse, in the fourth part of Tonson's *Miscellany Poems* which contained four contributions from his pen. These were, a translation of the story of Salmacis from the fourth book of Ovid's *Metamorphoses*, an English rendering of Virgil's fourth Georgic which was to gain some notoriety at a later date, and two original poems in English. Addison's part in this volume was so considerable that it could not fail to make his name known immediately in literary and fashionable society.

How Addison came to Dryden's notice can only be surmised. Congreve, like Addison, was indebted to the Duke of Ormonde and this might have opened the way for Addison to meet both dramatists. Addison remained grateful to Ormonde throughout his life. By the year 1694 He had established himself in the estimation both of Dryden and of Tonson, his publisher, with whom he was in regular correspondence in the year 1695 and by whom he was used as a source of information and perhaps as an agent in Oxford. Walking with his friend Thomas Yalden, a Demy of Magdalen and later a minor poet of some note, Addison turned the conversation to a translation of Ovid's *De Arte Amandi* which had been promised by Yalden, and reported to

Tonson in February that he had 'done Little of it'. In May of the same year he wrote to Tonson:

> Your discourse with me about translating Ovid, made such an impression on me at my first coming down from London, that I ventured on the 2nd Book, which I turnd at my leisure hours, and will give you a sight of, if you will give yourself the trouble of reading it . . . tho' I despair of serving you in this way. . . .

Addison need not have despaired, for Tonson published his lines nine years later.

The reference to London in this correspondence suggests that Addison had been journeying to the capital to further his literary ambitions. It was probably at this time that he lodged with Mrs. Benjamin Bartlett in College Street, Westminster, perhaps on the recommendation of Oxford friends from Westminster School to whom the locality would be well known. He may also have been engaged with his father in securing for his brother Gulston an employment with the East India Company at Madras, thus further relieving the financial position of the family. The Magdalen battels books are preserved only from the year 1696, when they show Addison as an almost continuous resident over long periods. But at this earlier date it is likely that he visited Tonson, and he had probably discussed with Dryden his contributions to the *Miscellany Poems*. The study at Magdalen was the scene of many exercises in translation. Amongst these was an ambitious project for an English version of Herodotus. Addison appears to have been acting for Tonson in bringing together a team of translators to handle the extensive Greek text. Five collaborators are mentioned, three of whom, including Charles Boyle, later Lord Orrery and a protagonist in the Phalaris controversy, were members of a Christ Church group of Latin poets with whom Addison was associated. A fourth was Doctor later Sir Richard Blackmore, who knew little Greek. Addison had already translated the 'Polymnia' but was dissatisfied with his work and promised to begin instead upon the 'Urania'. Tonson, however, seems to have insisted on seeing the 'Polymnia'. In this he was disappointed, for Addison reported the manuscript as lost upon the road from Oxford to London. But though the whole project miscarried, it remains interesting as evidence that Addison pretended to a substantial knowledge of Greek. One who knew him well but perhaps admired him overmuch, wrote that he 'caught the language and manner (of the ancient Greek and Roman writers) as strongly as other young people gain a French accent or a genteel air.'[1] But Macaulay came to the conclusion that he knew insufficient of the language to enable him to appreciate the originals in that tongue, or perhaps even to read them with facility. The truth probably is that Addison possessed a sound knowledge of Greek, but felt uneasy about his translation of 'Polymnia'; and that when he attempted the 'Urania' he became aware that his scholarship would not enable him to work to the standards which he set for himself in Latin studies.

Besides the translations, *Miscellany Poems* for the year 1694 had also carried the two English originals from Addison's pen. 'A Song for St. Cecilia's Day, at Oxford' is a failure as poetry but has some biographical interest. Daniel Purcell, brother of the more famous Henry, had been organist at Magdalen since 1689. In 1693 he had set Yalden's 'St. Cecilia' to music, doubtless for performance on 22 November, the day of the Saint. Addison's ode appears to have been written in 1692 and was probably set by the same hand. His early interest in the setting of poetry to music and therefore in music itself is thus probably due to the influence of the organist. But Addison had little understanding of music and his poem merely shows his treatment of a theme transferred from Latin to the vernacular. The 'Song' is made up of recollections of Dryden and of classical reading, platitudinous sentiments, and well-worn jargon from the common stock of poetical diction. Even in the ecstasy of admiration which followed Addison's death, the utmost that a panegyric-writer could find to say of the 'Song' was that 'the chorus is very transporting'.[2]

The other original contribution to the same volume was 'An Account of the Greatest English Poets', written at the suggestion of Henry Sacheverell, to whom it was addressed.

[1] Tickell, Preface to Addison's *Collected Works*, 1721.
[2] G. Jacob, *Memoirs of the Rt. Hon. Joseph Addison Esq.*, 1719, p. 31.

It is an immature production of which the author was evidently not proud, for he never reprinted it in his lifetime.[1] But the interest of the piece is greater than its merit, because it reveals something of Addison's taste in reading at this time. It begins with a natural and charming couplet, one of the few intimate touches in Addison's verse:

> Since, dearest Harry, you will needs request
> A short account of all the Muse-possest,

and leaves us in no doubt that 'Harry', whom Swift described after an evening's conversation as 'not very deep', and who in the previous year had been formally reprimanded by the Vice-President and three deans for what must have been serious misconduct,[2] was nevertheless an intimate friend.[3]

Beginning with Chaucer, whose works it will be remembered were admired by Dean Addison, his son finds that:

> . . . age has rusted what the Poet writ,
> Worn out his language, and obscur'd his wit:
> In vain he jests in his unpolish'd strain,
> And tries to make his readers laugh in vain.

Passing to Spenser's 'long-spun allegories' and 'dull moral' he finds that they 'Can charm an understanding age no more', and complains that the chivalry of the poet would not bear close inspection. In this catalogue of:

> . . . all the Muse-possest
> That, down from Chaucer's days to Dryden's times,
> Have spent their noble rage in British rhymes;

Shakespeare finds no mention at all. It must, however, be remembered that in the late seventeenth century the merit of Chaucer, Spenser, or Shakespeare was not tediously axiomatic. Chaucer must wait the day when the new age of enlightenment would take its own achievement so much for granted as to be able to contemplate its 'gothic' antecedents without embarrassment. Spenser has never been everyman's

---

[1] Though it reappeared in *Miscellany Poems*, 1716.
[2] Vice-President's Register, 29/1/1693.
[3] An inconclusive attempt has been made to throw doubt upon the identification of Addison's friend with the famous Henry Sacheverell.

meat; and Shakespeare was thought of as a dramatist. Addison's critical judgement cannot be dismissed entirely at this early stage; but it seems possible that he had as yet read little Shakespeare, and that, as Pope later hinted, he had never turned the pages of Spenser at all.

'Great Cowley', 'a mighty genius', draws upon himself the objection which so delighted Pope by its ineptitude:

> He more had pleas'd us, had he pleas'd us less;

and while Addison complimented the master upon his Pindarics, he went to some trouble to deplore the 'others', who:

> . . . in a labour'd strain,
> And forc'd expression, imitate in vain.

But the passage upon Milton is of quite another stamp, and it is evident that Addison had read the poet and was fired by his message:

> Whate'er his pen describes I more than see,
> Whilst ev'ry verse, array'd in majesty,
> Bold, and sublime, my whole attention draws.

But Milton was still obnoxious to many people as a republican, and Addison, though a Whig, was a monarchist:

> Oh had the Poet ne'er profan'd his pen,
> To varnish o'er the guilt of faithless men;
> His other works might have deserv'd applause!
> But now the language can't support the cause;
> While the clean current, tho' serene and bright,
> Betrays a bottom odious to the sight.

'Courtly Waller' provides Addison with an opportunity to show that, having disapproved of Milton's republican politics, he is nevertheless staunch to the Revolution Settlement:

> Oh had thy Muse not come an age too soon,
> But seen great Nassau on the British throne!
> How had his triumphs glitter'd in thy page,
> And warm'd thee to a more exalted rage!

The motive for publishing a piece concerned with literature thus reveals itself as being partly political. But returning to

the poets, Addison celebrated Dryden, editor of the collection in which this poem appeared, in a lengthy passage and
some of the worst verses. He probably disapproved of the
licentiousness of Dryden's plays and in later years he
incurred Tonson's displeasure by expressing openly criticism
which he now kept secret. He turned to Congreve and
flattered Dryden by praising his friend. From his Oxford
days Addison himself aspired to fame as a dramatist. The
great conflicts amidst which his adolescence had been spent,
and the ultimate triumph of reason over tyranny, provided
a sombre picture of the heroism, the vices and the hazards of
public life and the tragic destiny of great men. Against this
background, an intensive reading of the Latin classics projected the image of a patriot, fearless and upright yet human,
the image of Cato, which became increasingly the ideal of
Addison's life and the measure of his conduct. He was now
at work upon a tragedy[1] constructed around this original,
and showed it to Dryden, who made encouraging remarks
about the script while advising against its being acted. The
narrow scope and academic quality of Addison's work
during his Oxford period make it unlikely that his powers
were sufficiently developed or that his observation of the
world was mature enough to enable him to write a play
whose acting an experienced dramatist would sponsor.

One more 'poet' remained to claim attention and occupied
thrice the number of couplets afforded to Chaucer. This was
Charles Montagu, a brilliant financier but also a man of
sound scholarship, the younger son of a younger son, who
had risen fast to ministerial rank at the head of the Whig
party. Like many accomplished men of his time Montagu
amused himself by writing verses and was open to flattery
upon them. Addison celebrated him 'for wit, for humor,
and for judgment . . .'. So the literary lure led once more to
the political titbit. Yet the strangest feature of the poem lay
in the last six lines, wherein the author turned to take leave
of his friend:

> I've done at length; and now, dear Friend, receive
> The last poor present that my Muse can give.

[1] Tickell, Preface to Addison's *Works*, and Spence, p. 46 n., on the authority
of Edward Young.

I leave the arts of poetry and verse
To them that practise 'em with more success.
Of greater truths I'll now prepare to tell,
And so at once, dear Friend and Muse, farewell.

These cryptic couplets have been interpreted as a resolve to quit poetry for the Church, but such an explanation is unsatisfactory. There is no reason to suppose that in an age when the Church, scholarship, and poetry were closely related, entry into Holy Orders would have precluded Addison from rhyming. It is of course true that being descended from the parsonage on both sides of his family, he might well have had thoughts of an ecclesiastical career. Moreover his contemporaries felt his cast of mind to be naturally suited thereto: Mandeville described him as a 'parson in a tye wig'. That he was preparing to take his studies in divinity seriously is shown by his 'inception' in that faculty, which he made on 7 July 1694 along with West, Yalden, and Robert Welsted.[1] This step would be necessary not merely with a view to Holy Orders, but also if he was to seek further distinction at the university. He might study divinity without necessarily resolving upon a career in the Church. If Addison now thought as he later said, that 'an honest *Englishman* is a *Tory* in church matters and a *Whig* in politics', he may have understood the dilemma which would confront him in the Church and have realized the unsatisfactory prospects for a man with his own combination of views. Congreve is said to have urged him against taking Orders; but the whole course of Addison's intellectual expansion had been away from his father's world and towards that of letters and politics.

At some point in Addison's Oxford studies there came one of those difficult periods in the life of a young man when he hesitated in the choice of a career. He later reflected:

Irresolution on the Schemes of Life which offer themselves to our Choice, and Inconstancy in pursuing them, are the greatest and most universal Causes of all our Disquiet and Unhappiness. When Ambition pulls one way, Interest another, Inclination a third, and perhaps Reason contrary to all, a Man is likely to pass his Time but ill who has so many different Parties to please. ... One

[1] Vice-President's Register.

had better settle on a Way of Life that is not the very best we might have chosen, than grow old without determining our Choice, and go out of the World, as the greatest Part of Mankind do, before we have resolved how to live in it. There is but one Method of setting our selves at Rest in this Particular, and that is by adhering stedfastly to one great End as the chief and ultimate aim of all our Pursuits.[1]

If the year 1694 had been for Addison a period of 'Irresolution on the Schemes of Life' it is not difficult to see the reason why this should be so. Ambition no doubt drew him towards the lure of fame in a world of letters evidently ready to receive him; interest suggested a safe post in a rich Oxford corporation; inclination probably led to prolonged classical studies; and reason may have suggested preparation for eternal life. What then was the 'one great End'? It was the Roman concept of citizenship which had already impressed itself deeply upon Addison's mind. An upright character and conduct, good service to the State, with the embellishments of learning, culture, and urbanity, reveal themselves as parts in a single pattern of life. The concept was that of a virtuous layman, not of a pious priest; and it afforded full scope for the political ambition which fired him from his earliest days at Oxford.

The resolve which lay behind the last lines of the 'Account' did not long deter Addison from poetry and the further search for political patronage. In the year 1695 he addressed himself to a new patron, a powerful Whig politician, Sir John Somers, Lord Keeper of the Great Seal. A lawyer, who had raised himself by his own ability and courage, Sir John was one of the most remarkable men of his age. His achievement is an essential part of the Revolution Settlement and of the subsequent evolution of constitutional monarchy in Britain. When Addison had attained a pinnacle of fame, when Somers was dead, and when the time for flattery had passed away, the younger man looked back upon the patron of his Oxford days and thus committed him to posterity:

His Character was uniform and consistent with itself, and his whole Conduct of a Piece. His Principles were founded in Reason,

[1] *S.* 162.

and supported by Vertue; and therefore did not lie at the Mercy of Ambition, Avarice, or Resentment. His Notions were no less steady and unshaken, than just and upright. . . .

There is no question but this wonderful Man will make one of the most distinguish'd Figures in the History of the present Age; but we cannot expect that his Merit will shine out in its proper Light, since he wrote many things which are not publish'd in his Name; was at the Bottom of many excellent Counsels, in which he did not appear; did Offices of Friendship to many Persons, who knew not from whom they were derived; and performed great Services to his Country, the Glory of which was transferred to others: In short, since he made it his Endeavour rather to do worthy actions than to gain an illustrious Character.[1]

Horace Walpole added: 'One of those divine men, who, like a chapel in a palace, remain unprofaned while all the rest is tyranny, corruption and folly.'[2]

To such a man it was that Addison now wisely directed himself. The approach to Charles Montagu had been an indirect compliment embedded in an indifferent poem, and may have failed to attract attention. In later years Addison himself thought poorly of the 'Account', which he did not reprint in his lifetime,[3] and Montagu may never have seen it. In contrast, the approach to Sir John Somers was direct. Addison boasted in later life: 'I had a very early Ambition to recommend my self to Your Lordship's Patronage';[4] therefore his new 'Poem to His Majesty', who was a rugged Dutch soldier and would almost certainly not read it, carried a graceful verse letter of 'presentation' to the Lord Keeper. The choice of theme is interesting. Addison had followed Yalden when translating Ovid, and had invited comparison with him upon the 'St. Cecilia' motif. In this year Yalden produced a 'Pindaric Ode on the conquest of Namur', of the type criticized so severely in the 'Account'. On the theme of the king the two men now wrote in manners which again invited comparison and a dozen years later a poet writing of Oxford still thought of them together.[5] Upon this occasion the advantage undoubtedly lay with the

---

[1] F. 39.   [2] Catalogue of Royal and Noble Authors: 'Somers'.
[3] Spence, pp. 49-50.
[4] Remarks on Several Parts of Italy: Dedication.
[5] Tickell, 'Oxford'.

'Poem to His Majesty'. Its verse dedication desires the Lord Keeper to:

> *Receive the present of a Muse Unknown:*
> *A Muse that in advent'rous numbers sings*
> *The rout of Armies and the fall of Kings,*
> Britain *Advanc'd, and* Europe'*s Peace Restor'd,*
> *By* Somers' *Counsels, and by* Nassau's *Sword.*

The subsequent flattery was generous. Somers was assured of being himself a potentially immortal poet, unhappily frustrated by the distracting cares of State; and the piece ended with a plain and not unpleasingly candid picture of the expectant poet:

> *On You, my Lord, with anxious Fear I wait,*
> *And from Your Judgment must expect my Fate . . .*

Addressed to the arch-Whig, who had been counsel for the seven bishops, who had been deeply involved in the project for bringing over King William from Holland, and who before his appointment as Lord Keeper had been successively Solicitor and Attorney General to the new Government, such a declaration and such an appeal committed the author irrevocably not only to the Revolution Settlement but also to the Whig party, and published to the world yet more clearly than his previous writings had done that he looked to the Whig leaders for preferment. It is most improbable that he thought seriously of a career in the Church after 1695.

What then was the nature of the patronage which Addison sought from the great politicians to whom he addressed himself? It is possible to guess at the ambitions which lie concealed behind the 'Poem to His Majesty'. If much of the earlier verse is empty of thought and matter, mere whistling of the academic wind through a classical ruin, the same cannot be said of this piece. On the contrary, it is lively and topical; and in an age when news was hard to obtain and when comment came only in fugitive pamphlets, Addison shows himself well informed upon some of the economic and political issues of Europe. The whole piece betrays the interest of the author in his subject and the sincerity of his

views; for example, he writes upon the economic consequences of the sea war:

> Wheree'er the Waves in restless errors rowle,
> The Sea lies open now to either Pole:
> Now may we safely use the *Northern* gales,
> And in the *Polar Circle* spread our sails;
> Or deep in *Southern* climes, Secure from wars,
> New Lands explore, and sail by Other stars;
> Fetch Uncontroll'd each labour of the Sun,
> And make the product of the World our own.

A second feature of the piece is the pains which it takes to
impress upon the reader that the achievements of the
Government have suffered for lack of an adequate poet to
celebrate them. While thus careful to display his political
knowledge, and abstaining from dwelling upon his own
shortcomings as he had foolishly done in previous works,
Addison wrote:

> O that some Muse, renown'd for Lofty verse,
> In daring numbers wou'd thy Toils rehearse!
> Draw thee Belov'd in peace, and Fear'd in wars . . .

He may well have hoped that the Lord Keeper, a man of
literary parts, would recognize just such a muse in the lines
now before him.

At the age of twenty-four he was thus no longer in doubt
that there resided within him no ordinary talent; yet the
opportunity to exercise his ability did not obviously present
itself nor was he aware of the precise nature of his genius.
He had made remarkable progress towards literary recognition and already commanded the admiration and support of
the great poet of the last age and the friendship of the great
publisher of the present. Like many a young man, he now
mistook his talent, which was destined only to be revealed
to him after many disappointments. The success of his Latin
poetry, largely a technical feat, and the praise of his elders,
led him to think of himself as before all a poet. He certainly
saw no formidable rivals and had a competent hand at verse.
Thus he dreamed of becoming the court poet of a heroic age,
and, lacking the self-confidence of a man who has identified
his own genius, he waited 'with anxious fear' for Sir John

Somers's encouragement. It is, however, unlikely that political verse presented itself to Addison as an end in itself. It is
more probable that just as he had used his proficiency in
Latin poetry to open the gate at Magdalen, so he thought to
use his attainments in the vernacular as an introduction to
a larger society and greater objectives.

Dr. Lancaster had doubtless related how Sir Joseph
Williamson had sent him to Paris to study with a view to
official employment, perhaps in diplomacy. John Wallis, the
mathematician, whose son was at Magdalen and worked
with Addison upon Latin verses, had received a grant
for learning Arabic and Turkish. William Blaythwayt, an
eminent official, had been likewise favoured. Dean Addison
had been an intelligent traveller at government expense.
Dryden had offered good advice to the young and scholarly,
which Addison may well have applied to himself now that
he sought fame as an English poet:

> The *proprieties and delicacies of* English *are known to few; 'tis
> impossible even for a good Wit, to understand and practice them without
> the help of a liberal Education, long Reading, and digesting of those few
> good Authors we have amongst us, the knowledge of Men and Manners,
> the freedom of habitudes and conversation with the best company of both
> Sexes; and in short, without wearing off the rust which he has contracted,
> while he was laying in a stock of Learning.*[1]

Dryden himself had never been abroad and did not directly
counsel foreign travel; but the last line about 'rust contracted while laying in a stock of learning' described the
condition of an ambitious yet painfully academic young
don; and it was accepted that polish as opposed to rust
was to be acquired *par excellence* in France amongst the critics
and at the court, and in Italy in a cultured international
society. It therefore seems likely that at a time when he
decided to ally himself irrevocably with a political party,
Addison had made certain resolutions for his future. His
manner of life should be moral and rational but not ecclesiastical, his career should be one of public service, and letters
should be a means of advancement and an embellishment of
his leisure hours. In perfecting his achievement in all of these

[1] Preface to *Sylvae* (1685).

three compartments of existence foreign travel would be desirable, and the means to travel was probably the patronage which Addison sought.

The manner in which he made his way to the esteem and affection of his great patrons rests, like so much of Addison's early life, upon the slenderest evidence. We have it upon the authority of Steele in an open letter to Congreve that it was the latter who introduced Addison to Charles Montagu, a statement which would not have been made in such a manner if it were untrue. But nobody has allocated the credit for introducing him to Sir John Somers. A line in what Johnson called the 'kind of rhyming introduction' to the 'Poem to His Majesty' begged the Lord Keeper to:

> Receive the present of a Muse Unknown.

This suggests that Addison was not acquainted with the person addressed. Sir John judged the verses 'To the King' to have merit, and sent for their author.[1] Thus at the age of twenty-four, Addison had gained personal access to the two powerful political patrons who better than any others in that age could forward a young man's career.

It was at this point that the shy genius of the Water Walks drew with effect upon his reserves of character. Ministers were surrounded by a circle of adherents seeking to qualify for patronage through services of one kind or another; but there were few such folk in whose company these great men can have taken pleasure. Every witness who has spoken of Addison from intimate knowledge has told us of the almost magical attraction which he exercised in private and personal relationships. A brilliant mind, extensive scholarship, fortitude of character, and an elusive gift of humour, made him an admirable companion. As Addison later expressed it:

> The Mind never unbends it self so agreeably as in the Conversation of a well chosen Friend.[2]

His patrons found him such a man during his brief visits to London. Dryden, himself in need of patronage, who published his translation of Virgil in a magnificent folio in

---

[1] Tickell, Preface to Addison's *Works*.　　[2] *S.* 19.

1697, in the lengthy 'dedication' of the *Aeneid* which preceded his text, recorded that:

> Two other Worthy Friends of mine, who desire to have their Names conceal'd, seeing me straitned in my time, took Pity on me, and gave me the Life of *Virgil*, the two Prefaces to the Pastorals, and the *Georgics*, and all the Arguments in Prose to the whole Translation.

One of these two anonymous 'worthy friends' was Addison, who wrote the preface to the *Georgics*, possibly some time in the year 1693 and probably long before publication of the completed work. The finished translation also contained a 'Postscript to the Reader' which was written when much if not most of the book had been printed. In this postscript Dryden thanked by name various persons to whom he was indebted for help while engaged on his translation, most of them being noblemen and gentlemen of some importance. After mentioning these patrons, he went some way out of his course to include an acknowledgement of the merit of Addison's previous translation of part of the fourth Georgic. Pleading that Lord Roscommon and another anonymous translator had set a high standard, he wrote:

> The most Ingenious Mr. *Addison* of *Oxford* has also been as troublesome to me as the other two, and on the same account. After his Bees, my latter Swarm is scarcely worth the hiving.

Addison, the friend of Charles Montagu, for whom Dryden had a particular admiration, had now joined the little group of people in whom the reading public was interested and whom it was not only just but also fashionable to honour.

Macaulay dismissed Addison's translation as 'schoolboy lines' and Dryden's words as habitual courtesy. But the effect of his praise must have been to enhance very considerably Addison's growing reputation. Dryden's *Virgil* would pass automatically into the library of most wealthy noblemen or gentlemen who pretended to culture. The list of subscribers shows that it went on to the bookshelf of famous actresses and a great many wealthy citizens, and Dryden tells us, for example, that 'his Grace the Duke of Shrewsbury has procured a printed copy of the Pastorals, Georgics, and first six Aeneids, from my bookseller and has read them in the country . . . '. Addison was in fact deeply indebted to his literary father, for his name was now honourably associated with what then seemed to be one of the great literary undertakings of the age.

It may now be apposite to consider the merit of Addison's translations and their service to letters. Johnson thought them 'too licentiously paraphrastical' but 'such as may be read with pleasure by those who do not know the original'. By that time Pope had already pounced upon Addison's verse, some of which found a place in *Peri Bathous*. Bishop Hurd conceded that in the fourth Georgic, which Dryden so admired, Addison had 'the grace but not the energy of Virgil's manner', and thought that Book II of the *Metamorphoses* in its 'laboured ease resembles and almost equals the original'. Macaulay thought the translations 'of no value at all'. Pope, he pointed out, had taught mankind the art of writing heroic couplets, and thereby rendered all those produced before his time outmoded. But since Addison's day the technical quality of writing which the public could appreciate, and which in consequence authors were expected to maintain, had risen as considerably as had the extent of the apparatus available to the translator. Addison certainly never set himself any standard based upon an inviolable text. He was concerned to give his contemporaries a version which they might enjoy reading and to present to those not familiar with classical literature the beauties which were to be found therein. He had a robust contempt for the petty details of literary scholarship, which excused him from any necessity to satisfy the pedants:

Those of the graver sort have been wholly taken up in the Mythologies, and think they have appeared very judicious, if they have shewn us out of an old author that Ovid is mistaken in a pedigree, or has turned such a person into a Wolf that ought to have been made a Tiger.[1]

If Johnson's criticism is correct, Addison achieved the purpose which he had set himself; and making allowance for the considerable progress of scholarly education in the interval of time which separated the two men, we may suppose

---

[1] Notes to Ovid's *Metamorphoses*.

that his translations abundantly satisfied the needs of his own age.

As a critic of the classics Addison suffers likewise by comparison with the achievements of later times. Macaulay pointed out that in his notes to the translation of the *Metamorphoses*, Addison failed to call in aid the Greek poets who would have been much to his purpose. It is, however, difficult to think of any contemporary scholar who combined a profound knowledge of the Latin poets with an equal command of the Greek, and who was also able to translate and annotate in a manner acceptable to the general public. Johnson dismissed the preface to the *Georgics* as 'juvenile, superficial, and uninstructive, without much either of the scholar's learning or the critick's penetration'; but Dryden, who was a good judge of the merits of a piece intended for the many rather than for the scholarly few, was glad to find a place for it in his folio.

On St. Mary Magdalen day 1696 Addison had spoken the customary Latin oration in hall, no doubt because, in the absence of West, he was the senior Demy. On 30 July of the following year with West and Grandorge he was promoted from a demyship to a probationer fellowship.[1] He would now enjoy increased emoluments and privileges though losing his small share of the Higden scholarship. This financial gain may have permitted the sending of Lancelot, his younger brother, to The Queen's College, where he entered on 8 November that year. In the same year with the confidence born of a growing reputation he wrote a Latin poem of considerable merit: 'Pax Gulielmi auspiciis Europae Reddita.' This was addressed to Charles Montagu, who became more a friend and confidant than the Lord Keeper, who remained the benefactor at a distance. Yet at this time there can have been little intercourse with either statesman, for the battels books show Addison as constantly in residence at Magdalen from January 1696 until March 1698. The occasion of this poem was the Peace of Ryswick, and the introductory Latin letter to Charles Montagu emphasizes once more the lack of good poets to declare the noble theme of the day. With a growing appreciation of the scope of his powers, Addison may

[1] Vice-President's Register, 31/7/1697.

have felt more certain of excelling most of his competitors in Latin. Possibly he did not care to compete with Congreve in the vernacular, and judged his friend to be susceptible to the compliment of a choice of Latin for a piece which an anonymous correspondent of a nineteenth-century magazine dismissed as 'Praeclarum certè specimen adulationis'. His selection of that language would also enable the poem to reach an international circle of learned men, and thus to prepare the way for the fulfilment of his ambition to travel. The poem, when published in 1699, commended itself to contemporary taste as a fine piece of virtuosity. Edmund Smith, himself a considerable Latin poet, when dedicating his 'Phaedra' to Charles Montagu, referred to the 'Pax Gulielmi' as the 'best Latin poem since the Aeneid', which, even allowing for the fact that he had been an Oxford friend of Addison, was high praise from a man noted for his candour. Johnson thought that the piece 'cannot be denied to be vigorous and elegant'.

There was at this period a highly developed school of Latin verse writing in Christ Church and Magdalen. Addison had become a member of this group and the bulk of his surviving Latin poetry had already been written but had not been published by the year 1698. His reputation as a Latin poet was considerable, and he was now paid the unpleasant compliment of a large literary theft. Richard Wellington, a London publisher, produced a volume entitled *Examen Poeticum Duplex*, which was evidently intended to pass for a second volume of *Musarum Anglicanarum Analecta*, a collection of Oxford Latin verse the first part of which had appeared in 1692. Wellington's book contained a variety of pieces of which six appeared in Addison's name and were by him. A seventh, perhaps his best, appeared anonymously in an appendix at the end of the main work, amongst the rhymes of Westminster schoolboys.[1] Though published in London, the *Examen* appears to have been compiled in Oxford, from which place the preface was dated on 28 January 1698. Its appearance in July must have caused Addison and others great annoyance. Seven of his poems appeared in print for the first time without an opportunity

[1] 'Specimen Novum', p. 11, at the end of the *Examen Poeticum*, supra.

for correction by their author. Whether he was already at work upon a second volume of *Musarum Anglicanarum* in the capacity of editor, or whether he was goaded to undertake the task by the piracy, he produced such a book, which was registered on 9 February 1699. This was printed at the Sheldonian theatre for John Crosley and was also published in London by Timothy Child. The preface, in which Wellington was attacked, was by Addison, and the collection contained sixteen poems which had been included in the *Examen*. Eight of Addison's pieces appeared in this book, seven being from the *Examen*, but all of these had been extensively revised and in part rewritten. The eighth piece was the 'Pax Gulielmi', which was probably written too late for inclusion in Wellington's book. Most of Addison's contributors were Christ Church or Magdalen men, and in the preface he regretted the absence not merely of other Oxford but of Cambridge verse, which he could have obtained without much difficulty had he so wished.

The Christ Church poets were particularly prominent in the *Musarum Anglicanarum*. Amongst them were Hannes, Smith, Alsop, Friend, Boyle, Adams, and Smalridge. All are mentioned in Addison's surviving correspondence, and George Smalridge, who in 1693 had been appointed to a prebend of Lichfield Cathedral, was under the eye of Dean Addison and would be particularly known to Joseph for that reason. Addison was thus closely connected with this group, of which the most remarkable poet was Edward Hannes. The poem which had appeared anonymously in the appendix to Wellington's *Examen* but which Addison now claimed in the *Musarum Anglicanarum* was an alcaic ode addressed to Hannes in imitation of the latter's own lines to Sydenham. By a compliment to Charles Montagu it introduces the political element into what might have been a purely academic piece; and it displays Addison's skill in using the medium of a dead language to present trifling matters in an interesting manner. A second piece was addressed to Dr. Thomas Burnet, Master of the Charterhouse, whose *Telluris Theoria Sacra*, published in 1689, challenged the orthodox story of the creation and fall of man. Addison praised this work in superlatives unusual in his writing, and showed a warm sympathy with its rational spirit. He thus proclaimed himself out of sympathy with current ecclesiastical orthodoxy. Other pieces were the 'Sphaeristerium', a description of a bowling green, perhaps in imitation of the 'Sphaeristerium Suleianum' by a Cambridge poet, William Dillingham, and 'Barometri Descriptio' in the vein of Thomas Bisse with whom Addison was acquainted and who had written upon the microscope and the air pump. 'Machinae Gesticulantes, anglicè A Puppet-show' and 'Praelium inter Pygmaeos et Grues commissum' are mock heroics, which display a fine talent for humour and sentiment. The insignificance of the subjects in the two latter pieces proclaims them an exercise in elegance of style, ingenuity of description, and witty expression. In all of these they excel, foreshadowing in Latin the later development of Addison's genius in the vernacular. The 'Resurrectio delineata ad Altare Col. Magd. Oxon.', in serious vein, described the altarpiece of the college chapel; and finally, the 'Pax Gulielmi' was published here for the first time.

During the preparation of Addison's book a literary war had been in progress between the rival publishers.[1] This is revealed in the advertisement columns of the press, and it apparently ended in Wellington's defeat: though the *Duplex* is a scarce book, the *Musarum Anglicanarum* was continued and ran into four later editions.[2] Addison himself promised his readers a third volume of the *Musarum Anglicanarum*, but when it appeared it contained no poems by him and he is not known to have played any part in its preparation.

Other Latin verse has been ascribed to Addison.[3] Two pieces from the *Musarum Anglicanarum*, the 'Praelium Navale' appearing in the name of Hugh Parker, and the 'Cursus Glacialis' in that of Philip Frowde, both Magdalen men, both friends and perhaps pupils of Addison, may have been of his composing. It was not uncommon for a tutor to compose verses for recital by his pupils at university ceremonies,

---

[1] L. Bradner, 'The Composition and Publication of Addison's Latin Poems', *Mod. Philology*, xxxv (1938), 360–7.
[2] 1714, 1721, 1741, and 1761.   [3] L. Bradner, op. cit.

the real authorship of such pieces being widely known. There was also much give and take amongst the Latin poets. John Wallis, a member of Magdalen College, claimed in a letter which bears every mark of candour that he had contributed several lines to Addison's poetry in the *Musarum Anglicanarum*. He also alleged that other verses in the book had been written by him but sold to the person to whom they were attributed.[1] It would not therefore be surprising if Addison by including two pieces nominally those of younger Magdalen men was securing the publication of two more of his own poems.

The Latin verse of the Augustan period in Britain is dead as literature but remains of much interest. Speaking of the *Paradise Lost* and comparing it with the ancient poets, Addison remarked that:

So Divine a Poem in *English*, is like a stately Palace built of Brick, where one may see Architecture in as great a Perfection as in one of Marble, tho' the Materials are of a coarser Nature.[2]

It was upon intensive study of these 'marble' originals that much vernacular poetry of the eighteenth century was founded. If Addison's Latin verse now appears in the light of an exercise, it was certainly a good one. It enjoyed considerable popularity in later years. The 'Pygmaeos et Grues', for example, besides being several times reprinted, was translated anonymously in Addison's lifetime,[3] again shortly after his death by Thomas Newcomb and by Warburton, was commended in verse by Edward Cobden, and was 'imitated' by Beattie in the mid-century. Johnson thought his Latin poetry 'indeed entitled to particular praise' and remarked that Addison 'has not confined himself to the imitation of any ancient author, but has formed his style from the general language, such as a diligent perusal of the productions of different ages happened to supply'. Macaulay added that 'Purity of style and an easy flow of numbers, are common to all Addison's poems'; and a modern scholar observes that, without

---

[1] *Athenaeum* of 2/11/1889, p. 598.   [2] *S.* 417.

[3] *Miscellaneous translations from Bion, Ovid, Moschus, and Mr. Addison*, London, 1715.

indecency, they show a humorous management of common-place topics, such as is usually thought of as originating in the *Tatler*.[1] In Addison's best work this authority finds an element of imaginative fancy which separates it from all contemporary mock heroics and which exhibits a high degree of poetic genius. From much familiarity with the Latin originals Addison had not only acquired technical skill and a style of his own, but handled his medium so masterfully as to begin to reveal in a dead language the qualities of humour and satire which he was as yet too reticent to venture in English.

During the last period of his residence in Oxford Addison spared little time for the society of the great in London. His expenditure on battels was modest. He was perhaps intent upon saving money, or compelled by circumstances to an extreme economy, although this did not prevent him from having his portrait painted by William Sonmans, then work-ing in Oxford. When on 7 March 1698 he went down, it was for the first time for 113 consecutive weeks, and he remained away until 27 April. On 30 July of the same year with West and Grandorge he had been admitted a Fellow of the college upon the expiration of his probationary year,[2] and on the same date his brother Lancelot was elected to a demyship and took up residence in due course. This would further relieve the family finances. The brothers resided together at Magdalen until October when Joseph again went down, this time for five weeks until 27 November. He returned to spend Christmas in college. Meanwhile important plans had been laid, doubtless during his visits to London. It had been decided by his Whig patrons that this promising, politically devoted, and personally acceptable don should be given a treasury grant to enable him to travel abroad. The purpose of this generosity would be to improve his mind, to enable him to learn modern languages, and to prepare him for service to the Crown.

But the Government was not prepared to finance the whole expense of a grand tour. At a meeting of the Board of Treasury on 30 May 1699 it was agreed in the presence of

---

[1] L. Bradner, op. cit.
[2] Vice-President's Register.

the king that Mr. Addison should 'have £200 to travel'.[1]
It therefore remained necessary for some other source of income to be found, and Charles Montagu appealed to the
President of Magdalen with this end in view. It was normally
necessary for a Fellow of the college to take Holy Orders in
due course; nor was absence from Magdalen for lengthy
periods permitted without leave. A dispensation from taking
Orders was seldom granted; and in 1696 the college had
threatened two of its members with expulsion unless they
complied before Christmas.[2] Leave of absence was more
easily obtained, but had to be renewed every six months.
Dick Steele later recalled the 'warm instances made [by
Charles Montagu] to the Head of the College not to insist
upon Mr. Addison's going into Orders': and added that
his arguments were 'founded upon the general Pravity
and Corruption of Men of Business who wanted liberal
Education' (Dedication to the *Drummer*, 1722). Montagu,
he says, told the President that 'however he might be
represented as no Friend to the Church, he never would do
it any other Injury than keeping Mr. Addison out of it'. The
purpose of this approach was less to prevent Addison from
taking Orders, which at this time he can have had no thought
of doing, than to enable him to continue to enjoy the emoluments of his fellowship though remaining a layman and
while absent from the college travelling abroad. In this request Montagu was successful. It was on 5 August that the
President was translated to the bishopric of Lichfield where
Addison's father reigned as dean,[3] and gratitude to the
Government as well as civility to the dean of his cathedral
may have helped him to a favourable decision; for on 17
August it was recorded in the Vice-President's Register that
'Concessa est Mro. Addison, ab iis quorum intererat, dis-
pensatio, ne teneatur Sacris Ordinibus initiari'.

This was a wise as well as a fortunate decision, for Joseph
Addison had little relish of the stifling atmosphere of contemporary Oxford, and the few memories of the university
which he has preserved for us are those of affectionate
amusement, rather than of deeper preoccupation. He recalled
the peculiarities of senior Fellows, who, he thought, with

---

[1] *Cal. Treasury Books*, xiv. 90.   [2] Vice-President's Register.   [3] Ibid.

'superannuated Benchers of the Inns of Court . . . and defunct Statesmen' were really dead though refusing to admit as much.[1] On every hand he was offended by pedantry: 'a Form of Knowledge without the Power of it.'[2] Of documentary research he recorded with apparent surprise:

I have heard one of the greatest Genius's this Age has produced, who had been trained up in all the Polite Studies of Antiquity, assure me, upon his being obliged to search into several Rolls and Records, that notwithstanding such an Employment was at first very dry and irksome to him, he at last took an incredible Pleasure in it, and preferred it even to the reading of *Virgil* or *Cicero*.[3]

On 29 April 1699, therefore, the Magdalen battels book carried the word 'Exit' against Mr. Addison's account. He evidently lingered for his birthday which coincided with the May Day celebrations in College, and on 2 May took coach for London.[4] On that day he turned his back upon the cloisters for the world of great affairs; and although on the following 29 July the college gave Addison only the customary six months' leave of absence,[5] he had departed never to return. Indeed by 17 August when formal approval was given by the college to Charles Montagu's request, Magister Addison was already on his way to a foreign land.

---

[1] *T.* 110.   [2] *T.* 165.   [3] *S.* 447.
[4] J. Wallis, letter printed in *Athenaeum*, 2/11/1889, p. 598.
[5] Vice-President's Register.

III

A GRAND TOUR
1699–1703

THE Fellows of Magdalen had recently built a substantial fortified wall bounding the college upon those two sides which were otherwise unprotected. Amidst a hard world and violent events the community within walls and cloister lived a self-contained and usually sheltered life, drawing upon its own resources both material and spiritual. To leave this academic fortress for a long period of travel in foreign countries was more than a stimulus to fresh observation and reflection; it was a high adventure.

Upon such a journey finance would be a perpetual worry to Addison and it is likely that his father assisted him.[1] On 30 May the Board of Treasury had authorized payment of £200; but much remained to be done before he could touch the money. On 1 June a royal sign manual warrant was issued, on 9 June a money order, and on 7 July William Lowndes at the Treasury forwarded to the Auditor of Receipt a plan for disbursements of Civil Lists moneys proposed for the next twelve weeks, which included an item of £200 to Mr. Addison 'in one week'.[2] Thus in the late summer the intending traveller received what was in all probability the largest sum of money he had ever handled.

Addison had provided himself with copies of his new edition of the *Musarum Anglicanarum*, which would prove his claim to recognition by men of learning and letters, and the fame of which had preceded him in Europe.[3] He was to travel under the patronage of leading ministers of the Crown,

[1] Dr. Addison left a substantial sum in his will, but Joseph and Gulston received considerably less than Dorothy and Lancelot. This may suggest that money had been provided to start Joseph on his travels and Gulston on his career in India. Dr. Addison's will is in the Birmingham Probate Registry, probate of 7/6/1703.

[2] *Cal. Treasury Books*, 1698–9, pp. 90, 409.

[3] See Tickell's Preface to Addison's *Collected Works*.

and he would therefore be made welcome at English diplomatic missions. There was also the usual circle of Englishmen enjoying foreign travel, the tourists of their day, and these included several Oxford contemporaries.

In preparation for the ultimate objective of learned travellers, a visit to Italy, he had re-read much Latin poetry and had made copious notes of passages which might lend interest to a journey through the scenes of classical antiquity. He had visited Abraham Stanyan at the Secretary of State's office, and had received instruction from this Oxford contemporary in the forms of diplomacy and the course of English policy in Europe in recent years. The objectives of the journey were in fact nicely depicted in the mind of the traveller. The first was to fit himself for government service; he was 'sent from the University by King William, in order to travel and qualify himself to serve His Majesty'.[1] This task included speaking French, of which he understood not a word, although he had studied the French philosophers and had read widely if not profoundly in the critics and poets. His second desire was to justify the confidence of his political patrons and to secure their further support. But in the shadow of these designs a number of minor projects took shape, which if successful would contribute to advancement. Addison had studied the existing books of travel available to him, and had noticed that his mastery of the Latin poets would enable him to write such a book in English illustrated from that source. There also remained the project of a moral tragedy woven around the image of Cato, roughly drafted at Oxford, which might draw fresh substance from the stones of Italy. Beyond these precise projects lay a vista of opportunity for the exercise of poetic and literary talent. There was the chance to correspond with eminent men in England, who would be glad of first-hand intelligence from a reporter more able than the current news writers. There was also the opportunity to build up in Europe a circle of friends and correspondents who at a later stage might in their turn provide such a service to Addison himself.

On 19 August Lancelot Addison went down from Magadalen for a few days, possibly to bid farewell to his

[1] Bohn, vi. 634.

JOSEPH ADDISON AS A YOUNG MAN
by W. Sonmans, probably painted at Oxford previous to the year 1700
In the possession of Viscount Devonport

brother,[1] and it was probably late in the same month that Joseph Addison made his way to Dover. He beheld the ocean, as far as is known for the first time, and later recorded that 'I cannot see the Heavings of this prodigious Bulk of Waters, even in a Calm, without a very pleasing Astonishment'.[2] He experienced and later wrote of the sensation of vertigo as he stood on Dover cliffs, pointing his reading of *King Lear*. John Sansom, a friend since school days, had provided an introduction to a local resident, Mr. Breton, who entertained Addison while the packet waited for the wind, and smoothed the path of officialdom for an inexperienced traveller embarking for the first time.

At Calais while going ashore the new traveller in his clumsiness fell into the sea, from which he was rescued unhurt but wretched. Ashore he wrote to Congreve a letter eloquent of misery and homesickness. 'I have encountered as many misfortunes as a Knight-Errant' he complained, posting by day on lame horses and lying on hard beds at night, with unfamiliar words and faces on every hand and 'many other dismal adventures'. Arrived in Paris he sought to console himself with a visit to the opera. Here he might hope to find a congenial echo of Magdalen diversions. In 1697 Daniel Purcell, until recently the Magdalen organist, had set to music *The New World in the Moon*, an 'opera' by Settle, *Brutus of Alba* by Powell and Verbruggen, and in this year *The Island Princess* by Peter Motteux.[3] But the French opera, dominated by the spirit of Lully, in no way resembled Purcell's work which was more in the nature of masque. What he saw and heard disappointed and displeased this insular and rather priggish don upon whom the mood of disgust sat heavily:

Every man that comes upon the Stage is a Beau: the Shepherds are all Embroidered, Pluto has his Valet de Chambre, and a couple of riders appears in red Stockings. Alpheus throws aside his Sedge and makes Love in a Fair periwig and a plume of Feathers but with such a horrid voice that one would think the murmurs of a Country Brook much better music.

To crown all, 'Corelli has a very mean opinion of Harry

---

[1] Magdalen College battels book.   [2] *S*. 489.
[3] *Magdalen College Register*, ed. Bloxam, ii. 206.

Purcell's works';[1] that Harry, brother of Daniel Purcell, who had lately reset the 'Ode for St. Cecilia's Day' for performance in Oxford in November. This essay in misery culminated in the reflection that statues and pictures were the best company in Paris: 'what particularly recommends 'em to me is that they dont Speak French and have a very good quality, rarely to be met with in this Country, of not being too talkative.' Even the French genius for decoration eluded him; and noticing that the new column in the Place Vendôme had been erected before the buildings were completed he remarked to Sansom 'they have set up the Furniture before the House is half built'.

It was a fateful time for a homesick and insular Englishman to travel in Europe. Tension and foreboding dominated every capital. Death hung suspended over the childless King Charles II of Spain while the nations negotiated against time and circumstances to devise a disposal of his heritage which might avoid a general war. As Addison prepared to leave England a new agreement had been signed which would partition the Spanish heritage in a manner acceptable both to French and to Anglo-Dutch interests. Though these negotiations were conducted in secret, Addison was probably warned of their existence by Stanyan, and as he landed in France approaches were being made in Vienna and The Hague to secure general agreement. Amongst these dramatic events, and afflicted by insular malaise, Addison found a refuge for his wounded spirits at the British Embassy. Charles Montagu, Earl of Manchester, a relative of Addison's patron, was ambassador at this time, and had been requested to offer kindness to the young man in whose education the royal treasury had invested money. Manchester, a trusted friend of the king, with whom he had fought at the Boyne, was an able and experienced ambassador and Matthew Prior was his Secretary of Embassy. Thus Addison's first sight of diplomacy provided him an excellent model. He hastened to record his obligations to his two patrons. To the Lord Chancellor he wrote in terms of formal courtesy. To

[1] This familiar style in a letter of Addison's almost certainly indicates that Henry Purcell was well known to him, probably through the intermediary of Daniel.

the Lord Treasurer he wrote informally: 'modesty is so very
scarce that I think I have not seen a Blush since my first
Landing at Calais.' But a sensitive and observant mind soon
thawed before Gallic charm and wit, and 'the great kindness
and affability that is shown to Strangers'. He observed that:

tho . . . the English are a much wiser Nation the French are undoubtedly much more Happy. Their old men in particular are
I believe the most agreeable in the World. An Antediluvian could
not have more life and briskness in him at Three Score and ten:
for that Fire and Levity which makes the young ones Scarce
Conversible, when a little wasted and tempered by years, makes
a very pleasant and gay old age.

By November he was deep in French studies, and in a letter
to William Frowde, uncle of the reputed author of the 'Cursus
Glacialis', he complained that 'I am so Embarras'd with
nouns and Verbs that I have no time to think of Verse, but
am forc'd to Decline and conjugate words, instead of putting
'em into Rhime'. He lamented his bad memory: but like
many men who mistrust their memories he was a good
keeper of records, and he preserved drafts of his letters and
began to fill notebooks with his observations.[1]

The splendour of the royal palaces was Addison's
favourite theme. The 'fine variety of Savage prospects' at
Fontainebleau, and its 'artificial Wildeness', commended
themselves in a greater degree even than the magnificent
formality of Versailles, where:

the painter has represented His Most Christian Majesty under the
Figure of Jupiter throwing thunderbolts all about the Ceiling, and
Striking terror into the Danube and Rhine that lie astonished and
blasted with Lightning a little above the cornice.

In December he rusticated himself to Blois. There, he told
Congreve, 'all the languages of Europe are spoken except
English, which is not to be heard I believe within fifty miles
of the place'. And while thus immersed in their speech he
deepened his observation of the French people. "'Tis not in
the pow'r of Want or Slavery to make 'em miserable. There
is nothing to be met with in the Country but Mirth and

---

[1] These are known by report only. Unhappily for his biographer either
Addison or his executors were subsequently as careful to destroy them.

Poverty. Evry one sings, laughs and starves'; and of the women, 'Evry one knows how to give herself as charming a Look and posture as Sr. Godfrey Kneller could draw her in'. During his stay at Blois Addison was drawn into a quarrel which he afterwards regretted and which caused him to write a letter of apology for 'a mutual affront' offered 'in the heat of discourse'. Whatever the cause of trouble with a gentleman addressed as 'Monsr. L'Espagnol', it was certainly not on account of a lady. The Abbé Philippeaux, a resident of Blois who struck up an acquaintance with Addison, reported that 'he had no amour whilst here, that I know of; and I should have known it if he had had any'. Indeed the whole tenor of Addison's life in Blois struck the priest as eccentric and recluse:

> He would get up so early as between two and three in the height of summer, and lay in bed till between eleven and twelve in the depth of winter. He was untalkative whilst here, and often thoughtful; and sometimes so lost in thought, that I have come into his room, and staid five minutes there before he has known anything of it. He had his masters generally at supper with him; kept very little company beside.[1]

Addison cared little for Blois or its inhabitants. 'The Place where I am at present by reason of its Situation on the Loire and its reputation for the Language is very much infested with Fogs & German Counts' he reported to Stanyan. Any temptations to social relaxation were further put away by illness. To Charles Montagu he confided that he believed his trouble to proceed from the gout. To Adams, his fellow Latin poet from Magdalen, who had received his leave of absence a year before Addison did so,[2] who had been threatened with expulsion from the college for neglecting to take Orders at the appropriate time,[3] and who was now travelling in France, he reported that he had been 'lately very much Indispos'd with a Feaver . . . but am at present very well recovered, notwithstanding I made use of one of the Physicians of this place, who are as cheap as our English Farriers and generally as Ignorant'. Thus early in life

---

[1] Spence, p. 184.   [2] Vice-President's Register, 3/1/98.
[3] Ibid. 1696.

Addison's delicate health was accompanied by a distrust of and contempt for doctors, which became a credo:

As for myself, the only physic which has brought me safe to almost the age of man, and which I prescribe to all my friends, is Abstinence. This is certainly the best physic for prevention, and very often the most effective against a present distemper. In short, my Recipe is, 'Take Nothing'.

Magdalen was much in his thoughts. The translation of Bishop Hough from Oxford to Lichfield had necessitated the election of a new President. Addison was kept informed of the progress of events, and reported them to Adams with the slightly patronizing air of one who has left the little world of the cloister:

I hear there is at present a very great Ferment in Maudlin College which is workt up to a great height by New-nam Ale and frequent Canvasings. I suppose both parties before they engage will send into France for their Forreign Succours.

The implication was that Fellows who were abroad travelling would be entreated to return in the interests of one or other candidate for the vacant great office. Meanwhile Stanyan continued to coach Addison in his studies of diplomatic procedure, and elicited handsome thanks from his pupil:

I really think Myself very much obliged to you for your directions and if you would be a little particular in the names of the Treaties that you mention I should have reason to look upon your Correspondence as the luckiest Adventure I am like to meet with in all my Travails.

Stanyan also kept Addison informed of current political developments in England, which were such as to alarm dependants of the Whig ministers. The latter part of the year 1699 had been filled with bitter party warfare. Charles Montagu felt the pressure too heavy to bear and resigned from the Treasury in October. This would be a disconcerting blow to Addison, who wrote to Stanyan:

I thank you for yᵉ news and poetry you were pleas'd to send me, tho' I must confess I did not like Either of 'em. The Votes had too much Fire in 'em and yᵉ Verses none at all: however I hope the first will prove as harmless to Ministers of State as the others are to the Knights of the Toast.

Lord Somers remained in office and was the central figure in the Government and the principal target for political artillery.

Tormented by doubts about his political support, Addison fretted in the provincial isolation of Blois. A Capucin Father who announced that 'he did not question but laughter was the effect of Original Sin and that Adam was not Risible before the Fall' was matter for a passing comment. But his command of French had grown and he was impatient to converse with equals in a language which 'is indeed extremely proper to Tattle in'. It had been his intention to leave France for Italy some time before, but he had been delayed by his slowness in acquiring the language. Events at home and in Europe probably increased his anxiety to travel further while he might. Lord Somers was impeached and the king dismissed him in April. No longer able to rely on patronage, Addison sought pupils to accompany him to Italy, and awaited the conclusion of negotiations which would enable him to visit that country paying his way with his services. He continued to divert himself by observing French manners. Even the wild life of the countryside at this season of the year seemed to possess a quality particularly French: 'I cant but fancy the birds of this place as well as the men a great deal Merrier than those of our own Nation.' He met Edward Wortley a member of the Montagu family, and together the two young men undertook a tour in central France. Wortley was a man of wit and ability, condemned to future fame as the husband of a remarkable wife; but he was as yet a carefree bachelor, and the two men enjoyed themselves sightseeing and ridiculing the superstition of the devout or, in more serious mood, visiting La Trap. Addison was presented to the founder, then aged eighty, who had retired from office twenty years before. The abbey was occasionally visited by King James II, then in exile, and the father who accompanied Addison described the king's first visit.

At the end of the summer Addison was back in Paris, and his second stay in that city was much more agreeable than his first, for he was now at home in his surroundings and able to converse with freedom. Stanyan had come to Paris as Secretary of Embassy, and Addison continued his studies in the technique of diplomacy. He also enjoyed visiting the Sorbonne, and noticing that the public debates there were conducted with 'a great deal of Heat and false Latin'. He took particular pleasure in examining the royal collection of Greek and Roman medals. The contemplation of these originals suggested to him a scholarly hobby. Addison had a deep admiration for Sir Isaac Newton whose appointment as Master of the Mint by Charles Montagu indicated the importance which his patron attached to the coinage, which he himself had done much to restore. Addison may therefore have felt that his new hobby might in time bear fruit, and thenceforward upon his travels he made the study of medals his leisure amusement.

While Addison indulged the pleasures of observation in France, the Republic of Letters was enjoying some lively riots in England. In May 1700 Addison's master and friend, who had so long ruled supreme in English letters, at last vacated his throne. Dryden died leaving no successor to his bays, though himself intending them to fall upon Congreve. It was at this inauspicious moment that Dr. Blackmore took up his pen to attack the 'wits'. They were, he thought, useful members of society, destroyed by their pretensions to wit; Garth, for example, was a good physician lost to indifferent poetry. In this mood Blackmore prayed that heaven might guard 'poor Addison' from the same evil effects. This thrust drew upon him 'A Satyr upon a late Pamphlet entituled a Satyr against Wit' written by Steele, who on reading Blackmore's anonymous piece reflected what everybody knew to be the case:

> It must be Blackmore by his rumbling tone;

A minor battle ensued:

> Must I then passive stand! and can I hear
> The man I love abused, and yet forbear?
> Yet must I thank thy favour to my friend,
> 'Twas some remorse thou didst not him commend.

Thus fumed the angry Steele, and Blackmore rejoined with 'Discommendatory Verses to the Noble Captain, who was in a damned confounded pet because the author of the Satyr against Wit was pleased to pray for his friend'. John Dennis took part on Steele's side and others contributed as well. Blackmore was some eighteen years Addison's senior, and perhaps entitled to adopt an air of patronizing banter. In his time he had aspired to a demyship at Magdalen, but without success; and he took his degree from St. Edmund Hall. He may have watched with amusement the earnest pretensions of Joseph Addison. But he was a magnanimous man, and as Johnson observed, 'let it be remembered for his honour, that to have been once a school-master is the only reproach which all the perspicacity of malice, animated by wit, has ever fixed upon his private life'. The Steele–Blackmore hostilities, which continued far into the year 1700, must have impressed upon the reading public that Joseph Addison was important enough to provide a quarrel amongst the wits.

His Oxford studies in philosophy had prepared Addison to take advantage of a meeting with Malebranche; and his friendship with Dryden, who had drawn much of his critical apparatus from French sources, gave special significance to a conversation with Boileau whom he approached with the veneration due to a prophet. Of the two encounters Addison thought that with Malebranche the more interesting, that with Boileau the greater honour. Père Malebranche was at this time readily accessible to visitors, and according to his custom he welcomed Addison with conversation about his own works and read aloud the draft of an hypothesis of colours. Addison's philosophical reading enabled him to detect novelty in what he heard. He had declared of Descartes, 'Illustris ille vir, quem unum Galliae invidemus . . .'.[1] He was now interested to learn that Malebranche highly esteemed the English, amongst whom he had more followers than in France where the new philosophy was regarded as irreligious. He took notes of this interview which was one of the cherished incidents of his lifetime.

To Boileau, as doubtless to Malebranche, Addison went armed with a presentation copy of the *Musarum Anglicanarum*. This Boileau seems to have received civilly remarking that it had given him a new notion of the standards of

---

[1] 'Nova philosophia veteri praeferenda est.'

correctness in English scholarship and poetry. Johnson brushed this compliment aside, saying that Boileau had a contempt for modern Latin; and Macaulay thought him ignorant of English letters. But 'correctness' had not been a feature of English writers until recently, and Macaulay's observation emphasizes the probability that Boileau meant precisely what he said. At the age of sixty-four he was somewhat difficult of access. Addison reported that though deaf he talked 'incomparably well'. The conversation seems to have ranged over the merits of ancient and modern poetry. Boileau gave Addison a low estimate of modern poets, though praising Racine and those of his generation. Addison, who in temperament so much resembled Fénelon, asked Boileau his opinion of *Télémaque*, then a literary sensation, and was told that it gave a modern reader a better idea of Homer than any translation could do.[1] This observation made a deep impression upon Addison who himself knew the difficulties of translation. Boileau ventured another criticism which dwelt in Addison's mind throughout his lifetime. Fénelon, said Boileau, made his hero preach, while Homer showed his meaning in the character and actions of Ulysses.[2] The influence of Boileau's writings upon Addison, both as criticism and by example, was most powerful. That influence was deepened by this meeting which imprinted upon his genius not only the views but the personality of the great French critic.

These visits were the climax of Addison's stay in France, and by autumn his pupils were ready to leave for Italy. In the last week of November he passed through Orange, delighting in the triumphal arch of Marius and the Roman Amphitheatre and noticing with surprise the good relationship between the large Protestant colony and the Catholic community. On 29 November he was at Marseilles awaiting shipping. As he prepared for the voyage, he reflected that he was glad to turn his back upon the French:

I am at present very well pleas'd to Quit the French Conversation; which since the promotion of their young prince begins to grow Insupportable. That which was before the Vainest Nation

[1] Cf. also *T.* 156.   [2] Graham, p. 24.

in the World is now worse than ever; There is scarce a Man in it that does not give himself greater Airs and look as well pleas'd as if he had receivd some considerable Advancement in his own fortunes.

He had landed somewhat more than a year before with all the anti-French prejudices of a Whig implanted in the mind of one who still lived in the insularity and self-satisfaction of his own race. These ideas were unaltered and remained throughout life the basis of his political thought towards France:

The *French* are certainly the most implacable, and the most dangerous enemies of the *British* nation. Their form of government, their religion, their jealousy of the *British* power, as well as their prosecutions of commerce, and pursuits of universal Monarchy, will fix them for ever in their animosities and aversion towards us, and make them catch at all opportunities of subverting our constitution, destroying our religion, ruining our trade, and sinking the figure which we make among the nations of *Europe*. . . .

As we are thus in a natural state of war, if I may so call it, with the French nation; it is our misfortune, that they are not only the most inveterate, but most formidable of our enemies; and have the greatest power, as well as the strongest inclination, to ruin us.[1]

But across the barriers of political and doctrinal difference the sparkle of French civilization had made an irresistible appeal, and Addison remembered France with pleasure when the irritation of the moment was forgotten. Years later:

Seeing a Punch-Bowl painted upon a Sign near *Charing-Cross*, and very curiously garnished, with a couple of Angels hovering over it and squeezing a Lemmon into it, I had the Curiosity to ask after the Master of the House, and found upon Enquiry, as I had ghessed by the little *Agremens* upon his sign, that he was a Frenchman.[2]

But he reflected grimly that 'The Apothecary is perpetually employed in countermining the Cook and the Vintner'[3] and remained faithful to a diet of beef and mutton. He noted the Frenchman's familiarity with women and thought it conducive to good manners but never himself achieved it. He admired French affability, ease, and wit, but feeling himself

[1] *Present State of the War.*   [2] *S.* 28.   [3] *S.* 195.

outclassed by nimbler people, he distrusted them, and recalled Rochester's observation that 'French truth and British policy make a conspicuous figure in Nothing'. The splendour of the court, the beauty of the gardens, the nicety of taste, left an indelible impression. Counterpart of this admiration, was his annoyance at the jests which he endured at the expense of his compatriots. He found that a regular property of the stage was *'un gros Milord Anglois . . .* as if Corpulence was a proper Subject for Satyr, or a Man of Honour could help his being Fat, who Eats suitable to his Quality'.[1] He revenged himself by remarking that 'As a *British* Free-holder, I should not scruple taking place of a *French* Marquis; and when I see one of my Countrymen amusing himself in his little Cabbage-Garden, I naturally look upon him as a greater Person than the Owner of the richest Vineyard in *Champagne'*.[2]

Addison's judgement of things French, so acute, witty, and human, was superficial in the realm of art. He observed of French contemporary painting that a 'certain smirking air' was 'bestowed indifferently on every age and sex. The *toujours gai* appeared even in . . . judges, bishops, and privy counsellors. In a word, all men . . . were petits maîtres, and all women *coquettes*.' Of the opera his opinion mellowed after his first revulsion, as he learned to judge by new standards:

I remember the last Opera I saw in that merry Nation, was the Rape of *Prosperine*, where *Pluto*, to make the more tempting Figure, puts himself in a *French* Equipage, and brings *Ascalaphus* along with him as his *Valet de Chambre*. This is what we call Folly and Impertinence; but what the *French* look upon as Gay and polite.[3]

For the masters of French drama he had a deep respect increased by his esteem for Boileau; and the French contemporary stage seemed to him to have lessons for English dramatists amongst whom he aspired to figure:

I should . . . in this Particular, recommend to my Countrymen the Example of the *French* Stage, where the Kings and Queens always appear unattended, and leave their Guards behind the Scenes. I should likewise be glad if we imitated the *French* in

[1] F. 30.   [2] F. 1.   [3] S. 29.

banishing from our Stage the Noise of Drums, Trumpets, and Huzzas; which is sometimes so very great, that when there is a Battle in the *Hay-Market* Theatre, one may hear it as far as *Charing-Cross*.[1]

His own works bear innumerable traces of the influence of his stay in France, for, besides his memories, he bore away an accumulation of notes upon which he drew to the end of a life in which this was perhaps the most formative single year.

On 12 December Addison sailed from Marseilles upon the second part of his journey.[2] This was the portion of his travels to which he had looked forward with the keenest pleasure and for the full enjoyment of which he had made the most elaborate preparations. His vessel was a small single-masted ship, a tartane, such as was commonly used in coastal traffic in that part of the Mediterranean. With him travelled George Dashwood, son of the Lord Mayor of London and a commoner of Magdalen, who may have been Addison's former pupil. Apparently Dashwood did not impress continental Europe: 'C'est un bon gros et gras bourgeois fort porté pour les ancien droits de Londres. C'est pourquoy il a peur d'estre estime spirituel, à cause que c'est contre l'ancienne coustume des citoyens d'avoir de l'esprit.'[3] Also with the party as a pupil was Edward Montagu, a nephew of Lord Halifax. Addison's fees for conducting the two young men through Italy undoubtedly covered all his expenses and might be expected to show him a fairly substantial reward.[4] Their first day's sailing brought them to the small port of Cassis where with a countryman's eye Addison was quick to notice the abrupt change to the aromatic Mediterranean flora, contrasting strangely with the verdure of the Cherwell. He amused himself by gathering a handful of herbs and naming them. As he had walked in

[1] *S*. 42.

[2] He erroneously described his *Travels*, p. 1, 1st ed., as beginning in 1699, and in the title-page as in the year 1701. The events described in the book, however, begin 12 Dec. 1700. During the remainder of this chapter quotations not otherwise identified and not evidently from the Correspondence are taken from the *Travels*.

[3] Klopp, *Leibniz Werke*, ix. 47.

[4] Three years later he expressed disappointment at an offer of his expenses plus a hundred guineas annually for a single pupil. *Infra*, p. 86.

the shadow of Marius' archway at Orange he had felt himself drawing near to the classic ground of the Roman genius. Cassis brought to mind a passage from Claudian.

A second day's sail in the face of contrary winds forced the travellers into San Remo in Genoese territory. Sailing thence into the Gulf of Genoa, the little ship had the misfortune to encounter a violent storm, which it rode out for two terrible days. This was a grim experience for one not accustomed to the sea, sailing in a small craft and with a captain who, fearing all lost, flung himself upon his knees in confession before a friar. The experience sank deep in Addison's memory, and in later years he recalled and recorded the solemn thoughts which passed in his mind when:

> . . . *with affrighted Eyes*
> *Thou saw'st the wide extended Deep*
> *In all its Horrors rise!*
>
> *Confusion dwelt in ev'ry Face,*
> *And Fear in ev'ry Heart;*
> *When Waves on Waves, and Gulphs on Gulphs,*
> *O'ercame the Pilot's Art.*[1]

Provoked by the conduct of the master and by his own lively sense of providence he also turned this experience to account in prose:

> . . . there is not a more ridiculous animal than an Atheist . . . I was a shipboard with one of these Vermin when there arose a brisk Gale, which could frighten nobody but himself. Upon the rowling of the Ship he fell to his knees, and confessed to the Chaplain, that he had been a vile Atheist, and had denied a Supreme Being . . . a report immediately ran through the ship, that there was an Atheist upon the Upper deck. Several of the common seamen . . . thought it had been some strange Fish; but they were the more surprised when they saw it was a Man, and heard out of his mouth, That he never believed till that day that there was a God.

It was just such experiences of the world and observation of human nature which Dryden had in mind when he had spoken of wearing off academic rust.

An alteration of the wind carried the tartane into Monaco

[1] S. 489.

where Addison remembered Lucan's description of the harbour and drew a pen picture of the modern monarchy. From thence the party set out again for Genoa, hugging the coast. Even so the sea proved too formidable and the voyage was abandoned at Savona and continued over land 'over very rugged mountains and precipices'. Addison began sightseeing with the naïveté of a tourist; palaces, churches, Signor Miconi's famous collection of shells, and the Bank of St. George, all received attention. Good Whig that he was, he deduced the advantages derived by the people from the bank which had been a model for the Bank of England established recently by Charles Montagu. Training for diplomacy, he observed every aspect of the polity, remarking that where the Government is poor the people are generally rich. From Genoa the party continued by chaise to Pavia where Addison visited the tomb of the Duke of Suffolk who fell in the great battle, and also inspected the university. Throughout his travels he made a point of recording the traces of Englishmen abroad. But his main interest was in classical antiquity, and the precision of a don was offended by 'a Statue in Brass of *Marcus Antoninus* on Horseback, which the people of the Place call *Charles* the Fifth, and some learned Men, *Constantine* the Great'.

Travelling from Pavia to Milan, Addison looked forward with pleasure to visiting the cathedral and did so immediately upon his arrival. The profusion of marble delighted him, but the darkness and grime within was a disappointment. Unsophisticated, he consoled himself by counting the number of statues adorning the exterior, doubtless making a comparison with the array of statuary niches upon the west front of Lichfield Cathedral. Visiting the crystal tomb of St. Charles Borromeo, he reflected that 'such Publick spirited Virtues' as the saint possessed might lay a juster claim to canonization than 'a sour Retreat from Mankind, a fiery Zeal against *Heterodoxies*, a set of Chimerical Visions, or of Whimsical Penances, that are generally the qualifications of Roman Saints', thereby revealing to us how little he was able to comprehend the humanity of the Latin peoples and displaying the materialism which underlay his observation and thought. He noticed that while there were few reliquaries in Italy without a tooth or bone of Thomas à Becket, yet in the Ambrosian Library there was no picture of any learned Englishman except Fisher. He revenged himself by commenting that, as for books, they 'are indeed the least part of the Furniture that one ordinarily goes to see in an *Italian* Library, which they generally set off with Pictures, Statues and other Ornaments . . .', a reflection which moved a learned successor, John Breval, to remark that he could not have made much inquiry into the books and manuscripts which these libraries contained.

It was in Milan that Addison began to record comparisons between Gothic and classical styles of architecture. In spite of the friendly humble Gothic of Milston church, the splendid elegance of Salisbury and Lichfield, and the mature fifteenth-century dignity of Magdalen, Addison entered Italy prepared to ignore the Gothic as he had done in France. But the contrasts were too violent to escape him. He noticed a Carthusian convent by the roadside which struck him as 'extremely fine, and curiously adorn'd, but of a *Gothic* structure'. The cathedral of Milan seemed 'a vast *Gothic* pile'. Uncritically he identified Gothic with primitive clumsiness. Classical styles, on the other hand, were all sweetness and light, models for the dignity of Milton and the grace of Cowley. The mellow shadows of age on medieval marble were dismissed as 'that mouldy colour'; and though he betrays that something within him stirred at these southern relatives of the medieval buildings which had been his lifelong companions, he hardly questioned the opinion of the age in this as in many other matters. His was the generation which erected the New Building at Magdalen, rational antithesis of the founder's romantic fancy.

Luxuriating in the wealth of enlightened architectural models, Addison travelled on to Brescia and thence past Lake Garda to Verona, drawing upon his topographical collections from the Roman poets, and noticing the shortcomings of Bishop Burnet's prosaic account of these places. Against the background of antiquity, and what he considered, doubtless correctly, to be the low horticultural achievements of the Italians, he began to assess the character of the people. He contrasted with amusement the affected levity of France and the equal affectation of gravity in Italy, and cited the 'Young Men walking the Streets with Spectacles on their Noses, that they may be thought to have Impair'd their sight with much Study'. The Italian temperament was more congenial to him than the French, amongst whom he preferred the conversation of old men and clergy. He visited the tomb of St. Anthony 'where good Catholicks . . . smell his Bones, which they say have in 'em a natural perfume, tho' very like Apoplectic Balsom' and went on to transcribe and translate a passage from the life of the Saint which told of his address to a multitude of fish, commencing:

Altho' the Infinite Power and Providence of God (my dearly beloved fish) discovers it self in all the Works of his Creation . . . nevertheless the Goodness of the Divine Majesty shines out in you more eminently, and appears after a more particular manner, than in any other Created Beings.

At Padua he found a building wholly to his liking in Palladio's Sta. Justina: 'Handsome, luminous, disencumber'd' he commented. Signing the university register of English and Scottish students with his pupils on 9 January[1] the Oxonian noticed that the institution 'is of late much more reform'd than it was formerly, tho' it is not yet safe walking the Streets after Sun-set'; and with this comforting reflection passed on to Venice by river.

The great republic was a major objective for a pupil in diplomacy, and Addison set about a thorough study of its institutions beginning with an interview with Father Coronelli, the State geographer. He found the city 'very entertaining to a Traveller'. The lack of fencing upon the numerous bridges testified, he thought, to the sobriety of the citizenry; but he did not record whether it presented a hazard to a too convivial Englishman. Indeed the reserved, the shy, the prudent Mr. Addison also remarked that 'there is something more intriguing in the Amours of *Venice* than in those of other countries', but left us no hint of any

---

[1] *Registro dei viaggiatori inglesi in Italia*, ed. H. F. Brown, Venice, 1921, p. 313. Dashwood and Montagu signed 9 Jan. Addison's name is given as being put in in 'Aug', but this is certainly either a later and erroneous insertion, all the other names being dated, or a misreading or restoration of the entry.

experience upon which this judgement was founded. In this expansive mood, he went to the opera at the Teatro San Giovanni Grisogomo. The piece was *Cato Uticense* by Nori and Pollarolo.[1] He thought the music excellent, an opinion which in later years he chose to forget when conjecturing that the cat-call had its original in Italy. He was shocked at the weakness of the libretto and at the travesty of Cato's character, and doubtless thought again of the manuscript play in his baggage. He condemned the Italian comedy out of hand. 'Their Poets have no Notion of gentle Comedy, and fall into the most filthy double Meanings imaginable, when they have a Mind to make their Audience merry.' There is some evidence that Addison himself aspired to write a comedy at an early stage of his career.[2]

If his judgement of the stage was bold and correct, his comprehension of painting was narrow and formal. He enumerated and catalogued some of the pictures he saw. He noticed their profusion, thought that age mellowed their beauty, and passed on. His time was limited, for the scene in Europe continued to darken, while in England politics took a violent turn, Charles Montagu being threatened with impeachment, a word which still conjured visions of the scaffold. Addison therefore hurried his departure for Rome lest war or political misfortune should cut short his journey. Leaving Venice after enjoying the carnival, he passed on by ship to the Po delta and Ferrara where he paid homage at Ariosto's monument. Thence he travelled to Ravenna. After he crossed the Rubicon he paused in Rimini, to make an excursion to the village State of San Marino.

In the estimation of his nineteenth-century biographer Miss Lucy Aikin, the description of the republic which he wrote gained for its author as much reputation as any other production of his pen. The little community, doubtless surprised to receive such a visit, recalled the event when the historian Grote passed that way seventy years later.

From Rimini Addison travelled on through Pesaro, Fano, and Senigallia to Ancona. At Loreto he visited the lodgings of the English Jesuits, noticing that a monument to each of

---

[1] A. Zeitvogel, *Addison's Cato, eine geschichtliche und dramatische Quellen-untersuchung*, Darmstadt, 1934, p. 22. [2] p. 351 *infra*.

the English martyrs adorned the staircase. In the same place he was shown the Papal Treasury, where so vast an accumulation of wealth caused him to reflect upon what he had so far seen in Italy. He was on the whole disappointed with sightseeing, though this particular item exceeded his expectations. Yet as a good Whig he was pained to find so great an accumulation of wealth unused:

> It is indeed an amazing thing to see such a prodigious quantity of riches lye dead, and untouched in the midst of so much poverty and misery, as reign on all sides of them. . . . If these riches were all turned into current coin, and employed in commerce, they would make *Italy* the most flourishing country in *Europe*.

From Loreto Addison journeyed on through Recanati, Macerata, and Tolentino to Spoleto. He then viewed the Clitumnus and travelled to Terni, Narni, and Otricoli. The passage of the Apennines, though wearisome to the body, had delighted him. The variety of scene and climate and the profusion of unfamiliar plants continued to enthral him. As he drew near to Rome there ran in his head the lines written by Claudian travelling the same way:

> Inde salutato libatis Tibride nymphis,
> Excipiunt arcus, operosaque semita, vastis
> Molibus, et quicquid tantae praemittitur urbi.

He went first to St. Peter's, where he noticed that the admirable proportions of the building distinguished it from Gothic cathedrals in England which by their disproportion conveyed an impression either of height or of length. At the Rotunda he asked himself whether the form of the heathen or of the Christian temples was the more beautiful. He concluded that the 'variety of noble prospects' in a cruciform building outweighed the grand sweep of the Rotunda, and took occasion to reflect upon the pettiness of minute critics who search for little beauties in great buildings.

It was now Holy Week and, instead of remaining in Rome, Addison passed on to Naples. On his way he admired the beauty of the countryside but deplored its depopulation since Roman times. This he derived from the nature of the Catholic religion, which tended to enclose its people in

monasteries and its wealth in treasuries, while inviting
'swarms of vagabonds under the title of Pilgrims'. Thus the
Protestant Establishment, the Revolution Settlement, and
Whig economics were confirmed by observing their
opposites.

Upon the ancient road to Baiae, Horace and Silius Italicus
were Addison's particular companions; but in Naples he
was again face to face with contemporary politics. Holy
Week did not prevent a celebration of the accession of a
French prince to the Crown of Spain. Viceroy and cardinal
processed together, and relics and miracles were on every
hand. Both incurred Addison's disapproval. He noticed that
superstitions were tolerated in Naples which were un-
dreamed of in France, and detected the salutary effect of
a nearby reformed religion upon catholicism in the latter
country. He spent some time visiting the antiquities of the
region, and indulged in amateurish experiments amongst
the volcanic gases of the Grotto del Cani. He climbed Mount
Vesuvius, sinking knee deep in volcanic sand, and had the
good fortune to find the crater clear of mist and smoke. He
amused himself by rolling stones down on to the crater floor
and, finding that they did not sink into it, concluded the
matter to be solid 'and I question not but one might then
have crossed the bottom, and have gone up on the other side
of it with very little danger'. The experience much exceeded
his expectations, and provoked some yet more amateurish
explanations of the phenomena which he observed. Wishing
to view the place of retirement of Augustus and the residence of Tiberius, he visited Capri, sailing round the island
and exploring some of the ruins on foot. He then began
his journey back to Rome by sea, choosing the element
which had twice played him false so that he might follow
the voyage of Aeneas and enjoy Virgil's description of the
capes and headlands. He landed at Ostia and travelled thence
to Rome.

The classical concept of a good citizen, the statesman who
combined patriotism with urbanity, dominated the education of the young and men's judgement of one another for
two centuries, and was enshrined in ancient Rome. To
Addison, the student of Latin poetry, who took Cato for his

model of citizenship, a stay in the city must have been of profound and moving significance. Yet he had so far chilled his emotions and was so much master of his thoughts that no trace of sentiment is permitted to appear in the account of his visit. 'It is generally observed', he begins, 'that modern *Rome* stands higher than the ancient; some have computed it about fourteen or fifteen feet. . . .' The same self-possession led him to prefer the utilitarian structures of the commonwealth to the ornaments of the emperors, and to place both above the Christian antiquities 'so embroiled with legend and fable'. These conclusions were the result of a vigorous routine of sightseeing undertaken in spite of the heat of July, a season then considered unhealthy. Making copious use of his notes he paid special attention to statuary. Benefiting from his study of medals in France, he interested himself particularly in the domestic details of antiquity : the form of musical instruments, the varieties of dress, and the design of household articles. Embarked upon this inquiry, he decided to take formal instruction from Signor Ficoroni, an expert in medals, who later claimed that 'all Addison knew of Medals he learned of [me] in not above 20 lessons'. The pupil felt able to boast to Wortley : 'I . . . can count a Sum in Sesterces with as much Ease as in pounds sterling. I am a great Critic in Rust and can tell you the Age of it at first sight.' He loved medals with the affection of a connoisseur, they remained his hobby and he left a considerable collection at his death.[1]

Addison visited the churches of Rome and the Vatican Library. He saw 'the Pope officiate at St. *Peters*, where, for two Hours together, he was busied in putting on or off his different Accoutrements, according to the different Parts he was to act in them';[2] but it may be inferred that he did not have audience since he mentions the affability of Clement XI to such Englishmen as had been received but without recording his own impressions of the Papal Court. Amongst the English then in the city was the painter Jervas, who, engaged in studying the Italian masters, had the misfortune

[1] They were sold at Sotheby's Jan. or Feb. 1856; see *Gent. Mag.* iv, N.S., 1856, p. 163.
[2] *S.* 201.

to outrage Addison's sense of modesty as well as to win his admiration. 'Mr. Gervaise', he wrote to Bishop Hough, 'makes very great Improvements and 'tis thought will be an extraordinary Artist. He begins already to pity Titian. . . .' It seems that young Dashwood still accompanied Addison, and Edward Wortley also spent some days in his company. Addison's humour may be seen expanding in his correspondence as his travels progressed: 'I remember when our antiquary at Rome had led us a whole day together from one ruin to another, he at last brought us to the Rotunda; and this, says he, is the most valuable antiquity in Italy, notwithstanding it is so entire.'[1] Yet he was so earnestly bent upon self-improvement that he failed to think of himself in the posture of a satirist.

Addison made several excursions from Rome; to Tivoli, Frascati, Palestrina, and Albano, with many wayside stops and country walks evoking the spirits of the ancient poets. But by 1 October it was time to travel north. Imperial and French armies were already marching and counter-marching in the Italian plains. Addison may also have felt that the years of schooling at Salisbury, Lichfield, and the Charterhouse, a decade of learned life in Oxford, and two years of assiduous travel and study, had at last fitted him for government employment. Furthermore he had received no more grants from the Royal Treasury. His emotions on leaving Rome were heightened by the background of tragic events against which they were cast, and found expression in the best English poem which had yet come from his pen, a verse letter addressed to Charles Montagu, now Lord Halifax. As he travelled slowly northwards, the poem took shape in Addison's mind:

> While you, my Lord, the rural shades admire
> And from *Britannia*'s publick posts retire,
> Nor longer, her ungrateful sons to please,
> For their advantage sacrifice your ease;
> Me into foreign realms my fate conveys,
> Through nations fruitful of immortal lays,
> Where the soft season and inviting clime
> Conspire to trouble your repose with rhime.

[1] 'Dialogues on Medals.'

> For whereso'er I turn my ravished eyes,
> Gay gilded scenes and shining prospects rise,
> Poetick fields encompass me around,
> And still I seem to tread on Classic ground;
> For here the muse so oft her Harp has strung,
> That not a mountain rears its head unsung,
> Renown'd in verse each shady thicket grows,
> And ev'ry stream in heavenly numbers flows.

They were good lines, and 'classic ground' became so familiar to English ears that Miss Lucy Aikin in the nineteenth century thought it a trite phrase. But the couplets wear an uneasy air in English and seem to plead for the language which was their inspiration. In easier prose, Addison spoke to Bishop Hough of his admiration for the city he was now leaving:

> . . . I am in the pleasantest City I have yet seen. There are more statues in it than there are men in several others. The streets are markt out with Obelisks, Porphyry is as common as Free-stone, and one sees something in every wall that would be preserv'd in the Cabinets of other Countrys. There are Buildings the most magnificent in the world, and ruins more magnificent than they. One can scarce hear the name of a Hill or river near it that does not bring to mind a piece of a Classic Authour, nor cast ones Eyes upon a single Spot that has not bin the Scene of some extraordinary action.

If Addison had cared to compare his letters written at this time with his verses, he would surely have perceived in the latter all the marks of elegance and technical competence painfully achieved and in the former those of natural genius and grace.

He travelled north by way of Bolsena and Aquapendente to Sienna, where the cathedral drew from him yet another expression of affectionate contempt for Gothic:

> When a man sees the prodigious pains and expence that our forefathers have been at in these barbarous buildings, one cannot but fancy to himself what miracles of Architecture they would have left us, had they only been instructed in the right way.

It is, however, less remarkable that Addison thus expressed himself, or that in later life he wrote contemptuously of

'Times of Monkish Ignorance',[1] than that after swallowing the fashionable classical taste, he gave any thought to Gothic. But in spite of his prejudices, the romantic vision haunted his mind. Perhaps he recalled Lichfield, Milan, or Sienna when in later years he dreamed a literary dream:

. . . I discover'd in the Centre of a very dark Grove a Monstrous Fabrick built after the *Gothick* manner, and covered with innumerable Devices in that barbarous kind of Sculpture. I immediately went up to it, and found it to be a kind of Heathen Temple consecrated to the God of Dulness.[2]

In a yet more self-conscious strain, he made the crowning absurdity of his stage atheist an admiration for 'this *Gothick* Way of Building'.[3] And now, as he contemplated Sienna cathedral, he concluded that 'nothing in the world . . . [could] make a prettier show to those who prefer false beauties, and affected ornaments, to a noble and majestic simplicity'. And as though to match false values in things artistic with false standards in things spiritual, he added acidly: 'Over against this church stands a large Hospital, erected by a shoemaker who has been beatified, though never sainted.'

Leaving the cathedral of Sienna as it were in ruins, Addison continued to Leghorn, Lucca, and Florence. There he paused for an extensive view of painting, sculpture, antiquities, and manuscripts, and became acquainted with Antonio Mario Salvini, Professor of Greek in the university. He also made one of those personal political contacts which he was always assiduous to obtain. The Duke of Shrewsbury, a political moderate and a man whose influence in English politics was rarely but always decisively asserted, and who was much trusted by the king, was at present at Florence. He recorded in his journal that Addison, accompanied by George Dashwood, dined with him on 6 November.[4] Addison would probably be known to the Duke as one of those who had helped Dryden with his 'Virgil', the proofs of which he had read before the work was completed. The ducal party went to the opera, where Addison was amused

[1] S. 60.   [2] S. 63.
[3] *Drummer*, Act I, Scene I.   [4] H.M.C. 2, ii. 756.

at the poet's concern to defend his religious orthodoxy in a prologue disclaiming any real belief in the classical deities of the libretto. The duke was a noted conversationalist and doubtless appreciated Addison's talent as a foil, for the following day don and pupil again dined at his table and afterwards 'took the air'. Two days later the duke called upon the visitors and again took them to the opera, Addison's ninth in Italy. Yet again on 10 November Addison dined with the duke after accompanying him on a sightseeing expedition; and on 12 November each party called upon the other but they failed to meet. It seems likely that he made good use of these opportunities to forward his own aspirations to an employment. Addison certainly left Florence for Bologna feeling that his stay had been fruitful. Writing to Wortley he noted with satisfaction that he had had 'about three days conversation' with the duke. 'I find I am very much obliged to your-self and him. . . . I have taken care to manage my-self according to your kind intimations.' Perhaps Wortley had advised Addison to pay his court to the duke, who had written helpfully to his friend, Lord Manchester.

The campaign in northern Italy was now beginning in earnest and Addison passed hastily through Bologna, Modena, Parma, and Savoy to gain the neutral shelter of Switzerland. He crossed the Mont Cenis in December and was fortunate in anticipating the heavy winter snow. Nevertheless he shuddered upon the precipitous Alpine roads, and distracted himself from vertigo by meditating upon his life in Italy. He worked upon his verses to Lord Halifax and cast them into their final shape as a 'Letter from Italy':

> How has kind heav'n adorn'd the happy land,
> And scattered blessings with a wasteful hand!
> But what avail her unexhausted stores,
> Her blooming mountains, and her sunny shores,
> With all the gifts that heav'n and earth impart,
> The smiles of nature and the charms of art,
> While proud Oppression in her vallies reigns,
> And Tyranny usurps her happy plains?
> The poor inhabitant beholds in vain
> The red'ning Orange and the swelling grain:

Joyless he sees the growing Oils and Wines,
And in the Myrtle's fragrant shade repines:
Starves, in the midst of nature's bounty curst,
And in the loaden vineyard dies for thirst.

Oh Liberty, thou Goddess heavenly bright,
Profuse of bliss, and pregnant with delight!

Thus a good Whig was gratified to find that political virtue is rewarded with material prosperity. It was also never absent from Addison's mind that poetic virtue would be rewarded by a government employment, and he ended what was generally recognized as a fine piece of writing with a devastating attempt at flattery. Addison decried his ability to praise the king in proper terms, and thought his verses 'Unfit for heroes, whom immortal lays, And lines like Virgil's, or like yours, should praise.' It might be thought that he overestimated the vanity of his patron, who was a competent maker of verses; but the final couplet of the 'Letter from Italy' stands as a humorous comment upon the manners of the time.

In a letter to Wortley, Addison affected nonchalance and diffidence about his new piece:

During my passage o'er the mountains I made a Rhiming Epistle to my Ld. Halifax, wch perhaps I will trouble you with the sight of, if I don't find it to be Nonesense upon a Review. . . . You will think [it] I dare say as extraordinary a thing to make a Copy of Verses in a voyage o're the Alps as to write an Heroic poeme in a Hackney coach,[1] and I believe I am the first that ever thought of Parnassus on Mount Sennis.

It was banter to say that so carefully polished a piece was dashed off during an Alpine journey: but Wortley was now in London and the moment was propitious for him to show the 'Letter from Italy' to his influential friends, and perhaps to his cousin to whom it was particularly addressed. Both of Addison's political patrons were now in retirement, and were the subject of political attacks: but they retained the royal confidence and the king himself was master of diplomatic appointments.

As poetry the 'Letter' has secured a permanent place in the corpus of English verse. Johnson estimated it crisply

[1] A shaft at the unfortunate Blackmore.

as 'the most elegant if not the most sublime of his poetical productions. . . . It has always been praised but has never been praised beyond its merit. . . . It is more correct, with less appearance of labour, and more elegant with less ambition of ornament, than any other of his poems.' Macaulay, to whom its sentiments appealed, thought it Addison's best poem: 'quite as good as any poem in heroic metre which appeared during the interval between Dryden's death and the publication of the "Essay on Criticism". . . . It contains passages as good as the second-rate passages of Pope.' Even if the view were accepted that the Pope technique rendered obsolete all previously written English heroic couplets, the 'Letter' remains an interesting and beautiful poem. A century later it was still being studied and was translated into Latin as a compliment to a Lord Chancellor.

The passage over the Mont Cenis made a deep impression upon Addison. A year after the event he wrote from the security of sea-level to warn a friend against an intended journey to Italy by that route. 'Think but on Mount Cenni and, as you have not the brains of a Kite, I am sure it will deter you from so rash an undertaking.' It was therefore with relief that he now found himself in Geneva, where he reflected that 'the sight of a Plain is as agreeable to me at present as a shore was about a year ago after our tempest at Genoa'. Addison felt himself lucky to be alive after his journeys. He had escaped from his fall into the sea at Calais, from the storm in the Gulf of Genoa, from the pestilences of Rome in August, and from the precipices of the high Alps. In later life he grouped these events together as the principal dangers from which Providence had preserved him:

> *In foreign Realms, and Lands remote,*
> *Supported by Thy Care,*
> *Through burning Climes I pass'd unhurt,*
> *And breath'd in tainted Air.*
>
> *Thy Mercy sweetned ev'ry Soil,*
> *Made ev'ry Region please;*
> *The hoary Alpine Hills it warm'd,*
> *And smooth'd the Tyrrhene Seas.*[1]

[1] *S.* 489.

It was in such a mood of thankfulness, not unmixed with anticipation of blessings to come, that Addison delayed in Geneva. He dated a final draft of the 'Letter' 19 February 1702 and sent it to England. Meanwhile the good news of his appointment arrived. Prince Eugene, the Imperial commander, was preparing for a fresh campaign in Italy, and Addison learned from friends that King William had decided to appoint him a royal secretary to attend the prince in the field.[1] This was a diplomatic post of some importance, and afforded Addison an opportunity to prove his worth. He had made a careful study of the military and political dispositions of the Italian states which would now be serviceable to him, and success in such an employment might well lead to a safer and more agreeable post as secretary of an English Embassy.

It had taken a powerful combination of circumstances to obtain this employment for Addison. His scholarly and literary gifts and his personal charm and wit had been widely advertised for several years. His patrons, though not always in political favour, enjoyed the steady confidence of the king. The influential Duke of Shrewsbury had probably interested himself on Addison's behalf. Finally it was that other Charles Montagu, Earl of Manchester, the ambassador who had befriended Addison in Paris, who, acting in his capacity as Secretary of State for the Southern Department, made Addison's appointment. It was under Manchester's immediate supervision that Addison's work would now fall. Thus the principal purpose of so many years of industry and aspiration seemed to be achieved. Addison had first transformed himself from the status of a poor if promising student to the dignity of a don. Then for a further four years he had studied to transfer himself from the academic to the diplomatic world. If he now indulged in a moment of self-congratulation it was but a brief one, for on 19 March 1702 King William died, and with him died both Addison's new appointment not yet completed and the possibility of a further grant from the royal treasury. Addison had poured much verse to the late king, and had counted upon gaining promotion by his favour. But he also admired his manly

[1] Tickell, Preface to Addison's *Works*.

courage and statesmanlike vision with a deep and personal veneration. At a later time when praise of the royal memory could gain him no preferment, but rather the contrary, he wrote:

As this was the birthday of our late renowned monarch, I could not forbear thinking on the departure of that excellent prince, whose life was crowned with glory, and his death with peace. I let my mind go so far into this thought, as to imagine to myself what might have been the vision of his departing slumbers. He might have seen confederate kings applauding him in different languages; slaves that had been bound in fetters lifting up their hands and blessing him; and the persecuted in their several forms of worship imploring comfort on his last moments.

The new queen distrusted the Whig magnates who had been the political advisers of her brother-in-law, and gave her confidence to their political opponents. Lords Somers and Halifax were struck from the Privy Council. Thus at a blow the source of patronage fell into the hands of those who had no cause to reward a Whig verse-writer whose patron they had lately striven to impeach. Furthermore King William, who had little reason to trust the aristocracy, preferred to govern through permanent officials such as Williamson, Hedges, Blaythwayt, Lowndes, or Ellis. He had therefore encouraged those who might rise by merit from relatively humble origins and readily promoted them. Addison was such a man. But Queen Anne delivered unreserved power to her aristocratic advisers, who had less need of such men in high office. This diminished the prospects even of those not committed deeply to the Whigs, such as Lancelot Addison who had recently contributed to a volume of loyal Oxford verse.[1]

Joseph was now confronted with the problem of providing for his immediate necessities and seeking to rebuild his career. During his stay at Geneva he had made excursions round the lake and to neighbouring places of interest. It was probably at this time that his appreciation of natural scenery, always acute by the standards of his age, which was later reduced to principles, underwent a rapid development:

[1] *Exequiae desideratissimo Principi Gulielmo Glocestriae Ducis*, ab Oxon. Acad. 1700.

Our Imagination loves to be filled with an Object, or to graspe at any thing that is too big for its Capacity. We are flung into a pleasing Astonishment at such unbounded Views, and feel a delightful Stillness and Amazement in the Soul at the Apprehension of them. The Mind of Man naturally hates every thing that looks like a Restraint upon it. . . . On the contrary, a spacious Horison is an Image of Liberty, where the Eye has Room to range abroad, to expatiate at large on the Immensity of its Views, and to lose it self amidst the Variety of Objects that offer themselves to its Observation. Such wide and undetermined Prospects are as pleasing to the Fancy, as the Speculations of Eternity or Infinitude are to the Understanding. But if there be a Beauty or Uncommonness joyned with this Grandeur, as in a troubled Ocean, a Heaven adorned with Stars and Meteors, or a spacious landskip cut into Rivers, Woods, and Rocks, and Meadows, the Pleasure still grows upon us, as it arises from more than a single Principle.[1]

In words reminiscent of Dennis's 'a delightful Horrour, a terrible Joy', published ten years before[2] apropos the Savoy Alps[3] and prophetic of Byron's romanticism, he recorded that the high Alps filled him with 'an agreeable kind of horror'. He even departed so far from the taste of his age as to observe that he was able to conceive pleasure from 'the wildness of rocks and deserts, and the like grotesque parts of nature'. As Mr. C. S. Lewis observed,[4] Addison stood at the dividing line between the barbarous past, when man feared the violence of a nature which he could neither understand nor control, and the Wordsworth heyday when having as he thought understood and mastered it he exalted its beauty. But Addison now turned aside to speculate in semi-scientific fashion upon the melting of the snows and the fall of avalanches. He was the recipient of hospitality, for example, that of the Marquis d'Arzilliers, a French Protestant refugee, and of Jean Alphonse Turrettini, pastor of the Church and University of Geneva. The latter was a distinguished scholar and divine, who corresponded with Bayle and le Clerc, and from his learned antecedents of several generations, as well as by his merits, occupied a central position in European scholarship.

[1] *S.* 412.   [2] *Miscellanies in Prose and Verse*, 1693.
[3] See C. D. Thorpe, 'Two Augustans Cross the Alps', *Studies in Philology*, xxxii, 1935, p. 464.   [4] *Essays presented to D. Nichol Smith*: 'Addison.'

Addison now abandoned any thought of returning to England where his friends were powerless. After delaying in Switzerland, whence he wrote to Congreve on 1 August, he turned eastward and journeyed by way of Freiburg, Berne, and Zurich on his way to Vienna. The hostility of the Elector of Bavaria made it unsafe for English travellers to pass through his dominions, and the route selected was through the Tyrol. In November he wrote to George Stepney, the British minister at the Imperial Court, in terms which suggest that he had already been at Vienna for at least a month. It is therefore probable that his journey, upon which he admired the autumn tints of the Inn valley, took place some time in October. That he travelled in company is evident from the use of the plural in his letters, and one Charles Perrot was with him upon at least two occasions. George Dashwood temporarily disappeared from the scene in Switzerland where he probably joined his uncle, Chamberlayne Dashwood, the British minister. The latter presented Addison with a snuff-box shortly before his departure, perhaps as a small extra acknowledgement of his services to young George. Addison would need some means of paying his expenses, and it is probable that George Dashwood and Edward Montagu rejoined him as pupils when he left Switzerland.

Upon these fresh travels he set out with a variety of literary projects. He turned to the accumulated notes which were his material for a book of travels. This work, which appeared in 1705 as *Remarks on several parts of Italy &c. in the years 1701, 1702 and 1703*, was soon completed. The travels which it describes in fact took place in the years 1700, 1701, and 1702, and the narrative ends abruptly in the autumn of the last mentioned year. The book breaks off so suddenly and clumsily, leaving the reader sailing down the Inn somewhere below Kufstein, that so graceless a proceeding in an author usually preoccupied with form requires explanation. It is probable that Addison contemplated writing two volumes of travels. Having qualified himself by his journeys in France and Italy for service under the Secretary of State for the Southern Department, he now probably wished to extend the range of employments open to him by travelling and studying in the countries of northern Europe. As his journeys and studies in Italy had provided ample material for a first volume it may have seemed that his travels in the north would yield enough for a second.[1] His objects in writing a book of travels were precise. He had, he said, been at pains to study numerous existing books of travel, and felt that there was room for yet another.

So extensive was Addison's reading in Latin poetry that he found no difficulty in writing a book different from any other for so long as he travelled upon 'classic ground'. But when he leaves the poets behind him at the foot of the Alps, and without their aid describes his journey through Switzerland and Tyrol, the narrative becomes pedestrian. It may be, therefore, that when he reviewed his manuscript, he decided at least for the time being not to continue his narrative beyond Tyrol.

From the few letters preserved from this period of his life it is clear that Addison was also now casting his studies of medals into literary form. His first weeks in Vienna were spent upon this task. He selected the dialogue of Fontenelle's *Plurality of Worlds* as a model for what was admittedly a dry subject. But though different in form from the *Travels*, the *Dialogues* also depend for their merit upon the dexterity with which the author drew upon the resources of Latin poetry,

---

[1] If such was his belief, the form of the *Travels in Italy &c.* becomes intelligible. This volume covers the journeys in Italy, Switzerland, and as far as the approach to Vienna. France was doubtless excluded as too well known to travellers and because Addison's sightseeing there was not extensive. But it seems strangely illogical to have tacked Switzerland on to a single volume of travels in Italy largely concerned with classical antiquity. If, however, it was the intention to divide Europe into two parts, then Switzerland might be included as logically in the Latin as in the German portion. If there was any such project in Addison's mind, it may be that the title of the first and only published volume with the reference to the year 1703 and its curiously slipshod *Italy &c.* may have been intended to cover a second portion. Such an hypothesis, however, does not explain the discrepancy between the title of the work which gives 1701 for its beginning and the text itself which specifically takes 12 Dec. 1699 as its starting-point; nor was this apparent error corrected by Addison when he revised the text for a second edition in 1718. It is only possible to guess that for some reason not known to us the book was ultimately printed from an unfinished manuscript to which the publisher supplied a title in careless haste, the proofs of which were not seen by Addison; and that he did not care to make a subsequent alteration in a matter of purely personal chronology.

which he applied to explain the design and detail of ancient medals. The *Dialogues* are thus literary rather than antiquarian but, as Macaulay observed, owe little to Greek scholarship or to Latin prose writers. Finishing some first drafts, Addison submitted them to Stepney for an opinion. Stepney was a school and lifelong friend of Lord Halifax, a good scholar and a minor poet of some ability. With Addison he had been a fellow victim of Wellington's theft of Latin poetry for the *Examen Poeticum* in 1698. His advice on the drafts is not known, but the *Dialogues* were not published in their author's lifetime. Possibly Addison was advised of the insufficiency of his antiquarian knowledge, and for this reason had selected the dialogue form, which avoided the necessity for precision. It was suggested by Bishop Hurd[1] that the manuscript was never finished and should have included a fourth dialogue, placed between the existing second and third; he also thought that even the surviving portions as published by Addison's literary executors lacked the author's final correction. But Addison intended the *Dialogues* for publication, and when they appeared after his death they drew from the critical Pope a set of introductory verses including the following lines of praise:

> Touch'd by thy hand, again Rome's glories shine:
> Her Gods, and godlike Heroes rise to view,
> And all her faded garlands bloom anew.
> Nor blush, these studies thy regard engage;
> These pleas'd the Fathers of poetic rage;
> The Verse and Sculpture bore an equal part,
> And Art reflected images to Art.

Even the fastidious Gibbon read the *Dialogues* with pleasure, though offering the criticism that they were letters in disguise. Bishop Hurd thought them 'one of the most graceful' of Addison's works and 'next to Dryden's Dialogue on Dramatic Poetry, the best specimen in our language of this style of writing'.

In addition to the foregoing, Addison was now once more working upon his play *Cato*. Thus he set out upon his northern travels well stored with literary projects.

In Vienna he received many kindnesses from Stepney.

---

[1] See his edition of Addison's *Works*.

With Dashwood and Montagu he accompanied the minister on 30 November to dine with the Prince of Liechtenstein and subsequently at an opera at the Imperial Court, in celebration of the destruction of the Spanish Fleet at Vigo.[1] He was still in Vienna on 26 December, but reached Dresden by 3 January of the year 1703. Travelling through snow-bound country, he wrote bitterly to Stepney of his hardships:

Scarce anything we meet with except our sheets and napkins that is not white. I find very little difference in the straw beds of Saxony and Bohemia. About three nights ago we had the honour of a Cow for Chamber-fellow that bore with our company for the convenience of a stove. We are very seldom without the company of a cock that roosts under the same Roof and has bin as troublesome to us as ever he was to St. Peter. This all together has given me a great distaste of the Golden Age.

At Dresden letters from Stepney gained Addison entry to the Electoral Court where he had audience of the dowager electress, the Electress of Brandenburg, and the boy Electoral Prince, later King Frederick William I of Prussia. From thence he travelled to Hanover, where he was introduced at the court; and a list of English visitors enclosed with a letter from the electress to Leibniz dated 24 February gives his name with the comment: 'Il est fort bon, et ce qui est plus extraordinaire, fort modeste poëte. . . .'[2] He evidently paid a number of visits to the court for on 3 March the electress wrote to Leibniz: 'Le bel esprit Mr. Addison ne se manifeste gueres qu'en escrit (à ce que je crois); car il est fort "still" aupres de moi.'[3] Again on 7 March she reported: '. . . comme il est fort retiré, je n'en jouis pas beaucoup. Aussi je crois qu'il medite sur ce qu'il veut escrire.'[4] But if Addison's reserve prevented him from intimacy with the electress, it did not do so in the case of her retinue, or of the English Resident, Lord Winchilsea, of whom a contemporary recorded: 'C'est une bonne creature. Il n'est pas grand politique ny bon danseur. Et il a besoin d'un maistre pour regler sa teste aussi bien que ses pieds. . . .'[5] But Addison was already master of the ability to make himself agreeable to

[1] Stepney-Hedges, S.P. 80/19 letter of 2/12/02.
[2] Klopp, *Leibniz Werke*, ix. 7.
[3] Ibid., p. 11.   [4] Ibid., p. 14.   [5] Ibid., p. 47.

those whose tastes, temperament, and ability differed widely from his own, and later in the month he was writing to Winchilsea from Hamburg in terms which reflect their recent conviviality. The letter is almost entirely concerned with wine-drinking and is the first hint in a contemporary document that Addison might be other than a sober man.[1]

At Hamburg John Wyche, the English Resident in that city, succeeded Winchilsea as a partner in drinking Rhine wines. Addison's introduction probably came from Stepney, who had served a diplomatic apprenticeship as secretary to Wyche's father. The two men might equally well have been known to one another, at least by name, through Sir Joseph Williamson. That generous patron of young men, who was godfather to Wyche as he was to Addison, had died two years before. Wyche was a man of taste and parts. Hamburg was at this time the most important centre of opera in Europe outside Paris or Italy. Reinhold Keiser, manager of the theatre also a debauchee of the first order, set the pace in fast living for the opera circle of which the English Resident was a patron. Keiser was in due course the author of 113 operas, and his *Claudius* was performed in Hamburg this year. With him there worked Mattheson, a fine operatic singer. Young Handel, an unknown musician, arrived at Hamburg in the spring of this year, becoming associated with Mattheson and Keiser as an accompanist at the harpsichord, and being provided for by Wyche who made him tutor to his son, a post in which Mattheson succeeded him. It thus appears almost certain that Addison would now have an opportunity to study the Hamburg opera and conceivable that he met Handel at this time when both men were in the early stages of their careers. After his introduction to opera by Daniel Purcell, Addison had criticized it in Paris and Italy. He was now able to complete this study in the only other important European operatic centre.

From Leyden, where he had arrived by May 1703, Addison wrote to Wyche: 'My hand at present begins to grow steddy enough for a Letter so that the properest use I

---

[1] This is the only support for Spence's later allegation that Dryden, normally abstemious, had been led into intemperate habits during the last decade of his life in company with his Oxford admirer. Spence, p. 45.

can put it to is to thank the honest Gentleman that set it shaking.' The manner of his correspondence with the convivial Winchilsea and Wyche contrasts strangely with that of his letters to the virtuous Hough or the elegant Lord Halifax. It is not necessary to be told that Lord Halifax was powerful, scholarly, and vain, nor that the bishop was respected, scholarly, and modest, nor that Lord Winchilsea 'loved hunting and a bottle'. His letters accurately reflect the character of the person addressed. There was in Addison that flexibility and sensitiveness admirably suited to a diplomat, but strangely unharmonious with the concept of a modern Cato.

Much conviviality was trying to the body of one who as a child had not been expected to survive, who suffered from an irregular pulse, who had already been visited by the 'gout', and who was sufficiently hypochondriac to have a contempt for the medical profession. But if Addison recompensed himself for the rigours of travel in Germany by bouts of intemperate living, he also brought away pleasant memories of the land and its people. He recalled with delight that 'Ideots are still in request in most of the Courts of *Germany*, where there is not a Prince of any great Magnificence who has not two or three dress'd, distinguish'd, and undisputed Fools in his Retinue . . .'.[1] Perhaps he had approached with misgivings the native soil of the 'counts' who along with the fog had been so troublesome to him in Blois. But he found them agreeable enough in their own land, and found with pleasure that 'the blunt honest Humour of the *Germans* sounds better in the roughness of the *High Dutch*, than it would be in a Politer Tongue'.[2]

In Holland he was back in the home circle of English politics. Every important Dutch city was filled with English soldiers, merchants, and politicians engaged in the management of the war. But any pleasure which Addison may have felt at regaining the society of his countrymen was more than outweighed by news which reached him soon after his arrival from Germany; for on 20 April Dean Addison had died at Lichfield aged 71. He was buried outside the west door of the cathedral. Of Joseph's relatives, his father had

[1] *S.* 47.   [2] *S.* 135.

stood pre-eminent in his respect and affection. To him he owed much that was admirable in his character and education, and it does not appear that any difference had ever clouded their friendship. His death was a grievous loss, the more so because, knowing his parent to be declining, Addison was on his journey back to England, and thus narrowly failed to see him after the long interval spent in adventurous foreign travel. The dean had been ill for some time. He attended the annual formal chapter meeting at Lichfield on 26 September 1701,[1] but at the corresponding chapter on 25 September 1702 he was recorded as absent and confined to his deanery.[2] On 9 October he made a will.[3] Joseph was distressed to know that, quarrelling to the end, the dean had occupied his last months in a difference with his bishop, the friend and benefactor of the family who had added a benefice to the deanery. No single letter which passed between Joseph Addison and his father has been preserved, but when he knew himself to be dying Dean Addison had written to his son with advice. So scrupulously did Joseph conceal his emotions that we have no earlier insight into his thoughts than 24 August when he wrote to Bishop Hough in moving terms of sorrow:

My Lord,   Amsterdam August 24th 1703.

I have a long time denied myself the honour of writing to your Lordship, because I would not presume to trouble you with any of my private disappointments, and at the same time did not think it proper to give you a detail of a Voyage that I hope to present your Lordship with a general relation of, at my return to England. To finish the misfortunes that I have met with during my Travels, I have since my coming into Holland, received the news of my Father's death, which is indeed the most melancholy news that I have yet received. What makes it the more so is, that I am informed he was so unhappy as to do some things, a little before he died, which were not agreeable to your Lordship. I have seen too many instances of your Lordship's great humanity to doubt that you will forgive any thing which might seem disobliging, in one that had his spirits very much broken by age, sickness, and afflictions. But at the same time I hope that the information I have

---

[1] Lichfield Acta Capitularia, vii. 113.   [2] Ibid., p. 114.
[3] Birmingham Probate Registry, probate 7/6/1703.

received on this subject is not well-grounded, because in a Letter, not long before his death, he commanded me to preserve always a just sense of duty and gratitude for the Bishop of Lichfield, who had been so great a Benefactor to his family in general, and myself in particular. This advice, though it was not necessary, may shew, however, the due respect he had for your Lordship; as it was given at a time when men seldom disguise their sentiments. I must desire your Lordship to pardon the trouble of this Letter, which I should never have taken the liberty to have written, had it not been to vindicate one of the best of Fathers, and that to your Lordship, whom, of all the world, I would not have possessed with an ill opinion of one I am so nearly related to. If I can serve your Lordship in this country, I should be very proud to receive any of your commands, at Mr. Moor's in Amsterdam. I am my Lord,

Your Lordship's
Most dutiful, and Most obedient servant,
J. ADDISON

Upon this last occasion when Dean Addison and his son appear together before history, the father remained as ever, impetuous, tactless, and warmhearted, and Joseph cautious, prudent, and self-possessed.

It was thus a sorrowful and disappointed man who arrived in Holland during tulip-time and consoled himself by being 'very much pleased and astonished at the glorious Show of these gay Vegetables'.[1] But he soon engaged himself in literary activities in the centre of the European book trade, the more readily so because Jacob Tonson was now at Amsterdam conducting a series of business negotiations. Addison was soon a party to Tonson's projects, which included a monumental edition of Caesar. For this Addison endeavoured to secure from Leibniz an illustration of the European bison which he had apparently seen in the King of Prussia's collection of animals; and when a splendid folio appeared in the year 1711 and received a favourable review from Addison,[2] it contained a fine double-page engraving of 'Bos Gallicus sive Bisons' dedicated to Frederick, King of Prussia. Doubtless he also discussed with Tonson the publication of the *Travels* which he had already circulated

<hr>

[1] T. 218.   [2] S. 367.

in manuscript to several friends in Europe and England. Tonson also saw four acts of Addison's play which was still unfinished, and probably the draft of the *Dialogues*. In addition, *Miscellany Poems* for next year was now editing by Rowe for Tonson, and contained the 'Letter from Italy',[1] three translations from Ovid's *Metamorphoses*, and 'Milton's Stile Imitated'—a translation from the *Aeneid*, all from Addison's pen.

Bayle, author of the encyclopaedic *Dictionary* in folio, was living in Holland in retirement. Tonson had secured a royal grant of the sole right to print and sell an English edition of the *Dictionary* 'in view of the great Charge and Trouble in getting the said Work Translated and Augmented' and of 'the Encouragement such an Undertaking deserves'. Work upon this project was proceeding, many additions and alterations being made by Bayle himself, whom Addison probably now met in Tonson's company. In later years he was much indebted to 'the famous Monsieur *Bayle*',[2] 'a Man of great Freedom of Thought, as well as of exquisite Learning and Judgment',[3] and Tonson, who knew his habits of work, reported that Addison was often to be found with the folio volumes open before him. At this time he also formed an enduring and most valuable connexion with Jean le Clerc, scholar, critic, and editor. Both Bayle and le Clerc would probably have received an account of Addison from Turrettini. But the two men had quarrelled long and bitterly and continued to do so. This may have made it difficult for Addison to maintain much familiarity with both scholars. Le Clerc almost certainly read the manuscript *Dialogues* and it appears that Addison came to be much better acquainted with him than with Bayle. From this time onwards le Clerc praised Addison's writings in his *Journal Littéraire* which circulated throughout Europe.

Amidst so much literary activity Addison remained without employment. With George Dashwood he signed the 'Album Amicorum' of Frederick Ruysch at Amsterdam on 17 May; but the period of pupilage was about to end, if it had not already done so. And although his political patrons

---

[1] The title-page of the poem reads 1703 though the volume is dated 1704.
[2] *F.* 35.   [3] *S.* 451.

were now by a strange reversal of parts regaining in politics some of the power which they had lost in terms of royal favour, they were not yet in a position to promote their dependants. Tonson, whose peculiar merit lay in bringing together the great Whig patrons of learning and the men of letters who wrote for him, and in making them serviceable to one another, cast around to make some provision for Addison. 'Old Jacob' was the secretary and main motive force of the Kit-Cat Club of which the Duke of Somerset was a member. It is possible that Addison had already become a member *in absentia*, probably by Tonson's help, for it was in this year that he wrote lines to Lady Manchester designed to be inscribed on his glass according to the custom of the club. The duke was now inquiring for a tutor to travel abroad with his son the Marquess of Hertford. John Colbatch, a Cambridge scholar of some repute, had filled the tutor's post for two years and was now in touch with Addison in Holland while the latter was at Rotterdam and Delft awaiting passage. The duke was a ponderous and ineffective politician, notorious for his ill-temper and exaggerated self-importance. This disagreeable nobleman, who had once summarily dismissed Laurence Eusden, later Poet Laureate, from a similar post, with the comment that he had a groom fitter for the office, had now quarrelled with Colbatch and discharged him without compensation. Tonson then wrote to the duke suggesting Addison as a successor. This proposal the duke accepted with alacrity and replied to Tonson that he would be glad to see Addison in England to arrange details. For his part Addison, though consulted by Tonson, had left it to the duke to propose terms, thus putting himself in a false position when the proposal turned out to be disappointing:

I desire [wrote the duke] he may be more on the account of a companion in my son's travels than as a governor, and as such I shall account him: my meaning is, that neither lodging, travelling, or diet shall cost him sixpence and over and above that, my son shall present him at the years end with a hundred guineas, as long as he is pleased to continue in the service of my son ... I do desire his speedy answer, for to tell you plainly, I am solicited every day on this subject, many being offered to me ... but Mr.

Addison is my desire and inclination by the character I have of him.[1]

It was on 4 June that the duke wrote to Tonson and Addison replied to him direct on 16 June accepting the employment in terms of formal courtesy which made plain his dissatisfaction. He was so bold as to add:

I have lately received one or two Advantageous offers of the same nature, but as I should be very ambitious of Executing any of your Grace's commands so I cant think of taking the like employ from any other hands. As for the Recompense that is proposed to me I must take the Liberty to assure your Grace that I should not see my account in it but in the hopes that I have to recommend myself to your Graces favour and approbation.

Addison concluded that he would wait upon the duke in England in about a fortnight.

Somerset was furiously angry when he read an acceptance couched in such terms. Doubtless it was the hint that he would be fortunate to secure Addison's services which fired the ill-temper of this prickly nobleman. On 22 June he wrote to Tonson 'by this first post to prevent his [Addison's] coming to England on my account' and indignantly misquoted Addison's letter. It was not the age, nor was Addison the man, to produce a spirited reply to such an aristocratic salvo, and hurrying back from north Holland he wrote a lame apology which left the way open to the duke to forgive him with magnanimity. But the duke did not relent, nor did Addison apparently take up any of the 'advantageous offers' of which he had boasted. All his life Addison had been at pains to cultivate the friendship of the great, to flatter their vanity, to speak and write the appropriate word. Perhaps this was his first experience of their animosity, and he must have suffered acute anxieties conjecturing what the angry duke would report of the incident to his patrons in the Kit-Cat, Lords Halifax, Somers, and Manchester. Even Tonson, the assiduous collector and promoter of merit, could hardly be pleased at such clumsiness. He is never again recorded as offending one so far his social superior.

Lord Cutts, the hero of many engagements, was in Holland on military business. Addison had celebrated

[1] Bohn, v. 341–2.

Cutt's exploits in Latin verses addressed to the king at the time of the Peace of Ryswick:

> Hic, ubi saxa jacent disperso infecta cerebro,
> Atque interruptis hiscunt divortia muris,
> Vexillum intrepidus fixit, cui tempora dudum
> Budenses palmae, peregrinaque laurus obumbrat.

He now dined with the 'salamander', hinted a subscription to Tonson's *Caesar*, and doubtless discussed the affairs of Dick Steele, who was much indebted to Lord Cutts's patronage. Dick had entered the Tonson circle, and so intimate had he become therein that he now had an illegitimate child by one of the publisher's nieces. There was another illegitimate elsewhere, and besides that a book advocating strict morality called the *Christian Hero*, dedicated to Cutts, which annoyed the author's brother officers but ran through twenty editions in the century. Dick was languishing miserably at the Landguard fort after a London season in which he had written a successful play *The Funeral*, intrigued with Mrs. Manley who helped him to a midwife, borrowed money from Addison's friend Sansom, and narrowly escaped killing his opponent in a duel, upon which occasion Cutts had defended him warmly. He had now dissipated the rest of his money in alchemistic experiments designed to discover the philosopher's stone and unbounded wealth, and had finally quarrelled with Cutts, his principal benefactor, who cannot have given Joseph Addison an encouraging account of his progress.

Also in Holland at this time was Colonel, later Lord, Stanhope, fresh from the shame and glory of Vigo Bay, with whom Addison travelled from Rotterdam to Leyden. In September Addison was still in that country, drinking champagne with Lord Effingham at The Hague. At Amsterdam he saw the Gild plays which fired his sense of the bizarre:

> Their Actors are all of them Tradesmen, who, after their Day's Work is over, earn about a Gilder a Night by personating Kings and Generals. The Heroe of the Tragedy I saw was a Journeyman-Taylor, and his First Minister of State a Coffee-Man. . . . The Profits of the Theatre maintain an Hospital. . . .[1]

---

[1] *T.* 20.

George Downing, going to the English mission in Den-
mark, carried a letter for him to Wyche, wherein he complained of 'much noise and company'. Meanwhile at home
his father's affairs required attention. After the death of
Joseph's mother, the dean had married Dorothy Danvers,
daughter of a Leicestershire knight, for whom in her
widowed state his son may have felt responsible. The dean's
financial position had improved somewhat before his death,
possibly as a result of his remarriage, as well as by reason
of his three sons being at large in the world. His will had
been proved on 7 June 1703[1] with assets of £1927. 7s. 6d.
Dorothy Addison and Arthur Stevens, Vicar of Rugeley,
were named executors and obtained the probate. But Joseph
received only £100 in a legacy and an equal share with the
widow and children in the small residue. Gulston received
but £5 for a ring and a similar share; while Dorothy and
Lancelot were much more generously dealt with, the latter
receiving £400 to remain in trust until he should reach the
age of twenty-five. The dilapidations at Milston, however,
remained unsettled, the school fees unpaid. But there was
a continued improvement in the prospects of the Whigs, and
all these things drew Addison homewards. Early in the year
1704, probably in February and certainly before the second
week in March, he sailed from Holland in the Harwich
packet.

The memories of the Netherlands which dwelt in his mind
were relatively few, perhaps because he passed much time
in the company of his own countrymen. But with surprising
penetration, all the more remarkable in a Whig who was by
definition pro-Dutch, he perceived the economic weakness
which was to show itself so dramatically in the decline of
Dutch power during the eighteenth century:

Holland indeed florishes above the rest in wealth and plenty:
but if we consider the infinite industry and penuriousness of that
people, the coarseness of their food and raiment, their little indul-
gences of pleasure and excess, it is no wonder that notwithstanding
they furnish as great taxes as their neighbours, they make a better
figure under them. . . . But notwithstanding these circumstances
may very much contribute to the seeming prosperity of the *United*

[1] Birmingham Probate Registry.

Provinces, we know they are indebted many millions more than their whole republick is worth, and . . . we shall not think the condition of that people so much to be envied as some amongst us would willingly represent it.[1]

He was delighted with the monuments of the Dutch admirals:

which have been erected at the publick Expence, represent 'em like themselves; and are adorn'd with rostral Crowns and naval Ornaments, with beautiful Festoons of Sea-weed, Shells, and Coral . . .[2]

and he later compared them favourably with the monument to Sir Cloudesley Shovell erected in Westminster Abbey:

Instead of the brave rough *English* Admiral, which was the distinguishing Character of that plain gallant Man, he is repesented on his Tomb by the Figure of a Beau, dress'd in a long Perriwig, and reposing himself upon Velvet Cushions under a Canopy of State.[2]

In innumerable ways travel had broadened and diversified Addison's mind. But he found the Dutch gloomy: 'more famous for their Industry and Application, than for Wit and Humour', and noticed loftily that they 'hang up in several of their Streets what they call the Sign of the *Gaper*, that is, the Head of an ideot dress'd in Cap and Bells, and gaping in a most immoderate manner: This is a standing Jest at *Amsterdam*.'[3] Perhaps it was unfortunate that so exigent an observer of humanity did not visit Holland before instead of after paying homage in Paris, Venice, Rome, Naples, and Florence.

The four months preceding Addison's departure from Holland are a period of obscurity in his life, and in all probability they were one of privation and anxiety. But the circumstances of his return to England must have been far different from those which he had promised himself when setting out under such favourable auspices four years earlier. Of his emotions upon returning to familiar scenes and old friends he has left us neither record nor hint. Learned, widely travelled, deep in letters, beloved of many friends,

familiar with the diplomatic circle, he remained unemployed
and he crept back to England miserably poor.

> Thus Addison, by lords caress'd,
> Was left in foreign lands distress'd,
> Forgot at home, became for hire,
> A trav'lling tutor to a squire.

Swift was not just to Addison's patrons; and Addison himself later reflected that adversity of itself is not an evil and,
through Seneca, recalled the saying of Demetrius that
'nothing would be more unhappy than a man who had
never known affliction'.

IV

THE COCKPIT
1704–1708

B ACK in London Addison relished familiar sights and
sounds, such as the cries of the town, than which
'There is nothing which more astonishes a Foreigner,
and frights a Country Squire. . . .'[1] His name still appeared in
the Magdalen battels books, and he might have returned to
the college with honour, living in relative ease and elegance
amongst those who, like his brother Lancelot, had remained
cloister-bound. But instead of the Magdalen rooms which
might have been his, he took a third-floor garret off the
Haymarket, a poor habitation but within walking distance
of everything worth while in political, literary, and fashionable London.[2] Renewed intercourse with his old surroundings must have brought home to the returned traveller the
changes which had taken place in himself since last he
beheld them. Least important, perhaps, was an enhanced
pleasure in the classics, now conceived against the background of reality. In broader perspective he was aware of the
smallness of the civilized world, and at the same time of the
ties of culture which unite the peoples of Christendom even
in conflict. He had grown correspondingly tolerant of
foreign custom. 'We are all guilty in some Measure . . .
when we fancy the Customs, Dresses, and Manners of other
Countries are ridiculous and extravagant, if they do not
resemble those of our own.'[3] But this breadth of mind did
not extend to overcome the perennial English contempt for
foreign nobility : 'It is reported that *Talicotius* [a clap doctor]
had at one Time in his House Twelve *German* Counts,
Nineteen *French* Marquisses, and a Hundred *Spanish*
Cavaliers, beside One solitary *English* Esquire. . . .'[4]

[1] S. 251.
[2] Harte pointed out the place to Pope; D'Israeli: *Curiosities of Literature*,
p. 246, 2nd Ser.   [3] S. 50.   [4] T. 260.

On the other hand the spring in France and the winter in Italy had bred in Addison a discontent with the English climate, and it remained his settled opinion that the gloominess of our weather required the quality of humour in those called upon to support it.[1] It was in the quality of humour that he had benefited most from his travels. Four years of systematic observation of men and manners had sharpened his sight into the human mind and heart, and had thus laid the foundations of humour in thorough fashion. Politically he had also matured. The majestic tyranny of the French monarchy, the petty tyranny of the Italian states, the superstition and credulity of religious belief, the poverty of the papal subjects, the wealth of the merchant oligarchies, all tended to confirm his Whig and Revolution principles, his support of the reformed churches, and his admiration for the logic of human reason and for those philosophers who exalted its powers without excluding the divinity.

Thus it was a worldly wise Addison who in 1704 began to resume the threads of old friendships, and of others made during his travels. Under the tutelage of Lord Halifax and Jacob Tonson, he took his seat in the Kit-Cat Club, which, though charged by its enemies with godlessness and republicanism, was at once the most distinguished and the most powerful politico-literary society in England. He inscribed his glass to Lady Manchester. There were other less exalted meeting places. With Dryden dead, and the less sociable Congreve little inclined to reign in his place, Will's had declined. The St. James's Coffee House provided more congenial ground upon which to renew ancient bonds with Dick Steele when the latter's affairs permitted him to appear in London. Jonathan Swift was an occasional and little-known visitor there until he returned to Ireland in May without having made Addison's acquaintance. Joseph's brother Lancelot probably came to town to see him about this time. Usually a regular resident in college, he left Magdalen on 1 May, his brother's birthday, and did not return until ten days later.[2] London life was expensive, and Addison strove to earn his bread. Moreover he had to deal with difficulties at Milston. His father had held the living

---

[1] *S.* 179.   [2] Magdalen College battels books.

along with his deanery and the new incumbent sought to recover the dilapidations which had accumulated.[1] Poetry was not unprofitable, and Addison remained in close touch with Tonson. Writing to Ambrose Philips, whom he had met in Holland, he regretted that two of Philips's pastorals and a translation of his own from Horace had been too late for inclusion in the latest *Miscellany*. For the first time there appears in this letter an unmistakable note of the literary oracle patronizing a lesser man:

> Your first pastoral is very much esteemed by all I have shown it to tho the best Judges are of Opinion you shoud only Imitate Spencer in his beautys and never in the Rhime of the Verse for there they think it looks more like a Bodge than an imitation, as in that Line—Since chang'd to heaviness is all my Glee. I am wonderfully pleas'd with your little Essay of Pastoral. . . . Our poetry in England at present runs all into Lampoon which has seldom anything of true satire in it besides Rhime and Ill nature.

In the coffee house, serene amongst 'the best judges', the traveller returned fresh from converse with famous men of learning and letters throughout Europe, spoke with authority.

There was little relief for Addison from his financial anxieties. The school fees outstanding to Dr. Taylor could not be paid in cash and were gracefully discharged by the gift of a covered cup, perhaps part of his father's inheritance.[2] It was therefore security and an assured income which Addison sought. Dick Steele, with the same end in view, was striving to make himself serviceable to John Ellis, Member of Parliament for Harwich and Under-Secretary of State. Meanwhile the summer wore on and a sultry air of tension was finally broken on 13 August with the news of the great military victory at Blenheim. This had its poetic celebration in due course. John Dennis wrote 'Britannia Triumphans' which was not successful poetry and many others tried their hand; but it was generally felt that justice had not been done to the greatness of the event. Lord Halifax and Lord Treasurer Godolphin were now in

---

[1] *General Dictionary*, 1734, i, p. 262.
[2] Nichols, *Literary Illustrations*, iii. 241.

not infrequent, if not particularly friendly, personal contact, and upon one such occasion the project of a poem to celebrate the victory at Blenheim was discussed. Godolphin was advised by Halifax to approach Addison. Doubtless the 'Letter from Italy', published this year, was fresh in Halifax's mind. It is not improbable, however, that Addison had already set to work upon a new poem, with his patron's approval. He had celebrated the Boyne and the Peace of Ryswick; Blenheim provided a convenient further opportunity.

Finding the Lord Treasurer interested in his suggestion, Halifax stipulated that the Government themselves should approach Addison. He also protested to the Lord Treasurer against this neglect of promising men. Shortly thereafter, Henry Boyle, Chancellor of the Exchequer, formerly a member of the Board of Treasury which in 1699 had granted Addison his allowance to travel, a moderate Whig and fellow Kit-Cat, climbed to the third floor Haymarket garret to interview him.[1] As a result of this famous meeting Addison undertook to complete a poem to celebrate the victory. A rough draft was shown to the Lord Treasurer who signified his approval by appointing the poet a Commissioner of Appeal in Excise, an office within his own gift. Once more Henry Boyle had been the chosen intermediary, and on 6 November Addison wrote to him in terms of humble gratitude for 'your late generous and unexpected favour', and added with the eagerness of real satisfaction that he would that afternoon wait on Mr. Tilson at the Treasury to secure his patent of office.

Addison's appointment appeared in the *Diverting Post* for 11 November. Thus, for the first time after so many years of endeavour, he had obtained a small regular income from the Crown through the intermediary of his best loved patron, and the Lord Treasurer hinted better things to follow. The office to which Addison was appointed had become vacant on 28 October upon the death of John Locke for whom it provided a modest sinecure. Lady Masham, writing to Jean le Clerc three months later, remarked that it was 'a place honourable enough for any

[1] Budgell, *Memoirs of the Boyles*, 1732, p. 152.

Gentleman, though of no greater value than £200 per annum', and added that it 'required but little attendance'.[1] Meanwhile work upon the poem proceeded rapidly and an elaborate campaign of publicity in the press was prepared in advance of publication.[2] The *Diverting Post*, for example, carried advertisements on 28 October, 4 November, and 2 and 9 December. Tonson was to be the publisher and he knew how to manage such details. 'It is believ'd', ran one puff, 'that this Piece will be Perform'd with that Spirit and Fire, even to reach the Glory of that Celebrated Action, in the highest and most exalted Perfection.' Dick Steele had provided a more elegant advertisement in the opening lines of 'An Imitation of the Sixth Ode of Horace . . . Apply'd to his Grace the Duke of Marlborough':

> Shou'd Addison's Immortal Verse,
> Thy Fame in Arms, great Prince, Rehearse,
> With Anna's Lightning you'd appear,
> And glitter o'er again in War:
> Repeat the Proud Bavarian's Fall!
> And in the Danube plunge the Gaul![3]

Finally on 14 December *The Campaign, a poem, to His Grace the Duke of Marlborough, by Mr. Addison*, was published.[4] It was the day upon which the duke returned in triumph to London and the city was elated with gratitude and admiration.

The public was presented with some 470 lines in heroic couplets, and with a brief dedication to the Duke of Marlborough. It was and remains an easily readable piece, flattering the English public on matters in which they pride themselves, as the occasion demanded. If in the year of its publication it was sensational because topical, and if for two centuries it was influential because so widely discussed, today the *Campaign* is interesting because of the light which

---

[1] *ex* Fox-Bourne, *Locke*: from the Remonstrants Library MSS.

[2] For the circumstances of publication of the *Campaign* see R. D. Horn in *P.M.L.A.* Sept. 1948.

[3] *The Occasional Verse of Richard Steele*, ed. R. Blanchard, p. 14: first published *Diverting Post*, No. 2 (4 Nov. 1704).

[4] For a study of the early bibliography of *The Campaign*, see R. D. Horn, 'The Early Editions of Addison's *Campaign*', *Studies in Bibliography*, vol. iii (1950).

it throws upon the character and attainments of the author. The composition of such a piece at the request of the Tory Government was a highly delicate task for one who aspired to administrative office, who had been patronized by leading members of the Whig opposition, and who in return had been profuse in his verse adulation of them. Yet more delicate was the approach to royalty. The poet was called upon to celebrate events which owed their successful outcome in great measure to years of patient diplomacy and dogged fighting by King William, whom the queen remembered with distaste and jealousy. Addison was therefore faced with alternative courses; the first and simplest, to seize the opportunity given him to write a frankly Tory piece ascribing the victory to the duke, the queen, and the party in power; the alternative was to seek to please all parties at the risk of satisfying none, and it was this which commended itself. He therefore took the ingenious course of mentioning no living Englishman except the duke. There could thus be no cause for complaint, for the duke stood alone in military renown as did the queen, the other person mentioned, in royal authority. Thus the *Campaign* offended nobody though it did not satisfy extreme Tory opinion. It relied for its success upon its literary merit, upon the greatness of the occasion, and upon the propaganda with which it was launched upon the public.[1]

Unlike so much contemporary verse the *Campaign* avoids the classical ornaments; ancient gods fling no thunderbolts and play no part in the victory, nor does the hero himself slay thousands by his own sword. Instead a narrative is attempted, whose theme is the triumph of free citizens directed with reasoned courage and skill, over the superior forces of tyranny. The poet abstained from any analysis of the strategy of battle and concentrated his attention upon the character of the general which he was better equipped to judge. Addison himself expressed his purpose in lines which he reserved for the final passage and which would thus dwell in the mind of the reader:

[1] The disappointed Tories commissioned John Philips to write *Blenheim: A poem inscrib'd to the Rt. Hon. Robert Harley Esq.*, which made little impression on the public.

Thus wou'd I fain *Britannia's* wars rehearse,
In the smooth records of a faithful verse;
That, if such numbers can o'er time prevail,
May tell posterity the wond'rous tale.
When actions, unadorn'd, are faint and weak,
Cities and Countries must be taught to speak;
Gods may descend in factions from the skies,
And Rivers from their oozy beds arise;
Fiction may deck the truth with spurious rays,
And round the Hero cast a borrow'd blaze.
Marlbro's exploits appear divinely bright,
And proudly shine in their own native light;
Rais'd of themselves, their genuine charms they boast,
And those who paint 'em truest praise 'em most.

Abstinence from adornment and extravagance had been a restraint imposed by Addison upon himself so long ago as his early poem to the king. But an important difference between the two pieces is the wider understanding which had resulted from his travels. He could hardly have written a piece more reminiscent of personal experience: the suffering of the Protestants, the pomp and pride of France, the fears of the petty princes, the servitude of the peasantry, the ruined and overgrown cities and ravaged crops, the dashing of the sea against the Belgian dykes, all sprang from first-hand observation. Against this background of intimate knowledge of the European scene, it was possible not merely to portray the skill of the general, but to indicate the significance of his victory in the affairs of Christendom. As Johnson put it, the *Campaign* 'is the work of a man not blinded by the dust of learning: his images are not borrowed merely from books . . .'.

The success of the *Campaign* was immediate and a second edition was rushed through the press, followed by a third in which Addison made a number of corrections.[1] Hardly a contemporary voice was raised in deprecation. The public imagination was captured by the lines which describe the duke directing the course of the battle:

'Twas then great *Marlbro's* mighty soul was prov'd,
That, in the shock of charging hosts unmov'd,

[1] R. D. Horn, op. cit.

Amidst confusion, horror, and despair,
Examin'd all the dreadful scenes of war;
In peaceful thought the field of death survey'd,
To fainting squadrons sent the timely aid,
Inspir'd repuls'd battalions to engage,
And taught the doubtful battel where to rage.
So when an Angel by divine command
With rising tempests shakes a guilty land,
Such as of late o'er pale *Britannia* past,
Calm and serene he drives the furious blast;
And, pleas'd th' Almighty's orders to perform,
Rides in the whirlwind, and directs the storm.

With the latent quality of a journalist Addison thus associated his most telling simile with an event fresh in the public memory, the great storm of November 1703 which had wrecked ships by the score, blown down country mansions, and killed a bishop in his bed. So wide was the currency of the *Campaign* that the last line quoted above passed into the repertory of familiar quotation.

Immortal Rich! how calm he sits at ease,
Mid snows of paper, and fierce hail of pease?
And proud his mistress orders to perform,
Rides in the whirlwind, and directs the storm.[1]

Thus laughed Pope in the *Dunciad*: but long before that date the 'Angel' could be burlesqued without explanation or apology, and a crowd of humbler poets had already paid their tribute. William Harrison, a Fellow of New College, writing in 1706, observed of Marlborough that Addison alone 'Adorns thy laurels, and maintains his own'.[2] Blackmore rumbled:

How Addison excels in th' Epic Strain,
Learn from his finish'd poem, his Campaign;

while on the continent le Clerc wrote in the *Journal Littéraire*:

It is not properly an epic poem, but is an incomparable piece in heroic verse. . . . We may justly affirm that there is nothing wanting to the perfection of the poem; and that Mr. Addison, thus raised and supported by the nobleness of his subject, is as much

[1] *Dunciad*, iii, ll. 261–4.   [2] 'Woodstock Park.'

superior to himself, as he is in all his other pieces to the greatest part of the other poets of what nation soever.

Before long the *Campaign* was finding translators into Latin, in which tongue, like so much of Addison's poetry, it might well have been written. Nor did it escape the tribute of jealousy due to so monumental a success. In the *Consolidator*[1] Defoe wrote:

> Ad . . . son may tell his Master my Lord . . . the reason from Nature, why he would not take the Court's Word, nor write the Poem call'd *The Campaign*, till he had 200 *l.* per annum secur'd to him; since 'tis known they have but one Author in the Nation [Defoe] that writes for 'em for nothing. . . .

and he continued in verse in the *Double Welcome*:

> Let *Addison* our modern *Virgil* sing,
> For he's a poet fitted for a King,
> No Hero will his mighty Flight disdain,
> *The First*, as Thou [Defoe] *the Last* of the Inspir'd Train;
> Maecenas [Halifax] has his modern Fancy strung,
> And fix'd his pension, first, or he had never sung.

The criticism of later generations has assigned to the *Campaign* a less important place in English poetry than did the enthusiasm of the moment. Today even the considered praise of Voltaire seems exaggerated: 'monument plus durable que le palais de Blenheim . . . compté, par cette nation guerrière et savante, parmi les recompenses les plus honorables du duc de Marlborough.'[2] Macaulay thought the poem inferior to the 'Letter from Italy'. There was the inevitable revulsion against what had been too highly esteemed in popular opinion, and one pedant remarked to Johnson: 'If I had set ten schoolboys to write on the battle of Blenheim, and eight had brought me the "Angel", I should not have been surprised.' Horace Walpole delivered a balanced judgement of Addison's verse, particularly applicable to the *Campaign*. Writing to Lady Temple he remarked: 'Mr. Addison, with infinite labour, accomplished a few fine poems; but what does your ladyship think were his rough drafts?'

[1] 1705, p. 27.   [2] *Siècle de Louis XIV*, ch. xix.

After the *Campaign* no major poem came from Addison's pen for several years and it is more than a coincidence of fact that its writing marked the beginning of his material fortune and of his political and administrative career. From this time onwards he no longer felt the anxiety or the spur of privation, nor was he ever again far from the public eye. Not a 'poet born', he wrote poetry with difficulty, and henceforth it fell from him as a principal means alike of self-expression and of advancement. As Swift put it he:

> . . . wisely left the Muses Hill,
> To Bus'ness shap'd the *Poet*'s Quil,
> Let all his barren Lawrels fade,
> Took up himself the *Courtier*'s Trade,
> And, grown a *Minister of State*,
> Saw Poets at his Levee wait.[1]

Substantial reward soon followed the brilliant success of the *Campaign* and the glory which it shed upon a glorious victory. Throughout the winter and spring of 1705 the poem had been read in widening circles, with agreeable consequences. Jacob Tonson had recently published Addison's translation of part of the second book of Ovid's *Metamorphoses*. Anything from the pen of the author of the *Campaign* would be eagerly read, and he was also anxious to publish the *Travels*. The manuscript was sent to press to appear in the autumn[2] with a dedication to Lord Somers. Dick Steele had written a play with a title in his virtuous mood, the *Tender Husband*. This was perfomed at Drury Lane in April. Addison had spent some time with him upon the drafts and had made a number of corrections and suggestions. He now supplied a prologue to the piece commending the laudable purpose of the play, the ridicule of folly. When the script was published by Tonson in May, Steele replied with a dedication to Addison. It was a delicate attention to one accustomed to offer rather than to receive such tributes:

You'll be surpriz'd, in the midst of a daily and familiar Conversation, with an Address which bears so distant an Air as a

---

[1] *Swift's Poems*, ed. H. Williams (Oxford, 1958), ii. 482.
[2] Published 22 November.

publick Dedication. . . . My Purpose, in this Application, is only
to show the Esteem I have for you, and that I look upon my
Intimacy with You as one of the most Valuable Enjoyments of
my Life. At the same time I hope I make the Town no ill Compliment for their kind Acceptance of this Comedy, in acknowledging
that it has so far rais'd my Opinion of it, as to make me think it no
improper Memorial of an inviolable Friendship.

I should not offer it to You as such, had I not been very careful
to avoid every thing that might look Ill-natur'd, Immoral, or
prejudicial to what the Better Part of Mankind hold Sacred and
Honourable.

Thus early Addison was proclaimed not merely a man of
genius but an arbiter of morality. He was also becoming a
man of substance and in May this year he lent Steele £400
secured on Mrs. Steele's Barbados estate.[1] As well as cash,
Steele did in fact owe much in the play to Addison, and even
after so handsome a dedication he felt in later years that he
had not fully explained to the public the extent of this debt.[2]

While Addison's literary fortunes prospered, the political
scene had been altering fast in favour of his friends. The
election of May 1705 saw an increased Whig representation
in Parliament and the return of Lords Somers and Halifax
to the Privy Council. Addison had been promised further
reward by the Lord Treasurer and had certainly merited it,
and his friends were now in a stronger position to press the
Government on his behalf. On 3 July Narcissus Luttrell
noted in his diary: 'It is said Jos. Addison, one of the
commissioners of appeals, will succeed Mr. Ellis, under-
secretary to Sir Charles Hedges, Secretary of State.' This
was John Ellis, Member of Parliament for Harwich, to whom
Dick Steele had lately paid his court. The office of Under-
Secretary had grown during the seventeenth century from
a mere secretarial post to a position of executive authority.
As the Secretaries of State themselves became concerned
with major policy which had formerly been a royal preoccupation, so the Under-Secretaries took over from them
its day-to-day execution. This process was accelerated by
the accession of Queen Anne, who left to her ministers a

[1] See R. Blanchard, 'Richard Steele's West Indian Plantation', *Mod.
Philology*, xxxix, p. 285 n.   [2] *S. 555.*

greater degree of responsibility than their predecessors had ever possessed. The rumour which reached Luttrell's ears proving correct, Addison thus assumed a post of considerable and rapidly growing administrative importance, much beyond anything for which he had dared to hope two years ago when he would have accepted with delight any diplomatic post of the smallest consequence.

The emoluments of the office had been reviewed in 1702 when proposals to give an annual salary to the Under-Secretaries and their clerks, in consideration of 'their great trust, pains & attendance' and their small income, were put before the treasury.[1] The Under-Secretary subsisted mainly upon the fees for transacting home business, which at this time were estimated to amount to the quite substantial sum of £550 per annum.[2] On the other hand foreign business, which in its nature could carry no fees because they could not be collected, was now greatly increasing without any corresponding reward. This was still causing discontent in the Secretary of State's office nine years later.[3] But whatever the anomalies of the position, Addison was now placed in relatively affluent circumstances with an income in excess of anything he had previously enjoyed. The reason for his success, far beyond that of other men of letters, was that in addition to his literary ability he had systematically qualified himself to perform the duties of a substantial administrative post. The success of the *Campaign* had afforded him the opportunity to accept an office which in its nature could not have been open to a poet who had not so prepared himself.

Sir Charles Hedges, the Secretary of State for the South, Addison's immediate superior, was the minister responsible for relations with France and southern Europe, for the 'plantations', and for a share in home affairs, notably the maintenance of law and order and political matters. The Secretary was an experienced administrator, a royal servant in the tradition of Sir Joseph Williamson, rather than a minister in the modern sense. King William had preferred to rule through such men. Thus Addison now had an

---

[1] *Cal. S.P. Anne*, p. 47.
[2] M. A. Thomson, *The Secretary of State*, 1681-1782.
[3] S.P. 34/48, f. 278.

opportunity to serve his apprenticeship in central administration under a man who was a master of its details. Addison was an early example of the infiltration of Whigs into the Government at all levels; and his appointment to this minor but strategic post must have been a gratifying success for his patrons. But if he and his superior were not politically in accord, for Hedges was a moderate Tory, there was another bond. The Secretary was a Magdalen man and, not forgetful of the claims of the college, had in 1700 appointed as his chaplain Hugh Boulter, a Demy of the Golden Election and a Fellow of the college who was well known to Addison.

To enable him to discharge his duties, which included the taking of depositions on oath from those interrogated for political or State reasons, Addison was now put upon the Commission of the Peace. As he assumed his office, which included the drafting of documents of State and the transacting of business with other departments of government, with foreign representatives in London, and with English missions abroad, he was careful to circulate the glad news of his appointment and to invite a 'correspondence' for which he had laid the foundations during his travels. But the development in recent years which had transformed a purely secretarial office into an important executive post and had placed much patronage and influence as well as important responsibilities in the hands of its holder, had also required the appointment of men of wider outlook and greater ability than the clerical staff who had sufficed to fill it in the past. This naturally disappointed the office clerks, who had hoped to be promoted, and on 18 July J. de Fonvive protested to Robert Harley, the Northern Secretary, that:

The places of first clerks, called under-secretaries, ought to be naturally the preferment of other clerks after several years experience; but Mr. Hopkins,[1] Mr. Lewis and Mr. Addison are instances, besides many others, that those places do not require that such who have them should be brought up in the office.[2]

Thus Addison took a coveted place amongst the small group

[1] Hopkins, who had served with Secretaries Trenchard and Vernon, was later Addison's colleague as Under-Secretary for the South.
[2] H.M.C. *Portland*, viii. 188.

of administrators who were developing in the tradition of Pepys and Blaythwayt.

Amongst Addison's friends there was rejoicing at his good fortune, and none was more jubilant than Dick Steele. On 2 August he wrote to Edmund Revett in the peninsula:

Your friend Mr. Addison, who covers this to you, is secretary to Sir Charles Hedges in the room of Mr. Ellis. He may be a serviceable correspondent to you, and I am sure would be glad of an opportunity. Write to him what passes, and to me how you do under his direction.

Addison, who had so recently become an oracle in the world of letters, now found himself in a position to be consulted and besought by those who would rise or be rewarded in the world of politics and administration.

It was in the autumn of 1705 that the *Travels* came from the press. In spite of favourable circumstances, such as the curiosity aroused by the *Campaign*, the book at first sold slowly. The public had expected an account of persons and politics in contemporary Europe.[1] But when the purpose of the author was found to be elegance and scholarship, his book reached its true public and was rapidly sold out. The first printing ran up to four or five times its published price before a second appeared, and during the century it was translated into French as well as passing through numerous English editions after the author's death. Even the terrible Hearne relented somewhat. His first observation, made on 28 November, six days after publication, had read:

Mr. Addison's Travells is a book very trite being made up of nothing but scraps of verses, and things which have been observed over and over . . . though it must be acknowledged, that the book is written in a clean style, and for that reason will please novices and superficial readers.

By 12 January, however, he noted: 'Mr. Thwaites tells me' that Addison's book of travels is 'not so contemptible as most would make it.' This, from Hearne, was praise; and the book soon became notorious and popular enough to draw more than one pamphlet devoted to its praise or ridicule, such as *A Table of all the Accurate Remarks and New*

[1] Tickell, Preface to Addison's *Works*.

Discoveries in the Most Learned & Ingenious Mr. Addison's Book of Travels.

Such attentions only emphasized that the author of the *Travels* was big game for little men. But the charge of plagiarism brought by Hearne and others was less easily disposed of. Addison himself says that he had read extensively in the current literature of his subject. Johnson halted between the belief on the one hand that he had been anticipated by Leandro Alberti and the conclusion that he 'might have spared the trouble, had he known that such collections had been made twice before by Italian authors' and on the other the robuster view: 'Why, sir, all who go to look for what the Classics have said of Italy, must find the same passages.' He thought the book tedious, lacking in Italian learning though replete with French, and popular only because attached to Addison's reputation. But, he admitted, 'His elegance of language, and variegation of prose and verse, . . . gains upon the reader'. Macaulay, in an age when Greek scholarship had made large advances, was quick to notice Addison's poverty in this respect, as well as his failure to use Latin prose writers:

> In the gorge of the Appenines . . . he proceeds to cite, not the authentic narrative of Polybius, not the picturesque narrative of Livy, but the languid hexameters of Silius Italicus. On the banks of the Rubicon he never thinks of Plutarchs lively description; or of the stern conciseness of the commentaries; or of those letters to Atticus which so forcibly express the alternations of hope and fear in a sensitive mind at a great crisis. His only authority for the events of the Civil War is Lucan.
>
> All the best ancient works of art at Rome and Florence are Greek. Addison saw them, however, without recalling one single verse of Pindar, of Callimachus, or of the Attic dramatists; but they brought to his recollection innumerable passages in Horace, Juvenal, Statius and Ovid.

But the plentiful travel literature of the eighteenth century contains many passages in praise of Addison's book.[1] And it deservedly became the indispensable companion of every young man upon the grand tour. Its popularity was not

[1] e.g. H.M.C. XIV Report, pt. ix, Francis Hare, Bishop of Chichester, to his son, 30/6/1732.

confined to England; and when translated into French and published as a fourth volume of Misson's *Voyages*, it gained a place in the *Index Librorum Prohibitorum*. Jean le Clerc once more played the friendly critic; and amongst the reading public there were many who wanted the book on their family shelf, like the parson writing to Sir William Trumbull in 1708 who noted that 'Brown has Addison's travels for 4s'.[1]

In this year of good fortune for himself, Addison's friends also prospered. At The Queen's College, William Lancaster, who had first started young Joseph in the path of advancement, was elevated to become Provost of his Foundation. A genial, hard-living friend, Tidcomb, was advanced to Major-General. Abraham Stanyan had gone envoy to the Swiss Cantons. But Dick Steele continued his own enemy, quarrelling violently, persistently, and unnecessarily, with his former benefactor, Lord Cutts, who, he conceived, had used him 'like a scoundrel'. While Dick lost no chance to manifest his rash unbalance, Joseph impressed all men with his wisdom and judgement. Early in the year he supplied an epilogue to George Granville's 'opera' *British Enchanters*. Granville was an aristocratic dramatist and an active Tory politician. His desire for an epilogue to his 'opera' from Addison's pen is further measure of the esteem in which the author of the *Campaign* was held.

Though the machinery of the Government of which Addison was a member was relatively simple, the work which it performed was complex and diverse. Physically as well as administratively the Secretary of State's office at the Cockpit was the centre of government, attached to the Council Chamber and the Treasury, three minutes' walk from Parliament and four from St. James's. An examination of the office letter books[2] reveals the range of the business. Diplomatic documents of the highest importance, such as royal letters to foreign sovereigns, and instructions to English diplomatic representatives, were drafted, submitted, and dispatched from this office. Relations were maintained with the diplomatic corps in London, negotiations undertaken, and audiences arranged with the queen. The collection of

---

[1] H.M.C. *Devonshire*, i. 861–2.
[2] State Papers at the Public Record Office.

legitimate news through foreign correspondents, and the management of a system of espionage both at home and abroad, ran parallel with an outward news service to English representatives overseas. Some of the best work was done on a personal basis between the Under-Secretaries and their friends in service abroad. A special task was that of keeping the Admiralty informed of ship movements, which was done by correspondence with Josiah Burchett, the secretary and historian of that department. Relations were maintained with the royal government in Ireland, as also with the Board of Trade and Plantations on behalf of the colonial governments in America and elsewhere. A mass of detail connected with the work of the War Office and the administration of the war also fell to the Under-Secretaries. At home they were occupied with a great variety of domestic matters; and the negotiations for a union with Scotland which began at the Cockpit in April 1706, by adding greatly to the burden of the principals, much increased their own. There was responsibility for the gaols, and for much interrogation. There was already the perpetual battle against the Treasury personified in William Lowndes, the Secretary. Once sufficiently master of the process of administration to enable him to take his place amongst the key personalities of the government machine, Addison found his special knowledge and experience invaluable to him. It appears from the documents that he tended to be employed upon French matters. His personal contacts were of service to him almost at once, as for example in February, when he was corresponding with his friend Jean Alphonse Turrettini upon English policy towards the Protestants in general and Geneva in particular. When the opportunity offered, Addison soon found himself chosen for a 'mission' abroad.

Ever since it became apparent that Queen Anne was unlikely to have an heir, anxiety had been felt about the succession to the throne. The Act of Settlement of 1701 had attempted to secure the crown in the Electoral House of Hanover, whose members were descendants of King James I. Since that time the course of events in Europe had made it more than ever necessary to reinforce the safeguards contained in the Act of 1701, and it was now decided to send a second formal Embassy to Hanover on the pretext of presenting the Garter to the Electoral Prince, later King George II, but in fact to discuss the details of the arrangements for the succession laid down in the Regency Act and in recent amendments to the Act of Settlement. The Whig party was still rapidly gaining in power, and it was not therefore surprising to well informed opinion when the *London Gazette* for 12 April announced that Lord Halifax was 'sent by Her Majesty with a compliment to the Elector of Hanover, and the Princess Sophia, and with the Garter for the Electoral Prince' and 'is gone over this day to Hanover with the same convoy as the Duke of Marlborough'. Lord Halifax had put himself forward for the task, doubtless wishing to be in the graces of the future reigning family; and although leaving at short notice and 'only attended by those "liveries" which he had in town', he took his journey seriously enough to make a new will, witnessed by Jacob Tonson, two days before sailing. As his secretary he chose Joseph Addison, whom he succinctly described at this time as 'a Gentleman of learning and business', and who was already known at the Electoral Court. Also travelling with the party was young Lord Dorset, and Monsieur Falaiseau, a gentleman about the Hanoverian Court whom Addison probably met in 1703.

The mission had embarked at Greenwich on the evening of 12 April, the Duke of Marlborough sailing in the *Peregrine* Galley on his way to open the summer campaign. At six next morning the convoy passed the Nore and was escorted to the Gunfleet by H.M. Ships *Romney* and *Rye*. There on 15 April they joined the main squadron under command of Sir Edward Whitaker flying his flag in H.M.S. *Worcester*. This was Addison's fifth sea voyage, but the first occasion upon which he had put to sea with a fleet. As he beheld that noble spectacle he must have savoured the variety of the life opening before him. After putting into Lowestoft, the convoy sailed into Rotterdam on 25 April, and from thence Lord Halifax travelled to The Hague for consultations with the States-General and foreign diplomats engaged in negotiations upon the extent of the barrier of fortresses to be conceded to the Dutch as the result of a victorious war. Leaving The Hague on 6 May the party went to Amsterdam, where they were joined by Sir John Vanbrugh, Clarencieux King-at-Arms, who in virtue of his office was entrusted with the ceremony of presentation. They attended a service of the Portuguese Jewish community to hear prayers for success in the forthcoming campaign,[1] which were answered by the arrival of news of the great victory of Ramillies.

Meanwhile the prospect of the approaching visit had caused no joy in the Hanoverian Court, where the Electress Sophia had written to Leibniz: 'Mylord Halifax s'est offert a estre envoyé icy pour nous incommoder, et je crois que l'Electeur donneroit volontiers un présent à qui le voudroit empêcher.'[2] But considerations of policy prevailed over private annoyance, and a reception of suitable magnificence was made ready. After a wayside banquet at Stolftenau the party was welcomed at the frontier fortress of Diepenau on the evening of 28 May and arrived in Hanover late the following day. A private house had been prepared for its reception, with six coaches instead of the usual ceremonial provision of three, two electoral pages, and a detachment of foot-guards. The following day Lord Halifax was received in audience. As the party approached the electoral palace they were greeted with a roll of drums; at the head of the stairs stood the Grand Marshal, who conducted them into the presence; and going to table afterwards they were accorded the royal honours of trumpets and kettle drums. Addison was fortunate in being placed with Lord Dorset at the electress's table.[3] On 31 May Sir John Vanbrugh ceremonially presented the Garter, and thereafter followed a court ball, and a *Te Deum* to celebrate the victory at Ramillies.[4] In this favourable atmosphere diplomatic activity intensified. The King of Prussia arrived for the purpose of arranging a marriage for his heir, and there followed a further series of splendid entertainments. For these Lord Halifax delayed the departure of his mission, reflecting to Harley that he must not seem to run away from the king though he would not willingly go far out of his way to meet him.

[1] Luttrell, vi. 54.   [2] Klopp, *Leibniz Werke*, ix. 211.
[3] S.P. 81/162.   [4] Ibid.

Addison's friend and correspondent, Leibniz, was now in Hanover, and it is probably to this occasion that Addison's later mention of 'civilities' received there from him refers; for upon Addison's previous visit the philosopher had been in Berlin. He also met Schutz, son of the elector's confidential adviser. Addison had been chosen for the mission partly because of his command of French; for while the electress dowager spoke some English the elector could be reached only through the medium of French or German, and it was he who directed all matters of policy. These were priceless opportunities for Addison to prepare for the day when Queen Anne would die; and if he later grumbled that he was not paid for his services, he must have thought himself well rewarded at the time. He certainly carried away a happy recollection of the little court:

His Majesty [King George I] was bred up from his Infancy with a Love to this our Nation, under a Princess, who was the most accomplished Woman of her Age, and particularly famous for her Affection to the *English*. Our Countrymen were dear to Him, before there was any Prospect of their being His Subjects; and every one knows, that nothing recommended a Man so much to the distinguishing Civilities of His Court, as the being born in *Great Britain*.[1]

Years later he assured an English court official bound for Hanover that he would find the Electoral Court 'the most Agreeable place in the world'.

It was 13 June when Lord Halifax was able to leave for Utrecht. The mission had proved a personal success, in spite of the misgivings with which it had been at first regarded. Leibniz had enjoyed the visit: 'Il avoit avec luy Mr. Addison qui a bien du merite, le Roy d'Arms Mr. van Bruck, estant aussi poëte et Architecte; c'estoit une fort bonne compagnie.'[2] Lord Hertford, to whom but for his only recorded gaffe Addison would now perhaps have been tutor, arrived to join the party, which reached Utrecht on 17 June on its way to Marlborough's camp at Helchin. It was probably during this stay that the duke received a request from one P. H. Price for permission to dedicate to him a Latin translation of the *Campaign*.

[1] F. 2.   [2] Klopp, *Leibniz Werke*, ix. 226.

The business at Helchin, where the party arrived 15 July, was concluded by the 26th and Lord Halifax wrote requesting two frigates to convoy his return. With Addison he reached The Hague on 29 July to await the wind. But either the frigates were not available or the wind was contrary, for on 10 August they had not sailed. Meanwhile in Rotterdam Bayle complained 'Je n'ai pu avoir l'honneur de saluer My lord Halifax, ni Mr. Addison'.[1] He thought that Jean le Clerc had prejudiced the English against him. Lord Sunderland, a powerful Whig, had been brought to think that Bayle was in correspondence with the French Court,[2] and as lately as 23 July the scholar had written to Lord Shaftesbury asking for his intercession.[3] These circumstances perhaps made it inadvisable for Addison to pay him a visit, and on 28 December of this year Bayle died.

It is almost certain that Addison visited le Clerc, his friendly reviewer. Le Clerc had been at pains to build up one of the widest correspondences in Europe, upon which he founded his editing and writing. He now, through Addison, sought to know Lord Halifax, partly because he hoped to obtain literary or scholarly employment in England. As Barbeyrac put it, he received all visitors with 'gravité tempérée d'une honnête gaieté', and Addison was not the man to neglect so useful and engaging a friend. Holland was a delightful place in which to be delayed if one cared for books, and Addison killed time in the shop of Thomas Johnson, a well-known English bookseller. The days passed agreeably enough until the party sailed with the East India fleet from the Texel, arriving in London on 18 August. Perhaps on the voyage Addison heard first-hand news of his brother Gulston, growing rich on the Coromandel coast.

In his official capacity at the Cockpit Addison had many opportunities for acts of kindness; and a letter awaited him from a Monsieur le Moyne, a French prisoner, thanking him for his intervention with Secretary Harley with a view to a release. His friend Stepney had been sent British envoy

---

[1] Bayle, *Œuvres diverses*, iv. 877.
[2] L. P. Courtines, *Bayle's Relations with England*, p. 51.
[3] Ibid., p. 128.

to The Hague, and they began to exchange a series of lengthy news letters. The war was active in Spain, and Addison discharged much business in connexion therewith. This was a busy period, and Addison remarked to Stepney that he was 'very much straightened in time'. He had little time for literary matters but listened with approval to a reading of John Dennis's 'Battle of Ramillia',[1] which was dedicated to Lord Halifax. It is conceivable that Dennis wished to ascertain, through Addison, whether a dedication would be acceptable. Addison continued on intimate terms with his patron, who, writing to Lord Dorset in October, mentioned that they had read his letters together.[2] A source of satisfaction at this time was the election of Lancelot Addison to a fellowship at Magdalen. Though he showed no extraordinary qualities, Joseph's youngest brother had built up for himself the reputation of a sound classical scholar.

In the autumn there occurred a change of ministers. The Secretaryships of State were highly coveted by the party managers, and the Whig leaders had long wished to appoint one of their number to counterbalance the Tory influence of Robert Harley who, in the Northern Secretaryship, much outweighed Addison's modest superior. Hedges was dismissed, and the queen was brought to appoint in his stead Charles Spencer, third Earl of Sunderland, who took the oaths of office and was sworn of the Privy Council on 3 December. That night Addison was busy issuing the necessary warrants and writing notes to British envoys abroad to inform them of the change in high direction. The appointment of Under-Secretaries lay in the hands of the Secretary of State, and such a change was hazardous for those in the subordinate posts. Lord Sunderland inherited two Under-Secretaries from his predecessor: Tucker, the senior, and Addison. Tucker and also the First Clerk in the office lost their places; but Addison was continued and Thomas Hopkins appointed his colleague. Lord Sunderland was cordially disliked by the queen, and his appointment had been secured, after a long struggle, by an ultimatum to her supported by Addison's two principal patrons. If the new

---

[1] Dennis, *Critical Works*, ed. Hooker, ii. 24.
[2] H.M.C. *Stopford Sackville*, i. 34.

Secretary of State was not particularly well acquainted with Addison, no doubt Lords Halifax and Somers interceded for his retention in office. His position would be delicate, for Lord Sunderland was on bad terms with his father-in-law, who had been celebrated in the *Campaign*.[1] Nevertheless, Addison must have congratulated himself upon surviving a moment of peril as he prepared to serve a new master.

Two years younger than Addison, Lord Sunderland, though a good scholar, lacked the intellectual distinction of Halifax, the judicial calm of Somers, or the debonair charm of Wharton. He was a plump, unlovely young man of an earthy quality. Yet he possessed formidable talents and advantages. Amongst the former was a ruthless and single-minded devotion to Whig principles, and that restless yet determined energy which makes a good administrator; among the latter was a political heritage of great distinction from his father and his marriage with Lady Anne Churchill, second daughter of the Duke of Marlborough, a popular Whig lady. Dick Steele, who came to know him well, praised the 'candour and openness of heart which shine in all your actions . . . '. Moreover, Sunderland exercised 'a winning condescension to all subordinate to you' which 'made business a pleasure to those who execute it under you'. An excellent linguist, like several of his political friends he was 'perfectly accomplished in the knowledge of books and men'.[2] As the youngest member of the Whig Junto he was distinguished as the first to hold high office under Queen Anne. Thus it was that Addison for the first time became directly associated with one of the great political figures of the age, not as a literary companion, but in the day-to-day management of national affairs. It had been good to be the helper of Sir Charles Hedges, the faithful servant of State; but it was better to be political factotum of the Earl of Sunderland, a great magnate, deep in the counsels of national and international politics.

This event occurred at a time when Addison was maturing an important venture in the arts. At Magdalen he had been associated with Daniel Purcell, who had set several 'operas' to music, including, since Addison left England in 1699, *The*

---

[1] Churchill, *Marlborough*, ii. 295-6.   [2] Dedication to *Spectator*, vol. vi.

Grove, or Love's Paradise, by John Oldmixon.[1] In the course of his travels he had visited each of the three principal seats of opera. In both French and Italian schools he had been quick to notice many real and some fancied faults and absurdities; yet the fact remained that in England there was as yet no opera at all in the continental sense, though for some time past any play which included songs and dances had been given that name. But several poets were feeling their way towards an operatic performance. Peter Motteux produced the *Temple of Love,* translated from the Italian with songs and dances, at the Haymarket in 1706. He also translated Stampiglia's *Camilla* which was set to music from Buononcini by Nicolo Haym and produced at Dorset Garden. Congreve, and Sir John Vanbrugh, who had travelled so recently to Germany with Addison, had opened the Haymarket Theatre with a so-called 'pastoral opera'. There was also Granville's recent *British Enchanters* to which Addison had supplied the epilogue. This piece had 'infinitely arrided both sexes, and pleas'd the Town as well as any English Modern Opera'.[2] But the most interesting experiment had been in January 1706 when Thomas Clayton produced *Arsinoë, Queen of Cyprus* at the same theatre. This was an opera in the continental sense, not merely a play with musical interludes. Clayton had been a member of the Royal Music for ten years previous to 1702, when he paid a visit to Italy. Returning to England, he brought with him a number of Italian songs of original merit, and also the score of an opera by Thomas Stanzani which had been produced at Bologna in 1677 and which he used as the foundation for *Arsinoë.* But Clayton was at once a composer of low merit and an able self-advertiser. When his *Arsinoë* was produced on 16 January 1706, either because of the novelty of the event, or because of the advertisement which it received, or because of merit in the imported songs and score, it ran for fourteen nights, was revived after a short interval, and, as Addison put it, 'was the first opera that gave us a taste of Italian music'.

No doubt it was the appetite of the public for something

---

[1] *Magd. Col. Reg.* ed. Bloxam, ii. 206.
[2] Downes, *Roscius Anglicanus,* p. 49.

more spectacular than drama, the success of *Arsinoë*, and reflections upon the weakness of its libretto, which encouraged Addison to write an opera in English for the London stage. He was certainly encouraged by Steele who in 1705 in his epilogue to *The Tender Husband* had urged the public:

> No more th' Italian squaling Tribe admit,
> In Tongues unknown; 'tis Popery in Wit.

But he recognized that although concert music was popular in England, there was no educated musical public. Even four years later he reflected sadly that:

> At present, our Notions of Musick are so very uncertain, that we do not know what it is we like; only, in general, we are transported with any thing that is not *English*: . . . In short, our *English* musick is quite rooted out, and nothing yet planted in its stead.[1]

He was equally clear that opera is essentially national, that the French and Italian operas differed from one another, and that neither being translated to London could give rise to an English opera. Reflecting upon the example of Lully, he remarked that the great Frenchman:

> . . . acted like a Man of Sense in this Particular. He found the *French* Musick extreamly defective, and very often barbarous: However . . . he did not pretend to extirpate the *French* musick, and plant the *Italian* in its stead; but only to Cultivate and Civilize it with innumerable Graces and Modulations which he borrow'd from the *Italian*. By this means the *French* musick is now perfect in its kind. . . .[2]

Addison's purpose, reflected in these later writings, was to construct an opera which should be essentially English, while borrowing technique from foreign sources.

With a dramatic rather than a musical approach to his subject, Addison attached an overriding importance to the libretto. He felt himself well able to supply the deficiency which he had noticed in Italian pieces. It was, he thought, imperative that the audience should fully understand the

[1] *S.* 18.   [2] *S.* 29.

libretto; therefore any direct transfer of a foreign opera to the London stage would be not only unacceptable but ludicrous. Partial translation, which had been attempted, in which 'The King or Hero of the Play . . . spoke in *Italian*, and his Slaves answer'd him in *English*'[1] seemed yet more ridiculous. Nor could a satisfactory answer be found in full translation, for Addison perceived that even a skilful translator could not hope to adapt the temper of the libretto in English to that of music originally written for Italian words. Worse still, an unskilful translator could make sorry havoc:

I have known the Word *And* pursu'd through the whole Gamut, have been entertain'd with many a melodious *The*, and have heard the most beautiful Graces, Quavers and Divisions bestow'd upon *Then, For*, and *From*; to the eternal Honour of our *English* Particles.[2]

Having rejected transfer or translation, Addison described his purpose as an attempt to write a piece 'which should give a more natural and reasonable Entertainment than what can be met with in the elaborate Trifles of that [the Italian] Nation'.[3]

The French opera, on the other hand, suffered from an artificiality and anachronism which could be rectified without difficulty. 'Common Sense . . . requires, that there should be nothing in the Scenes and machines which may appear Childish and Absurd.'[4] There remained the question of form. It so happened that a set of such rules lay readily available in the formula of the Italian opera, which to suit musical convenience had assumed a stereotyped structure. This prescribed to the librettist six principal characters, three of each sex, thus providing for the full range of voices. Superimposed upon the unities of time, place, and action, this convention served the Italian opera well enough, and Addison appears to have accepted it without question.

His English opera was therefore to have a theme which would be readily understood, which would not be rendered ridiculous upon the stage, which would be conveyed in sound English poetry while conforming with the conventions of Italian operatic production, and which should be

[1] *S*. 18.   [2] Ibid.   [3] Ibid.   [4] *S*. 5.

matched with music written to the temper of the verse and giving adequate expression to the poet's thoughts.

It would be . . . strange, to represent visible Objects by Sounds that have no Ideas annexed to them, and to make something like Description in *Musick*. Yet it is certain, there may be confused, imperfect Notions of this Nature raised in the Imagination by an Artificial Composition of Notes; and we find that great Masters in the Art are able, sometimes, to set their Hearers in the heat and hurry of a Battel, to overcast their Minds with melancholy Scenes and Apprehensions of Deaths and Funerals, or to lull them into pleasing Dreams of Groves and Elysiums.[1]

Unhappily when Addison selected a musical partner with whom to found an English opera his choice fell upon no such 'great master in the art'. Never sure of his judgement in music, he appears to have been unduly impressed with the success of Clayton's venture in *Arsinoë*. Perhaps Clayton's recent visit to Italy and his consequent ability to understand the poet's purpose in terms of the Italian opera were decisive. Addison needed a technician versed in Italian methods, and it is difficult to think of another Englishman whom he might have employed for the purpose. Daniel Purcell, otherwise an obvious choice, would be excluded for his limited view of the opera and lack of knowledge of the Italian models upon which Addison was working.[2] It is therefore idle to condemn the choice of Clayton if, as seems likely, Addison's project could not have been undertaken at all without his aid. Nevertheless the misalliance had fatal consequences, for it prevented Addison from exploiting the excellent musical executants then available in London. A contemporary authority considered them 'inferior to few in Italy, and some Hands would make it [the "band"] one of the best in the World'.[3] Clayton's musical partners, Charles Dieupart

---

[1] *S.* 416.

[2] In 1706 John Dennis wrote that there appeared to have been of late years a combination of all sorts of people to set up operas, by which he probably meant works of the type of D. Purcell; while his title referred to 'Operas after the Italian manner, which are about to be established on the English stage' by which he probably meant works of the type of *Rosamond* or *Arsinoë*, J. Dennis, *Essay on the Opera*; Dennis: *Critical Works*, ed. Hooker, ii. 385.

[3] *A Comparison between the French and Italian Musick and Operas*, London, 1709, pp. 52–53.

and Nicolo Haym, were respectively distinguished at the harpsichord and violoncello, but could achieve nothing without good music.

During his first years as Under-Secretary, therefore, Addison wrote an opera called *Rosamond*.[1] As his theme he had selected the ballad of that name. Fair Rosamond Clifford, daughter of Walter, Lord Clifford, was the mistress of King Henry II and mother by him of Walter Longspee, Earl of Salisbury, and of Geoffrey, Archbishop of York. It was a tale inscribed in the chronicles and printed deep in the folk memory, thus familiar to most hearers and suited to Addison's purpose of intelligibility. It had also the advantage of a strongly 'English' flavour while the simplicity of the plot lent itself to unity of action. The choice also made it possible to place the scene in Woodstock Park, once part of a royal residence, where Blenheim Palace was now building. This would be familiar ground to Addison from his years of residence in Oxford and he probably remembered the grass-grown mounds of the labyrinth said to have enclosed Rosamond's bower, which Hearne recalled as still visible ten years later. This choice had the triple advantage of offering a delicate compliment to the Duke of Marlborough, of providing a strong topical interest for the public, and of giving scope to the action while enabling the unity of place to be observed. In conformity with Italian usage, six principal characters covering the range of voices were readily at hand: King Henry and Queen Eleanor, Fair Rosamond and a Page, and Sir Trusty, Keeper of the Bower, with his wife Grideline. The action takes place within a single day and thus observes the unity of time. In the original ballad, however, a serious obstacle was presented by the death of Rosamond. French ideas of 'correctness' did not favour killings upon the stage: furthermore, the ballad was essentially tragic, whereas Addison sought to give to his libretto a sprightly air which would have been incongruous with a tragic ending. Therefore instead of murdering Rosamond at the hands of the injured queen, Addison permits her to end her days penitently but comfortably lodged in the nunnery at Godstow, while King Henry and his spouse are reunited

[1] Tickell, Preface to Addison's *Works*.

in conjugal bliss, the curtain falling upon them with a final chord of virtue in duet:

> *Who to forbidden joys wou'd rove,*
> *That knows the sweets of virtuous love?*

He did not forget the liking of the crowd for the sensational and was careful to provide a 'machine'. In act three 'a cloud descends, in it two Angels, supposed to be the guardian spirits of the British Kings in war and peace'. Furthermore, the same act included a 'grotto', an innovation generally associated with Alexander Pope and a later generation. Thus the critics and the crowd were considered and edified. Within the critical and moral limitations which he imposed upon himself, Addison produced a delightful libretto full of good song-writing. In an effective passage complimenting the duke and Vanbrugh, his architect, the building of Blenheim is described:

> Behold the glorious pile ascending!
> Columns swelling, arches bending,
> Domes in awful pomp arising,
> Art in curious strokes surprising.

Some of the best lines are the humorous ones, showing Addison in his lightest vein, which he never resumed. Sir Trusty, awaking after a draught of what he wrongly believed to be poison, fancies himself dead:

> In which world am I! all I see,
> Ev'ry thicket, bush and tree,
> So like the place from whence I came,
> That one wou'd swear it were the same.
> My former Legs too, by their pace!
> And by the Whiskers, 'tis my face!
> The self-time habit, garb and mien!
> They ne'er would Bury me in Green.

Other passages are reminiscent of the ballad:

> *Grideline:* My stomach swells with secret spight,
> To see my fickle, faithless Knight,
> With upright gesture, goodly mien,
> Face of olive, coat of green,

> That charm'd the ladies long ago,
> So little his own worth to know,
> On a meer girl his thoughts to place,
> With dimpled cheeks and baby face;
> A child! A chit! that was not born
> When I did town and court adorn.
>
> *Page*:   Can any man prefer fifteen
> To venerable *Grideline*?

A competent musician could have turned all of this and most of *Rosamond* to good account, but Clayton failed his poet, producing:

> ... a confus'd Chaos of Musick, where there is every thing, and nothing, and ... the only thing to be lik'd in it is that it is short; ... if a Reward was to be ordain'd for him that made the worst Musick in all the World, the Author of Rosamond wou'd have reason to say he had not lost his Labour. ... [1]

Possibly it was of Clayton that Dennis was thinking when he wrote 'tho' the Opera in Italy is a Monster, 'tis a beautiful harmonious Monster, but here in England 'tis an ugly howling one'.[2]

The public had high expectations of the partnership between the author of the *Campaign* and the 'composer' of *Arsinoë*.[3] But when *Rosamond* was produced by public subscription at Drury Lane on 4 March 1707, it was a bitter disappointment. In vain did the celebrated Mrs. Tofts take the part of the queen, and Gallia, a well-known Italian, that of Rosamond. King Henry was entrusted to Hughes and Sir Trusty to Leveridge, with Mrs. Livesay as Grideline. All were excellent performers,[4] but, as a contemporary forcibly put it, *Rosamond*:

> ... struggled through and mounted the Stage on purpose to frighten all England with its abominable Musick; and this was the celebrated *Rosamond*, with the Expectations of which the Town had been full for a year together. The Author of *Arsinoë* compos'd this Piece, which those, who had any skill in Musick, foretold before its appearance, was to be but of a short continuance. The Event justified their Conjectures, for after the third Night it

---

[1] *A Comparison* ..., p. 69.
[2] Dennis, *Critical Works*, ed. Hooker, i. 392.
[3] H.M.C. *Egremont*, ii. 215.   [4] Genest, ii. 356.

expired, and 'tis generally thought it wou'd not have liv'd so long, had not the good natur'd Physicians supported its Spirits with a little Aurum Potabile.[1]

Rosamond is not known to have been revived in the author's lifetime or to Clayton's setting.

Addison did not consider that the failure of his ambitious venture was a reflection upon his poetry, which he immediately published 'Inscrib'd to' the Duchess of Marlborough. This abrupt phrase evidently gave rise to comment, for the second edition, also published in 1707, was 'Humbly Inscrib'd to' the same person. The dedication was criticized by Johnson on the ground that the duchess was a woman of no taste in poetry or letters; but the choice was probably made on other grounds. Addison was now closely associated with Lord Sunderland, whom the queen hated with the passion of one injured in family life. Sunderland, besides being personally distasteful to her, had opposed the financial provision made for Prince George in 1702. Addison may have felt himself precluded from coming to royal notice by this association. It would therefore be politic to court the queen's principal confidante, who was also the mother-in-law of his political superior.

In retrospect, *Rosamond* was a daring performance. When in later years Arne set it to music the resulting work was widely performed, at least six occasions being on record between 1733 and 1747; and Macaulay tells us that the songs were sung at hundreds of harpsichords daily throughout the length and breadth of England. The Victorian critics treated the piece with overmuch gravity. But Johnson thought highly of it:

The opera of *Rosamond*, though it is seldom mentioned, is one of the first of Addison's compositions. The subject is well chosen, the fiction is pleasing, and the praise of Marlborough, for which the scene gives an opportunity, is, what every human excellence must be, the product of good luck improved by genius. The thoughts are sometimes great, and sometimes tender; the versification is easy and gay. . . . The whole drama is airy and elegant; engaging in its process, and pleasing in its conclusion. If Addison had cultivated the lighter parts of poetry he would probably have excelled.

[1] *A Comparison* . . ., p. 68.

The failure of his experiment caused Addison some bitterness. He permitted himself several attacks upon contemporary opera which, though universally condemned by the critics and dramatists, yet succeeded in gaining a foothold in London. Undoubtedly thinking of his own work he wrote:

some Attempts of forming Pieces upon *Italian* Plans . . . alarm'd the Poetasters and Fiddlers of the Town, who . . . laid down an establish'd Rule, . . . *That nothing is capable of being well set to Musick, that is not Nonsense.*[1]

He was at pains to catalogue the spectacles of the town pleasing to ladies as follows: 'The dancing Monkies are in one Place; the Puppet Show in another; the Opera in a third; not to mention the Lions . . .'[2] In so far as he apportioned blame for the failure of *Rosamond* it appears to have fallen upon the public rather than upon Clayton, with whom he remained on friendly terms for a number of years.

One happy result of Addison's opera was that it brought notice to Thomas Tickell, a member of The Queen's College, Oxford. He was a man of agreeable and unassuming temper, and considerable poetic ability. He had already praised Addison, formerly a member of his college, in a poem 'Oxford', published this year and addressed to Lord Lonsdale, a magnate of the north-west, from which the Tickell and Addison families sprang. He now addressed to Addison a set of verses upon *Rosamond* which were printed in the sixth volume of *Miscellany Poems* in 1709. The elder poet liked Tickell's lines well enough to print them with *Rosamond* beneath the dedication in the third edition in 1713, when at the height of his literary reputation. If the two men were not previously acquainted, these lines must have brought Tickell to Addison's notice. They betray so full an understanding of the purpose of the author of *Rosamond* that it is possible that the writer was already in the confidence of the person he addressed:

> *The* Opera *first* Italian *masters taught,*
> *Enrich'd with Songs, but innocent of thought.*
> Britannia's *learned theatre disdains*
> *Melodious trifles, and enervate strains;*

[1] *S.* 18.   [2] *S.* 31.

And blushes on her injur'd stage to see
Nonsense well-tun'd, and sweet stupidity.

There is no doubt that by these verses Tickell sought to win Addison's patronage. Much as before him Addison to Dryden, so now wrote Tickell to Addison:

Accept, great monarch of the British *lays,*
The tribute song an humble subject pays.
So tries the artless Lark her early flight,
And soars, to hail the God of verse, and light.
Unrival'd as thy merit be thy fame,
And thy own laurels shade thy envy'd name:
Thy name, the boast of all the tuneful choir,
Shall tremble on the strings of ev'ry Lyre;
While the charm'd reader with thy thought complies,
Feels corresponding joys or sorrows rise,
And views thy Rosamond *with* Henry's *eyes.*

After making allowance for the flattery of verse compliments, these lively lines makes it clear that Addison already occupied a highly distinguished place in contemporary letters. This distinction rested entirely upon his poetry, and he had not yet produced any of the works by which he is now chiefly remembered.

Addison continued to discharge routine duties of state, while Lord Sunderland was principally engaged in piloting the union of England with Scotland through a difficult passage in the House of Lords. He corresponded on terms of familiarity with those much his social superior. Horatio Walpole proceeding envoy to Madrid, becalmed off Yarmouth, wrote to him of 'good victuals, good drink & good company but all these in perfection without the prospect of dear Liberty are but poor comfort to a W[hi]g'.[1] The Earl of Manchester, Addison's one-time patron in Paris, now going to Vienna upon important negotiations, corresponded with him at length.[2] Addison confided to George Stepney that he often drank the latter's health with Lord Halifax, hinted the private doings of great names, and forwarded a letter to the electress in Hanover to oblige Lord Hertford. Lord Halifax, as well as Lord Sunderland, was

[1] Blenheim MSS. C.I. 39.   [2] Ibid. C.II. 8.

now on bad terms with the Duke of Marlborough. Dexterously Addison steered his course amongst warring magnates. He was an extremely busy man who had become important rather quickly, and it is not surprising that in January Congreve wrote to Joseph Keally in Ireland: 'I have made your compliments to Mr. Addison, having seen him by accident. It is not so familiar a thing to see him as it was ten years ago.'[1] It appears from his correspondence that Addison was at pains to keep his literary and his political activities separate, and that it was the latter which prevailed now and for some time to come. For example, throughout his correspondence in the winter of 1706, when he wrote many letters in informal terms addressed to men of wit and culture holding official positions, there is no hint that he was engaged upon a major operatic experiment. Yet in the few surviving letters upon literary topics there is hardly a notice of affairs of State although Addison daily handled the greatest issues in Europe. If it be asked what was the relationship between these two worlds, then it is necessary to recall once more the concept of the Roman citizen and statesman, a man of public business with elegant accomplishments of learning and letters. In this spirit the Under-Secretary found time from his duties to pen a prologue for 'Phaedra and Hippolytus', written by his Oxford friend and fellow Latin poet, Edmund Smith. The play was acted four times in April of this year, and published with the prologue in 1707.[2] Matthew Prior supplied an epilogue. Smith had been expelled from Christ Church two years before after many crosses with authority. Addison is reported to have tried to assist him by suggesting that he write a *History of the Revolution*. To this 'Rag' had replied by asking what he should do with the character of Lord Sunderland. Addison turned this objection aside by inquiring when Smith was last drunk; and in fact he drank himself to death three years later, leaving the history unwritten. The worlds of business and letters came together occasionally, as in the case of Jean le Clerc, with whom Addison continued to correspond. Le Clerc was

[1] Berkeley, *Lit. Relics*, 351.
[2] Advertised in the London *Gazette* of 16 June 1707 for publication on the following day.

endeavouring through the agency of Addison and Lord Halifax to secure an appointment as librarian to Queen Anne. In this, unhappily, he failed, and England was thereby deprived of the services of a most eminent scholar.

Towards his official duties Addison adopted a peculiarly personal attitude. Looking back on his period of subordinate office he thus recorded his thoughts:

> I am perswaded there are few Men, of generous Principles, who would seek after great Places, were it not rather to have an Opportunity in their Hands of obliging their particular Friends, or those whom they look upon as Men of Worth, than to procure Wealth and Honour for themselves. To an honest Mind the best Perquisites of a Place are the Advantages it gives a Man of doing Good.
>
> Those who are under the great Officers of State, and are the Instruments by which they act, have more frequent Opportunities for the Exercise of Compassion, and Benevolence, than their Superiors themselves.[1]

He was in precisely such a position under a 'great officer of state', and his opportunities 'for the exercise of compassion and benevolence' and to 'oblige his particular friends' were many. Numerous, sometimes mysterious, were those who applied to him; for instance Jezreel Jones who in July wrote recommending Mr. Bobbin who had something important to communicate to Lord Sunderland.[2] Doubtless it was into Addison's ear that Bobbin poured his confidence. Such a purveyor of mystery was immortalized in the forty-sixth *Spectator*, and on picking up and reading the shorthand jottings for that paper which its author had let fall in the coffee-house, advised that it should be carried to the Secretary of State. But amongst the 'particular friends' Dick Steele was one ever willing to receive compassion and perpetually in need of being 'obliged'. Having found and recently lost a wife of some means, he had not yet obtained the government employment to which he also aspired. He had therefore applied for a loan to his more fortunate friend, again offering as security his late wife's estate in Barbados, the 'Content Plantation', with its 'sugar works Negro's Cattle and other

---

[1] S. 469.   [2] Blenheim MSS. C.L. 39.

appurtenances'.[1] On this impressive sounding security which yielded £858 per annum, although it was encumbered by other debts of considerable size of which he may not have known, Addison lent Dick Steele £1,000, the transaction being completed by an indenture to which the late Mrs. Steele had been a party, signed on 6 December 1706.[2] This large sum must have absorbed most of Addison's savings, and the fact that he could now make such an advance reveals the frugality with which he had lived in recent years. But it was now possible to provide for Dick at public expense.

The post of Gazetteer, in modern terms editor of the *London Gazette*, was a minor place worth about £60 per annum and under the immediate control of the senior Secretary of State. It had been usual for the Secretary for the South to be the senior, and, if he vacated his office as in the case of Sir Charles Hedges, for the Northern Secretary to transfer to fill it. But for Sunderland's benefit, this rule, never a strict one, was suspended, and he had been appointed direct to the South and ranked as senior. It was thus Sunderland who controlled the *Gazette*, and Addison who discharged the routine work of keeping it supplied with reliable foreign and domestic news.[3] The post of Gazetteer was now given to Steele and, to make it apparent that it was no sinecure, a salary of £300 was attached to it. The appointment became effective on May Day 1707, Addison's birthday, and no doubt there was a double celebration. Steele did not know how he had come by this good fortune and with characteristic haste precipitated himself and his thanks upon Secretary Harley who, with surprise and amusement, referred him to Arthur Maynwaring, a literary Whig politician who worked powerfully and often anonymously behind the scenes. Maynwaring was a friend of Addison, and it is hard to disbelieve reports that the Under-Secretary had played a part in the appointment.[4] Dick was certainly a 'man of worth',

---

[1] P.R.O. Chancery Pleas C 6/352/2 where the transaction is described. I am indebted to Professor A. L. Cooke, who brought the document under reference to my notice.

[2] See R. Blanchard, 'Richard Steele's West Indian Plantation', *Mod. Philology*, xxxix. 281.

[3] For examples of news dispatches coming into the Under-Secretaries' office for the *Gazette*, see Blenheim MSS. C.II. 18 *et al.*   [4] Macaulay.

the *Gazette* needed new life, and Addison might well think that he would supply it.[1] It would, however, be heavy-handed to approach his superior to plead the appointment of his particular friend, and he may have preferred to use the agency of Maynwaring.

The two men were now closely associated in this aspect of Addison's work, and Steele threw himself into his task with zeal. He proposed a scheme of reorganization, wrote to negligent correspondents, and grasped the editorial reins with a masterful hand. But his eager journalistic genius was soon driving the *Gazette* in a manner unsuited to so staid an official vehicle. Trouble followed; the Prince Consort took offence; even Addison criticized the Gazetteer's handling of the news;[2] and Steele came to realize, bitterly, that what was required by officialdom was colourless reliability.

Addison lodged with Steele through the summer, but must have found him an uncomfortable companion. While still trying to realize money from the West Indian estates which had belonged to his first wife, Dick now began to court a second, also the possessor of a modest fortune. He lay awake at might, rose to survey the dawn, fidgeted at any time, and never ceased to require money. Ever since Addison had escaped from actual want, he had been called upon to relieve the constant need of his friend. To Dick Steele money meant little; when he received it, he spent it, and borrowed more. Perhaps Addison was glad to get away towards the end of summer to stay for a week with Lord Halifax in the country, then to pass on to visit his political head at Althorp, while Dick Steele carried his courting to a successful con-clusion on 8 September when he bought a licence for his marriage to Molly Scurlock. Dick decided to leave his lodg-ings and to set up house, but could not take away his furni-ture until Addison had found quarters elsewhere. The latter, back in London, probably visited George Stepney who had returned mortally ill from his embassy and died in Chelsea on 27 September. His death was a personal loss to the Kit-Cats, and particularly to Addison.

---

[1] For an interesting comment on the qualities requisite, see H.M.C. *Portland*, viii. 187-8, J. de Fonvive—Robert Harley 18/7/05.

[2] H.M.C. viii, ref. p. 49.

Addison's prosperity was increasing and it was time to seek a more dignified dwelling in keeping with the coach and four which he maintained. On 29 October he left Dick Steele's lodgings, and their period of domestic intimacy ended. The winter was one of intense activity, and Addison turned his pen to a pamphlet. It had been an unfortunate year, with no victory comparable with Blenheim or Ramillies, and a disaster in Spain. The Government therefore became yet more dependent upon the support of the Whigs, the only party prepared to give wholehearted approval to another year of campaigning in Europe. In November Addison finished a pamphlet entitled *The Present State of the War and the Necessity of an Augmentation considered*. It was published late in the year 1707. This piece, written by an Under-Secretary, though anonymous, would be taken as a statement of government and party policy, even at a time when collective responsibility was not understood. It has the strength and weaknesses of a document written with such advantages and limitations. It is elegant, clear, logical devoid of malice, and unamusing. The classical Whig case is argued with clarity; France is the 'constant and most dangerous enemy to the British nation': if united with Spain she must be so powerful that no peace treaty could be relied upon: there must therefore be no peace 'without an entire disunion of the French and Spanish monarchies'. The war has brought great successes, but they will be valueless if not secured by further operations which should take the form of land battles fought with British levies. The Whig economic argument, 'wealth and power are but different names for the same thing', is carefully reasoned. The whole piece shows a wide grasp of the great European struggle, such as could only be possessed by one at the centre of affairs and who also knew and understood Europe at first hand.

From Lord Sunderland's office the political machinations of the Northern Secretary, Robert Harley, were being narrowly watched; he was felt to be intriguing against his colleagues. There had been friction between the Duke of Marlborough and Lord Halifax. There was increasing tension in home affairs as the Union Bill approached its final stages and as secret reports came in of an intended French invasion designed to raise both Jacobites and opponents of the Union. In a long series of letters to Lord Manchester at Venice Addison reported upon angry debates at St. Stephen's. Amidst so many anxieties he can hardly have noticed the publication of a second Latin version of the *Campaign* by an Oxford hand. A political crisis arose in February of 1708, when the Government secured evidence of Robert Harley's intrigues. For the moment he had overplayed his hand, and the Captain-General, the Lord Treasurer, and their Whig and moderate Tory colleagues united angrily against him. Simultaneously he made a foolish mistake, permitting himself to be double-crossed through negligent handling of his agents and a consequent leakage of information from his office to the French Government. The queen was given to understand that the alternative to dismissing her Secretary for the North was the loss of most of her ministers, including the two men who had borne the main burden of the war; and in face of this threat she had no choice but to submit. On 7 February Addison wrote to Lord Manchester: 'I can tell your Lordship what is a Secret here at present that the Queen has just now demanded the seals of him [Harley].' The new Secretary was Henry Boyle of the Kit-Cat Club, who had climbed the stairs to commission the *Campaign*.

All this was excellent news to Addison, who on 13 February purred to Lord Manchester that: 'This revolution has already had the good Effect to Unite all old friends that were falling off from one another, and in all probability will produce a good new Parliament'; for the hazard of a general election, upon the outcome of which the places of the Under-Secretaries and others would depend, was now fast approaching. It was thus in a mood of satisfaction, though in an atmosphere of intense political excitement, that Joseph Addison dined at the George in Pall Mall at two o'clock on 1 March. The company was Richard Steele, Jonathan Swift, recently returned from Ireland, who had sought an interview and been asked to dinner, and Philip Frowde, one-time Magdalen pupil now a minor poet. It would be interesting to know whether the Under-Secretary confided in his companions that he was about to stand as a Whig candidate at the coming election. If this decision had not in fact yet been taken, it was probably hastened by the events of the next few days which greatly increased the political excitement and improved the Whig electoral prospects.

Evidence coming into the Secretary of State's office from the informers whom Addison was engaged in interrogating removed any doubt as to the purpose of a French expedition assembling at Dunkirk.[1] On 2 March Addison wrote to Lord Manchester warning him that an invasion of Scotland was expected, and commented like a good party man:

> We . . . are very happy in a Ministry that can take such vigorous and speedy Methods for our Defence and Security. . . . They say our new Admirals [probably the reconstituted Board of Admiralty] who are all active men have very much contributed to the manning and equipping so many of the queen's ships with such an unusual Expedition.

On 6 March the Pretender sailed from Dunkirk with 5,000 men aboard a French fleet under Admiral Forbin, with the Firth of Forth his destination. Sir George Byng was waiting off the port with a British squadron and the two fleets disappeared into the mists of the North Sea leaving the world in an agony of suspense, and no place more so than the office at the Cockpit, where heroic measures had now to be taken.

The ensuing two weeks were probably the busiest in Addison's life up to the present time. From his office there poured forth a stream of emergency orders sent by express to all parts of the kingdom.[2] Every available man under arms was mustered and set marching north to join the troops in Scotland. The Irish Government was ordered to send troops immediately to Carrickfergus and to raise more to follow. The Commissioners of Transports were instructed to assemble shipping at that port with a fortnight's provisions to await convoy to an unknown destination. Next day these orders were countermanded by instructions that the ships be ready to sail immediately, if necessary without convoy

[1] S.P. Dom. 34/9.
[2] The following account of Addison's duties as Under-Secretary is based upon the Letter-books at the Public Record Office, especially S.P. 44/106, 67/3.

and with only five days' provisions. Troops and ordnance were assembled in Holland and sailed from Ostend. It was reckoned that the Duke of Argyll would have 20,000 foot and 3,000 horse at his command by these measures, but nobody knew how much support the Pretender would find in Scotland. Addison, however, viewed the military situation with some confidence. He warned Burchett at the Admiralty that conditions for a landing there might prove so unpromising that the expedition would sail past the Forth and make an attempt in Ireland, where measures had already been taken to meet such a contingency. Meanwhile the Under-Secretary's office, which was particularly concerned with internal political matters, saw to the disarming of Irish Catholics, and the stopping of all persons going to Scotland without passes. At last a message came through from the Mayor of Berwick to the Secretary of State reporting Sir George Byng's squadron offshore, and this was followed by an express from the admiral which arrived on 16 March as Addison sat writing to Lord Manchester. This brought the joyful news that Sir George was 'in full chase' after the French, north of the Forth. Then came further news of the capture of the *Salisbury* with Lord Griffin and other leading Jacobites on board, and instructions were sent forthwith to the Mayor of Hull to prepare to receive the prisoners, who were to be delivered to the Secretary of State. The mayor did well and received a letter of thanks from Lord Sunderland. Meanwhile the French fleet managed to outpace Sir George and sailed back to Dunkirk.

Amidst the rejoicing in London it now fell to Addison to countermand the emergency measures and to arrange for the reception of the prisoners. A party of about fifty were on their way, and Lord Griffin arrived and was interrogated by the Secretary of State himself before being committed to the Tower. At this moment Lord Manchester's servants were detected smuggling cloth in Venice in the ambassadorial gondola, and in the consequent measures diplomatic privilege was infringed by the Venetian Government. There followed one of those protocol disputes which have been the delight of diplomats in all ages. Invasion or no invasion, it fell to Addison to manage the matter so that

Lord Sunderland might discharge official wrath upon the Venetian Ambassador in London. Under the strain of an enormous burden of detailed administrative work Addison's eyesight failed him, and he was forced to employ an amanuensis. The physical strain told upon his system generally, and he suffered from lameness. But casting his mind over the menacing events of the past few weeks, and their fortunate outcome in which he had played such an important administrative part, he comforted himself that they had wrought favourably upon the political situation. 'It is believed', he told Lord Manchester, 'that this Intended Invasion will have a great Influence on the Elections for the ensuing Parliament.' When, therefore, the old House was dissolved on 4 April, the candidates of the Whig party faced the polls with the tide of events running in their favour.

It is an instance of Addison's reticence about his personal affairs, and of the manner in which he isolated his activities one from another, that in the long series of letters which he was addressing at this time to his former benefactor and fellow Kit-Cat, Lord Manchester, he did not mention that he was to be a candidate at the election. The manner in which he secured nomination as a candidate at Lostwithiel is not known, but Edward Wortley may have helped him. Wortley had recently been distinguishing himself in the Commons where, as Addison put it, he 'spoke incomparably well'; and, after an absence of seven years, his name again appears in the list of those to whom Addison addressed letters, precisely at this time and in connexion with the issue of writs for the election. The two friends were now intimate once more, and had he not been prevented by business, Addison would have spent a month of summer leave at Wortley's country seat.[1]

That he should have sought to enter politics at this point of his career is not surprising. At a time when the distinction between the permanent official and the legislator was not well established, it was quite usual, and in some cases perhaps

---

[1] Arthur Maynwaring, who was highly influential behind the scenes of Whig politics and who was also largely concerned in distributing patronage to Whig authors, himself stood not far away at West Looe and may have helped Addison to a seat.

indispensable, for the holders of important administrative posts to sit in Parliament. William Lowndes, Secretary of the Treasury, William Blaythwayt, Secretary at War, Josiah Burchett, Secretary of the Admiralty, all sat in the Commons, although from their long years of service to successive governments they resembled permanent rather than Parliamentary Under-Secretaries. Even six serving admirals were in the House. The significance of Addison's candidacy is therefore not so much that he had ambitions to enter another sphere of public life, but that a seat in Parliament had become a desirable and perhaps a necessary adjunct of his administrative career.

The small Cornish borough of Lostwithiel returned two burgesses and lay in strong Tory territory. In 1705 it had elected Russell Robartes and Robert Molesworth, but by order of the House of Commons Molesworth was struck out and James Kendall seated in his stead. Besides Addison, the candidates now were Russell Robartes, Francis Robartes, and James Kendall. Francis was also a candidate for Bodmin which he had represented in the last Parliament. A son of the first Earl of Radnor, a Fellow of the Royal Society, a Teller of the Exchequer, and author of a 'Discourse concerning the musical notes of a Trumpet' as well as of other musical researches somewhat unusual in this period, he was a man of distinction. The two Robartes were in the Tory interest and James Kendall was Addison's Whig colleague. A combination of circumstances, including ambiguities real or alleged in the borough franchise, and a persistent political intriguer in the office of mayor, had made the electoral history of Lostwithiel in Queen Anne's reign a chequered one. The Borough Charter laid it down that the mayor, six capital burgesses, and seventeen assistants should vote for the two members. There were thus twenty-four votes, which were sometimes regarded in the nature of personal property. The right of the franchise was not unlike an option; it was something which might be exercised for the financial profit of its holder; and viewed in this light the practice of purchasing votes, which was common in this period, assumes a rather less sinister appearance than is sometimes attached to it. But by no means every vote was for sale, and the state of public opinion had a profound and sometimes decisive effect upon the outcome of elections. It was, however, by a manipulation of the franchise that Addison won his seat, the first alleged irregularity being the manner in which the mayor, Alexander John, secured himself in office for five years, it being alleged by his opponents that there ought to be a new mayor every year. Thus seized of the key post, he advanced the view that once an assistant had been chosen, he need not be confirmed annually at the meeting prescribed by the charter, nor could he be displaced without just cause shown. The mayor had therefore evidently assembled a Court of Assistants who were politically reliable and who maintained him in office. After the charter meeting of 1707, which would determine who should exercise the franchise at this election, the Mayor had struck out the names of a capital burgess and five assistants, who according to his interpretation of the charter were not properly chosen, and had replaced them, presumably, by his own supporters. There were thus two rival registers of electors, and the persons named in both presented themselves to vote.

The declaration of the result took place on 17 May 1708. When the votes were counted, the mayor excluded those who upon his view of the charter were not entitled to the franchise, and computed the results as follows:

James Kendall, Esq.	13 votes	Elected
Joseph Addison, Esq.	13 votes	Elected
Hon. Francis Robartes	6 votes	Not Elected
Hon. Russell Robartes	4 votes	Not Elected

But according to the Tory view of the franchise the results of voting were quite different and should have been declared as follows:

Hon. Francis Robartes	20 votes	Elected
Hon. Russell Robartes	17 votes	Elected
James Kendall, Esq.	5 votes	Not Elected
Joseph Addison, Esq.	4 votes	Not Elected

According to these later calculations, nine persons had been admitted to vote who had no qualification, and fourteen who should have been admitted had been excluded. For the moment, however, the decision rested with the

mayor, whose duty it was to make a return to the High
Sheriff of Cornwall, and he declared James Kendall and
Joseph Addison duly elected.[1]

These were but the opening shots in a lengthy political
duel which continued intermittently for some years after
Addison's disappearance from the scene. His own part in
the proceedings would hardly require him to be present at
so artificial a contest; and although he was absent from town
from the beginning of May until the 20th of the month it is
unlikely that he made the long journey to Cornwall. Instead
he was thinking of hiring a coach and going to Bath with
Colonel Frowde, uncle of his Magdalen pupil, Philip, 'to put
myself in good humour for the rest of the year'. Philip was
also about town, and, as Swift found him, 'just as he was,
very friendly and *grand rêveur et distrait* . . .'[2] and a good
listener to other people's poetry. He wrote two tragedies
and was an intimate friend of Addison at this time. In fact
Addison probably left town for a change of air after the
strenuous work of the winter, and to oblige his colleague
Hopkins who wished to go away later. It is evident that
Mayor John was quite capable of managing affairs in the
borough of Lostwithiel, and Addison's view of the matter
was probably that of most candidates in such circumstances;
he had secured a nomination, he would meet the expenses,
and unless his personal intervention became necessary he
would leave the conduct of the election to the local managers. In later years Addison estimated that his first five
election campaigns cost him about £1,200. Lostwithiel
would be rather more costly than the average of the succeeding four contests which were fought by different electoral tactics; so that a guess at the expenses on this occasion
might put them at £350. With so small an electorate no
problem of organization would be involved, and no doubt
a portion of this sum was laid out by Mayor John to those
who supported his view of the franchise.

Having been declared elected, Addison could not act as
a Member of Parliament until he had taken the oath and his
seat. This he could not do until the House reassembled,

[1] For the preceding and other details, see *House of Commons Journals*, xvi.
249–50.   [2] Williams, i. 92.

which would not be until the autumn. Meanwhile the next move lay with his opponents who, if they wished to do so, might petition the House of Commons to avoid the election. On 20 May, when the Cornwall results were known, George Granville, for whose 'opera' Addison had written a prologue and who had been acting as a political organizer for the Tory party in the county, reported the position to Robert Harley. Things had gone badly. Harry St. John had been defeated, and at Tintagel the seat had been lost because, although one named Hooker had been secured in the seat for two years past as the result of a local bargain, on the morning of the election an interest of importance had suddenly switched to his opponent. 'Addison', said Granville, 'has likewise been brought in at Lostwithiel by an interest carried on in another name and transferred by surprise in the same manner.'[1] It would appear, therefore, that Mayor John had laid his plans with care and success, taking his opponents by surprise; they therefore decided to present a petition against both the successful candidates, and spent the early summer preparing the documents. Petitions were drawn up in the names of the defeated candidates and in that of the corporation. But two further events also complicated the situation. Francis Robartes had been returned at Bodmin and, if successful in his petition, would have to elect to serve for one place or the other, thus vacating a seat; and James Kendall, Addison's partner at the poll, had died. Rumours were current of an agreement between Addison and Francis Robartes, which would secure them both in their seats while Russell Robartes would elect to serve for Bodmin; but this would depend upon the consent of Canon Kendall, a relative of the deceased man, who fell heir to his interests in the borough. Francis Atterbury, Addison's Oxford contemporary, a strong Tory and now Dean of Carlisle, was apparently used by Robert Harley to sound the canon. In July he wrote that the chances of such a compromise were small, but hinted strongly in favour of seeking such a solution:

Upon turning this matter over in my head I see but one way wherein it is possible for Mr. Addison and Mr. Roberts to join:

[1] H.M.C. *Portland*, iv. 489.

and that is if Mr. Roberts should whisper to him, that if he will quit his pretensions to a choice, upon the foot he now stands, and give in to Mr. Roberts petition, he shall be brought in upon a new foot by Mr. Roberts interest; and that his election shall be secured to him not only in this but in future parliaments. It is possible there may be persons that for the good of the common cause may set such an accommodation on foot, ere the matter is ripe for a decision in Parliament.[1]

An alternative plan put forward was for the petitions to proceed and for an attempt to be made to introduce Harry St. John at Lostwithiel, if he could find no better opportunity elsewhere.

When the news of Addison's election reached him in London, probably about 21 May, it cannot have afforded him any undue satisfaction, except possibly that of being returned simultaneously with Lord Hertford as whose tutor he had been rejected five years before. Dick Steele, however, hurried off to congratulate his friend 'with some persons concern'd . . . immediately'. Addison was now living at Sandy End, near Fulham, where his lameness had benefited either from the country air or from his holiday.[2] He had entered into a friendly relationship with the household of the widowed Countess of Warwick, who lived in the stately manor of Holland House. Twice in May Addison found time to write lengthy letters to the young earl, now aged eleven. These are enigmatic documents. Far from being jottings of a man who had worked until his eyesight broke down, who suffered from rheumatism or gout, who carried the major administrative burden of a great office of State, who was too busy to visit a friend in the country, and who had just been elected to Parliament, they breathe leisure and detachment. These letters insinuate solicitude for the young earl's education, alike in the classics and in bird-nesting, and anxiety to please him, indeed to have his company whenever the boy chooses to avail himself of the services of a learned lover of nature. A bachelor of thirty-six writing to a boy of eleven is not in the most happy of postures; but they are charming letters.

According to Oldmixon Addison, after returning from

---

[1] H.M.C. *Portland*, iv. 500.　　[2] E.B. i. 101.

his travels, took upon himself the care of the education of the young earl. A study of his administrative career and political standing makes it improbable that he was engaged as a paid tutor. Although it is conceivable that such an arrangement may have been envisaged before his return to England, as a means of providing himself with a livelihood. But he could not now have spared the time for such a task, nor was there any financial motive for his doing so when, since the *Campaign*, his pen might have been turned to more remunerative work. It is also known that in 1710–11 the duty of tutoring young Warwick was discharged by John Pountney, his mother's chaplain.[1] Pountney's expenses in this respect are entered in the countess's household account books but there is no mention of Addison therein during these early years. This omission and Addison's many commitments at the time, taken with the tenor of his letters to the young earl and his reputation as a scholar, make it more likely that Oldmixon's comment meant simply that Addison advised Lady Warwick upon her son's education and followed it with a personal, almost a fatherly, sense of responsibility.

Lady Warwick was a daughter of the aristocratic family of Myddelton of Chirk, and a connexion by marriage with the Montagu clan. Baptized at Chirk Castle on 7 January 1680, and thus eight years younger than Addison, she was the only survivor of several children and suffered a sickly childhood. Her father died when she was four years old and she retired from Chirk Castle to live more modestly with her mother at Plas Cadwgan, Denbighshire. When she was fourteen, her mother also died and Sir Orlando Bridgeman, a maternal uncle, became her guardian. As sole heiress of both parents, she had a moderate but respectable fortune. In January 1697 she married Edward Rich, sixth Earl of Warwick and by the terms of the marriage gave £16,000 to her husband and placed a further £10,000 in a marriage trust. The earl was one of the 'roaring boys' of the late Restoration, whose rakish career reached a climax when he was tried before the House of Lords in 1698 on a charge of murder. When found guilty of manslaughter, he pleaded the

---

[1] For details concerning the Countess of Warwick, see Arthur L. Cooke, 'Addison's Aristocratic Wife', *PMLA*, lxxii (1957), pp. 373–89.

benefit of his peerage and it was granted. The stern warning of Lord Chancellor Somers that such a plea can be made once only proved superfluous, for on 2 August 1701 he died 'very penitent', leaving his widow aged twenty-one with a son, aged four, and, it is to be feared, with an unfavourable view of the benefits of marriage. Lady Warwick had in fact suffered a collapse in health after the long strain of the trial with its attendant gossip and publicity, and had even been reported dead.

In these adverse circumstances there is nevertheless some evidence that Lady Warwick was being courted in the year 1705. Narcissus Luttrell had written in his diary on 1 August 1704 that 'Ld Hallifax' would marry the Countess. Thomas Hearne, in his diary for January 1705, wrote, ' 'Tis certain that Jo. Addison is marry'd to the Countess-Dowager of Warwick', then altered the opening to read: ' 'Tis reported for certain . . .'. It is not difficult to see that the Countess would be flattered to have two such men interested in her, even if she was not interested in marriage, nor to guess the advantage which Addison might have over his patron. In 1705 he was thirty-three and Halifax was forty-three. For the young widow, whose expenditures on newspapers and books indicate an active interest in literature and politics, Addison must have appeared attractive. Unlike Halifax, he was not her social equal but he was in the prime of life, still quite handsome and, importantly, the exact opposite of her former husband: he was shy, charming, and mature. It is safe to assume that Addison, who had a proper reverence for the great, would find it congenial to have an entry to the establishment at Holland House. While none of the evidence proves conclusively that this most secretive man was already designing to marry, it is remarkable that a busy official three days after his election to Parliament should have 'employed the whole neighbourhood in looking after birds-nests', should set a friend to searching the book-shops for a Statius 'to look in the beginning of the Achilleid for a Birds-nest which if I am not mistaken is very finely described', and should have had leisure to listen pensively to the nightingale 'that has a much better voice than Mrs. Tofts, and something of the Italian manner in her divisions'.

There is in fact no reason why the romantically inclined should not conclude that Joseph Addison was in love.

Back in the office Lord Sunderland congratulated the Duke of Newcastle on the success of the elections, which had resulted in 'the most Whig Parliament that ever was . . . if our friends will stick together, and act like men, I am sure the Court must whether they will or no, come into such measures as may preserve both us and themselves'.[1] But from Scotland there came on to Under-Secretary Addison's desk long dispatches from a humble informer and correspondent, the same Defoe who had grudged him his Commissionership of Appeals, telling in pungent phrases of trouble in that kingdom. In London the grim business of examining and trying the captured rebels kept the office busy and gave Addison material for thought upon the philosophical side of politics, while he arranged for the foot-guards to attend Lord Griffin's execution.[2] There was little time for diversions, but Addison was constantly in company with the Gazetteer. Mrs. Steele approved of her husband's closest friend, her 'favourite Mr. Addison', but grudged the hours that Dick spent in his company. Unable to compete with the friendship of many years, she followed her husband to Sandy End, where the couple lodged near Addison. Her 'favourite' was also her 'rival' she said. It was a business as well as a private association. Sometimes Addison sent the *Gazette* to press.

There was also still the financial tangle between the two men. In the previous November this had involved Addison in some hasty explanations about a note inadvertently left lying out, for which he made himself responsible in Steele's default.[3] On 25 June Addison surrendered his place as Commissioner of Appeals, by an instrument dated 14 May and passed under the Great Seal. His successor was Walter Hungerford, who presumably purchased the office for a considerable capital sum.[4] The expense of his election, immediately followed by the sale of his place, suggest that Addison was short of money. This may throw some light

[1] B.M. Lansdowne MSS. 1236, f. 243.   [2] Never carried out.
[3] R. Blanchard, 'Another Steele Letter', *Review of English Studies*, Apr. 1947.
[4] *Cal. Treasury Books*, xxii. ii. 285.

upon the fact that he apparently pressed Dick Steele hard to repay the loan of £1,000. This he obtained from Steele on 19 or 20 August, but not apparently in discharge of the mortgage, as will be seen presently. He was probably coming to the conclusion that loans to his friend were a mistaken kindness. A story survives that he went a step further in forcibly selling Steele's home 'The Hovel' at Hampton Wick, upon which he had secured a loan, to bring his friend to his financial senses. Johnson regarded this incident as authentic. 'Sir, it is generally known, it is known to all who are acquainted with the literary history of that period. It is as well known as that he wrote "Cato".' Johnson had it from Savage who had it from Steele 'with tears in his eyes'. He was also told by Benjamin Victor who was told by Wilks, the actor, who was a friend of Steele. The amounts given are variously £1,000 and £100, and after realizing his debt Addison is alleged to have returned the balance. But it appears that Steele's house was not now sold. Whether upon a later occasion Addison took the action described, or whether these stories are exaggerated accounts of threats which he used upon this occasion to compel Steele to a repayment, awaits determination. That he was capable of such a proceeding if convinced of its wisdom is beyond doubt. His attitude towards Steele's importunities was now hardening; and in November of this year Dick wrote ruefully to his wife: 'I am by applying to my Adversary prepar'd for ending my present calamity, but was deny'd by my Friend.'

The loan made by Addison upon the security of the Barbados estate now had some complicated legal consequences. Steele had not paid the interest thereon, and had not repaid the principal, not at least in legal form, though it is likely that he had privately reimbursed Addison who gave him a formal discharge dated 6 August. The tenant of the property had come forward as a purchaser and Dick had sold it for £9,300, perhaps partly as a means of recouping himself the money repaid to Addison as well as of settling his debts, and £2,000 was paid in cash on or before the day of the sale. To facilitate the transaction in view of various encumbrances on the estate, on 5 or 6 August he had conveyed it to trustees who, amongst other undertakings, agreed to pay off Addison's mortgage at request. Addison thereupon tendered to the trustees, Messrs. Rowland Tryon, John Walter, Stephen Clay, and William Leche, a surrender of his interest and demanded repayment of the outstanding capital, interest, and costs. The trustees and Walker, however, raised legal objections and withheld payment. A clear issue now arose, and Addison applied to the Lord Chancellor for a Writ of Subpoena, which would enable him to bring the parties before the court and thus to establish the facts upon which his case would rest. The persons against whom the writ was requested were Richard Steele, George Walker, and the trustees, being all those who under any legal interpretation of the facts might be liable to repay the money or against whom a foreclosure might be obtained, and whose evidence might be material. If this writ was refused, no trial of the main issue could take place. The proceeding was not hostile to Steele, who was undoubtedly joining Addison in seeking to make the purchaser or his trustees discharge the mortgage, as the latter had agreed to do in the deed of purchase.

On 7 December Tryon put in a plea on behalf of the trustees resisting Addison's demand for a writ upon a variety of grounds and raising a number of legal obstacles, and it does not appear that a writ issued or that a hearing of the main point in dispute took place in Chancery. Evidently, therefore, Steele had sold his estates, subject to encumbrances, on 5–6 August. According to his letter to his wife dated 20 August he then 'paid Mr. Addison His whole thousand pound [but not apparently any interest] and have settled every man's payment except one which I hope to perfect tomorrow'. He could not have legally paid off Addison's mortgage after disposing of the security upon the terms that it should become the responsibility of the purchasers, who doubtless deducted something on that account from the purchase price arrived at; but he evidently used the proceeds of the sale, or such part as was paid immediately, to make a general settlement with his creditors including £1,000 paid to Addison by private arrangement. He then, in collusion with Addison, sought to enforce his

bargain with the trustees to recover, through Addison, his
£1,000 with interest and costs. The litigation apparently
failed, but it is possible that some settlement was eventually
arrived at. Steele had repeated dealings with Tryon; and
when in the latter part of 1711 he wrote to his wife, 'Addison's
money you will have to-morrow noon', it may be that his
friend had managed to recover something for him.[1]

Jonathan Swift was upon the fringe of the two men's
friendship. He wrote to Ambrose Philips in July:

> The triumvirate of Mr. Addison, Steele, and me, come together
> as seldom as the Sun, Moon and Earth. I often see each of them,
> and each of them me and each other; and when I am of the number
> Justice is done you as you would desire.[2]

It is not likely that he in fact saw Addison often at this time,
but he evidently took pride in placing himself upon an equal
footing of intimacy with the two other members of the
'triumvirate', who enjoyed a political and literary reputation
with which his own was as yet in no way comparable. As
the year wore on he grew more closely acquainted and
assumed more authoritatively the posture of disposing of
the Under-Secretary's favour. On 14 September he wrote
to Ambrose Philips:

> I am glad at heart to see Mr Addison who may live to be service-
> able to you, so mindful in your Absence. He has reproached me
> more than once for not frequently sending him a Lettr to con-
> veigh to You. That Man has Worth enough to give Reputation to
> an Age, and all the Merit I can hope for with regard to you, will be
> my advice to cultivate his Friendship to the utmost, and my
> assistance to do you all the good Offices towards it in my Power.[3]

Such 'good offices' were in fact needless, for Addison corresponded familiarly with Philips, addressing him with the
unusually affectionate 'My Dearest Friend' towards the end
of the year. Indeed this seems to have been a time of intimate
friendship in Addison's life and the man whom Swift
thought to possess 'Worth enough to give Reputation to

---

[1] The foregoing is the interpretation placed by the author upon Addison's
Chancery pleading at the P.R.O. No. C6/352/2 discovered by Professor
A. L. Cooke, to whom he is much indebted. See also R. Blanchard, 'Richard
Steele's West Indian Plantation', *Mod. Philology*, xxxix. 281 et seq.
[2] Williams, i. 91.   [3] Ibid. i. 98.

an Age', wrote in a copy of his *Travels in Italy*: 'To Dr. Jonathan Swift, the most agreeable companion, the truest friend, and the greatest genius of his age, this book is presented by his most humble servant the author.'[1] The burden of official duties had eased a little after the crises of invasion and election. On 9 September Addison took Dick Steele in a coach and four to visit his sister Dorothy in the country. This was one of the rare occasions upon which there is a record of his associating with immediate relatives. Dorothy Addison had married the Reverend James de Sartre, a native of Auvergne, who had lived as a Protestant refugee in England since 1691 or earlier. At that time de Sartre was accusing Bayle, whom he had known in youth, of having had early Jesuit connexions.[2] Like most of those related to or connected with Addison, he subsequently obtained promotion, in this case to a prebend at Westminster. With Dorothy he moved into what Swift described as 'a delicious house and garden' in the Close. There was also much entertaining at Addison's retreat at Sandy End, and there were visits to Steele's villa at Hampton. Ambrose Philips was back in London. Even Addison's old friend Congreve was occasionally to be met with. Leibniz in Germany was not forgotten in correspondence, and Colonel Hunter, governor-designate of Virginia, was an intimate at this time. But this interlude was short for the political situation was once more threatening.

The victory of Oudenarde on 30 June did something to appease critics of the Government, but the Secretary of State was dissatisfied with the administration of Lord Treasurer Godolphin. Scotland was mismanaged, the invasion not well handled, the pardoning of Lord Griffin inexcusable; the Treasurer and the Duke of Marlborough would probably arrange to bring in the Pretender when the queen died, unless vigorous measures were taken to safeguard the Protestant succession.[3] In October there was a stormy interview between seven Whig magnates and the Lord Treasurer, in which they complained of the incom

[1] E. Ball, *Swift's Verse*, p. 63; Forster, *Life of Swift*, p. 160.
[2] L. P. Courtines, *Bayle's Relations with England*, p. 51.
[3] B.M. Lansdowne MSS. 1236, f. 244.

petence of the administration, particularly that of the drunken Prince Consort at the Admiralty. Dissatisfied with the Treasurer's answers, they decided to oppose the court candidate for Speaker.[1] Then the Prince Consort died and the political deadlock was broken, once again to the advantage of the Whigs. The queen was too disturbed to withstand political demands. Lord Sunderland, in whose office the arrangements for the prince's funeral were proceeding,[2] reported on 4 November that Her Majesty had agreed to the appointment of Lord Wharton as Lord Lieutenant of Ireland, and Lord Somers, Lord President of the Council.[3] On 16 November Parliament met and the Speaker was not opposed. The Whigs now enjoyed more power than at any time since King William's day.

In the Commons Addison's opponents at Lostwithiel proceeded to introduce their petitions. These were presented on 22 November and ordered to be heard on 26 February of the following year. There were so many petitions before the House that a group of members introduced a Bill 'for preventing bribery and corruption in Election of Members to serve in Parliament'. But Addison's thoughts were now turned in another and a new direction. On the same day that the petitions against his election were presented in the House of Commons *the supplement* had carried the news that the Right Honourable the Earl of Wharton had been appointed to succeed the Earl of Pembroke as Lord Lieutenant of Ireland. This had been foreshadowed by Addison to Lord Manchester as long ago as 9 March, and was the outcome of an agreement between the Whigs and the Lord Treasurer. Two days later, the day on which the petitions against Addison were deferred until February, Lord Somers's appointment also appeared. Addison's friends were returning at last and in force to the seats of power, and in their triumph they did not forget him. Indeed his notable service as Under-Secretary at a critical time, with his stature as a man of letters, entitled him to consideration. On 6 December he was appointed Secretary of the Irish Government.

[1] Ibid., f. 246.   [2] S.P. 44/106, 411.
[3] B.M. Lansdowne MSS. 1236, f. 252.

It is now opportune to look back over the past four years. The man whom we have been studying differs from the long-accepted picture of Joseph Addison. During these four busy years, after lengthy and careful preparation in England and abroad, he raised himself to an executive post of high trust, requiring administrative abilities of the first order. We have seen how he raised himself to a pinnacle of literary eminence by the publication of the *Campaign*, and how in the intervals of business he managed to produce an opera and some minor pieces. But as the pressure of government business became heavy his literary activities ceased almost entirely. The vision of a poet philosopher discoursing leisurely over coffee or claret to a circle of literary friends has no place in this period of Addison's life. The coffee, the claret, and the friends were there; but a busy official of government had little time or thought to spare for them.

V

IRISH EMINENCE
1708–1710

THE office of Lord Lieutenant of Ireland carried with it such incomparable power and patronage in that kingdom that the prospect of a new incumbent created a speculative boom in new appointments. Of the Irish offices, that most interesting to semi-professional administrators was the Secretaryship. The Secretaries of State in England had enlarged their function from that of confidential secretary to the king into a directorate of high policy through a great department. Similarly the Secretary in Ireland had become a powerful figure in the politics and administration of the kingdom. Though wholly subordinate to the Lord Lieutenant and not yet, as Lord Chesterfield put it, a 'first minister',[1] the holder of this office was already, though incorrectly, referred to as the Secretary of State. For a post of such power, whose revenues from fees and other sources amounted to about £2,000 per annum, there were numerous competitors. On this occasion Swift reported to Archbishop King in Dublin that 'One Mr. *Shute* is named for Secretary to Lord *Wharton*: he is a young Man, but reckoned the shrewdest Head in England'.[2] This was John Shute, a friend of Locke, who had played an important part in the negotiations which took place in Scotland at the time of the Union. His experience with the Scottish politicians would be useful in the complicated problems of religion in Ireland. There was also a report that Addison's experienced colleague Hopkins might be selected for the vacant post. Lord Wharton was ruthless and efficient and insisted upon being well served. It was therefore a tribute to the success with which Addison had discharged his duties as Under-Secretary when he was chosen to go as Secretary to Dublin.

The appointment was made on 6 December 1708, but was

---

[1] *Chesterfield Corr.* ed. Dobrée, i. 121.   [2] Williams, i. 115.

not at first published; nevertheless it immediately bore fruit in an application from Dick Steele for the post of Under-Secretary which would now fall vacant. He scribbled to his wife:

I will not defer telling you that there is a thing in Agitation that will make me happy at once. Your rival A ... n will be remov'd and if I can succeed Him in His Office It will answer all Purposes.

On 14 December Addison proposed to his new chief that he should use his influence with Lord Sunderland on Steele's behalf, and on 23 December Narcissus Luttrell heard the rumour that Steele would be appointed. But Lord Sunderland had other views, and on 28 December Peter Wentworth wrote to his brother, Lord Raby, in Berlin:

Mr. Addison is certain of going over Secretary to Lord Wharton, and Mr. Steel put in for his place, but Lord Sunderland has put him off with a promise to get him the next place he shall ask that may be keep [*sic*] with the Gazette.[1]

Dick had none of the qualities which the post required; he was not diligent, tenacious, reserved, or tactful. Yet on this occasion Addison permitted affection to prevail over reason, and recommended his friend for the post. But the vacant Under-Secretaryship went to John Pringle of Haining, one of the new Scottish Members of Parliament who sat for Selkirk in the Union House.

Addison was now the centre of a considerable business in patronage and found himself much occupied, and Steele was helping him in the emergency. On 18 December, for example, he was upon 'extraordinary business' all day on his friend's behalf, and dined with him that night. Jonathan Swift, who had been disappointed of going Secretary to Lord Berkeley the British envoy in Vienna, was also seeking preferment. Archbishop King now suggested to him that he should come to Ireland as the Lord Lieutenant's chap-lain; but if he made any attempt to secure the post he, too, was disappointed.[2] The claims of Peter Desmaizeaux, a friend of Addison's, and correspondent of Bayle, later troublesome to Steele, were also put forward for an employ-

---

[1] *Wentworth Papers*, p. 68.   [2] Luttrell, vi. 386.

ment. It was about this time that Richard Smallbroke, a
Demy of the 'Golden Election', became chaplain to Archbishop Tenison; and though there is nothing to connect his
appointment with Addison, it is remarkable that several of
his Magdalen colleagues had received promotion at a time
when he was well placed to speak an influential word. Finally
the news of his own advancement, which had been known in
an inner circle of friends, was made public in the press for
23 December.[1] Narcissus Luttrell had received the information two days earlier, and he also noted that Alexander
Denton, Member of Parliament for Buckingham, would go
as the Lord Lieutenant's private secretary.[2]

While Joseph prospered he had not been forgetful of his
brothers. Gulston had followed an adventurous and profitable career since his entry into the service of the East India
Company. He was now a member of the Presidential Council
at Madras, and had been seven years married to a widow,
Mary Brooks, whose brother was an influential merchant in
India. The Governor at Fort St. George and President of
the Coromandel Coast was 'Diamond' Pitt, who had ruled
there with an autocratic sway since 1697. He had recently
defied the besieging armies of the Great Mogul, and had
crowned a profitable term of office by the purchase of the
fabulous diamond which bears his name. Quarrelling with
the Court of the Company in London, Pitt had been dismissed, and Joseph Addison had thereupon used his
influence to secure the governorship and presidency for his
brother. In this he was successful and the *Post Man* for
30 December carried an announcement that the Directors
of the East India Company had chosen Mr. Gulston Addison
'an eminent merchant residing at Fort St. George, Governor
and President of that place in the Room of Thomas Pitt
Esq, who 'tis said, hath desired leave to come home.'[3]
Addison evidently took some interest in the affairs of the
presidency, for he was instrumental in sending Brudenell
Baker, son of a prebendary of Lichfield, to employment at
Madras.

The two brothers changing employments at the same time
had caused some confusion in the public mind, and Peter

[1] *Post Boy*, 2132.   [2] Luttrell, vi. 386.   [3] *Post Man* 1697

Wentworth had gained the impression that it was Gulston who was to go to Ireland as Secretary. On this point Addison set him right when they discussed the matter on 20 December, and Wentworth was much impressed:

Since I writ this I am told a great Peice of News that Mr. Addison is really a very great man with the juncto, and that he has got his elder brother who has been a factor abroad in those parts, to be Governor of Fort St. George, and the Great Pitts is turn out, his son here had a great while constantly voted with the Torys which has been a help to Mr. Addison. It seems Mr. Addisons friends can do what they please with the cheif of the East India Company, who I think have the liberty of naming their Governor, and by management with them this place is got which they say some years are worth 20,000 pound.[1]

With Lancelot a Fellow of Magdalen, and Dorothy married to a man of some distinction in the Church, Addison could feel satisfaction at the provision made for his family and free to attend to his own affairs in which there was much to be done before he could leave for Ireland.

The election petitions against him in the House of Commons were still pending. In spite of the fact that he had already begun to transact affairs for Lord Wharton and that Pringle's appointment was noticed by Luttrell on New Year's Day,[2] he was not yet relieved of Lord Sunderland's business. In the absence of a chief governor, Ireland was ruled by a panel of Lords Justices. Their secretary, Joshua Dawson, had held that and parallel offices for twenty years and was established in Dublin with a wife and seven children. Dawson was known to Addison by correspondence through Lord Sunderland's office in connexion with Irish business.[3] He was the experienced official on the spot, the element of continuity in changing administrations, and could be invaluable to Addison in introducing him to the complexities of his new post. On the other hand Dawson also had an interest in commending himself to the new Secretary. Edward Southwell, who had many Irish connexions, reported to Dawson that he was approaching

[1] *Wentworth Papers*, pp. 75–76.   [2] Luttrell, vi. 391.
[3] S.O. 1/15, ff. 450–1; S.P. 44/243, ff. 174–5.

Addison on his behalf through the agency of Swift and good claret.[1] Another London correspondent let Dawson know that Mr. Addison was 'a civil good natured man'.[2] Daniel Pulteney, who knew Addison well, was even more explicit and comforting: 'I do not know a better tempered, obliging and ingenious gentleman than he is, and you will be as easy under him as yourself can wish, for he designs to continue you in your present station.'[3] On 11 January there began a correspondence between the two men, Addison's first letter assuring Dawson of his employment.

The art of governing Ireland, which Addison was now to learn, lay in the skilled management of the legislature, and in this the Secretary was the chief instrument of the Lord Lieutenant. It was not desirable that the Dublin Parliament should meet until Lord Wharton was there to manipulate it. Therefore amongst the earliest instructions sent over by Addison was an order of prorogation. Addison was fortunate in having the advice in London of George Dodington, the outgoing Secretary. It was necessary to take measures to safeguard shipping in St. George's Channel, where privateers were active, to draft the new establishment of government, to rectify accounts with the treasury, to settle a new Mutiny Bill, and to obtain new liveries for the Lord Lieutenant, a ticklish demand to which the Treasury replied with characteristic sang-froid that it was impossible that the former ones should be worn out in the space of three years.[4] Addison became accountable as from 4 December, the date of Lord Wharton's patent, but was troubled to find that Dawson had allowed his predecessor the fees for the whole of his last quarter. Dawson was now made to know that he would expect similarly favourable treatment when he in turn should vacate his place. Addison called for the accounts of his predecessor 'which may give me some Light into the nature of the Office', by which he probably meant that he would thus be able to estimate the revenues accruing. But amidst so much business he did not forget to write a short

[1] F. Elrington Ball, *Correspondence of Jonathan Swift* (1912), i. 179 n.
[2] Cit. H. Wood, *Roy. Soc. Antiq. Ireland*, xxxv. 133.
[3] Cit. Murray, 'Addison in Ireland', *19th Cent. Rev.*, vol. lxxv.
[4] S.P. 67/3.

but affectionate latter to Lord Warwick on his birthday, 20 January, enclosing a silver pen.

As time drew on he sent orders for a yacht to be ready in Chester-water at the end of March, to convey the Lord Lieutenant; and about the middle of the same month he instructed Dawson that his lodgings, the official quarters of the Secretary in Dublin Castle, should be made 'inhabitable'. In response he was assured by the Constable that they were in 'good forwardness, and I believe will pretty well serve your occasions during your stay here'. They consisted on the ground floor of an office, waiting room, paper closet, and another small room, with suitable offices for Under-Secretaries and clerks; while upstairs there were panelled dressing and 'lodging' rooms, and a drawing-room 'with hangings'. The stables accommodated ten horses. Captain Pratt, the Constable, who became a personal friend, occupied the next lodgings.

In all of these proceedings Jonathan Swift took a personal interest. He had become more closely acquainted with Addison during the autumn and winter, and immediately after his friend's appointment he had written to Archbishop King:

Mr. Addison, who goes over first Secretary, is a most excellent Person; and being my most intimate Friend, I shall use all my Credit to set him right in his Notions of Persons and Things. I spoke to him with great Plainness upon the Subject of the Test; and he says he is confident my Lord *Wharton* will not attempt it, if he finds the Bent of the Nation against it. I will say nothing further of his Character to Your Grace at present, because he hath half persuaded me to have some Thoughts of returning to *Ireland*, and then it will be Time enough: But if that happens otherwise, I presume to recommend him to Your Grace as a Person you will think worth your Acquaintance.[1]

Swift thus already saw himself pulling the strings of Irish policy and patronage through the hands of his 'most intimate' friend. Thereafter his correspondence reveals him attempting to use Addison to persuade the Lord Lieutenant to procure a remission of the 'first fruits' paid by the Irish clergy, in which he was unsuccessful.

[1] Williams, i. 118.

Swift complained much of Addison's obsession with business:

'I know no People', he wrote to Colonel Hunter, then a prisoner in France after capture by privateers on his way to govern New York, 'so ill used by your Men of Business as their intimate Friends. About a fortnight after Mr Addison had received the Letter you were pleased to send me, he first told me of it with an Air of Recollection, and after ten days further, of Grace, thought fitt to give it me.'[1]

And again:

Mr. *Addison* hath been so taken up for some Months, in the amphibious Circumstances of premier C—— to my Lord *Sunderland*, and Secretary of State for *Ireland*, that he is the worst Man I know either to convey an idle Letter, or deliver what he receiveth; . . . The best Intelligence I get of public Affairs is from Ladies . . . and Mr. Addison is nine Times more secret to me than any Body else, because I have the Happiness to be thought his Friend. . . . I pray God, too much Business may not spoil *Le plus honnête Homme du Monde*; for it is certain, which of a Man's good Talents he employeth on Business, must be detracted from his Conversation.[2]

It will be noticed that in the three quotations above Swift is in each case careful to impress his correspondent with the intimacy of his friendship with Addison of which at this time he seems to have been particularly proud.

From Ireland came proposals for yet more business. Joseph Keally, an Oxford man, close friend of Congreve, a relation of George Berkeley, and of whom Addison and Steele spoke with evident affection, was Member for Doneraile in the Irish Parliament. Addison had exchanged civilities with Keally in the autumn, and now received from him the offer of a seat in the Dublin House if he should wish for one. Such a position carried with it considerable privileges and was regarded as a valuable property. The suggestion came through Steele, who replied that Addison was already provided. In fact he was to stand for the vacant seat at Cavan borough, which would be filled when Parliament met.[3] From Daniel Pulteney at The Hague came a

[1] Williams, i. 119.   [2] Ibid. i. 132–4.   [3] *Gents. Mag.* 1790, i, vol. lx.

request for help in private business in Ireland,[1] and from Ambrose Philips a copy of his 'Winter Piece', which Addison corrected and approved. There was also family business to be put in order before he could leave for Dublin. There were debts outstanding to his sister Dorothy in Lichfield, probably in connexion with the dean's estate. Arthur Stevens, an executor, was charged with handling these matters;[2] and about the middle of March Addison himself was in the country, possibly at Lichfield, while Charles Delafaye at Lord Sunderland's office answered correspondence on his behalf.[3]

As the date of departure for Ireland, already postponed, finally drew near, Addison's activity became feverish. On 6 April he was authorized by a queen's warrant to be sworn a member of the Irish Privy Council.[4] On the same day with Edward Wortley he stood godfather to Dick Steele's daughter Elizabeth at St. James's, Piccadilly. He was importuning Burchett for an appointment to meet Brigadier Macartney to settle details of the now imminent journey to Ireland, and was urging the College of Heralds to complete the new blazons required by the Lord Lieutenant, probably as a result of his recent election to a Garter,[5] in time for use at the arrival ceremonies. Finally on 9 April Addison left London for Winchendon, Lord Wharton's country seat, whither the Lord Lieutenant himself had gone some three days before. The following afternoon the party set out for Northampton on its way to Chester.[6] Included in the retinue were Alexander Denton, M.P., private secretary, Thomas Ellis and Mr. Mitchell, gentlemen ushers, Dr. Lambert, first chaplain, and Captain Goring, aide-de-camp.[7] The journey to Ireland was notoriously hard and it was only by 18 April that the party arrived at Chester where the *Charlotte* yacht awaited them. On 20 April, the wind being favourable, they embarked at Park Gate and sailed under convoy of Her Majesty's ships *Hampshire* and *Speedwell*.[8]

The chief personage sailing aboard the *Charlotte*, to whose

---

[1] S.P. 67/3, f. 387.   [2] Blenheim MSS. D.I. 32.
[3] S.P. 63/366.   [4] S.P. 67/3, f. 394.
[5] *Supplement*, 189.   [6] Ibid. 193.   [7] Ibid. 194.
[8] *London Gazette*, 4534; *Supplement*, 194.

fortunes those of Joseph Addison were now attached, was one of the most remarkable Englishmen living:

> Thomas, Earl of Wharton, Lord Lieutenant of Ireland, by the Force of a wonderful Constitution hath some Years passed his Grand Climacteric, without any visible Effects of old Age, either on his Body or his Mind, and in Spight of a continual Prostitution to those Vices which usually wear out both. . . . His behaviour is in all the Forms of a young Man at five and twenty. Whether he walketh, or whistleth, or sweareth, or talketh Bawdy, or calleth Names, he acquitteth himself in each beyond a Templar of three Years standing. . . . With a good natural Understanding, a great Fluency in Speaking, and no ill Taste of Wit, he is generally the worst Companion in the World; his Thoughts being wholly taken up between Vice and Politics; so that Bawdy, Prophaneness and Business, fill up his whole Conversation. . . . He is without the Sense of Shame or Glory, as some Men are without the Sense of Smelling.[1]

Thus wrote Jonathan Swift towards the end of the year 1710. A more friendly biographer merely suggested that this master of political technique had accepted the Lord Lieutenancy to recoup his expenses at the recent election. Swift's bitterness at not receiving any promotion from the Government had probably been accentuated by the feeling that so profound a student of men as of women penetrated and disliked his character. Steele and Addison, whose talent it was to analyse the positive in men, judged Lord Wharton as follows:

> You are so throughly acquainted with the Characters of Men, and all the Parts of Humane Life, that it is impossible for the least Misrepresentation of them to escape Your Notice. It is Your Lordship's particular Distinction, that you are Master of the whole Compass of Business, and have signalized Your Self in all the different Scenes of it. We admire some for the Dignity, others for the Popularity of their Behaviour; some for their Clearness of Judgment, others for their Happiness of Expression; some for the laying of Schemes, and others for the putting of them in Execution: It is Your Lordship only who enjoys these several Talents united. . . . Your Enemies acknowledge this great Extent in Your Lordship's Character, at the same Time that they use their utmost Industry and Invention to derogate from it. But it is for Your

---

[1] Swift, *A Short Character of Thomas Earl of Wharton.*

Honour that those who are now Your Enemies were always so.
You have acted in so much Consistency with Your Self, and
promoted the Interests of Your Country in so uniform a Manner,
that even those who would misrepresent Your generous Designs
for the Publick Good, cannot but approve the Steadiness and
Intrepidity with which You pursue them.[1]

Though the lampoon and the courtly dedication contrast
so sharply, they together portray a vigorous, able, and steadfast politician, a subtle judge and ruthless manipulator
of men. Lord Wharton's appointment was the high water-
mark of Whig power in Queen Anne's reign, and Addison
was carried to Dublin upon that favourable tide.

It was a troubled kingdom of which the Lord Lieutenant
and his Secretary were now to assume the government.[2]
The bitter heritage of civil war and religious strife had given
Ireland her peculiar political structure. The Protestant
interest could be counted upon to resist Jacobite and Catholic
invasion or sedition and it was Whig policy to strengthen it
by every possible means. Such a policy took for granted and
sharpened the already bitter hatred of the Catholic Irish.
Lord Wharton was thought to support the dissenters who
wished for a repeal of the Test Acts. He saw a real need
for an attitude of tolerance towards the dissenting sects, for
its expression in sound legislation, and for the just administration of the law. Consequently his appointment had raised
a pitch of excitement unusual even in Ireland, and it provoked violent hostility amongst the clergy of the established
Church:

> Republicans, your tuneful Voices raise,
> And teach the People, who to thank and praise.
> L—d Wh——n first, for b'ing High-Church's Terror,
> And confuting that antique vulgar Error,
> That poysnous Creatures could not in I—land live,
>   'Till he came thither, . . .[3]

In the month of February 1709 there had been reports of
duels, brawls, and courts martial, symptoms of the accumulat-

---

[1] Dedication to *Spectator*, vol. v.
[2] For an examination of Wharton's Viceroyalty, see L. A. Dralle's 'Kingdom
in Revision', *HLQ*, 1952.
[3] *A Collection of Poems for and against Dr. Sacheverell*: 'The Thanksgiving.'

ing troubles which broke out in the 'Whiteboy' riots in 1711.[1]
Trinity College, a stronghold of the doctrines of John Locke,
had been torn by political faction and rebuked by the queen.[2]
Early in March, partly to maintain order and partly to deter
invasion, troops had been recruited all over the kingdom.[3]
Then followed a grain famine[4] and soon after the arrest of a
papal agent selling Jacobite literature in Cork.[5] Rumours of
an invasion by the Pretender were increasing and the coastal
defences were being manned.[6] As the *Charlotte* sailed there
were reports of a landing by French privateers at Youghal[7]
and three days after her safe arrival the Holyhead packet
was captured and the mails jettisoned.[8]

The party from the *Charlotte* landed at Ringsend on 21
April, and the elements favourable to Whig policies saw to
it that the Lord Lieutenant received an impressive welcome.
Soon after dawn three great guns gave notice of the yacht
being sighted. These were answered by the castle battery.
As the party landed a further nine guns discharged and
members of the Privy Council of Ireland waited in attendance with 'great numbers of the Nobility and Gentry in
their Coaches'. The Sheriffs and four troops of horse escorted
the Lord Lieutenant and his train to the accompaniment of
State trumpets and kettle-drums, the streets were lined with
infantry, and there were repeated salvoes of cannon. The
Lord Mayor, Recorder, and Aldermen of Dublin in their
robes offered dutiful submission, and at the Council Chamber the oaths were administered, and proclaimed by a further
discharge of artillery. The cavalcade then proceeded to the
castle attended by the Privy Council, Officers of State, and
Guard of Battle-Axes. At the castle the Archbishop of
Dublin, on behalf of the clergy, and St. George Ashe,
Bishop of Clogher, Swift's old tutor, on behalf of the university, and the nobility and gentry on their own account,
approached their chief governor to render dutiful submission. Doubtless the archbishop looked with curiosity
upon the Secretary of whom he had received so warm a
commendation from Swift. The day concluded with ringing

[1] See many references in contemporary press.   [2] *London Gazette*, 4517.
[3] *Supplement*, 186.   [4] Ibid. 196.   [5] Ibid. 206.
[6] Ibid. 207.   [7] Ibid. 198.   [8] Ibid. 202.

of bells, bonfires, and other demonstrations of joy.[1] Before
he retired to the lodgings which had been prepared for him,
after one of the most memorable days in his life, Addison
managed to deliver a kind remembrance to St. George
Ashe from his old pupil, to whom he also found time to
write in the midst of much business the following day.

One of his first official acts was to sign a proclamation
further proroguing Parliament.[2] It was the same House of
Commons which had been sitting at infrequent intervals
since the beginning of Queen Anne's reign and much tension
and bitterness was pent up therein. Lord Wharton reported
dryly to Lord Sunderland that parliamentary business would
be carried on 'as amicably and quietly, as could be expected,
from a number of men, that hate one another as heartily as
'tis possible to imagine, and yet are pretty equally divided'.[3]
It was desirable to seat Addison as soon as possible after the
session was opened on 5 May, because he had an important
constitutional function to perform as the mouthpiece of the
administration in the Commons chamber. On the first day
of the sitting a writ was issued for an election at Cavan
Burgh to fill the vacancy caused by the death of Robert
Saunders. The other Cavan seat was occupied by Thomas
Ash, and it may be that Addison had obtained his nomination through the agency of Swift's friend St. George. As he
awaited his election, Addison watched with admiration the
dexterity of his master in managing Parliament. He reported
to Lord Sunderland that he 'has so well succeeded . . . that
it is believed that he has broken all the parties that some had
endeavoured to form against him . . .'. To Lord Halifax he
wrote:

His Excellency . . . has addressed himself to all sorts of men . . .
with unspeakable application . . . gains ground daily and I question not but in a new Parliament where parties are not settled and
confirmed he will be able to lead them into anything that will be
for their real interest and advantage.

To the Lord Treasurer Addison also wrote by request.
Perhaps that shrewd Tory valued a private account, however

---

[1] *London Gazette*, 4536; *Supplement*, 202.
[2] Steele, *Tudor and Stuart Proclamations*, ii. 194; *Supplement*, 202.
[3] Blenheim MSS. V.I. 23.

circumspect, of the conduct of his unwelcome Whig colleague. The volume of writing, both official and private,
was a burden to Addison's eyesight, which again failed him.

His election at Cavan passed successfully. It is estimated
that in 1692 the choice of a Member of Parliament for at
least 176 Irish boroughs was mainly a matter of nomination
by a patron. In others the choice rested with a handful of
burgesses who were members of the established Church.[1]
Addison took his seat in the Commons on 13 May,[2] doubtless receiving a warm welcome from Joseph Keally. But
Irish politics shocked him. Swift recalled that:

> Mr. Addison, when he first came hither . . . was extremely
> offended at the conduct and discourse of the chief managers. . . .
> He told me they were a sort of people who seemed to think, that
> the principles of a Whig consisted in nothing else but damning
> the Church, reviling the Clergy, abetting the dissenters, and speak-
> ing contemptibly of revealed religion.

Government business necessitated Addison's immediate
appointment to a place on the Committee of Public Accounts
where he would act in the capacity of a government watch-
dog, a task for which his experience of administration as
Under-Secretary, so greatly in excess of that possessed by
most of his parliamentary colleagues, would particularly fit
him. There continued to be a great deal of work and ceremony, so much so that Thomas Ellis the Usher, after a hard
Sunday on duty, including a State attendance at divine
service, was found dead in bed.[3] Addison nevertheless found
time to write to young Lord Warwick:

> I give your Lordship a thousand thanks for your kind Letter
> and must desire you will give me the like Instances of your friend-
> ship as often as your time will permitt; which will be some amends
> for the Losse of your Dear Company. . . . pray my Dear Lord let me
> know what pretty story you read last in Ovid, . . . Pray my Dear
> write anything so you do but write. . . . Do me the Honour to
> give my most Humble Respects to My Lady and to believe me
> always. . . .

---

[1] Lecky, *Ireland in the 18th Century*, p. 195.
[2] Happenings in the Irish Commons are all stated on the authority of the
Journals, unless another reference is given.
[3] *Supplement*, 212.

He even remembered to ask the young earl his opinion of 'a paper called the Tatler' which had appeared for the first time two days after Addison left London.

In Parliament Addison noticed how Lord Wharton 'took off the leaders' of those who might obstruct supply, and secured the passage of Ways and Means resolutions without a division. His opinion of Archbishop King mounted daily and he wrote to Lord Godolphin:

The Arch Bishop . . . is a great speaker both in ye House of Lords, and at the Council table. He seems to have joined a Good Knowledge of the World to a great Deal of learning. . . .

The archbishop had stifled an attempted political attack on the Government in Convocation by 'terrifying some and soothing others'. The complexities of Irish politics and their relationship with those of England can be followed in detail in the ample records of the period preserved in the Public Record Office, but are beyond the scope of this work. Addison was greatly extending his knowledge of political management and of the character of mankind. He served upon a number of committees, notably that appointed to consider a proposal to address the queen against any reversal of the outlawries of 1641, a highly dangerous political topic. As a member of the Privy Council he signed many official documents. He expostulated with the Admiralty for sufficient protection to be afforded to shipping in St. George's Channel, strove to mollify his Irish colleagues in their desire for an Irish arsenal which was felt in London to threaten the principle of Poyning's Law,[1] and steered a dexterous course on behalf of his superior in the proposal to codify the laws against the Catholics and in a quarrel between the two Houses of the Irish Parliament. Edward Young was acting as his secretary, and travelled to London on business.[2] Addison was soon sufficiently master of affairs to be left in Dublin in charge of the Lord Lieutenant's interests, for, as he reported to Lord Sunderland: 'His Exeye not having absented himselfe from the prayers in his Chappell one morning since his arrivall in this Kingdome, he is this day gone to the Curragh which is our Irish New Markett, and will stay

[1] S.P. 67/3, f. 400.   [2] Blenheim MSS. C.I. 23.

there during this Short Recess . . . .' On his return Lord
Wharton surveyed with satisfaction the manner in which the
dangerous opening weeks of his government had passed,
though he still feared that the zeal of the Protestant dissenters
might wreck his delicately balanced political machine.[1] It was
therefore doubtless a relief to Secretary Addison to inform
the reassembled House of Commons on 29 June that
Parliament stood adjourned.

During the short but eventful session Addison had discharged a number of official duties in the Commons which
involved him in addressing the House. He can have had
little leisure for private friendships, though in the course of
politics he must have seen much of Archbishop King and the
Bishop of Clogher. Jonathan Swift had decided to leave
England, where he had failed to win the confidence or
the patronage of the ministry, and to return to Ireland.
Addison wrote to the captain of the *Wolf* to accommodate
his friend at Chester, but the letter missed, and Swift landed
from another vessel two days after Parliament rose. He went
straight to his living at Laracor, and did not put in an
appearance in Dublin, causing the Secretary to expostulate,
'I think it is very hard I should be in the same Kingdome
with Dr. Swift and not have the Happinesse of his company
once in three days'. Hurrying to see the Lord Lieutenant
at his country residence at Chapelizod, Addison declared his
intention of paying a call on his return. But the political
quicksands were shifting once more, drawing the Lord
Lieutenant and Secretary back to England, and thus inter-
rupting what might have been a period of rest and fruitful
literary recreation.

It was on 5 July that Alexander Denton set out from
Dublin with the Irish Bills for approval in London and
with two important letters to Lord Sunderland. In them
Lord Wharton made it plain that he feared his administration was being undermined by political intrigue at home,
and he earnestly entreated to be allowed to return to England in September.[2] Of necessity Addison would go with
him, to transact the numerous matters of detail which arose
between the two governments. The leave asked for was

[1] Ibid. V.I. 23.   [2] Ibid. C.I. 23.

granted,[1] but the Bills were amended in such a way as to cause deep offence in Ireland and to increase the suspicion that Lord Wharton's policy was not supported from home.[2] It was no doubt to counteract as far as possible the reports of local political opponents that Addison took much time and trouble in writing letters to Lords Sunderland and Godolphin.[3] It now appeared that places on the Irish establishment were being filled from London without reference to the Lord Lieutenant, which, he protested, if it continued, would soon render him insignificant in Ireland.[4] If ever the seats of power had appeared desirable to Addison, he can by now have had no doubt about the cares and frustrations which beset the greatest of their occupants. In fact, Lord Wharton was in conflict with the queen's personal wishes, and Lord Sunderland warned him that 'any people that are in her service, that shall countenance so extravagant a proceeding [i.e. the enacting of the Irish Bills as sent to London] must expect her severest resentment'.[5] This was final, and Lord Wharton was left to deal with the Irish Parliament as best he could, and to prorogue it if necessary in the last resort. It did in fact prove necessary to prorogue Convocation, where serious trouble was making, and this was done by a letter from Addison. Thereupon the Archbishops of Tuam and Armagh complained of the irregularity of such a proceeding. To this Lord Wharton rather lamely replied that the letter had not been written on his instructions, but that no other means could be used because the Archbishop of Armagh was out when Addison had called upon him. The Upper House now met and asked for an explanation, but this proved to be a squib amongst the major fireworks of a violent day's proceedings (5 August) at the end of which the queen's writ of prorogation until 4 October was read, thus releasing the Secretary from an embarrassing situation.

In Parliament the crisis broke when Alexander Denton arrived back with the Bills from England. Addison noticed that the House was fuller than he had ever seen it, when, to smooth the way, he announced the queen's favourable answer to addresses upon the subject of outlawries. The controversial Money Bill was then read and the attack upon it opened. But writing that night, 9 August, Addison was able to tell Lord Sunderland that the prospects of its passage were good. He thought the debate, which was renewed two days later, 'as good a one as any I ever heard...' though it had kept him in suspense from eleven in the morning until seven at night. The Bill then passed by a large majority thanks to 'an unspeakable diligence in all my Lord Lieu^{ts} friends to work this point to his Satisfaction'. Even Lord Wharton was pleased. 'I am extreamly oblig'd to your Lordship', he wrote witheringly to Sunderland, 'for your concern you are pleased to expresse, for my tottering Administration here; ... there never was anything so laboured as the throwing of [the bill] out hath been, ...'[1] Throughout this period Addison's letters show him steadily supporting Lord Wharton's point of view; presenting it in his own fashion to the ministers to whom he wrote in London; even venturing to play upon their feelings, as when he described to the Lord Treasurer the manner in which that minister had been attacked by opponents of the Lord Lieutenant, and the zeal with which he had been defended by Archbishop King.

As the summer drew to its close, Lord Wharton and Addison had the satisfaction of seeing that they had triumphed over their opponents. The House of Commons passed a resolution thanking their chief governor for his Administration, which was dispatched to Dick Steele as material for the *Gazette*; and on 30 August the session was closed. All that remained was for Addison to sign a number of proclamations, to settle the appointment of Lords Justices to administer the kingdom in the absence of Lord Wharton, and to make arrangements for the homeward journey, now authorized.[2] There followed a fortnight of relative freedom, in which Addison found time to pay a visit to the scene of the Battle of the Boyne, dear to good Whigs, and to drink a glass to the memory of that King William who by a small pension had set him at large in the world and to Charles

---

[1] Blenheim MSS. C.I. 23.   [2] S.O. 1/15, ff. 485–6.

Montagu to whom he owed that favour. For a few days Swift and Addison had leisure to converse before he sailed from Ringsend. The Lord Lieutenant's party landed at Park Gate in time to see over 2,000 Protestant Palatines, whose settlement in Ireland Addison had been industrious to promote, travelling in the opposite direction. As Lord Wharton observed, it was better to spend money settling loyal people than purchasing the doubtful adherence of papists. Sixty years later, Arthur Young found the descendants of the people for whose settlement Addison and the Council had petitioned[1] living as good and industrious farmers.

Making the tedious journey to London, the Secretary doubtless looked forward with pleasure to a reunion with Dick Steele, the more so since during the summer the latter had founded and managed the most successful English periodical yet to appear from the press. The *Tatler* had begun publication on 12 April, and although Tickell recorded that Addison had no knowledge of the project and only detected his friend as the principal author by reading in the sixth number a reflection upon Homer and Virgil which he himself had made,[2] it is improbable that the paper's appearance can have greatly surprised him. The two men had already collaborated in management of the *London Gazette*. Addison was aware of the unwelcome restraints under which his friend laboured in editing that periodical, and he probably knew that Lord Halifax, Arthur Maynwaring, and others were interested in Steele's project. The *Tatler* was a remarkable production, and in the light of Dick's authorship Addison doubtless looked at it with particular interest. It was not entirely new in any respect; there was news, gossip, wit, and edification, each of which had been attempted before in a periodical. The exceptional feature of the *Tatler* was its air of gentlemanly unconcern, its appeal to the world of fashion and hence, subtly, to that of unfashion. It was the pleasantest of entertainment; tactfully it chatted to the ladies with the sure touch of one who had spent much time and study how to please them. It flattered the intelligence of the reader by dealing in serious as well as trifling matters. It exactly fitted the appetite of the town which its author knew

[1] H.M.C. 8th Rep., p. 47.   [2] Preface to Addison's *Works*.

so well. Yet its avowed objects were to reform as well as to entertain, a difficult combination of purposes, but one for which the time was ripe. Steele's whole life had been torn between noble aspirations and abject failings; he now drew upon his own soul.

To the ninth *Tatler* Swift, who was then still in England, sent a few verses. To the eighteenth, dated 20 May 1709, Addison himself had found time to make a considerable contribution. He wrote with elegant ease about trifles. Dick invited more. Numbers twenty and twenty-four were Joseph's work and he helped with hints elsewhere. His remarks upon 'pretty fellows', product of several years of silent observation of high society, helped the *Tatler* publishing thrice weekly to take the town by storm. Gratefully, Dick had printed a laudatory critique of the *Campaign*, in which the simile of the angel was described as a 'Sublime Image . . . as great as ever enter'd into the Thought of Man'.[1] When Addison reached his lodgings in St. James's Place the paper was the universal topic of conversation. Those not in the secret attributed the authorship to Swift, to Steele, even to Yalden. It had wide and influential support, but by far the best piece of fortune in the paper's career was Addison's arrival in town with his volumes of notes, the collection of many years' observation, and some further contributions which he brought from Jonathan Swift. He readily fell into the mood of the *Tatler*. Back in May he had written:

May-Fair . . . is now broke, . . . But it is allow'd still to sell Animals there. Therefore, if any Lady or Gentleman have Occasion for a Tame Elephant, let them enquire of Mr. *Pinketh-man*, who has one to dispose of at a reasonable Rate. The Downfall of *May-Fair* has quite sunk the Price of this noble Animal. . . .[2]

In July he had followed in the same vein with an inventory of the playhouse:

Three Bottles and a half of Lightning.
One Shower of Snow in the whitest *French* paper.
Two Showers of a browner Sort . . .
A Rainbow a little faded.
A Set of Clouds after the *French* Mode, streak'd with Lightning, and furbelow'd . . .

[1] T. 43.   [2] T. 20.

A Basket-Hilt Sword, very convenient to carry Milk in . . .
A Wild-Boar, kill'd by Mrs. *Tofts* and *Dioclesian*.
A Serpent to sting *Cleopatra*.
A Mustard-Bowl to make Thunder with.
Another of a bigger Sort, by Mr. *D——is*'s Directions, little
    used . . .
The Whiskers of a *Turkish* Bassa . . .
A Suit of Clothes for a Ghost, . . .[1]

These were the raw materials of satire, fresh in spirit. Even
the glance at Dennis's ponderous technique and lack of
popularity was hardly exceptionable. But they were no more
than Dublin reactions to Steele's London venture. Now in
daily conversation with his friend, Addison could colla-
borate instead of merely contributing, thus renewing upon
more fruitful ground the intercourse of the years.

In contrast with the gay virility of wit which was the
property of Steele, the second *Tatler* from Addison's pen in
London sounded the note of grave humour which was
peculiarly his own. 'There are two kinds of Immortality;
that which the Soul really enjoys after this Life, and that
imaginary Existence which Men Live in their Fame and
Reputation';[2] there followed not a sermon but a 'dream'.
Perhaps doubting the success of this kind of writing,
Addison returned to flippant topics for two more October
Tatlers before once more making trial of the previous
formula, a semi-philosophical introductory paragraph
followed by a 'fable'. On this occasion, however, he selected
a subject susceptible of lighter handling, namely 'love'. Still
uneasy with this form of paper, he followed it with an
explanation: 'I have been always wonderfully delighted with
Fables, Allegories, and the like Inventions, which the politest and the best Instructors of Mankind have always made
Use of.'[3] This predilection for allegory and fable sprang
from the memory of his father's scholarship in the affairs of
Barbary, and the words spoken to Addison by Boileau, that
precept is never so effective a medium of persuasion as
example; and its indulgence now led him into some facile
writing of little value.

[1] *T.* 42.   [2] *T.* 81.   [3] *T.* 90.

But divining that a diversity of resources is the secret of a successful periodical, Addison turned to his knowledge of classical literature, now not drawn upon for some years. He used the classical veneer to cover the foundation of morality, and pointed his lesson wittily at the majority of the inhabitants of London, who, he maintained, because employing their minds to no useful purpose, were really 'dead' without being aware of the fact:

It is said of *Xerxes*, That when he stood upon a Hill, and saw the whole Country round him covered with his Army, he burst out in Tears, to think that not one of that Multitude would be alive a Hundred Years after. For my Part, when I take a Survey of this populous City, I can scarce forbear weeping, to see how few of its Inhabitants are now living. . . . I have more Hopes of bringing to Life those that are young, than of reviving those that are old.

Then followed a 'classical' allegory of Hercules, and the final thrust:

I have translated this Allegory for the Benefit of the Youth of *Great Britain*; and particularly of those who are still in the deplorable State of Non-Existence, and whom I most earnestly entreat to come into the World.[1]

Finding a balance amongst the literary temptations besetting him—too serious a sermonizing on the one hand, too flippant a trifling on the other—Addison was arriving at a temper in writing calculated to appeal to an audience which was wider, more serious, more middle-class than the reading public of the past. He spoke, in fact, to the bourgeois stratum of society which was fast emerging.

Steele recognized his friend's talent, and decided to use it to the full while it was readily available. For Addison it had been an unproductive literary year.[2] He was therefore fresh and fertile in imagination; while Steele had begun to feel the burden of writing most of the papers which had appeared since April, and was glad to be relieved. During the winter he was to turn over the main share of the *Tatler* to Addison

[1] *T.* 97.
[2] It had seen the first printing of his translation of *Horace*, Ode III, Book III, under Rowe's editorship in the sixth of Tonson's *Miscellanies*.

who, in December 1709, contributed to seven out of eleven numbers, in January seven out of thirteen, and in March and April a further series of fourteen out of twenty. With the gesture of a man seeking to bolster his self-esteem after many attacks upon it by loans and their accompanying un-pleasantness, Steele paid Addison in full for his contribution. The Secretary might well have forgone his fee, for he was now a relatively wealthy man: but that powerful sense of his due which led him to exact payment of every commission as a moral right, may have prevented him from waiving his claim on this occasion.

The *Tatler* was but one of many matters awaiting Addison's attention when he returned to London from Dublin; and although it is undoubtedly that in which posterity has taken the greatest interest, it was not the most immediately pressing. From his lodgings Addison followed the preparation of the proceedings against him in Parliament which was soon to assemble a few minutes' walk from his door. One of the original signatories of the Lostwithiel petitions had died since they were presented, and this appears to have been used by Addison as a pretext for delay. While he was in Ireland he had hit upon the expedient of securing an office, acceptance of which would automatically void his election and would therefore also stop the petitions. He would thus be able to offer himself for Lostwithiel on the same footing as before, or perhaps for another less troublesome seat, while at the same time securing a personal advantage in an in-creased income. He had accordingly arranged to purchase the office of Keeper of the Records in Bermingham's Tower, that is to say, Keeper of the Irish Public Records. This was a sinecure place with a nominal salary of ten pounds. He now applied for substantial duties to be attached to the post.

Like most public records at this time, those in Dublin were in poor condition, badly housed, and disordered. Addison proposed that they should be examined, digested, transcribed, and catalogued. He may well have taken these proposals seriously, for there had been a project to establish an Irish State Papers Office in 1699,[1] and in March 1706 a Committee of Lords sitting in London had reported in

[1] Cal. S.P. Dom. 1699–1700.

favour of rehousing the English Public Records.[1] In August of the same year Sir Christopher Wren submitted a report to the Lord Treasurer proposing that the latter records be housed in the rooms at the Cockpit which had been fitted up for use by the Commissioners of the Union.[2] Both rooms and report would be well known to Addison and he probably now copied this scheme. He also had before him the enthusiasm of Lord Halifax, who had been instrumental in the publication of Rymer's *Foedera* and who was an amateur of ancient documents. Addison therefore drafted a petition and forwarded it to the Lord Treasurer who in turn passed it to the Lord Lieutenant for his observations before it should be submitted to the queen. Johnson comments that the office was little more than nominal, and Swift (later) described the transaction in acid terms when he spoke of the difficulty of getting a place in Ireland because the reversions were held by absentees:

Mr. Addison was forced to purchase an old obscure Place, called Keeper of the Records in Bermingham's Tower, of Ten Pounds a Year, and to get a salary of £400 annexed to it, though all the Records there are not worth Half a Crown, either for Curiosity or Use.[3]

It is probable that Addison took his office more seriously than Johnson or Swift believed to be the case, and certain that the Records were of much value. Some months hence it was reported from Dublin that six great guns had been brought down to the castle yard from the Black Tower where they had been many years, because 'they are fitting . . . a fine place for the Records of this Kingdom'.[4] But however conscientiously Addison may have performed his office, there lay many exasperating delays and difficulties between him and its quiet possession.

Lord Wharton inclined to think that Addison's acceptance of office as Secretary in Ireland might in itself be sufficient to invalidate his membership of the English Commons if he chose to put forward that objection; but the law as to which offices disqualified a Member if accepted subsequently to his election was not clearly defined at this period. He was

[1] S.P. 45/21. [2] Ibid.
[3] *Drapiers Letters*, IV. [4] *Supplement*, 411.

therefore anxious to regularize his position as Keeper of the
Records, which would apparently disqualify him, as soon
as possible; and for this purpose he needed a valid surrender
thereof from its previous holder, Cusack Baldwin. Baldwin
lived in Ireland, and in negotiation with Dawson, who acted
on Addison's behalf, made full use of his nuisance value
before completing his part of the transaction. As September
wore on into late October and Baldwin still evaded completion, Addison's letters to Dawson grew more querulous.
Lord Wharton was willing to countenance the transaction,
and the Lord Treasurer and Lord President were both also
well disposed; but meanwhile the proceedings in Parliament
approached and it was only Baldwin and his son interested
in the reversion who delayed:

> I must ... desire you to conclude it upon their own terms rather
> than let it be deferred a moment longer, and to send one to him,
> wherever he resides, if he is not at Dublin. For I shall be under
> the greatest difficulties Imaginable unlesse I receive His Resig-
> nãcon before yᵉ sitting of our parlament having thought of no
> other Expedient.

Thus wrote Addison to Dawson, and, beginning to doubt
his correspondent's energy or goodwill, he added, 'If you
have not time yourself to negociate this businesse I believe
you may find some among my friends that would lend a
helping hand to it'. The affair was becoming sufficiently
embarrassing for him to have to resort to deceiving his
superiors, to whom he had not apparently revealed the fact
that he had not completed his purchase. He now asked
Dawson to write private matters in separate documents, and
suggested that he burn letters received, which Dawson did
not do. In his anxiety, Addison even told Lord Wharton
part of the truth, but added that he was assured of Baldwin's
consent, which was not the case.

Meanwhile the machinery of the petitions ground on. It
was 16 November when they came before the House and
were referred to the Committee of Privileges and Elections.
A week later the objection that a signatory was dead failed
to postpone a hearing. Addison redoubled his efforts to
perfect his title as Keeper of the Records, writing to Dawson

that he already passed in that capacity. 'Let me beg you to send me Mr. Baldwin's Surrender and to comply with his Terms whatever they are'. His patent was signed in London on 2 December but this could not, of course, validate a flaw in his title to the office. Finally on 19 December it was ordered that the Lostwithiel report be presented to the House. This was done next day, when the committee report, with the arguments put forward by counsel, was debated. It found that Joseph Addison and his late colleague, Kendall, had been declared elected on an incorrect interpretation of the borough franchise. The House adopted the report of the committee without a division, thus confirming the view which Addison appears always to have taken, that he had no chance of winning his case. He was accordingly declared 'not duly elected' and ceased to have any connexion with the borough. The case had been important enough to attract Luttrell's attention, and continued to trouble Parliament for several years, though its further repercussions did not concern Addison. He might console himself that he was rid, albeit involuntarily, of a difficult seat. There was a further consolation at this time; as he remarked to Dawson, 'I am very well pleased to see our accounts [i.e. takings in fees] rise so well under the present administration'.

It was now equally urgent for Addison to expedite his transaction with Baldwin, though for a different reason. If he were to offer himself for another parliamentary seat and to be elected, and subsequently to perfect his title to the Keepership of the Records, this would invalidate his election. He would not wish to re-enter Parliament until this unsatisfactory affair was settled. He therefore continued to importune Dawson to procure Baldwin's agreement, and put his more personal affairs into the hands of Eustace Budgell, who was a grandson of his uncle, William Gulston, now Bishop of Bristol. Budgell records that 'my principles and part of my education' derived from Addison,[1] who now gave permission to his cousin to occupy his rooms at the castle in Dublin.

In London a first-class political crisis was forming and

---

[1] Budgell, *A Letter to the Craftsman*, 1730, p. 35; see also *Liberty and Property*, 2nd edn., p. 144.

there was a threat that the Lord Lieutenant would be impeached by political opponents for alleged financial irregularities. A change of governor was the very least that was forecast. By late October, however, the crisis seemed to have passed for the time being; Lord Wharton went down to Winchendon and Addison hastened to assure the staff in Dublin that 'the present Lord Lieutenant is better fixed than Ever, and as we have often thought in our private discourse I find it is the opinion here of those that are the best judges that he will be long Liv'd'. Rumours in any case did not abate routine administration, which continued as of course, including much correspondence about the settlement of the Palatines.[1] There was also the perpetually interesting topic of fees. Unable to forget the poverty of his early years, Addison was insistent upon his due:

I must desire You to make them pay the fees that are usual on this Occasion as well as all . . . fees for the future; and I am sure no body can be so unreasonable as to think I do amisse in taking what is my Due when I take nothing but what is so.

Not forgetting the material perquisites of office, he suggested that Dawson should send him a Hogshead of 'Irish Wine', that is to say, claret imported into Ireland, duty free to a Privy Councillor, or smuggled. He added a hint that any trouble might be avoided, by the connivance of the Commissioners of Revenue, if the wine was packed in boxes or hampers, and urged dispatch in 'this piece of Friendship'.

It was a time when wine would be welcome, for Addison was back amongst convivial friends. On 5 October he had dined with Lord Halifax, Dick Steele, Arthur Maynwaring, Lord Essex, and Lord Edward Russell. The conversation turned upon the brilliance of Jonathan Swift, still at Laracor without preferment. Next day Lord Halifax wrote to Swift: 'Mr Addison and I are enter'd into a New Confederacy, never to give over the pursuit, nor to cease reminding those, who can serve you, till your worth is placed in that light where it ought to shine.'[2] Addison also wrote on the same day, and two days later, after he had left town, Steele forwarded the letter: 'I assure you no man could say more in

[1] S.P. 67/3; S.O. 1/15.   [2] Williams, ii. 150.

praise of another than he [Addison] did in your behalf at that noble lords table on Wednesday last . . . .' Addison had returned from Ireland determined to achieve something on his friend's behalf and had made this dinner the occasion for influential men to hear his case. But Swift did not commend himself to those who must be his colleagues rather than his dining companions. Proposed as a Dean of Derry by Lord Berkeley some years before, he had been rejected by the bishop in revealing terms:

> I have no objection to Mr. Swift. I know him to be a sprightly ingenious young man; but instead of residing, I dare say, he will be eternally flying backwards and forwards to London; and therefore I entreat, that he may be provided for in some other place.[1]

Addison's endeavours apparently now met the same fate as those of Lord Berkeley.

While Swift languished in Ireland, his friend Ambrose Philips was back in London accompanying Daniel Pulteney, also back from service abroad. They joined the circle expecting the 'Irish Wine'. Moved by Addison's reported solicitude on his behalf, Swift assured Philips: 'You have the best friend in the World, Mr Addison, who is never at ease while any man of worth is not so.'[2] There was plenty of discussion in the literary circle besides the merits of Swift and the current excitement of the *Tatler*. Mrs. Manley, once famous for her neck, bosom, and accessibility to men of wit and means, had recently published the *New Atalantis* libelling all and sundry. From Lord Sunderland's office, where Dick Steele, one of her former admirers, still edited the *Gazette* and where Addison was still a frequent visitor on business, there went out on 20 October a warrant to arrest her printer and publisher.[3] No work such as hers would have been complete without a reference to Addison, and Mrs Manley gave him generous praise in order the more effectively to attack his patrons:

> O Pity! that Politicks and sordid Interest should have carried him out of the Road of Helicon, snatched him from the embrace of the Muses, to throw him into an old withered Artificial States-

---

[1] Orrery, *Letters*, No. 3.   [2] Williams, i. 153.
[3] S.P. 44/78, ff. 64-65.

man's arms. Why did he prefer Gain to Glory? . . . Virgil himself,
nor Virgil's greater Master Homer, could not boast of fairer
Qualifications than Maro [Addison]: Maro! who alone, of all the
Poets, truly inspired, could . . . turn away his eyes from the
delicious gardens of Parnassus, of which he was already in possession, to tread the wandering Maze of Business. Farewell Maro,
till you abandon your artificial Patron, Fame must abandon you.[1]

Indeed Addison's only surviving poetical production of
this year was his belatedly published translation from Horace
and an unauthorized re-publication of the 'Letter from Italy';
and in terms of the estimate of posterity Mrs. Manley was
undoubtedly correct in her judgement.

One of Addison's earliest friends also made ready for
trouble. Henry Sacheverell, the 'Dearest Harry' of Magdalen
days, had become a Fellow of his college, and, making the
Church his profession, had proceeded Bachelor and Doctor
of Divinity and in the current year had been elected bursar.
He was not, therefore, without distinction. Like Addison he
sought to forward his career by making use of his talents in
politics, but the pulpit was necessarily his battleground and
he enlisted in the Tory interest. It was on 5 November, fit day
for incendiarism, that he preached before the Lord Mayor
at St. Paul's, in the Whig City of London, the sermon which
attacked and outraged the Government to such a degree
that it led to his impeachment in a famous State trial. For
Addison, who had once shared rooms with the central
figure in this drama, the situation was particularly interesting, all the more so in that Lord Wharton was a principal
advocate of bringing the doctor to trial before the House of
Lords while Dr. Lancaster, now Vice-Chancellor of the
university, was Sacheverell's bail.[2] Thus one benefit which
Addison might count from his unseating in Parliament was
his absence from the Commons during the critical period of
the trial, in which interest and reason might have directed
his actions in one direction, honour and sentiment in another.
But at this moment his attention was fully occupied in a
different and more immediately personal matter.

In the month of December 1709, in rising political excitement, the impeachment of the Lord Lieutenant was again

<hr />

[1] New Atalantis (1736), ii. 218–19.   [2] Post Boy, 2292.

threatened. So far as he could ascertain the substance of the charges, Addison thought there was little in them. But, he decided, 'for my own part, tho perhaps I was not the most obliged person that was near his Lordship, I shall think myself bound in Honour to do him what Right I can in case he should be attacked'; and he instructed Dawson to prepare the necessary documents for a defence. It is possible to catch in the foregoing declaration of cool loyalty the first notes of disappointment; it is the complaint of a man who although fabulously successful by the standards of his contemporaries, still thinks himself rewarded rather below his deserts. Then, the political danger to Lord Wharton passing off once more, the Secretary was not called upon to draw his pen in defence of a master who had obliged him only in the second degree.

The routine work of the office was particularly heavy at Christmas time, and Addison, whose eyes were troubling him again, was making much use of Edward Young his secretary, Tickell's friend from All Souls. Writing on Addison's behalf, Young tactfully reminded Dawson of his 'kind offer' of wine which the Secretary had 'forgot' to mention. A major negotiation was on foot between the Dublin Government and the London departments, in the course of which an attempt was being made to regulate the relationship of the two on a more satisfactory footing. New model instructions to the Lord Lieutenant, probably drafted with Addison's help and under his supervision, were put forward for agreement.[1] One of the new articles[2] provided that no places were to be sold and that buyers were to be ejected if discovered, a provision which if applied might have cut short the Baldwin affair. A series of new appointments in Dublin was to be negotiated under the new instructions.[3]

Overshadowing these administrative matters came the report of a French squadron off Kinsale, and precautions were taken to set the Kingdom of Ireland in a state of readiness. In this task Addison already had much experience dating from the Pretender's attempt on Scotland two years

---

[1] Blenheim MSS. C.I. 23.   [2] No. 20.
[3] S.P. 67/3, ff. 448–54.

earlier.[1] Further afield, though not any longer within Addison's field of administration, his friend Hunter, now Governor of New York, was facing the problem of accommodating Palatine refugees, and doubtless Addison watched this matter with professional interest.[2] Perhaps it was a relief when Lord and Lady Wharton went down to Winchendon once more for the New Year.[3] The Lord Lieutenant was not an easy man to serve, and the Secretary commented to Dawson: 'My Lord Lieut^nt accompanys all the Reports from Ireland with a Letter of his own which gives me as much trouble as a Report would do. If any Fee is due for it you will deduct it in its proper time.' Nevertheless he still looked to Lord Wharton for help in the affair of the records, who on 27 January 1710 reported to the Lord Treasurer upon his petition for an increase of salary, recommending £500 per annum.[4] The document was minuted 'To be laid before the Queen, 400 li year', thus evidently suffering at the hands of the Treasury, but in that form was approved by a signet warrant, the salary being payable from Christmas.[5] It was a time of financial good fortune for the Charterhouse friends, for it was announced three days later that Richard Steele, Esq., was made a Commissioner of the Stamp Office.[6] From Magdalen a fellow Demy of the 'Golden Election', Hugh Boulter, had been appointed to the living of St. Olave's, Southwark, in 1708, by the influence of Lord Sunderland, and it is likely that Addison had assisted his cause. Another Demy, Richard West, who had been Addison's immediate senior on the college books and closely associated with him, had also prospered. In 1697 with Robert Welsted, also of Magdalen, he had edited Pindar, and in 1699 Theocritus. In 1706 he had been appointed by the Crown to a prebend of Winchester. In January 1710 he was invited to preach before the House of Commons on the anniversary of the death of King Charles I. A strong Whig, he urged that the observance which was the occasion of his sermon be abolished. This caused such a stormy debate in

[1] S.P. 44/210, f. 201; S.P. 104/22.   [2] S.P. 44/102, f. 190.
[3] Post Boy, 2285.   [4] S.O. 1/15, ff. 528-9.
[5] Cal. Treasury Papers, 1709-10, cxx. 22; 1704-9, p. 163.
[6] Supplement, 319; Evening Post, 73; Post Boy, 2296, 2298.

the chamber on the motion to thank the preacher and to print his sermon that it was only carried with difficulty.

The *Tatler* flourished; but Addison dropped his contributions on 14 February and did not resume them until 16 March. This was because of one of those sudden turns of fortune which sometimes make previous disaster appear a blessing. In the autumn he had striven to prevent an election petition succeeding against him in his Lostwithiel seat, but without success. Now he was offered a far better opportunity to enter Parliament at Malmesbury. Captain Henry Mordaunt, one of the two sitting Members for the borough, lay dying of smallpox, and on 24 February the press carried the news of his death.[1] He was, the announcement ran, 'very much regretted on account of his great merit'.[2] But on 18 February it had been decided that Joseph Addison was to put up in his stead; and that day was spent in renewed endeavours to obtain the documents necessary to prove a good title to the Keepership of the Records before the election should come on, so that its subsequent perfection would not unseat the holder. The opportunity had come at short notice: 'I find that I am very likely to set up for a member of Parliament very suddenly . . .', Addison wrote. Mordaunt had sat for the borough since 1698, when it had been Lord Wharton's steward who bluntly explained that whoever expected to be returned for Malmesbury would pay him £400 for the privilege.[3] The borough remained dominated by the Wharton influence well into the next reign,[4] and Addison's political chief was now advising him how to clear the legal obstacles to his sitting in Parliament. Addison was therefore put forward as candidate by the chief to whom he so recently thought himself but moderately indebted.[5] It would be useful to the Lord Lieutenant to have his Secretary in the Westminster House as well as in that at Dublin. Another circumstance may have assisted Addison in obtaining the seat. Sir James Rushout, his Magdalen pupil, had been an important magnate at Malmesbury as Lord of the Manor, and lived at Northwick

---

[1] *Post Boy*, 2307; *Evening Post*, 84.   [2] *Post Man*, 1851.
[3] Porritt, *Unreformed House of Commons*, i. 354.
[4] Bohn, vi. 644.   [5] Spence, p. 350.

Park to which the lordship attached, until his death in 1705.
He was now about to be succeeded by his brother Sir John,
who would come of age next year, and who must have been
known to Addison at least by repute. His influence with the
burgesses may have worked in the same direction as that of
Lord Wharton, and it is on record that Addison sometimes
stayed at Northwick Park from about this time onwards,[1]
probably in connexion with the political management of the
borough.

The historian of the unreformed House of Commons[2]
alleges that the Malmesbury election of 1698 was the first
instance which he had been able to find of a nomination
offered for sale. It may have been an isolated case, but the
practice was growing, and at Malmesbury in 1722 blackmail
and promises backed up by purses of 500 and 1,000 guineas
were stated to have been made use of for a single, though
doubtless a crucial, vote.[3] Malmesbury was an even smaller
corporation than Lostwithiel, the franchise resting with an
alderman and twelve burgesses:[4] so that one voice might
decide the issue and each would be of value. If therefore the
seat did not cost Addison much money, this was because he
was already supported by the principal interests in the
borough. Even so, he was forced to draw upon his Irish
account for £200 which was, he thought, somewhat near to
the limit of his balance.

Addison went down to Malmesbury some time after 21
February and was back in London again by 16 March. The
circumstances were not good for electioneering. As before
at a time when he was overburdened with work, his eyesight was out of order. Furthermore the Sacheverell trial
was in progress and opinion was running strongly towards
the Tory party. It was on 2 March that the writ for the
election was issued and the following day the riots accompanying the trial were at their height. On 4 March Addison
was at Malmesbury, writing to 'Dear Dick' to approve his
Tatler upon courtship.[5] In London three days later, Lord
Sunderland was calling out the trainbands, the horse guards,

---

[1] Aikin, *Life of Addison*, ch. ix.   [2] Porritt, op. cit.
[3] *Commons Journals*, xx. 78.   [4] Beatson, *Parliamentary Register*, iii. 286.
[5] Blenheim MSS. Cat. item, F.I. 89.

and the horse grenadiers, in case of trouble on the queen's birthday.[1] Thus it was in indifferent health, amidst a rush of business, and against a tide of Tory opinion, as well as at short notice, that Addison was elected Member of Parliament for Malmesbury on 11 March 1710. On his return to London he took his seat unchallenged, on 20 March was appointed to his first committee, and on 5 April to a second.

The latter committee was constituted to consider amendments made by the Lords in a Bill to encourage learning by vesting the property in printed books in their authors or publishers. Together with the university burgesses, Addison was doubtless chosen a member thereof for his particular qualifications. It is likely that Wellington's theft of almost all of his best Latin poetry twelve years before, at a time when he could ill afford to forgo any financial reward, had remained a green wound in his memory. He had been joint author of a paper in the *Tatler* the previous December, which drew attention to the impunity of literary pirates,[2] against which he could now legislate. It was also with satisfaction that he dispatched a parcel of commissions to Dawson 'to swell our next reckoning', for even under favourable circumstances an election was an expensive process.

Meanwhile the affairs of Ireland needed the attention of its chief governor, and on 4 April Addison wrote to Dawson that Lord Wharton thought of crossing at the end of the month, and asked for the yacht and convoy to be made ready. A series of prorogations kept the Irish Parliament and Convocation out of mischief until the Lord Lieutenant could arrive to manipulate their activities.[3] The religious problem of Ireland was in a particularly agitated phase.[4] Perhaps because of many preoccupations, and because he shrank from using his eyes more than necessary, for they still troubled him, Addison had run into arrears of correspondence with his friends. During the previous summer he had exchanged at least half a dozen letters with Swift.[5] During the past winter there is no trace of correspondence,

[1] S.P. 44/108, f. 233.   [2] *T.* 101.
[3] *Supplement*, 333, 363; S.P. 67/3, ff. 461, 465, 469–70.
[4] S.P. 67/3, f. 473.   [5] Williams, i. xxiii.

although he had entered the autumn with a debit balance of letter writing to Laracor. He now wrote to make amends:

I have run so much in debt with you that I dont know how to excuse myself. . . . I hope to have the happiness of waiting on you very suddenly at Dublin, and do not at all regrette the leaving of England whilst I am going to a place where I shall have the satisfaction and Honour of Dr. Swift's conversation. . . . I must beg my most Humble Duty to the Bishop of Clogher. I heartily long to eat a dish of Bacon and Beans in the best company in the world. . . . I am forced to give myself Airs of a punctual Correspondce with you in discourse with your friends at St. James's Coffeehouse, who are always asking me Questions about you when they have a mind to pay their court to me. . . .

Then he added as though in after-thought '. . . if I may use so magnificent a Phrase', and continued, 'Pray Dear Doctour continue your friendship towards one who loves and esteems you, if possible, as much as you deserve'. But he addressed the 'Dear Doctour' as 'Sir', though he wrote to the Captain as 'Dear Dick'.

Ambrose Philips was also much in Addison's thoughts, who spent some pains trying to secure for him a post as Queen's Resident either at The Hague or in Switzerland. Daniel Pulteney, Lord Sunderland, and Lord Somers were all approached; but he evidently failed to carry conviction, for the solemn poet with the red stockings obtained no promotion as yet. To Joseph Keally, who had recently been with him in England, Addison sent welcome hints of an approaching promotion to a Commissionership of Appeals in Excise in Ireland, and thereafter begged him to 'sound Baldwin to the bottom'. The question of the keepership now appeared even more complicated, since Addison's title had not been perfected in time, and it might be necessary for the office to be held upon his behalf by another until the next election should occur, lest his seat at Westminster be forfeit. Keally, the experienced Irish politician and lawyer, was an effective instrument for dealing with Baldwin, who certainly understood how to exploit a nuisance. Addison also reported to Keally upon their friend, Benjamin Hoadly, since 1704 rector of St. Peter-le-Poor, as Whiggish a parson as Sacheverell was Tory. Having attended to these personal details, he drew £130 on government funds to reimburse his expenses on public account. Of this amount a proportion was put upon the Secret Service account by authority of the Lord Lieutenant, which indicates that it had been laid out upon political objectives. On 30 April Addison left London to meet Lord Wharton at Chester. The main party arrived there on 4 May and embarked in the Dublin yacht next day to sail under convoy of H.M.S. *Seaford*.[1]

In Dublin preparations were making for a State welcome; but the press carried reports of the drinking of the Duke of Ormonde's health in several places, an indication of the resentments which were pent up against the administration.[2] Joshua Dawson returned from the north to meet the party. His failure to settle the Baldwin affair had irritated Addison and perhaps he attempted to placate his superiors in another commodity; for the newspapers reported that plenty of wine had been sent over to the castle.[3] The Lord Lieutenant arrived with new instructions[4] and a considerable alteration had just been made in the composition of the Privy Council in the light of the past year's experience. It was 7 May when the party landed at Ringsend[5] and Addison almost immediately signed a proclamation further proroguing Parliament until 19 May.[6] It then opened in fair humour, and Addison, sitting on the two most important current committees, was able to tell Lord Sunderland that the Speaker, then a key party man, was elected with only two dissentient votes, one being that of Lt.-General Stuart who 'talks much of a new Ld Lieutenant and is very active to oppose the present Government as much as his parts will give him leave'. The principal embarrassment was now not so much the internal position in Ireland as the persistent rumours of the approaching fall of the Whig ministers in London. The Duke of Shrewsbury, Addison's host in Florence a decade before, had been sworn a member of the Privy Council, and the appearance of this independent magnate at the centre of affairs was taken as a portent.

Nothing is more disquieting to administration than the

[1] *Gazette*, 4688, 4887.   [2] *Supplement*, 363.   [3] Ibid. 356.
[4] S.P. 67/3, f. 467.   [5] *Post Boy*, 2339.
[6] Steele, *Tudor and Stuart Proclamations*, ii. 196; *Post Boy*, 2341.

threat of a change of high direction. But Addison had to continue to administer a mass of business, and to conduct much parliamentary management, as well as Privy Council matters.[1] He was again a member of the Committee of Public Accounts and on 5 June, after acquainting the House with the queen's reply to its addresses, was appointed one of the drafting committee for the address of thanks. The day following he reported from the Committee of Accounts[2] and two days later joined the controversial committee considering the manufacture of arms in Ireland. This body reported in favour of praying the queen that half of the arms required for the establishment should be Irish made, and Addison explained to Lord Sunderland that it was 'utterly impossible' to prevent their coming to this conclusion: 'H. Ex^cies friends would entirely lose themselves should they offer to oppose it'. More satisfactorily, he soon afterwards completed a favourite project when he signed the proclamation authorizing the immediate settlement of Protestant Palatines.[3] The session had gone well and on 18 June Addison wrote to Lord Sunderland: 'we now look upon the business of the session to be over.' On 24 June on behalf of the Lord Lieutenant he formally declared Parliament adjourned until 1 August.

But in England the political foundations of Lord Wharton's power were being sapped away. Ever distrustful of the Whig ministers, and particularly of Lord Sunderland, and daily more irritable under the tutelage of the Lord Treasurer and the Duke of Marlborough, the queen had been listening to Tory advice. After the fiasco in which the Sacheverell trial had ended and the swing of opinion to the Tories, supported by the Duke of Shrewsbury's advice and authority, and urged forward by backstairs counsels, she now struck the first blow. On 13 June she dismissed Lord Sunderland, 'a man who I took into my service with all the uneasiness imaginable',[4] and replaced him in due course by Lord Dartmouth, a moderate Tory. Archbishop King brought the latest news from court to Dublin where he arrived on 16

---

[1] e.g. Blenheim MSS. C.I. 24.   [2] *Gazette*, 4706.
[3] Steele, *Tudor and Stuart Proclamations*, ii. 197.
[4] H.M.C. viii. 43.

June[1] and five days later Addison sat writing the last of his unofficial reports to his former master:

Tho' one may Congratulate your Lordship upon your withdrawing from so great a Scene of Cares and Business Your Lordship must give us leave to Console the publick upon this Occasion. I shall not presume to trouble your Lordship with my own private Concern for this piece of News, but your Lordship will Easily guess it, when you Consider your own great Goodness towards me, and with how much Gratitude and Respect I ought to be and am, My Lord. . . .

In spite of official denials[2] it was evident in Dublin that ministers were now exposed to the malice of their enemies, and Addison's fortunes, which had risen to a high peak with those of the Whig party, now seemed likely to fall with them. There were, however, two causes for private satisfaction at this time. The first was that on 15 June Lord Wharton was elected High Steward of Malmesbury by the comfortable margin of ten votes over the Duke of Beaufort, an event which confirmed Addison's position in the borough.[3] The other was that on 29 May Baldwin at last executed a 'surrender' of his office. Joseph Keally witnessed the document, as well as Dawson and Budgell, which probably indicates that he had been instrumental in bringing the negotiations to a conclusion. The way was now open for Addison to perfect his title as the Keeper of the Records in Bermingham's Tower. It only remained to act in England upon the now completed purchase. But Baldwin had put a high price on his consent; it was £230 and a reservation to himself and his son of the right to act as Addison's deputies.[4] Yet in one respect the delay had enabled fortune to play into Addison's hands. Some months previously the completion of his purchase would probably have necessitated the most careful manœuvres to avoid his being thereby unseated at Westminster. Now it was coming to be generally believed than an election must ensue before many weeks were out, and no action could be taken against him while Parliament was not sitting. In this fashion, so unlooked for, the problem which had caused so much worry was laid to rest.

[1] *Supplement*, 381.   [2] S.P. 104/136.
[3] *Dawks's News Letter*, 15/6/10.   [4] Aikin, *Life of Joseph Addison*, ch. ix.

The Lord Lieutenant would return to England soon in the ordinary course of events, and in the threatening political situation it was most necessary that he should do so. Addison may thus have promised himself some final leave during the recess. Swift was at Laracor: 'I love your company and value your conversation more than any man's . . .' wrote Addison, who was admitted to intimacy with Stella and Dingley. 'Mr. Addison immediately found her out', Swift observed of Stella after her death. It was Addison's delight to entice one who was very emphatic in a wrong opinion by agreeing therein until a point of patent absurdity was reached. This tactic evidently entertained Stella in the several days spent together at Clogher with St. George Ashe and at Finglas with Dillon, his brother, the rector there. Swift came seldom to court at the castle, and even Addison sighed: 'to tell you truly, I find the place disagreeable, and cannot imagine why it should appear so now, more than it did last year.' He had attempted to improve matters. Lord Wharton invited Clayton to Dublin and to produce an 'opera', which must almost certainly have been at Addison's suggestion. But it was in the country that the long discussions of literary matters took place, such perhaps as that upon Swift's 'Baucis and Philemon'. Swift, who never varied in his admiration for Addison, did not hesitate on his friend's advice to 'blot out four score lines, add four score, and alter four score'.[1] As might be expected in such an exchange, the poem lost in fire, gained in elegance.

Addison judged it prudent to take steps in England to improve the terms of his keepership before any more of his political patrons should lose office. He wrote to the Lord Treasurer pointing out that he had as yet only a queen's letter placing him upon the establishment at £400 per annum and that his office might be terminated at pleasure. This, he explained, was because he had not had a copy of his patent by him at the time of his Malmesbury election, a statement which, while literally true, was certainly misleading. He now asked for a grant of the place during good behaviour, in effect for life, pointing out that Lord Wharton had recom-

---

[1] Patrick Delany, *Observations*, 1754, p. 19. He omitted 96, added 44, and altered 22. Forster, *Life*, 1875, p. 165.

mended such a grant at a salary of £500, and that for many years every holder of the office of Secretary in Ireland had received a profitable place as his reward. To this request Lord Godolphin wrote replying that he would 'move' the queen favourably next time he should wait upon her. By 1 August Addison was writing to correspondents in terms which clearly indicated that he did not expect to continue long in office, and the local scene in Ireland was again becoming gravely disturbed, breaking out in such disorders as the defacing of King William's statue on College Green. The sword was bent, the truncheon gone, the face daubed with mire, and a rope hung round the effigy's neck. The defacers left 'a Sirreverence' on the back of the horse.[1]

In the midst of these events, private news of a most disturbing nature had reached Addison. On 17 July 1709 Captain Tolson of the *Heathcote* went ashore at Fort St. George with the letters which dismissed Governor Pitt and appointed Governor Gulston Addison. A stormy scene had ensued, but next day Governor Pitt submitted to the will of the directors. 'I think they have made a very good choice in their Governor, but God deliver us from such a Scandalous Councill. . . .'[2] On 3 July 1710 the news sheets back in England carried the announcement that 'Mr. Addison, Governor of Fort St. George for the United East India Company, being dead, his fortune, which is very considerable, devolves upon his brother Joseph Addison Esq., now Secretary of State in Ireland'.[3] It had been on 24 October 1709 that four East India merchants in Madras, members of, or associated with, the 'scandalous Councill', had hastily signed a letter to Joseph Addison to catch the *Heathcote*, then on the point of sailing back to England. 'The death of Governor Addison (which is heartily lamented by all that ever knew him) occasions you this trouble.' The writers were Gulston's trustees, and with their letter went a copy of the will and letters from the dead man to his brother and sister. The full story did not come to Addison's knowledge until the arrival of the next ship. In fact, the joyful news of Gulston's promotion had, as his widow Mary put it, 'found

---

[1] *Evening Post*, 139; *Post Boy*, 2362.
[2] *Diary of W. Hedges*, Hakluyt Soc. ii. cxx.   [3] *British Mercury*, 43.

him in a condition not fit to enjoy it'. The ship which brought the letters summarily dismissing Governor Pitt and appointing Gulston had found him already sick of a fever, and when she sailed home the new Governor was dead. His widow thought his death had been hastened by the difficulties of dispatching the vessel, and the outgoing Governor suspected poison.[1] The will and codicil were dated 16 October and left a legacy of 14,000 pagodas to Mary Addison, £1,000 to Dorothy Sartre, and the residue to Joseph. This residue was to be invested in diamonds whose purchase was to be entrusted to one Sunca Rama, and to be shipped home in that commodity. Dorothy's legacy was to be paid in the same way. Mary Addison regretted that her husband had made no mention of his brother Lancelot in a will bearing all the marks of haste, and she stated that she would leave him a legacy of 3,000 pagodas. She also regretted that her husband had not been able to express to his brother Joseph the deep sense of gratitude which he felt for 'all the pains you took to advance him'. Long before these tidings arrived in Britain, however, Mary had followed her husband to the grave[2] leaving a legacy to Joseph as well as that promised to Lancelot.

Lancelot had continued a Fellow of Magdalen, holding various college offices. In December 1705 Hearne had noted in his diary that he had 'written nothing yet though as to parts qualified for it'. Praise from Hearne taken with Lancelot's authorship of a poem upon the death of the Duke of Gloucester, and with the fact that Addison had not provided for him by means of Whig or other patronage until this time, may indicate that he had Tory sympathies. It will be recalled that under his father's will Lancelot would inherit £500 absolutely when he attained the age of twenty-five unless an advance was made to him under certain conditions before that date. In 1705 Lancelot celebrated his twenty-fifth birthday and presumably inherited his capital. On 29 July 1706 he became a probationer Fellow of his college and was confirmed in his fellowship a year later. Meanwhile on 31 January 1707, after obtaining his fellowship, he was granted six months' leave of absence by the

---

[1] H.M.C. *Fortescue*, i. 43.   [2] 1 Feb. 1710.

college. This was renewed year by year, and he never returned to Magdalen.[1] He had, it would seem, resolved to seek his fortune in the world with his small but not inconsiderable capital to venture, and Gulston's promotion to Governor provided an opportunity. He had therefore left for India where he arrived by 30 July 1710. But he was inexperienced in business and his brother and sister-in-law were dead before he reached Madras. There seemed to be little point in his remaining in India, and Joseph looked about for an opportunity to promote him elsewhere. It so happened that on 10 July Dr. Cresset, who had been at the Hanoverian Court with Addison in February 1703,[2] had been appointed and was preparing to proceed to the Courts of Hanover and Wolfenbüttel as British Resident.[3] A few days after the news of Gulston's death had arrived in Dublin, the press carried an announcement that 'Lancelot Addison, Esq is made Secretary to Mr. Cresset'.[4] This was a shrewd move on Addison's part, for not only was it an important post to which his brother was appointed, but it would provide him with a reliable source of information and advice in the Hanoverian capital close to the prospective King of England. But disappointment followed Addison's brothers, for on 26th of the same month a further announcement informed the public that Cresset had been taken ill after kissing the queen's hand and had died.[5] Lancelot's appointment thus failed.

Discussing his own position with Swift, the Secretary expressed his sense of personal loss and disappointment in the death of Gulston, but welcomed the consequences of his inheritance. As Swift expressed it in a letter: 'I long till you have some good account of your Indian affairs, so as to make public business depend upon you, and not you upon that.' This prospect was particularly welcome at a moment when by the change of political fortunes it seemed likely that Addison would lose his employments and that his patrons would lose their power to assist him to others. But

the whole of his considerable Indian interests now lay in the
hands of the trustees, who were many months distant by sea.
There was no prospect even of sending written instructions
to them before Christmas, and no reply could be hoped for
within a period of a year. Of necessity the men who traded
in India were hard and none too scrupulous merchant
adventurers. To control their actions was impossible; even
to secure the protection of the law would be difficult. To one
who for most of his life had dwelt in extremely narrow
circumstances and often in debt, who still saw every small
fee due to him punctually paid, who had never known
extravagance himself or approved that of his friends, the
anxiety of the position must have been tormenting. But
there was nothing to be done for the moment except to
await further and fuller news.

In all of these circumstances Addison was anxious to be
back in London as soon as possible. The Lord Lieutenant
himself felt that he was being detained in Ireland of set
purpose so that his influence might be neutralized as the
political crisis approached.[1] The greatest blow yet to fall
had been struck on 1 August when the queen had let it be
known that Parliament would soon be dissolved; and six
days later she followed this up by dismissing the Lord
Treasurer, who had served her throughout her reign. Unhappily he had not had time to redeem his promise about
a life tenure and increase in salary for the Keepership of
the Records. But Addison was already preparing to leave
Dublin in order to look to his electoral interests at Malmesbury. On 5 August he had written to Keally: 'We are still in
great uncertainties as to the dissolution of the English
parliament. . . . If tomorrow's letters bring news of it,
several gentlemen will leave this country with the first fair
wind, and among the rest, your humble servant.' The news
of the Lord Treasurer's dismissal served the same purpose,
and Addison obtained leave to go.

As he waited in the lodgings at the castle for a favourable
wind, he occupied his time writing letters and performing
agreeable tasks. His friend the Marquis d'Arzilliers, who
had been hospitable to him in Geneva when he was but a

[1] S.P. 63/366.

poor travelling scholar, had died leaving a widow in hard circumstances, perhaps in England. One of Addison's last acts in Dublin was to procure a letter from the Lord Lieutenant to the Treasury recalling her husband's past kindness and supporting her petition for assistance.[1] He wrote to Ambrose Philips in Copenhagen about poetry:

I am very much obliged to you for sending me ... the Copy of your Pastoral. I have read it over with abundance of pleasure, and like extremely well the alterations you have made in it. You have an admirable hand at a Sheep-Crook, tho' I must confess ye Conclusion of your poeme would have pleas'd me better had it not bin for that very reason that it was the Conclusion of it. I hope you will follow the example of your Spencer and Virgil in making your Pastorals the prelude of something greater.

By 16 August he had crossed to Chester, to be greeted by the ominous news that Robert Harley, formerly excluded from the Government for plotting against Whig ministers, had been sworn a member of the Privy Council.[2]

Behind him in Ireland Addison left many friends. He appears to have been a popular holder of his office. Writing after him, Swift assured the departing Secretary:

I am convinced that whatever Governmt come over you will find all marks of Kindness from any Parlmt here, with respect to Your Emplymt, the Toryes contending with the Whigs, which should speak best of You ... if you will come over when you are at Leisure, we will raise an Army, and make you King of Ireland. Can you think so meanly of a Kingdom as not to be pleased that every Creature in it who hath one Grain of Worth has a veneration for you.[3]

Sir Andrew Fountaine protested to Swift that summer:

because there is never a B[isho]p with halfe the Wit of St. George Ash, nor ever a Secretary of State with a quarter of Addisons good sense, therefore you cant write to those that love you as well as any Clogher or Addison of 'em all.[4]

In England Addison's arrival at his lodgings in St. James's Place was eagerly awaited by the editor and principal author of the *Tatler*.

[1] *Cal. Treasury Papers*, 1710, cxxiii. 9.   [2] *Gazette*, 4730.
[3] Williams, i. 169.   [4] Williams, i. 164.

During the summer Dick Steele had published the first two collected volumes of this paper, with dedications to Arthur Maynwaring and Edward Wortley, and a subscription list which, as he put it, included practically every name 'now eminent among us for Power, Wit, Beauty, Valour, or Wisdom . . .'. It did indeed contain the names of 128 peers, 21 peeresses, and 6 bishops. He had restated the aims of his paper: 'to expose the false Arts of Life, to pull off the Disguises of Cunning, Vanity, and Affectation, and to recommend a general Simplicity in our Dress, our Discourse, and our Behaviour.' In the preface to the fourth volume he acknowledged to his readers his indebtedness to an anonymous contributor:

. . . I have only one Gentleman, who will be nameless, to thank for any frequent Assistance to me, which indeed it would have been barbarous in him to have denied to one with whom he has lived in an Intimacy from Childhood, considering the great Ease with which he is able to dispatch the most entertaining Pieces of this Nature. This good Office he performed with such Force of Genius, Humour, Wit, and Learning, that I fared like a distressed Prince who calls in a powerful Neighbour to his Aid; I was undone by my Auxiliary when I had once called him in, I could not subsist without Dependance on him.

Shortly after Addison's departure for Ireland in the spring, Steele had taken the opportunity to portray his friend in the *Tatler* in terms which show us Joseph Addison as he approached the climax of his powers of intellect and force of character:

Aristaeus is in my Opinion a perfect Master of himself in all Circumstances: He has all the Spirit that Man can have, and yet is as regular in his Behaviour as a meer Machine: He is sensible of every Passion, but ruffled by none.[1] In Conversation, he frequently seems to be less knowing to be more obliging, and chuses to be on a Level with others rather than oppress with the Superiority of his Genius: In Friendship, he is kind without Profession: In Business, expeditious without Ostentation. With the greatest Softness and Benevolence imaginable, he is impartial in Spight of all Importunity, even that of his own good Nature. He is ever clear in his Judgment; but in Complaisance to his Company, speaks with

---

[1] Addison was apparently well known for his abstention from the use of oaths (Blanchard, p. 88), letter attributed to Henry Newman, secretary to the Society for Promoting Christian Knowledge.

Doubt, and never shows Confidence in Argument but to support the Sense of another. Were such an Equality of Mind the general Endeavour of all Men, how sweet would be the Pleasures of Conversation?[1]

Upon his arrival in London, however, Addison had many preoccupations more pressing than the *Tatler*. On the passage to Chester he had been turning over his financial position, and from that town he had written to Dawson on the important matter of fees: '. . . I desire you will let me know at the End of Every month what have been the profits . . . every month, and to send me with the Account a bill for Such Sum as may be due to me.' Amongst outstanding transactions was one, equally unofficial and unfortunate, in which he had invested in a consignment of shoes, probably for sale to the regiment which Lord Wharton had been authorized to raise. These had been damaged by storm, and their disposal remained uncertain except that it would involve a loss. He resolved bitterly against 'ever sending any more ventures to sea'. Another financial worry was in connexion with Edward Young's expenses on duty in London. Addison had lent him £62 out of his own pocket. He now instructed Dawson to retain this for his own credit, otherwise Young 'will be obliged to pay me in London'. But in the case of Budgell, who now seems to have returned to England, Addison, contrary to all principle, waived his fee for a licence of absence from Ireland, though he probably reconciled this procedure with his rule of taking his due by considering that it was in consequence of his own change of fortunes that Budgell was now recalled. Addison's eyes still troubled him, and on his return he had put himself in the hands of Dr. Garth, kindly and learned physician and poet. Garth sent him to the country, on this occasion to Chelsea, where he went on 26 August for a few days' rest. This afforded him some relief, and Young took over his routine duties.[2]

But the menacing political situation made this no time for sickness. Swift wrote from Ireland:

I believe you had the displeasure of much ill news almost as soon as you landed. Even the moderate Tories here are in pain

---

[1] T. 176.   [2] *Gents. Mag.* (1803), lxxiii, pt. 2, p. 623.

at these revolutions. . . . My Lord Lieutenant asked me yesterday when I intended for England. I said I had no business there now, since I supposed in a little time I should not have one friend left that had any credit; and his Excellency was of my opinion.[1]

Lord Wharton did not expect to hold office much longer, and did not wish to do so now that his political associates were falling. In London Addison was conducting political negotiations on his behalf. The two men seem to have been on fairly intimate terms. It had been Lord Wharton's custom to take Addison down to his seat at Winchendon when he was in England,[2] and the Secretary was by now deeply versed in the intricacies of politics. Congreve told Joseph Keally: 'It is impossible any change can be in the Court and Mr. Addison not able to inform you.'[3] Addison reported, for example, that '. . . Mr Bertie, . . . upon my acquainting him with your Lordship's concern for his brother's election . . . said, his brother was so tired of sitting in the House, that he would not be in it again upon any consideration'. Finally on 8 September the Lord Lieutenant himself arrived in London where the hour of the dissolution of Parliament was anxiously awaited. Addison, who had abandoned any thought of continuing in office in Ireland, warned Dawson that an election would necessitate drawing upon his Irish account. With Lord Wharton came Jonathan Swift, who had taken Addison's advice as to the desirability of being in London at this juncture.

On the political battlefront Matthew Prior, who had aspired to the Under-Secretaryship which Addison had obtained, was writing violent attacks in the weekly *Examiner* upon the tottering Whigs in general, upon the Kit-Cat Club in particular, and upon Addison's medical adviser, who had written a poem in commendation of the fallen Lord Treasurer, in person. On 14 September, at the suggestion of Arthur Maynwaring,[4] Addison published the first number of the *Whig Examiner*, a line-by-line rejoinder to the *Examiner* of an unwonted acerbity, on behalf of party, club, and doctor. Like

[1] Graham, p. 464.   [2] Spence, p. 350.
[3] Berkeley, *Literary Relics* (1789), p. 372.
[4] Oldmixon, *Life and Posthumous Works of Arthur Maynwaring Esq.*, 1715, p. 158.

most rejoinders, it ignored a principal rule of political controversy, that against making excuses, which are seldom
believed and merely remind the public of what they would
otherwise probably forget. Nevertheless, Gay reported that
the papers were 'writ with so much Fire, and in so excellent
a Stile, as put the *Tories* in no small pain for their favourite
Hero'.[1] The second number appeared on 21 September, the
day upon which the dissolution of Parliament was announced.
These papers were designed as election propaganda; but
though reprinted next year with the *Medley* they were not
particularly popular. Meanwhile, although amidst the political confusion a group of Tory magnates took office in the
Privy Council, the queen begged Lord Wharton to remain
in place until a successor could be found, and this he agreed
to do. Addison noticed grimly that the Duke of Somerset,
who had helped to precipitate the crisis, had misjudged the
situation: 'he seems to have pulled down the pillars like
Sampson to perish among those he destroyed.' He summed
it up to Congreve in a line from Dryden's 'Oedipus': 'One
but began to wonder, and straight fell a wonder too.'[2]

At the Malmesbury election Addison was unopposed.
This was doubly fortunate since his eyes were too troublesome for him to be able to carry any extra burden. His
success was partly attributable to careful management. Both
a Mr. Collins and a Mr. Brown had been entered as surgeon's
mates in Sir John Wittewrong's regiment in Ireland, and
when Lord Wharton's regiment was raised they became
Surgeons therein. It is unlikely that either person ever saw a
surgery or went to Ireland; but Addison confided in Dawson:

> I must acquaint you as a secret that these two good people
> happen to be my principal friends at Malmesbury for which reason
> I am their agent in this particular matter and more solicitous than
> ordinary on their account. . . . Nobody knows how soon one
> may have occasion to make use of them.

This method of rewarding his principal local supporters
must have reduced very considerably Addison's election
expenses at a time when he was again pressing Dawson on

[1] Gay, *Present State of Wit* (1711), pp. 8-9.
[2] Berkeley, *Literary Relics* (1789), pp. 374-5.

finance. But to achieve an unopposed return a visit to Malmesbury had been necessary. On 27 September he was still in London, dining with Swift. Next day there appeared the third *Whig Examiner*, which extolled the virtues of General Stanhope, then a candidate at Westminster, in the character of 'Alcibiades'. On 29 September Addison entertained Swift, and Jervas, whom he had met in Rome, at the retreat which he commonly used at Chelsea. He then evidently left town for Malmesbury. The fourth *Whig Examiner* appeared on 5 October, mainly devoted to a vindication of the foreign policy of the late Government, and, in the heat of the elections, taking a passing glance at Henry Sacheverell: 'I think there are none of our present writers who have hit the sublime in nonesense, besides Dr. S——l in divinity and the author of this letter [the *Examiner*] in politics.' It was on 9 October that Addison, along with Thomas Farrington, was declared duly elected for Malmesbury, and on the night of 12 October the news appeared in the London press.[1] Addison was then back in town dining with his physician and Jonathan Swift. Up and down England the strength of popular feeling in both parties had been expressed in scenes of violence at the polls, particularly at Chippenham, neighbour Wiltshire borough to Malmesbury. But Swift reported after dinner to Stella: 'Mr. Addison's election has passed easy and undisputed; and I believe, if he had a mind to be chosen king, he would hardly be refused.' On the same day appeared the fifth and last *Whig Examiner*, an excellent paper expressing the Whig view of the monarchy:

Passive-Obedience and Non-Resistance are the Duties of *Turks* and *Indians* . . . the proper Measures of our Duty and Obedience . . . can never rise too high to our Sovereign, whilst he maintains us in those Rights and Liberties we were born to.

Johnson esteemed the *Whig Examiners* highly, but Macaulay, the better judge of political writing, thought they had 'as little merit as anything that Addison wrote'.[2] It was alleged by Oldmixon that Arthur Maynwaring and not Addison was

[1] *Dawks's News Letter*, 12/10/10; *Evening Post*, 182; *Gazette*, 4755.
[2] See notes in his copy of Addison's *Works* in B.M.

generally thought to be the author,[1] and that he did in fact
write considerable portions of the paper.[2] Maynwaring
certainly had a close connexion with its successor, the *Medley*,
and it seems unlikely that Addison himself wrote the attack
upon Sacheverell noticed above.

Addison's Irish Secretaryship was now drawing to its
close. Writing confidentially to Dawson he had told him of
what had passed between the Lord Lieutenant and the queen
on 22 September. Dawson, Addison thought, had made
indiscreet use of this information; and as a result the Lords
Justices were disputing the validity of the Lord Lieutenant's
instructions in view of his alleged resignation. But the news
had been published on 23 September independently of
Addison or Dawson.[3] Addison was himself in some doubt
as to the position, and felt bound to excuse himself to Lord
Wharton, who resolved the matter by announcing his intention of acting until superseded. It was not until 13 October
that the Duke of Ormonde, once Addison's patron at
Oxford, was appointed to the Lord Lieutenancy[4] and it only
remained for the Secretary to clear up arrears of business,
and to recover any fees outstanding. He arranged with
Dawson for a renewal of his licence of absence and reminded him of the favour shown to the last outgoing
Secretary in his receiving a full quarter's fees though retiring
before the end of the period, and of his promise that
Addison should have the same indulgence in his turn. The
new Secretary, Southwell, was, he observed, a wealthier man
than he; besides, he hinted, a day might well come when he,
Addison, would be better able to repay Dawson in favours.
Meanwhile a bill for £405 had been acceptable and: 'I hope
to have another as soon as you can make up your accounts.'
The Irish interlude had not been unprofitable; and in
five years of subordinate office Addison had learned much
about the human mind and heart, and in particular that
'our Admiration of a famous Man lessens upon our nearer
Acquaintance with him'.[5]

[1] Oldmixon, *Life and Posthumous Works of Arthur Maynwaring Esq.*, 1715,
p. 167.   [2] Ibid., p. 163.
[3] *Evening Post*, 174.   [4] S.P. 67/3, ff. 506–7.   [5] *S.* 256.

VI

A SPECTATOR IN THE WILDERNESS
1710–1712

AFTER the election and the resignation of Lord Wharton, Addison was confronted with a new and menacing future. His patrons, so long powerful, were out of favour and office. For the first time since his appointment as Under-Secretary in 1705 he had no regular employment, and in terms of finance the Keepership of the Records contributed only a fraction of his former income. Even that office was at the mercy of political opponents. Of all his patrons only Lord Halifax perceived that the new Government might with skill be modified to form a coalition in which Whig elements would play a part. But tentative approaches to Harley failed of success, partly because Lord Halifax could carry no important section of his party with him. Even Addison's innate moderation, which he had elevated into a principle of conduct, had nothing in common with the opportunism of Harley. Inevitably his mind turned away from politics and towards literary pursuits both as a means of livelihood and because the *Tatler* provided an immediate outlet for his talent.

During September he had contributed four papers to Steele's periodical. Thereafter had followed a barren period of a month, occupied in electioneering, at the end of which he again became a regular contributor. Steele had welcomed his friend's return by the announcement: '*The Season now coming on in which the Town will begin to fill, Mr.* Bickerstaff *gives notice, That from the First of* October *next, he will be much wittier than he has hitherto been.*'[1] During the summer there had been a noticeable falling off in the quality of the papers. Steele had felt tempted to enter the political arena, and the Tory *Examiner*, with which he consequently became embroiled, referred scornfully to his reinforcements from Ireland. Addison turned the paper away from politics

[1] T. 217.

Sir   (V)   3.

Mr Frowde tells me that You design me the Henour
of a Visite to-morrow morning but my Lord Sunderland
having directed me to wait on him at Nine a clock I
shall take it as a particular favour if You will give
me Your Company at the George in Pal-mal about
two in the After noon when I may hope to enjoy
your Conversation more at leisure which I set
a very great value upon. I am

                Sir

Mr Steele & Frowde
will Dine with us.

                   Your most Obedient
                   Humble Servant

Feb. 29. 1707/8

                     J. Addison.

A LETTER FROM ADDISON TO SWIFT

British Museum, Add. MS. 4804

and wrote of the adventures of a shilling, or the ignominies suffered by great men's chaplains. On the first subject he took the opportunity to praise John Philips, author of the 'Splendid Shilling'. Philips had been put up by the Tory party to write a rival poem to the *Campaign*, and was now dead. The paper upon chaplains took the form of a letter protesting against the custom of dismissing that functionary from the table before the dessert. An incident of this kind in the Duke of Somerset's household had recently resulted in the resignation of the reverend man and this paper would be taken by the public as an entertainment at the duke's expense under cover of anonymity. For Addison it was a return to a favourite theme of his father's, who in *A Modest Plea for the Clergy* in 1677 had deplored the manner in which they were disparaged, not merely by the ignorant, but by 'the Refin'd and Philosophical persons of the Age'. Four of Addison's papers were devoted to an imaginary 'Court of Honour', sitting in judgement upon offences against good manners and written in the facetious vein of the 'dreams' into which Addison fell so easily and sometimes disastrously in his early prose work. He contributed at least seven papers in November and five in December.

That Addison wrote his periodicals with great facility we know on the authority of Steele. That he was able to do so was doubtless the result of his wide experience of the world, his penetrating and practised eye for the weaknesses and foibles as well as for the nobility of mankind, and of his systematic accumulation of notes, drafts, and letters, some of which he transcribed almost verbatim. He wrote a compact and carefully finished hand, which did not lend itself to speed. Perhaps for this reason, and also to rest his eyes, it was Addison's habit, once he had decided upon the matter and form of a paper, to walk about the room dictating to a secretary. According to both Steele and Pope he drafted fluently and rapidly, it appearing to help him if he was pressed for time. But he corrected his drafts slowly and meticulously.[1] In the original sheets of the paper there are

[1] For an examination of the errata in the *Tatler,* see F. W. Bateson, 'The Errata in the *Tatler*', *R.E.S.*, vol. v, and Miss Rae Blanchard's rebuttal, *R.E.S.*, vol. vi, pp. 183–5.

numerous alterations; not merely printing corrections, but second thoughts. For example 'fawning as a Lap-dog' is excused as a misprint for 'fond as an Alderman'. These 'errata' have been shown to occur mainly in Addison's papers and there is little doubt that they are the result of his own revision. A story that he would sometimes stop the press to insert a correction is supported by the fact that the *Tatlers*, being printed in more than one impression, errors occasionally find correction in one batch and not in another. This supports a hint of Steele's that Addison sometimes himself sent the paper to press. A careful censorship of advertisements took place and he wrote some of the witty mock announcements which were a feature of the paper. It was by now an undertaking of considerable size, extending to the provinces, and a large share in its conduct was Addison's chief preoccupation in the autumn of the year 1710.

The change in his employment resulted in a corresponding alteration in daily habits of life. It is to this period, when he held no public office demanding his day-to-day presence, that the popular vision of a literary Augustan presiding at the coffee-house most properly belongs. 'In Proportion, as Conversation gets into Clubs and Knots of Friends, it descends into Particulars, and grows more free and communicative',[1] Addison observed. Jonathan Swift was in London, an admirable ingredient for any such group. He dined with Addison and Edward Southwell, the new Secretary going to Ireland, and heard that Steele had lost the *Gazette*. Though he gave occasional help to the *Tatler* his friendship for Steele, never warm, cooled fast; but he was on cordial terms with Addison, to whom he ordered his mail to be directed at St. James's Coffee House. Neither of the chief authors of the *Tatler* could now serve as a post box at the Secretary of State's office, and Swift had failed to secure promotion from their patrons in their day of power. The recent protestations of Lord Halifax in his favour had brought no benefits. Addison, who had read a great deal of history, both ancient and modern, and who had a poor opinion of contemporary English historians engrossed in 'bare matters

[1] *S.* 68.

of Fact',[1] may have considered for him the post of historiographer. 'Our Country, which has produced Writers of the first Figure in every other kind of Work, has been very barren in good Historians.'[2] He thought them singularly blameworthy for their neglect of commerce.[3] The writing of history he considered as an art:

> It is the most agreeable Talent of an Historian, to be able to draw up his Armies and fight his Battels in proper expressions, to set before our eyes the Divisions, Cabals and Jealousies of Great Men. . . . We love to see the Subject unfolding it self by just Degrees, and breaking upon us insensibly. . . .[4]

The requisites of an historian he catalogued as:

> . . . Purity and Elegance of Stile, . . . Nicety and Strength of Reflection, . . . Subtilty and Discernment in the Unravelling of a Character, . . . Choice of Circumstances for enlivening the whole Narration.[5]

Jonathan Swift possessed just these talents. For his part, Swift would have been thankful for a prebend at Westminster; but either post was now beyond the power of his Whig friends to procure. He was still friendly with them, but found himself in a new situation. As he put it to Archbishop King on 9 September: 'Upon my Arrival hither, I found myself equally caressed by both Parties.'[6] Next evening he sat late with Addison, and again the night following. Addison liked to speculate in the lottery and four days later they went together to see it drawn at Guildhall. Thence they went to dine at the retreat at Chelsea 'where Mr. Addison often retires . . .'. 'I loved it mightily today', wrote Swift to Stella.[7] Three days later they were again dining together at Chelsea. Swift went home inspired to write on English style for the *Tatler*, the discussion having turned upon the structure of the language.

It was during Addison's absence from town at Malmesbury that Swift was received by Harley and came away captivated. When Addison returned his friend was a changed man. They dined together at a city merchant's on 19 October,

---

[1] S. 409. [2] F. 35. [3] F. 41.
[4] S. 420. [5] F. 35. [6] Williams, i. 173.
[7] Quotations from Swift without reference in this and succeeding chapters are from the *Journal to Stella*.

and with Wortley the night following over a bottle of 'Irish' wine. Two days later Swift visited Addison to talk about Steele's place at the Stamp Office, which was now in peril. He affected to dispense the favours of the Tory leaders to his Whig friends. Surprised and hurt that he was not appreciated in this new character, he reflected of Addison that '. . . party had so possess'd him, that he talked as if he suspected me, . . . So I stopt short in my overture and we parted very dryly'. Next day he went to the coffee-house:

. . . where I behaved myself coldly enough to Mr. Addison. . . . We dine together to-morrow and next day by invitation; but I shall not alter my behaviour to him, till he begs my pardon, or else we shall grow bare acquaintance. I am weary of friends . . .

On 24 October he dined with Addison at Sir Matthew Dudley's, and the next day with Addison and Steele, Mrs. Sartre being there: 'I am not fond of her . . . a sort of a wit, very like him'. Three days later he dined with Garth and Addison at 'a hedge tavern', and the day following with Addison at Lord Mountjoy's. On the last day of the month he dined at Addison's lodgings; the company 'were half fuddled, but not I; for I mixt water with my wine, and left them together between nine and ten'. Two days thereafter Swift took an irrevocable step, already some time in contemplation. Secretly he had assumed the conduct of the *Examiner*, and in his first number he gave vent to his dislike for his late Whig associates:

It is a Practice I have generally followed, to converse in equal Freedom with the deserving Men of both Parties; and it was never without some Contempt, that I have observed Persons wholly out of Employment, affect to do otherwise: . . . But several of my Acquaintance, among the declining Party, are grown so insufferably Peevish and Splenatick . . . that I find myself disposed to share in their Afflictions, . . . To offer them Comfort one by one, would be not only an endless, but a disobliging Task.[1]

It is most likely that Swift had Steele particularly in mind, yet he dined with him in Addison's company two days later. Again on 8 November he dined with Addison, Vanbrugh,

[1] *Examiner*, 13.

and other Whigs: 'I was weary of their company and stole away at five.' Two days later he dined at Addison's lodgings with Garth and Steele and stayed late. On 16 November after a dinner he returned with Addison to the coffee-house and 'loitered till 9', remarking afterwards, 'Mr. Addison and I meet a little seldomer than formerly, although we are still at bottom as good friends as ever; but differ a little about party'. Then on the last day of the month in the *Examiner*[1] all of his pent-up resentment burst forth upon the late Lord Lieutenant.

Borrowing Addison's device of 'Alcibiades'' speech in the *Whig Examiner*, Swift imitated Cicero's impeachment of Verres as a means of vilifying Lord Wharton in the most extravagant terms. This proceeding must have been peculiarly embarrassing to Addison, who may have had suspicions but no proof as to the authorship of the piece. Not content with this, Swift also wrote an anonymous pamphlet attacking the same nobleman by name. In the presence of such violent hatreds it is apparent that the catalogue of dinner assignations noticed above was the reflection of doubt and hesitation in Swift's mind before he finally broke with his old associates and cast in his lot with the Tory party. It is not surprising that by 12 December he recorded: 'Mr. Addison and I hardly meet once a fortnight; his Parliament and my different friendships keep us asunder.' Yet three days later he again intervened with Harley on Steele's behalf about the Stamp Office, but found his action not appreciated:

I believe Addison hindered him out of mere spight, being grated to the soul to think he should ever want my help to save his friend; yet now he is soliciting me to make another of his friends queen's secretary at Geneva; and I'll do it if I can, it is poor Pastoral Philips.

Swift had become intolerable to his friends in his desire to offer them patronage.

Meanwhile the new Parliament met on 25 November and Addison was appointed one of the members to tender the oaths. Russell Robartes, his old opponent, was forced to

petition once more against the Lostwithiel returns, and
Addison must have congratulated himself upon his move to
a safer seat. The political atmosphere was still violently
charged, and in clearing up arrears of Irish business he asked
Dawson to send him various documents which would be
required in case Lord Wharton were impeached. He felt
that such proceedings would be welcome, as serving to
reveal the baselessness of the charges. For his own affairs,
he was warned that he might be accused of countersigning
documents of State in improper circumstances. This might
result in the loss of his office as Keeper of the Records, to
which there were several Tory aspirants. He had therefore
prudently made his peace with the new Lord Lieutenant
through the intermediary of his own successor, and the
duke had assured him of continuance in his place. There
remained the outstanding matter of the shoes, and Addison
pressed Dawson to recover and forward every available
balance to him in England, where 'there are great advantages in this juncture to be made of money . . .'. Though
forsworn to merchant adventuring since the episode of the
shoes, Addison was engaging in some form of financial
speculation, perhaps in the stocks.

In the private circle he was intimate once more with Lord
Halifax and Congreve, and he was still striving to provide
for Ambrose Philips in diplomatic service. 'I have spoken
to Dr. Swift (who is much caressed and invited almost every
day to dinner by some or other of the new ministry) . . .
and he has given me a kind of a promise . . .' he wrote to
Philips. But his eyes troubled him greatly, and prevented him
from maintaining his correspondence with his friends. He
was in depressed spirits, and confided in Keally, to whom he
wrote with more than usual expansiveness: 'I have had
incredible losses since I saw you last; but this I only communicate to yourself.' He proposed going to Bath in the new
year in hopes of benefiting his sight, and from thence to
Ireland to defend his keepership, if it should be necessary.

It was on 2 January of 1711 that Steele published his last
Tatler and Addison had arranged to leave St. James's Place
for Bath next day. In a joint enterprise in which he was so
intimately concerned, it is incredible that it should be stopped

without his knowledge, particularly in view of the fact that he had arranged to leave town the day following publication of the last number. But in a word-splitting quarrel with Tickell in later years, in which the latter alleged that the *Tatler* had ended without Addison's 'participation', Steele implied that this was the case by suggesting instead the word 'knowledge'. But there were several reasons, well known to Addison, why the *Tatler* should now come to an end; and it is noticeable that Steele makes no assertion of fact but merely challenges Tickell's motive and innuendo. And although Swift wrote to Stella that Addison was as surprised as he to find the *Tatler* ended, the two men were not now on such terms that Addison would have disclosed so important a secret, and it is unlikely that Steele's action was unexpected by his partner. Knowing of his friend's impending departure, Steele probably gave way to boredom and wrote *finis* to his work. It had certainly become irksome to him; he was under pressure from the Government to abstain from politics in which the *Tatler* had been deeply engaged, and Addison's contributions had, as he later told Congreve, raised it 'to a greater thing than I intended it for the elegance, purity, and correctness which appear'd in his writings, were not so much my purpose'. Furthermore, having paid his contributors for their work, Dick regarded the paper as his own property. He had founded it and had himself supplied about 188 numbers to Addison's 42. He might thus feel free to dispose of it. Addison, for his part, doubtless found it uncongenial to participate in a venture which had many critics and enemies as well as imitators.[1] He had enumerated some of

these my doughty Antagonists, I was threatened to be answered Weekly *Tit* for *Tat*: I was undermined by the *Whisperer*, haunted by *Tom Brown's Ghost*, scolded at by a *Female Tatler*, and slandered by another of the same Character, under the Title of *Atalantis*. I have been *annotated, retattled, examined* and *condoled* . . . .[2]

There had also been more serious collisions with outraged individuals who, both with and without justification, thought themselves attacked. Addison had now participated

[1] See W. Graham, *English Literary Periodicals*, for an account of the latter.
[2] T. 229.

long enough in the *Tatler* to perceive its limitations, and also the possibilities of an improved paper.

The last number came from the press with Dick Steele's name at the foot, and contained a handsome, though anonymous, acknowledgement of Addison's help:

. . . the most approved Pieces in it were written by others, and those which have been most excepted against by my self. The Hand that has assisted me in those noble Discourses upon the Immortality of the Soul, the glorious Prospects of another Life, and the most sublime Ideas of Religion and Virtue, is a Person who is too fondly my Friend ever to own them: But I should little deserve to be his, if I usurped the Glory of them. I must acknowledge at the same Time, that I think the finest Strokes of Wit and Humour in all Mr. *Bickerstaff*'s Lucubrations are those for which he is also beholden to him.[1]

Addison himself insisted upon preserving his anonymity to the end. Writing later this year John Gay recorded that Swift had generally been thought to be Steele's principal assistant, but that it was now known to have been Addison:

who refuses to have his Name set before those Pieces, which the greatest Pens in *England* would be Proud to own. Indeed, they could hardly add to this Gentleman's Reputation; whose Works in *Latin* and *English* Poetry, long since convinc'd the World, that he was the greatest Master in *Europe* of those Two Languages.[2]

But it had been Dick's vision, enterprise, and courage which had evoked his friend's talent in prose satire, and Addison's peculiar nature which inspired the devotion and self-abasement of his partner. Their paper had achieved European fame and had many translators and imitators, and Addison's anonymity increased his literary glory.

Three continuators took up the vacant title in an attempt to exploit its fame. Only one of these, William Harrison, writing with Swift's encouragement, survived for any length of time. The son of the Master of St. Cross and a New College friend of Tickell and Edward Young, he had praised Addison in a poem, 'Woodstock Park', at the time of the *Rosamond* venture, and by him had been brought to the

[1] T. 271.   [2] Gay, *Present State of Wit* (1711), p. 15.

notice of the literary circle. He had also obtained a post as tutor to the son of the Duke of Queensberry, a colleague of Lord Sunderland as Secretary of State, who would be known to Addison. Harrison's *Tatler* appears to have met with no objections from the original authors, and with little success. John Gay observed that he and his colleagues appeared to think that their predecessors had succeeded by devices. Accordingly 'they were continually talking of their *Maid, Night-Cap, Spectacles,* and *Charles Lillie*'.[1] But, as Gay put it, the success of the *Tatler* had been due to 'the Conjunction of those two Great Genius's (who seem to stand in a Class by themselves, so high above all our other Wits) . . .'.[2]

With the new year the time approached when Addison would be able to take action to recover his interest in Gulston's estate. The *Lichfield* was to sail to India in February, and with her Bernard Benyon, one of the trustees, who had been to England on business and with whom Addison had been able to consult. Accompanying Benyon to India was Edward Harrison, the newly appointed Governor of Fort St. George. The trustees in India were Edmund Montague, an official of the East India Company, Robert Raworth the Receiver of Customs at Fort St. George, and Edward Fleetwood, a business associate of Gulston Addison. There was no alternative but to act through the agency of the men at Madras, hoping that they would respect the trust of their dead friend, and that Addison's influence in England, which had been seen to be so powerful with the Company, might prove a consideration with them. In this frame of mind Addison wrote to the trustees by the *Lichfield* a letter which was affable in the extreme:

If so great a Affliction to his whole family and myself in particular could be alleviated by any Consideration, it would be by his haveing left his affairs in the Hands of Trustees who have so universal a Character among all that know them of being Gentlemen of Probity and Honour.

But Addison prudently made the new Governor his attorney, and let his trustees know his desire that they should 'consult with my Honoured Friend . . .'. They were to pay to

[1] Ibid., p. 18.   [2] Ibid., p. 21.

Harrison any sums due, but to send home duplicates of his accounts. Addison's anxiety spoke aloud in the last paragraph, echoing the solicitude of the letters to Dawson upon financial matters:

> I must not conclude my Letter without... desireing the Continuance of your good offices that I may receive with as much speed and safety as possible all that was intended me by the Will of my dear Brother deceased. And if I can any way be Serviceable to any of you in this Country. . . .

Of the executors it was Benyon who assumed the main duties of carrying out the will, and to him Addison gave special instructions. There were many complications and it is evident that Addison had taken professional legal advice. John Pitt, a cousin of Governor Pitt, had died in India in 1703 and his widow had died three years later, naming Gulston Addison an executor. Gulston had traded with a portion of her estate, and the Pitt family now threatened to claim against Gulston's estate for losses incurred. Mrs. Pitt, on the other hand, had made a will leaving Gulston a cash legacy and Joseph alleged that she owed his late brother a debt. He evidently anticipated litigation in London, and wrote his instructions to Benyon in the strain of a man determined to forgo nothing to which he might be entitled. Benyon was to sell the 'great house', convert all available cash into diamonds, and ship them home at the rate of two to three thousand pagodas value by each ship. Addison intended to insure himself for so much cargo by each vessel sailing from Madras after the arrival of the *Lichfield*.[1] Foreseeing the possibility of his interests drifting into disaster in case Governor Harrison should die, he made Bernard Benyon and the Reverend George Lewis joint attorneys in that event. Against the possibility of a disagreement between Governor Harrison and the trustees he provided secret instructions to the latter to be held in reserve. He provided for the death or departure of both Harrison and Benyon by requesting and empowering Lewis to act alone; and finally, in the event that Lewis himself should be unable to act, he requested him to leave the power in the hands of his own

[1] B.M. Egerton MSS. 1972, ff. 39-40.

attorneys or trustees. Having thus made every provision which prudence could devise to bring home the funds as quickly as possible, Addison delivered the packets of instructions to Harrison and Benyon, who were preparing to sail in February.

Almost immediately after the *Tatler* ceased publication Addison and Steele began to prepare a new periodical, which would be the logical expansion of the partnership envisaged by Steele at the time of the *Tender Husband*, begun in a technical sense with the production of the *Gazette*, developed in a literary one in the *Tatler*, and founded upon a lifelong friendship. The *Tatler* had begun primarily as Steele's venture; but when the two men worked together it was the mind and character of Addison which predominated; and he it was who set the tone for the new periodical in the sense that his partner had done for its predecessor. No man's mind could have been more amply provided for the task. Founded in the best scholarly tradition of the day, broadened by travel throughout Europe, matured by the carrying of responsibility in high administrative duty, embellished by conversation with men and women of wit and fashion, he was splendidly equipped to evoke the genius of the age, and thus to precipitate the elements which were latent in the social and political atmosphere. Confident in their abilities, and in spite of the misgivings of their friends, the two men decided to publish a paper which would appear, not thrice weekly as the *Tatler* had done, but daily.

It was on 1 March 1711, as the spring season in town approached, that the first number of the *Spectator*, strictly anonymous, appeared on the streets of London.[1] It was an explanatory piece by Addison intended to introduce the publication. He was particularly interested in the technique and methods of controversy, and was at pains to explain the purpose of the *Spectator* upon numerous occasions, of which this was the first. Whereas the *Tatler* had turned upon the lucubrations of Bickerstaff, the *Spectator*, as its name implied, was the work of a more vague, and therefore more flexible,

[1] Throughout this chapter I am indebted to the Introduction and notes in Donald F. Bond's monumental edition of the *Spectator* (Oxford, 5 vols., 1965).

imaginary personage who recounted the words and deeds of others. This device immediately broadened the scope of the publication and made its literary form more pliable. Next day appeared the second paper, by Steele, in which were roughed out the portraits of the members of a 'club', or society of gentlemen who were the familiar associates of Mr. Spectator. This idea was not new in literature. Defoe had used it in his *Review*; Addison himself had adopted something similar in his as yet unpublished 'Dialogues upon Medals'. In that case, three learned gentlemen who were 'capable of entertaining themselves on a thousand different subjects, without running into the common topics of defaming public parties, or particularly persons', had retired together in the manner of the *Decameron*, though in a more scholarly spirit, to pass away the heats of summer. Like the earlier trio, Mr. Spectator's more numerous club forswore party politics and personal attacks.

The *Spectator* would be considered by the public as a successor to the *Tatler* from which it had so evidently grown, but Addison was at pains to dissociate himself from the *Tatler*'s politics and even from its preoccupation with minutiae:

> I must . . . once for all inform my Readers, that it is not my Intention to sink the Dignity of this my Paper with Reflections upon Red-heels or Top-knots, but rather to enter into the Passions of Mankind, and to correct those depraved Sentiments that give Birth to all those little Extravagancies which appear in their outward Dress and Behaviour.[1]

Suitably to this graver turn of wit, the form of the paper was adapted to convey a more elaborate train of thought. Whereas the *Tatler*, except for the last months of publication, usually consisted of several separate articles, the *Spectator* from the first number was a single piece, thus imposing a greater strain upon the resources of its authors.[2] And in other respects the continuity of the two publications was maintained; and the authors evidently expected and desired that

[1] *S.* 16.
[2] For a detailed study of this development, see P. Greenough, *PMLA*, xxxi (1916), 633–63.

the readers of the *Spectator* who had previously enjoyed the *Tatler* would understand allusions to the earlier periodical, especially to the more popular numbers such as Addison's paper on 'pretty Fellows'.[1] Like the *Tatler*, the *Spectator* had a missionary purpose; it sought to expose and reform, to instruct and polish; but its form and purposes had been thought out with greater care and precision.

Addison recognized that humour was an indispensable ingredient of success. He therefore proposed 'to enliven Morality with Wit, and to temper Wit with Morality'.[2] 'I would not willingly Laugh but in order to Instruct . . .'.[3] To laugh was all the more necessary because the paper was addressed particularly to women as well as to men; and in an age when the majority of them played little part in politics and had a poor education, this required a light touch upon some serious topics. Like the *Tatler*, the *Spectator* was written for both the coffee-houses and the tea-tables, but especially the latter: 'There are none to whom this Paper will be more useful, than to the female World.'[4] 'I shall take it for the greatest Glory of my Work, if among reasonable Women this Paper may furnish *Tea-Table Talk*.'[5]

Addison reiterated his good purposes, of which he was rather oppressively aware: 'the great and only End of these my Speculations is to banish Vice and Ignorance out of the Territories of *Great Britain*.'[6] To Lord Somers the authors explained the *Spectator* as 'a Work, which endeavours to Cultivate and Polish Human Life, by promoting Virtue and Knowledge, and by recommending whatsoever may be either Useful or Ornamental to Society'.[7] Lawrence Eusden, later Poet Laureate and a friend of Addison, described his purpose in turning from verse writing to prose essays in accurate couplets:

> Next, Human follies kindly to expose,
> You change from numbers, but not sink in prose:
> Whether in visionary scenes you play,
> Refine our tastes, or laugh our crimes away.[8]

[1] *S*. 323. [2] *S*. 10. [3] *S*. 179.
[4] *S*. 10. [5] *S*. 4 by Steele. [6] *S*. 58.
[7] Dedication to *Spectator*, vol. i.
[8] *Verses to the author of the Tragedy of Cato*, 1713,

But it was Addison himself who best expressed his purpose to posterity:

It was said of *Socrates*, that he brought Philosophy down from Heaven, to inhabit among Men; and I shall be ambitious to have it said of me, that I have brought Philosophy out of Closets and Libraries, Schools and Colleges, to dwell in Clubs and Assemblies, at Tea-Tables and in Coffee-Houses.[1]

In his double design of rendering learning polite and society decorous Addison was powerfully influenced by his visit to Europe and by his meetings with and study of Boileau and Bayle. Macaulay found such an influence 'in part salutary in part pernicious'. Of reformist extremes, however, Addison was not on the whole guilty. His good judgement and acute sense of humour preserved him from falling into excess of zeal. But he regarded himself as a pioneer in his kind of writing:

When I broke loose from that great Body of Writers who have employed their Wits and parts in propagating Vice and Irreligion, I did not question but I should be treated as an odd kind of Fellow. . . .[2]

He gloried in the novelty of his venture, yet the reformation of manners was not a new idea. Several societies for that purpose already existed in William III's reign.[3] But Addison was appealing by a new method to a new and wider public to many of whom the idea was still unfamiliar.

Addison was at pains to disclaim all personalities in his writings:

I promise . . . never to draw a faulty Character which does not fit at least a Thousand People; or to publish a single Paper, that is not written in the Spirit of Benevolence and with a Love to Mankind.[4]

And again later:

I have shewn . . . with how much Care I have avoided all such Thoughts as are loose, obscene, or immoral; and I believe my Reader would still think the better of me, if he knew the Pains I am at . . . that nothing may be interpreted as aimed at private Persons.[5]

[1] *S.* 10.   [2] *S.* 262.   [3] Bond, i. 35.   [4] *S.* 34.   [5] *S.* 262.

Lampooning had attained such proportions that it was with some difficulty that the public could be persuaded that the *Spectator* contained no hidden meanings or covert attacks.

Addison also laboured his political neutrality:

> . . . my Party-Correspondents, . . . are continually teazing me to take Notice of one anothers proceedings. . . . However, as I am very sensible my Paper would lose its whole Effect, should it run into the Outrages of a Party, I shall take Care to keep clear of every thing which looks that Way.[1]

After a considerable period of publication he surveyed his social and political chastity with satisfaction:

> . . . on the one Side, my Paper has not in it a single Word of News, a Reflection in Politicks, nor a Stroke of Party; so, on the other, there are no fashionable Touches of Infidelity, no obscene Ideas, no Satyrs upon Priesthood, Marriage, and the like popular Topicks of Ridicule; no private Scandal, nor any thing that may tend to the Defamation of particular Persons, Families, or Societies.[2]

A strict adherence to these standards provided the severest test of the ability of the authors.

In his own mind Addison classified his readers as the mercurial and the saturnine, the gay and the grave:

> the former call every thing that is Serious Stupid. The latter look upon every thing as Impertinent that is Ludicrous. Were I always Grave one half of my Readers would fall off from me: were I always Merry I should lose the other.[3]

He thus presented himself to the public as compelled to be witty for moral purposes, an attitude which doubtless amused those who knew his natural capacity for raillery.

In other ways Addison sought to make his precepts upon serious topics acceptable. The 'dream' and 'vision' were pressed into service. Wishing to speak of the well-worn subjects of the uncertainty and brevity of human life, and of the relative merits of the hereafter, he lent entertainment to his theme by an ingenious allegory, filling out a whole paper.[4] As he expressed it, perhaps recalling his conversation with Boileau on the subject of Télémaque: '. . . a Man improves more by reading the Story of a Person . . ., than by the

[1] *S.* 16.   [2] *S.* 262.   [3] *S.* 179.   [4] *S.* 159.

finest Rules and Precepts of Morality.'[1] It was a device which fell naturally into Addison's cast of mind, and he extended its use, sometimes making it serve as a protection when writing on subjects which he did not well understand.

For somewhat similar reasons, although Addison made little use of letters sent in by correspondents,[2] the device of a letter written in reality by the authors of the paper was extensively used:

> I often chuse this way of casting my Thoughts into a Letter, for the following Reasons; First, out of the Policy of those who try their Jest upon another, before they own it themselves. Secondly, because I would extort a little Praise from such who will never applaud any thing whose Author is known and certain. Thirdly, because it gave me an Opportunity of introducing a great variety of Characters into my Work, which could not have been done, had I always written in the Person of the *Spectator*. Fourthly, because the Dignity Spectatorial would have suffered, had I published as from my self those several ludicrous Compositions which I have ascribed to fictitious Names and Characters. And lastly, because they often serve to bring in, more naturally, such additional Reflections as have been placed at the End of them.[3]

Addison thus devoted much thought to the form of the paper and to the techniques which he employed and was conscious of the many problems which he must face in order to sustain success:

> ... those who publish their Thoughts in distinct Sheets, and as it were by Piece-meal, ... must immediately fall into our Subject and treat every Part of it in a lively Manner ... Our Matter must lie close together, and either be wholly new in itself, or in the Turn it receives from our Expressions. Were the Books of our best Authors thus to be retailed to the Publick, and every Page submitted to the Taste of forty or fifty thousand Readers, I am afraid we should complain of many flat Expressions, trivial Observations, beaten Topicks, and common Thoughts, which go off very well in the Lump.[4]

Indeed the *Spectator* not only commanded admiration, but created an aura of superior sense and taste. In his Oxford days Addison had admired Virgil's strategy: '... the Mind,

---

[1] *S.* 299.   [2] *Infra*, p. 217.   [3] *S.* 542.   [4] *S.* 124.

which is always delighted with its own discoveries, only takes the hint from the Poet, and seems to work out the rest by the strength of her own faculties.'[1] This device served an excellent purpose in the *Spectator*, and also helped to make a policy of restraint acceptable to readers, for, he remarked: 'As nothing is more easie than to be a Wit with . . . Liberties, it requires some Genius and Invention to appear such without them.'[2]

In practice it was easier to avoid personal attack than political innuendo. Anonymity had made it possible to deliver lofty moral discourses with an air of authority and condescension. It also gave rise to rumour and speculation as to the person of the author, which was excellent publicity, a fact of which Addison was well aware.[3] But anonymity was no defence against political susceptibilities. Addison's thought was so political that he wrote veiled political propaganda as early as the third *Spectator*. In this paper he 'dreamed' a dream upon the beauties of credit a month before a crucial Bank Election in which a Tory victory would most likely have assisted a Jacobite restoration. Trevelyan quotes the essay to illustrate Whig fears that a return of the Stuarts would mean the repudiation of government debts contracted since the Revolution. But Addison's moderation, also evident here, is characteristic: he points out the dangers to public credit both of Jacobitism and of republicanism.[4] The device of a dream enabled him to make certain premises and to attach consequences to them without any logical sequence of reasoning, the simplest and most effective of all forms of political propaganda when directed to a relatively uninstructed audience.

The subject of finance and commerce, lying within the sphere of banking, was peculiarly the province of the Whig magnates of the city. From his contact with these men Addison derived an admiration for the great institutions of commerce, such as the Bank and the Exchange. The essays which he wrote praising trade and merchants establish a continuous if muted political theme in the *Spectator*. In the sixty-ninth number Mr. Spectator visits the city:

[1] *Essay on Virgil's Georgics.*   [2] *S.* 179.
[3] *S.* 542.   [4] Bond, i. 14, n.1.

There is no Place in the Town which I so much love to frequent as the *Royal Exchange*. It gives me a secret Satisfaction, and, in some measure, gratifies my Vanity, as I am an *Englishman*, to see so rich an Assembly of Country-men and Foreigners consulting together upon the private Business of Mankind, and making this Metropolis a kind of *Emporium* for the whole Earth.

Much in advance of his time he deplored the gentlemanly snobbery which looked down on commerce: 'How many Men are Country-Curates, that might have made themselves Aldermen of *London*, by a right Improvement of a smaller Sum of Mony than what is usually laid out upon a learned Education.'[1]

And if he found such affectation foolish in the aristocracy, he noticed that it was inexcusable in the wives of the merchant community. Putting his views into the mouth of a self-made city magnate he caused him to complain of his wife:

She makes an Illumination once a Week with Wax-candles in one of the largest Rooms, in order, as she phrases it, to see Company. At which time she always desires me to be Abroad, or to confine my self to the Cock-loft, that I may not disgrace her among her Visitants of Quality.[2]

None of the papers on trade could be read by High Tory country gentlemen without distaste. But Addison evidently felt it legitimate to praise what he thought commendable in politics.

In May 1712 the *Spectator* made its most daring venture into the current political battles. William Fleetwood, Bishop of St. Asaph, published a collection of sermons with a Preface in which he strongly defended the Hanoverian claim to the throne and warned against Tory hostility thereto. Probably with Addison's approval,[3] Steele reprinted the entire Preface on 21 May. In June Fleetwood wrote to Burnet concerning the sermons and said: 'The *Spectator* has conveyed above

---

[1] *S.* 21. [2] *S.* 229.

[3] It seems rather unlikely that Steele would have entered into a political skirmish of this kind without consulting Addison. Nor would Addison be likely to dissuade him since, in the third *Spectator*, he had complained about the government's, and indirectly the queen's, failure to invite Prince George to England. See Bond, i. 17.

14,000 of them into other People's Hands, that would other-wise have never seen or heard of it.'[1] According to Nichols, this paper (*S.* 384) 'was not published till 12 o'clock, that it might come out precisely at the hour of her Majesty's break-fast, and that no time might be left for deliberating about serving it up with that meal, as usual.' This was not the first time the *Spectator* entered into political disputes of a topical nature. A week before the queen dismissed the Duke of Marlborough from his offices in December 1711, Addison published an essay on fame.[2] In the context of current politics, it is not difficult to see that he is attacking Tory writers who denigrated Marlborough:

> Others there are who proclaim the Errours and Infirmities of a great Man with an inward Satisfaction and Complacency, if they discover none of the like Errours and Infirmities in themselves; for while they are exposing another's Weaknesses, they are tacitly aiming at their own Commendations who are not subject to the like Infirmities, and are apt to be transported with a secret kind of Vanity, to see themselves superiour in some Respects to one of a sublime and celebrated Reputation.

Even the members of the 'club' had political roles. Sir Roger de Coverley, the principal member, was the embodi-ment of a Tory squire. Skilfully Addison took Steele's original, filled out the character, and made some important changes. Sir Roger, who was drawn by Steele to be 'rather beloved than esteemed', was re-drawn by Addison to be esteemed rather than imitated.[3] With a few strokes Addison and his friends created the image of a man generally beloved, in whose soul there was no positive vice, a man above all harmless. It was the picture of one to whom nobody could take exception, indeed all must recognize in him the endearing foibles of mankind. The *Spectator* went down to Sir Roger's country seat for a visit and recorded his daily

---

[1] Fleetwood's estimate of the *Spectator*'s reading audience may be optimistic. For details concerning *S.* 384, see Bond, iii. 440-1.

[2] *S.* 256. This essay was written some years before and the Dykes Campbell manuscript (see *infra*) contains an early draft. However, Addison's decision to publish the essay at this time would have given his general remarks a specific meaning for his readers.

[3] For a full discussion of the development of Sir Roger's character, see Emile Legouis's *Dernière Gerbe* (Paris, 1940), pp. 85-104.

life.[1] Sir Roger was then brought to town and taken on frequent occasions to the 'club'; he went to Spring Garden,[2] to the theatre,[3] to Westminster Abbey,[4] to see Prince Eugene on his visit to London,[5] and upon a dozen other adventures. Yet in spite of his good nature, Sir Roger was a man to whom nobody would entrust private business or public affairs. The Whig merchant Sir Andrew Freeport, on the contrary, though less prominent in the 'club', was clearly a man of substantial wisdom, a man of prudence to whose advice and ability all would defer. His comments on trade offer a contrast to Sir Roger's outdated views on the importance of the landed interest.[6] Sir Andrew gave the *Spectator* the opportunity to defend the merchant class against the attacks of Tory writers without seriously violating its professed neutrality. Another member of the 'club', Will Honeycomb, was a man on whom 'Time has made but very little Impression, either by Wrinkles on his Forehead, or Traces in his Brain.'[7] He was conceived as a parody of the Restoration dandy, the ladies' man whose gossip and fashions are behind the times. Like Sir Roger, he is a kindly caricature of the nostalgic Tories who tried to live in a fast disappearing pre-Revolution society.

Addison had expected that his paper would call forth critics in spite of the precautions taken. This was the more likely because it was generally associated with Steele in the public mind. It was therefore a wise decision, so characteristic of Addison, so unlike Steele, to ignore any critics who might appear:

I have been very often tempted to write Invectives upon those who have detracted from my Works, or spoken in derogation of my Person; but . . . the work wou'd have been of very little use to the Publick, had it been filled with Personal Reflections and Debates, for which reason I have never once turned out of my way to observe those little Cavils which have been made against it by Envy or Ignorance.[8]

For materials Addison had his accumulation of drafts and notes. He also had a hint from Swift of which he made use, causing the doctor, who attributed the paper to Steele,

[1] S. 106.   [2] S. 383.   [3] S. 335.   [4] S. 329.
[5] S. 292.   [6] S. 2.   [7] Ibid.   [8] S. 335.

to remark to Stella: 'I repent he ever had it.' He made frequent use of Bayle's dictionary as a source of raw materials, using both the French edition of 1702 and Tonson's English edition published in 1710.[1] He also drew upon his own travels,[2] as well as his extensive reading of travel books. His knowledge of oriental fable, which dated back to his father's studies in Tangier, was another useful source. The *Spectator* also invited the private contributor, who was thus encouraged:

if he has started any Hint which he is not able to pursue, if he has met with any surprizing Story which he does not know how to tell, if he has discovered any epidemical Vice which has escaped my Observation, or has heard of any uncommon Vertue which he would desire to publish; in short, if he has any Materials that can furnish out an innocent Diversion, I shall promise him my best Assistance in working of them up for publick Entertainment.[3]

But it was Steele rather than Addison who made use of readers' contributions. John Scott's *The Christian Life*, one of Addison's favourite books, was used for several essays.[4] Locke's *Essay concerning Humane Understanding* was also a source.[5] Even the Bills of Mortality which Addison read regularly were used to give the paper a topical air.[6]

Addison's method of writing the *Spectator* varied with the subject matter. The nature of his topics required more elaborate preparation than did most of those treated in the *Tatler* and where he wrote upon serious and philosophical subjects, the order and structure of the paper were considered in advance in much detail. Where he was in lighter vein, he would 'throw together . . . Reflections . . . without any Order or Method' as though thinking aloud to his reader.[7] This was a natural development of his method of dictating. A secretary took down the first draft and Addison and others corrected and added copiously.[8] In a paper pro-

---

[1] Bond, ii. 365. [2] Bond, i. 59; ii. 390. [3] *S.* 16.
[4] *S.* 111, *S.* 447. [5] *S.* 62. [6] *S.* 289. [7] *S.* 249.
[8] See *Some Portions of Essays contributed to the Spectator, etc.*, ed. Dykes Campbell, Glasgow, 1864 (privately printed) and facsimile in Catalogue No. 71 (1950) of Martin Breslauer, Bookseller (23 Museum Street, London W.C. 1), illustrating a MS. now at Harvard, which would repay detailed analysis. For details concerning another MS. at the Bodleian Library, see

duced daily there were inevitably times when the press was kept waiting for material, and when minutely examined some of Addison's *Spectators* can be seen to show signs of haste in composition. In general, however, they were written and corrected with meticulous care; and alterations were made, as in the case of the *Tatler*, both in the press in the form of errata, and as revisions in the course of subsequent editing and collection. This process of polishing did not diminish the freshness of Addison's style. On the contrary, he attained the ideal of classical prose, 'the perfect adaptation of language to subject-matter without too obvious effect.'[1] The influence of his prose style in modern literary history can hardly be overestimated and its importance in the eighteenth century is established with authority by Samuel Johnson's tribute:

His prose is the model of the middle style: on grave subjects not formal, on light occasions not groveling; pure without scrupulosity, and exact without apparent elaboration; always equable, and always easy, without glowing words or pointed grace; he seeks no ambitious ornaments, and tries no hazardous innovations. His page is always luminous, but never blazes in unexpected splendour. It was apparently his principal endeavour to avoid all harshness and severity of diction; he is therefore sometimes verbose in his transitions and connections, and sometimes descends too much to the language of conversation: yet if his language had been less idiomatical it might have lost somewhat of its genuine Anglicism. What he attempted, he performed; he is never feeble, and he did not wish to be energetick; he is never rapid, and he never stagnates. His sentences have neither studied amplitude, nor affected brevity; his periods, though not diligently rounded, are voluble and easy. Whoever wishes to attain an English style, familiar but not coarse, and elegant but not ostentatious, must give his days and nights to the volumes of Addison.[2]

M. C. Crum, 'A Manuscript of Essays by Addison', *Bodleian Library Record*, v (1954), 98–103, and R. D. Chambers, 'Addison at Work on the *Spectator*', *Modern Philology*, lvi (1959), 145–53.

[1] Bond, i. lxix. For a full analysis of Addison's style, see Z. E. Chandler, *An Analysis of the Stylistic Technique of Addison, Johnson, Hazlitt, and Pater* (University of Iowa Studies, Humanistic Studies, IV, no. 3, 1928), and J. Lannering, *Studies in the Prose Style of Joseph Addison* (Essays and Studies on English Language and Literature, ed. S. B. Liljegren, IX, Uppsala, 1951).

[2] *Lives of the English Poets*, ed. G. B. Hill (Oxford, 1905), ii. 149–50.

At the head of each *Spectator* there appeared a Latin or Greek motto. These were apparently not collated with their texts and were often inserted from memory or slightly altered to suit the context. They were not accompanied by translations.

> When I have finished any of my Speculations, it is my Method to consider which of the Ancient Authors have touched upon the Subject that I treat of. By this means I meet with some celebrated Thought upon it, or a Thought of my own expressed in better Words, or some Similitude for the Illustration of my Subject. This is what gives Birth to the Motto of a Speculation . . .[1]

More than half of the mottoes are drawn from Horace and Virgil.[2] For many men these quotations would have been familiar from their school days. Even those who could not read them would be flattered by the assumption of learning in the reader. For the erudite, however, the motto served as a title and sometimes as an ironic comment upon the subject of the essay.

Of those who worked with Addison in the *Spectator*, Dick Steele took by far the largest share. With his experience of producing the *Gazette* and the *Tatler*, he probably undertook the technical management and production of the paper. There were four persons responsible for the business side and all were experienced technicians: Samuel Buckley and Jacob Tonson (the younger) as printers, with Anne Baldwin and Charles Lillie as distributors. Buckley was the successful publisher of the first daily newspaper in England, the *Daily Courant*, and Anne Baldwin, with her husband Richard, had published the popular *Post-Man* from 1694 to 1700. Charles Lillie was a perfumer in the Strand who had taken a prominent part in the distribution of the *Tatler* and Jacob Tonson, nephew of Addison's publisher of the same name, had taken over the collected volumes of that paper by the middle of 1711. Professor Donald Bond's careful examination of the typographical features of the original sheets indicates that Tonson shared the printing from the paper's beginning, although his name does not appear in the colophon until number 499.[3] In fact, for most of the run of 555 numbers the

---

[1] *S.* 221.
[2] For a commentary and list of the sources of the mottoes, see Bond, v. 225–32.
[3] Bond, i. xxvii–xxviii.

two printers worked in exact alternation, but after sixteen months this arrangement was changed to permit each to prepare three consecutive numbers. Steele, whose essays were usually printed by Buckley, was responsible for the issues appearing on Mondays, Tuesdays, and Wednesdays, while Addison, whose essays were usually printed by Tonson, wrote for the latter half of the week. As might have been expected in such experienced hands, the organization appears to have worked smoothly and efficiently even when the *Spectator*'s circulation rose to 4,000 or more copies daily.[1]

Addison signed his papers only with one of the four letters which spelled the name of the muse Clio. Had all of his papers appeared under the same initial their authorship could hardly have been in doubt. Steele's papers were signed 'R' and 'T' and those by Eustace Budgell 'X'. In answer to those who speculated as to the meaning of these signatures, Addison referred to an ancient philosopher who carried something hidden under his cloak, and who replied to inquiries as to what it might be: '*I cover it . . . on purpose that you should not know.*'[2] In the original series of 555 numbers, 249 are signed with 'C', 'L', 'I', or 'O' and 251 are signed 'R' or 'T'. Tickell included two *Spectator* essays with no signatures in his edition of Addison's *Works* and Professor Donald Bond concludes that Addison and Steele, with 251 papers each, contributed about ninety per cent. of the whole. About two-thirds of the essays with Steele's signature, and one-fifth of those with Addison's, are made up of contributed material, mostly letters, with varying amounts of editorial comment. Addison thus contributed more than twice as many original essays as Steele, that is to say, 202 as compared with 89. After establishing these statistics, Professor Bond concludes that 'while it is true to say the two men shared equal responsibility for the 555 numbers, Addison's contribution in the form of original essays looms much larger.'[3]

As the paper proceeded Addison filled out so naturally the beginnings of characters and projects begun by Steele, and Steele fell so easily into the mood and style of his friend, that a remarkable degree of uniformity of writing was achieved. This, with one or two references of a personal

[1] Bond, i. xxv–xxvii.   [2] *S.* 221.   [3] Bond, i. lix.

nature, which would lead readers to think of Steele and of the *Tatler*, was responsible for the *Spectator* being principally attributed to him by the contemporary reading public. Therefore when it had run for 382 numbers he disclaimed the principal share in the work:

The *Spectator* writes often in an Elegant, often in an Argumentative, and often in a Sublime Stile, with equal Success; but how would it hurt the reputed Author of that Paper [himself] to own that of the most beautiful Pieces under his Title, he is barely the Publisher?[1]

The subject matter of the *Spectator* was the whole field of human activity. To describe its content would be to analyse the society of an age. Addison took pride in 'the Variety of his Subjects, with those several Critical Dissertations, Moral Reflections'.[2] The lighter *Spectators*, for which the *Tatler* had prepared the way, were directed mainly at women readers. Such a one was the 'Diary of Clarinda', 'placed in a modish State of Indifference between Vice and Vertue, and . . . susceptible of either'.[3] Against the more general and masculine failings he turned a graver humour, when, for example, he ridiculed numerology, lotteries, and lucky numbers:

These Principles of Election are the Pastimes and Extravagances of Human Reason, which is of so busie a Nature, that it will be exerting it self in the meanest Trifles. . . . The wisest of Men are sometimes acted by such unaccountable Motives, as the Life of the Fool and the Superstitious is guided by nothing else.[4]

Addison's intimate knowledge of classical authors enabled him to illustrate his papers freely from this source, and thus to introduce his readers to a superficial acquaintance with works of which they probably knew only the authors' names. A series of papers upon the subject of 'Lover's Leap'. for example, afforded an opportunity to discourse upon the beauties of Sappho, Plutarch, and Theocritus.

Criticism was a large part of the purpose of the *Spectator*. As a critic Addison was sometimes novel and often much in advance of the taste of his age. But he also served in popular form the ponderous theories of the scholars, whose work

[1] *S*. 382.   [2] *S*. 101.   [3] *S*. 323.   [4] *S*. 191.

when thus presented penetrated into places where the original was never studied. A good example of Addison's method is his famous comment: 'I must entirely agree with Monsieur *Boileau*, that one Verse in *Virgil*, is worth all the *Clincant* or Tinsel of *Tasso*.'[1] More than a half century later Hurd was to write that 'Mr. Addison, who gave the law in taste here, took it up, and sent it about the kingdom in his polite and popular essays. It became a sort of watchword among the critics; and, on the sudden, nothing was heard on all sides, but the *clinquant* of Tasso.'[2] It will be recalled that in his criticism of Latin poetry Addison's purpose was to assist the reader, particularly the reader of a translation, to an appreciation of the beauties of the original. Dryden had taught him to insist upon this main purpose. His purpose in English literary criticism was therefore wider to the extent that he now sought, not merely to educate and correct the taste of the reading public, but also that of the community of authors. 'I shall endeavour as much as possible to establish . . . a Taste of polite Writing', he declared;[3] and he thought this the more necessary because of the shortcomings which he detected in the public taste:

> *Ned* is indeed a true *English* Reader, incapable of relishing the great and masterly Strokes of this Art; but wonderfully pleased with the little *Gothick* Ornaments of Epigrammatical Conceits, Turns, Points, and Quibbles, which are so frequent in the most admired of our *English* poets, and practised by those who want Genius and Strength to represent, after the Manner of the Ancients, Simplicity in its natural Beauty and Perfection.[4]

This was a comprehensive restatement of his estimate of English taste, formerly expressed in his 'Notes' to Ovid's *Metamorphoses*, and repeated on many occasions in different forms throughout his life.[5] It was a judgement which applied equally to architecture as to literature. The rules by which he determined 'simplicity in its natural beauty and perfection' were those which he had observed in their application in the Latin poets and in Roman buildings. He had learned them as precepts at the feet of Dryden, who had taken much of his critical scholarship from French sources.

[1] *S.* 5. [2] *Works* (1811), iv. 314. [3] *S.* 58. [4] *T.* 163. [5] e.g. *S.* 62.

It had therefore been an easy transition for Addison to pass on to Boileau, Bouhours, and the contemporary French critics. He had compared his conclusions with those reached by John Dennis, and had adopted much from his writings.

Addison envisaged 'natural' genius as born in every age, but it was its added good fortune if it should happen to be born in one which was 'polite', that is to say one which understood the rules of reason as applied to literature.[1] Nor were natural genius and the polish of learning alone sufficient to satisfy his canons of judgement, which exacted also the patina of urbanity, the quality which Dennis's critical writings lacked. He quoted approvingly from Roscommon:

> None yet have been with Admiration read,
> But who (beside their learning) were well-bred.[2]

Because his insistence upon rules was tempered with good sense, Addison's criticism was acceptable to his contemporaries. As Macaulay expressed it, his critical papers are 'always luminous and often ingenious'; and Addison himself despised the unimaginative critic:

> . . . there is not a more importunate, and conceited Animal than that which is generally known by the Name of a Critick. This, in the common Acceptation of the Word, is one that, without entering into the Sense and Soul of an Author, has a few general Rules, which, like mechanical Instruments, he applies to the Works of every Writer . . .[3]

He elaborated his theme by pointing out that the lazy and ignorant critic condemns by rules culled at second hand from other writers, while the scholarly critic appraises from the study of originals. The ancient and great masters of criticism used their art to discover and illustrate beauty wherever it was to found.[4] In fact, as Saintsbury pointed out, it was Addison's peculiar characteristic that with his correctness he combined freedom, and with precision, independence of judgement. Addison's critical writings were doubly welcome because of their wit and humanity. Lady Mary Wortley Montagu, who disliked Addison in retrospect, expressed grudging admiration for this quality:

[1] S. 160.   [2] Quoted in the *Lover*, No. 39.   [3] T. 165.   [4] S. 592.

Thus Addison, 'tis true, debauch'd in schools,
Will sometimes oddly talk of musty rules,
Yet here and there I see a master line,
I feel and I confess the pow'r divine.
Inspite of interest, charm'd into applause,
I wish for such a champion in our cause.

His wit, and his agreement with Bouhours and Boileau that 'no Thought can be valuable, of which good Sense is not the Ground-work'[1] made Addison a critic calculated to please the majority of English readers: while his basic belief in French critical principles, including those of Le Bossu and Rapin as well as the others, made him the most acceptable of English writers in France in his own lifetime and in that of Voltaire.[2]

Addison's bookseller reported that his papers of criticism were selling better than could have been expected.[3] He had analysed the ballad of *Chevy Chase*, an original with which most readers would be familiar, but which they were startled to find treated as literature. He opened himself to the critical wrath of Dennis,[4] and to such parodies as *A Comment upon the History of Tom Thumb*, which advertised his work rather than damaging it. Ignoring such incidents, though noting some of the criticism for correction in the final revision of his works,[5] he wrote three principal courses of papers on literary topics. These were published either on Saturdays, or in consecutive series to enable the train of thought to remain unbroken. The most important of these was his series upon the 'Pleasures of the Imagination', which, though belonging to the realm of philosophy rather than of literature, contained much critical work. Next in importance were his papers upon the *Paradise Lost* of Milton, a poet who was widely read by the public but only rarely commended by the critics. This was not a new development in Addison's taste. At Oxford he had praised Milton in his 'Account'; he had 'imitated' his style in translating Virgil, had noticed it in the *Travels*, and praised it in the *Tatler*,[6] while he thought

[1] *S.* 62.
[2] For a detailed study of Addison's criticism, see L. A. Elioseff, *The Cultural Milieu of Addison's Literary Criticism* (Austin, 1963).
[3] *S.* 58.   [4] Dennis, *Original Letters*, 1721, p. 166.
[5] E. B. Reed, *Mod. Phil.* vi. 1908.   [6] *T.* 114.

(erroneously) that in the *Spectator* he quoted Milton more frequently than any other poet.[1] Tickell tells us that his materials for the Milton papers had been collected for some years and this fact perhaps may account for Addison's ignoring the critical work which Dennis had published on Milton,[2] but he was also addressing a public much wider than any that Dennis could reach. His examination of the *Paradise Lost* was thorough, painstaking, and interesting, and was in part responsible for giving that work the place in popular esteem which it has occupied ever since. Indeed, Addison's Milton papers are themselves the subject of a considerable literature, and were translated into Italian and German.

The third series of critical papers dealt with the nature of wit. Here Addison's missionary purpose was especially pronounced. He consistently sought by criticism and example to prune from contemporary humour all 'Gothic' excrescences. Under this epithet he included quaint conceits and artificial turns, puns, rebuses, and other forms of wit not founded in reason,[3] observing that a pun can be neither translated nor engraved.[4] He likewise excluded from true wit all ill nature, and any immoderate quality conducive to laughter as opposed to mirth.[5] When stripped of such defects, the central structure of wit was that proposed by Locke, founded in the similarity of ideas. He tried to relate the concept of wit thus simplified to that of 'truth', in a genealogical parallel:

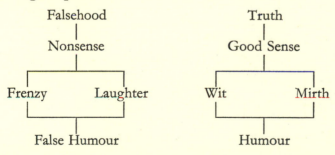

But his expansion of critical theory lay in the realm of demonstration rather than of exposition. His own works

[1] S. 262.   [2] Bond, i. 201.   [3] S. 47, 61, 440.
[4] 'Dialogue on Medals', II.   [5] S. 47, 249.

were the most effective criticism of the faults of others, and Felton truly commended him for rescuing the art 'from Pedantry, Dulness, and Ill-Nature' and establishing it in 'a Place among the politest Parts of Learning'.[1] Later generations have discounted Addison's critical writing; but, as Macaulay observed, 'he was not so far behind our generation as he was before his own'.

Addison's criticism was by no means confined to literature; indeed his literary analysis was the elaboration of the process of reasoning which he applied to any given human activity. Thus, if his purpose in examining the *Paradise Lost* was to 'particularize those innumerable kinds of beauty . . . which are essential to poetry, and which may be met with in the works of this great author',[2] when writing of architecture he sought to perform a similar service. Nor did he fail to use all his resources of ridicule where he thought that he detected false taste in the other arts, as in daily matters of human conduct. The opera, now succeeding under Handel's direction, gave him, as he thought, opportunities for attacking those false qualities which he had tried to reveal by contrast of example in *Rosamond*.[3] The list of topics to which Addison turned his critical apparatus would be a lengthy one if completed.

The success of the Milton papers may have encouraged the authors of the *Spectator* to deepen their tone. The range of the paper in 'philosophic' subjects was considerable, and while some of Addison's writing seems trite today, its successful presentation of speculative topics in a popular daily periodical was an extraordinary triumph. Much of his writing was upon matters which had been declaimed from the pulpit to drowsy congregations for many years but which now received a new life and interest because presented as a part of daily conduct as lived by the 'polite'. The obligation to charity,[4] the attributes and consequences of greatness,[5] the shocking nature of conceit both in the eye of God and man, the nature of good and bad fortune,[6] and of good and evil

[1] *A Dissertation on Reading the Classics and forming a just style*, 1713.
[2] *S*. 369.
[3] Addison devoted *S*. 18 to a history of Italian opera in England. See Bond, i. 78–82.
[4] *S*. 177. [5] *S*. 101. [6] *S*. 293.

actions,[1] the virtues of cheerfulness[2] and compassion,[3] the contrast of discretion and cunning,[4] the futility of apprehension,[5] the greatness of indifference to praise or censure,[6] the virtues of good nature[7] and forgiveness,[8] the hollowness of fame[9] and the elusive nature of happiness,[10] the relationship of luxury to avarice,[11] the place of motive in human nature,[12] the moral dangers of wealth and poverty and the advantages of a middle state,[13] self-control distinguishing the wise man from the fool,[14] self-criticism indispensable to right living,[15] self-esteem more important than public esteem,[16] the nature of the superiority of one man over another,[17] the tendency of the mind to vacancy[18] and sloth,[19] the nature and causes of jealousy,[20] the definition of virtue[21] and its profitable consequences,[22] the nature of time,[23] the value of truth[24] and of integrity when associated with urbanity,[25] and the glory of a proper uniformity in a man's actions.[26] Such multifarious speculations, scattered throughout the *Spectator*, testify to the truly missionary spirit of its authors. This was most strikingly expressed in the series of eleven papers upon the 'Pleasures of the Imagination',[27] to which the *Spectator* was wholly given over for a fortnight in a most daring experiment in serial writing. They were well received and were greatly admired until the present century. Addison's concept of the imagination was not precise; and much ink has been spent upon these papers. They were closely allied with his literary criticism, and their purpose was to encourage and assist the reader to develop his faculties of mind in such a way as to enlarge the field of sensibility, and thus of true pleasure.

With so many striking features to commend it, the *Spectator* was immediately and universally successful, and the authors, aware of the contagious nature of fashion, lost no chance to advertise their achievement. As early as the tenth paper, Addison wrote:

[1] S. 213	[2] S. 387.	[3] S. 397.	[4] S. 225.
[5] S. 505.	[6] S. 255.	[7] S. 177.	[8] S. 181.
[9] S. 256.	[10] S. 15, 163.	[11] S. 55.	[12] S. 213.
[13] S. 464.	[14] S. 225.	[15] S. 399.	[16] S. 122.
[17] S. 219.	[18] S. 471.	[19] S. 93.	[20] S. 170, 171.
[21] S. 93.	[22] S. 243.	[23] S. 94.	[24] S. 407.
[25] S. 557.	[26] S. 349.	[27] S. 411–21.	

It is with much Satisfaction that I hear this great City inquiring Day by Day after these my Papers, and receiving my Morning Lectures with a becoming Seriousness and Attention. My Publisher tells me, that there are already Three Thousand of them distributed every Day: So that if I allow Twenty Readers to every Paper, which I look upon as a modest Computation, I may reckon about Three-score thousand Disciples in *London* and *Westminster*, who I hope will take care to distinguish themselves from the thoughtless Herd of their ignorant and unattentive Brethren.

The estimate of twenty readers per paper was probably optimistic. But at this time a sheet of printed matter was relatively more valuable and prized than today and only a small percentage of the papers would be wasted. The number of roughly bound collections of the original *Spectator* which are still in existence is some evidence that they were carefully preserved. Furthermore, by the time that No. 29 appeared it was already the custom to sell sets of back numbers. It was also common in an age when literacy was not the rule for the paper to be read to groups in coffee-houses and taverns as well as in the home. The circulation soon spread to the provinces, where it was sometimes read aloud to village groups and sponsored by 'polite' societies. The 'Gentlemen's Society' at Spalding was founded on 3 November this year with the encouragement of Addison and Steele. It met at Mr. Younger's Coffee House, Spalding, and provided that atmosphere of self-improvement which the *Spectator* sought to promote.[1] In Scotland—weighty testimonial!—it is reported to have been read aloud after church on Sunday.[2] As the paper grew in fame and circulation the public formed the habit of collecting the numbers and binding them by subjects, a fact which Addison was quick to notice and to encourage. He kept a vigilant eye upon the popularity of different types of material and upon the sales of the paper, consulting his publisher at every stage.

It is not surprising that the preparations for this great literary venture should have occupied most of Addison's time during the first few months of the year 1711. There

---

[1] 'Some Account of the Gentlemen's Society at Spalding', by Mr. Gough and J. Nichols; Nichols, *Literary Anecdotes*, vi. 2, 28.
[2] *Addisoniana*, ii. 8.

were nevertheless some details of Irish business still to be wound up. There were also occasional meetings with Swift by chance at the coffee-house, where, as Jonathan put it, they 'talk'd coldly'. 'All our friendship and dearness are off:' he wrote to Stella in January, 'we are civil acquaintance, talk words of course. . . Is it not odd? But I think he has used me ill, and I have used him too well, at least his friend Steele.' He wrote of the continuator of the *Tatler*: 'little Harrison, a young poet whose fortune I am making.' Since his adoption by the Ministry Swift had become intolerable in his self-importance and patronage. In February he dined with Addison after an interval of three weeks. 'I have represented Addison himself so to the Ministry, that they think and talk in his favour, though they hated him before. —Well; he is now in my debt, and there's an end; and I never had the least obligation to him, and there's another end.' The dinner must have been an uncomfortable one, and it is not surprising that the next record, in March, was to the effect that another three weeks had gone by without a meeting. Swift was trying, he said, to prevent Steele's dismissal as Gazetteer, but suspected Addison of advising Steele against making his peace with the Ministry. If this suspicion was correct, it was honest and politically wise advice that Addison gave his friend. But Swift again recorded defiantly: 'All our friendship is over.' He seems to have felt the publication of the *Spectator* a special offence to himself, as a refusal to submit to the Government; and the Ministry may indeed have frowned upon the rebirth of the *Tatler* in an improved and reinvigorated form which might yet run to politics. Of the *Spectator* Swift wrote:

I believe Addison and he [Steele] club. I never see them, and I plainly told Mr. Harley and Mr. St. John, ten days ago, before my Lord Keeper and Lord Rivers, that I had been foolish enough to spend my credit with them in favour of Addison and Steele: but that I would engage and promise never to say one word in their behalf, having been used so ill for what I had already done.

In April he assured Stella that 'I never see him or Addison' and, evidently feeling uncomfortable in the presence of his former friends, told Archbishop King, 'I have left off going to Coffee-Houses'.[1] In May he gave instructions to Stella, 'send nothing under cover to Mr. Addison, but to Erasmus Lewis Esq.; at my Lord Dartmouth's office'.

Meanwhile in February Governor Harrison had sailed for Madras and at sea off Portsmouth wrote to Addison a friendly reassuring letter. There was nothing for it but to await news of the Governor's arrival in India. Between the *Spectator* and Parliament Addison was fully occupied. In April there also appeared the third and fourth collected volumes of the *Tatler*, published with dedications by Steele to Lord Cowper, the fallen Lord Chancellor, and to Lord Halifax. To the latter he took the opportunity to express a sense of the service performed by him in encouraging men such as Addison to enter public affairs:

it is to you we owe, that the Man of Wit has turned himself to be a Man of Business. The false Delicacy of Men of Genius, and the Objections which others were apt to insinuate against their Abilities for entring into Affairs, have equally vanished. And Experience has shown, that Men of Letters are not only qualify'd with a greater Capacity, but also a greater Integrity in the Dispatch of Business.

One of the 'Men of Letters' now attacked the *Spectator*. In No. 40 Addison had published a paper upon the drama and began with an attack upon 'a ridiculous doctrine in modern criticism' that dramatists 'are obliged to an equal distribution of rewards and punishments, and an impartial execution of poetical justice'. Such a rule, he argued, was contrary to nature and reason. This was a reference to the writings of John Dennis, who had propounded such a theory since the year 1701. Dennis, who was considerably Addison's senior, and who had striven unsuccessfully for the scholarly and literary prizes which Addison had easily won, had never been a familiar member of literary or fashionable society, but had remained its distant and ill humoured, though scholarly, critic. His works were read only by the literary or the learned, and much of them was translated into popular form by Addison in the *Spectator* at a later date. Dennis was now in poor health and withdrawing into a surly isolation.

But he respected Addison's ability, and undoubtedly thought Steele responsible both for passing gibes at critics in the *Tatler* and for the present attack on his theory of poetic justice. He had in fact already conducted an acrimonious quarrel with Steele to whom he now wrote two letters in a strain of angry protest.[1] A week later Addison published a *Spectator* in which he commended a couplet written by Dennis in a translation of Boileau:

> Thus one fool lolls his tongue out at another,
> And shakes his empty noddle at his brother,

a quotation which would infuriate the critic, who though he might apply it to himself could hardly object thereto. Then Addison ended his paper with a paragraph directed at 'butts':

those honest Gentlemen that are always exposed to the Wit and Raillery of their Well-wishers and Companions; . . . and, in a word, stand as *Butts* in Conversation, for every one to shoot at that pleases. I know several of these *Butts*, who are Men of Wit and Sense, though by some odd turn of Humour, some unlucky Cast in their Person or Behaviour, they have always the Misfortune to make the Company merry. . . . A stupid *Butt* is only fit for the Conversation of ordinary People: Men of Wit require one that will give them Play, and bestir himself in the absurd part of his Behaviour.[2]

This was a deliberate baiting of the critic, who wrote caustically to Steele, and thereafter took upon himself the duty of defending the public against what he considered to be the ill-grounded remarks on drama and literature appearing in the *Spectator*.[3] The development of the controversy provided advertisement for the *Spectator*, while a quarrel with Dennis could make no important enemies for its authors. It was a battle between comparable intellects but characters of great disparity.

In later life Steele claimed that he had shielded Addison from 'the Resentments which many of his own Works would have brought upon him at the time in which they

---

[1] Dennis, *Original Letters*, 1721, pp. 407 et seq. [2] *S.* 47.
[3] e.g. his attack on *Spectators* 70 and 74, see Hooker, *Critical Works of John Dennis*, ii. 29–40.

were written. . . . Many of the Writings now published as his, I have been very patiently traduced and calumniated for. . . .'[1] This was certainly the case with some of Addison's *Tatlers*, such as No. 229, which was attacked by the *Examiner* with round abuse of Steele, and it was also the case in the poetic justice controversy. Whether Addison exacted and Steele submitted to this arrangement because of the sensitiveness of the former, or because of Steele's indifference to attack, or because Addison wished to preserve a strict anonymity, or because Steele considered himself responsible as publisher of the paper for what appeared therein, it was evidently a clearly understood arrangement between the two men. For his part, Addison may have comforted himself that, as Swift put it, he 'bridled' Steele in point of party, and thus saved his friend from at least as many troubles as he created.

As summer approached, Addison and Steele opened a second phase of their attack upon the Italian opera, which had secured a triumph with the appearance of Nicolini in Handel's *Rinaldo* the previous February. In May they followed the *Spectator* attacks with a series of concerts organized by Steele and Clayton. These were performances of English poetry set to music, a rational answer to Handel's challenge. But though lavishly advertised in the *Spectator* they failed to impress the public.

Addison now seems to have withdrawn almost entirely from political activity. As he later expressed it in sentiments more appropriate to his own character than in the mouth of Cato:

> When vice prevails, and impious men bear sway,
> The post of honour is a private station,[2]

or, in the *Spectator*: 'It is my Duty to speak Truth, tho' it is not my Duty to be in an Office.'[3] He played little part in Parliament, and in the unlikely event of any intercession being required to secure him in his office Lord Halifax was in frequent touch with the Ministry on financial matters, and was the only great Whig to attend the Tory Lord Treasurer when he took the oaths of office.[4] Thus the *Journals*, a poor record of Parliamentary activity, probably in this case give

---

[1] Dedication to the *Drummer*, 1721. [2] *Cato*, Act IV, Scene IV.
[3] *S.* 507. [4] *Evening Post*, 282.

a correct impression when recording only that Addison sat upon a committee appointed on 10 May to hear a Scots petition. On 12 June the House rose until the autumn and Addison apparently went to the country for a rest. Knowing the appetite for green fields which sweeps the town in July, he prepared for that time a series of country adventures for Sir Roger. He had probably taken advice on this when he dined with Jacob Tonson and Dick Steele at an Ordinary near the Temple on 2 June; and when he returned to London at the end of the month, he was ready to entertain the town with an account of Mr. Spectator's stay with the knight, beginning on 2 July.

The booksellers reported that the country papers were well received and, always ready to exploit the advantage of success, Addison noticed this fact in his paper and reported 'several having made up separate Sets of them, as they have done before of those relating to Wit, to Operas, to Points of Morality, or Subjects of Humour'.[1] The series ran inter-mittently until he summoned Mr. Spectator back to town at the end of the month with a letter from Will Honeycomb, the fashionable and rakish member of the club:

Dear Spec,

I suppose this Letter will find thee picking of Daisies, or smell-ing to a lock of Hay, or passing away thy time in some innocent Country Diversions of the like nature. . . . Thy Speculations begin to smell confoundedly of Woods and Meadows. If thou dost not come up quickly, we shall conclude thou art in Love with one of Sir Roger's Dairy Maids. . . .[2]

Addison had hardly returned to town with his 'country' papers after his short holiday when the Irish Parliament, of which he was still a member, began its sitting. This caused him some uneasiness and he wrote to Dawson asking whether his absence from Ireland might 'produce anything' to his disadvantage. The new draft Irish Establishment contained the authorization of his salary as Keeper of the Records, and he feared the possibility of its being disallowed in his absence and given to another. But he evidently hoped that Dawson would feel able to advise him that a visit to

[1] *S.* 124.   [2] *S.* 131.

Dublin was not necessary. His presence in England was, he said, 'very much for the convenience of my affairs', which in all probability meant for the conduct of the *Spectator*. Dawson apparently acted on the hint, for Addison paid no visit to Ireland this year.

It was a time of some anxiety. Writing with unusual candour to Wortley in July, Addison had reflected upon his causes for melancholy. There was the loss of his place as Secretary, with its revenues. The news coming from India about Gulston's estate was discouraging and his attempt to foreclose Dick Steele's Barbados estate in the hands of the trustees had not succeeded. It was probably to the former though perhaps to the latter of these interests that he referred when he lamented to Wortley the loss of an estate in 'the Indies' worth £14,000. He feared, as he told Wortley in an excess of pessimism, that he would lose his Irish place, and, in addition, he had just resigned his fellowship. Ever since leaving college in 1699 his leave of absence had been renewed at six-monthly intervals, the last occasion being on 31 January 1711.[1] But he now resigned, voluntarily, on 14 July of that year.[2] A number of his contemporaries had already done the same, having departed for benefices or employments; Watkins, Smallbroke, and Boulter, for example, resigned in 1709. Addison had been fortunate in being permitted to remain on the foundation during twelve years of absence and not in orders, but he could do so no longer. At the same time the financial speculations which had caused him to request all available funds from Dawson so that he might make use of opportunities offering had not prospered, for, he said, 'stocks sink every day'. Finally, 'what is worse than all the rest', he had lost his 'mistress'.

It has been assumed that this reference is to Lady Warwick, but there is no evidence that this is the case. Addison was much occupied with thoughts about women; in his writings he showed a deep interest in the details of their dress and behaviour; his attitude towards them was paternal, condescending, but not unsympathetic. Yet no shred of evidence indicates that he was associated with any woman upon more than a social footing. In his letter to Wortley,

[1] Vice-President's Register. [2] Ibid.

Addison is obviously bantering himself upon his misfortunes, which he exaggerated. He was able to put up a
bond for £1,000 not long after this declaration of financial
calamities.[1] In this context the reference to his mistress
wears an air of banter which suggests that it did not proceed
from any heartfelt emotion. It is consistent with a reverse in
a half-serious courtship of a fashionable and wealthy woman,
and as such Lady Warwick might be described.

Having decided to remain in England, Addison contemplated spending a month in the country with Wortley, who
proposed a visit together to Newcastle, a project which they
had previously discussed. Alternatively he proposed a visit
to his seat, Wortley, in Yorkshire, where 'perhaps we may
contrive how you may pass your time'.[2] Addison was in the
mood for an outdoor life. His instinct to draw close to wild
nature was seldom far beneath the surface of a man about
town. Wortley tolerated this eccentricity: 'I am not sure we
shall easily have leave to lodge [sleep] out of this house,
but we may eat in the woods every day if you like it. . . .'[3] In
the event Addison decided to set off with Ambrose Philips
early in August to Bath. He hoped to benefit his eyes, which
remained troublesome. Shortly before leaving town he had
met Jonathan Swift for the first time for many weeks, at the
house of Jacob Tonson junior. Possibly Addison was
invited so that he might persuade Swift to intercede to
prevent Tonson from being deprived of the *Gazette*, of which
he was the publisher. 'Mr. Addison and I talked as usual',
Swift reported. Also back in town was Henry Newton, an
old friend and correspondent who had been four years envoy
in Tuscany.[4] Hearing that Addison had gone to Bath,
Wortley wrote again offering hospitality including the
services of one who 'writes a better hand than your own
secretary'.[5] The reference was probably to Ambrose Philips,
who at this time wrote a crabbed and 'fantastic' hand,[6] or to
Captain Edward Addison, whose employment would be

---

[1] B.M. Egerton MSS. 1971, f. 7 *et al.*
[2] *Addisoniana*, i. 236.   [3] Ibid.
[4] *Flying Post*, 3085, and see Graham, 'Addison and Sir Henry Newton',
N. & Q. clxx. 110–11.
[5] *Addisoniana*, i. 238.
[6] M. G. Segar, *Poems of Ambrose Philips*, xxxv.

consistent with Joseph's readiness to prefer his own family and who wrote little better than Philips.

It was early in September when Addison and Philips returned to London without having visited Wortley. From Ireland had come the good news that the salary of the Keeper of the Records had been included in the civil list reported to Parliament. Another satisfactory development had been the final settlement of the transaction of the shoes: Dawson was now in a position to render an account for such money as had been salvaged from the misfortune. Meeting Addison and Philips in the Park, Swift went back to supper with them. The atmosphere was more friendly and he reported: 'we were very good company, and yet know no man who is half so agreeable to me as he is.' Swift stayed till midnight. Wortley was still pressing Addison to stay with him in the country, but as October drew on and the session of Parliament approached, any idea of leaving London had to be abandoned. Addison therefore reciprocated with a suggestion that he move from his lodgings to a house in Kensington Square where Wortley should stay with him. This offer was accepted, with the proviso that Addison 'be nice in the choice of a cook', a caveat which indicates that his taste for plain cooking did not commend itself to all of his friends. The two men were intimate, and it is likely that Wortley took Addison into his confidence when he courted Lady Mary Pierrepont, with whom he eloped the following August. The remainder of the year 1711 was spent in parliamentary duties and in the affairs of the *Spectator*. Financial worries continued to press upon Addison's mind and he urged Dawson to send his remittances as soon as they should fall due. Then, just before Christmas, there befell a stroke of fortune. The author who inveighed against the enjoyment of dreams of future wealth before it was secured, who had nevertheless speculated in shoes in Dublin and in stocks in London, drew a £1,000 prize in the lottery. 'I cannot forbear telling you . . .', he wrote to Dawson in a burst of candour. It was timely relief, for though the *Spectator* prospered extraordinarily, further bad news was on the way from India.

Governor Harrison and Bernard Benyon had arrived in Madras on 10 August. Five days later Benyon wrote to

Addison an account of the state of his affairs. Of the executors, Fleetwood had died and Raworth had been obliged to leave Madras. The condition of the estate was one of confusion and obscurity, and so far there were not enough assets to pay off the debts. Much money lay out upon ventures, in one of which Gulston had been concerned with Governor Pitt. Benyon suggested that Addison take the best legal advice procurable; meanwhile he proposed realizing everything he could secure and lodging the proceeds with the Company. Governor Pitt, who sat with Addison in the House of Commons, was now readily accessible for consultation; but the estate was enmeshed in claims and cross claims with that of John Pitt, whose heir was a minor. The assets included Gulston's 'great house . . . untenanted and running to ruin'. After so much ill news there followed a postscript in which Benyon added with the air of a man writing in a land where life was cheap: 'I had almost forgot to advise you of the death of your Brother Lancelot', and suggested that it would be prudent to send out letters of administration to recover the legacy bequeathed to the dead man by Mary Addison. Lancelot had been buried on 13 July 1710, and Magdalen College had given him further leave of absence on 30 July of the following year and did not record his death until 29 December.[1] His death removed from the scene in India one person upon whose loyalty Joseph could depend. He died leaving such wealth as he possessed to his surviving brother and sister. Perhaps it was the bad news from India which provided material for the hundred and ninety-first *Spectator*:

It should be an indispensable Rule in Life to contract our Desires to our present Condition, and, whatever may be our Expectations, to live within the Compass of what we actually possess: It will be time enough to enjoy an Estate when it comes into our Hands. . . .

It was about the autumn of 1711 that Addison made the acquaintance of Alexander Pope, but the name of this brilliant young poet would have been known to him for several years. Pope had been introduced to the wits at Will's,

[1] Magdalen College, Vice-President's Register.

but their diet and hours did not suit his constitution. George Granville had been slightly known to Pope since 1706, and Edmund Smith probably met him the following year. Both were friends of Addison. Moreover, Jacob Tonson had recognized and applauded Pope's genius in the same year and doubtless mentioned his name at the Kit-Cat. Pope also knew Dr. Garth, to whom his 'Autumn' had been dedicated, and Garth was Addison's physician and friend. The young poet had been at work for some years upon the manuscript of his 'Pastorals' which, according to his own report, had passed through the hands of Congreve, Maynwaring, Garth, Halifax, and, surprisingly, Wharton, before publication in Tonson's *Miscellany* in 1709. Therefore when the *Essay on Criticism* appeared in May 1711, Pope's name would be well known and Steele had been corresponding with him and had noticed him favourably in the *Tatler*. Furthermore, Pope's new poem had been severely criticized, and thus advertised, in a pamphlet by Dennis.

Addison probably read the *Essay on Criticism* the more attentively because Pope in his 'January and May', published in Tonson's *Miscellany* two years previously, had made rather free with some lines from the 'Letter from Italy'. Pope's early poetry was shot through with reminiscences of his reading of Addison. In later life he recalled, 'I used formerly to like Mr. Addison's Letter from Italy extremely, and still like it the most of all his poems',[1] a statement the truth of which is evident from a collation of the works of the two men. Addison now reviewed Pope's *Essay* extensively in a *Spectator* whose keynote was the opening sentence: 'There is nothing which more denotes a great Mind than the Abhorrence of Envy and Detraction. This Passion reigns more among bad Poets than among any other Set of Men.' In his heaviest style he continued:

I am sorry to find that an Author, who is very justly esteemed among the best Judges, has admitted some stroaks of envy and detraction . . . into a very fine Poem . . . which . . . is a Masterpiece of its kind.[2]

Thereafter the *Essay* was highly praised, in an examination

[1] Spence, p. 316.   [2] *S.* 253.

which discovered that the poetry and the expression were admirable though the sentiments, excusably, were not new. The passages to which Addison took exception in Pope's poem were those which reflected upon Dennis's critical tantrums. Perhaps he intended to placate Dennis, assuming that Pope would be sufficiently grateful for the praise to overlook the rebuke. But the pontifical air of the paper was precisely such as would wound and enrage the abnormally sensitive younger poet, and Addison had barbed his rebuke with an apt quotation from Denham:

> Nor is thy fame on lesser ruins built,
> Nor needs thy juster title the foul guilt
> Of Eastern kings, who to secure their reign
> Must have their brothers, sons, and kindred slain.

The reproof sank very deep, and, deeply resented, failed of any reforming effect. In the privacy of his study Pope worked upon couplets which indignantly rebutted the charge:

> Nor fame I slight, nor for her favours call;
> She comes unlook'd for, if she comes at all:
>
> Or if no basis bear my rising name,
> But the fall'n ruins of another's fame;
> Then, teach me, heaven! to scorn the guilty bays.

But to an extremely ambitious young man the words of praise in the leading periodical of the day were as welcome as the rebuke was offensive; and, thinking Steele the author, Pope wrote him a letter of thanks. He even showed his disclaimer verses to Steele,[1] who thought them inoffensive and passed them on to Addison. Steele replied urbanely to Pope's letter, promising him an introduction to the real writer of the paper. Pope and Addison, when introduced, were ill adapted to agree together. Addison's genius lay in his judgement, self-command, correctness, and a wit which tolerated human weakness while deploring it; Pope's lay in his impulsive, affectionate, yet intolerant spirit and brilliant poetic gifts. Addison at a pinnacle of worldly repute had the failings

[1] Prior to 12 Nov. 1712; see Ault, *New Light on Pope*, generally on this transaction.

of success latent in his character; Pope resented his rebuke but accepted his praise.

The complex feelings of the young poet probably gave Addison little thought, for this was a busy time for the *Spectator*. In addition to the daily publications, the first two collected volumes were ready for subscribers on 8 January 1712. The dedications, written by Steele but doubtless approved by Addison, were to the two men who had made his fortune: Lords Somers and Halifax. The volumes were well advertised and were soon sold out. With the new year the paper gathered new strength. Sir Roger came to town to 'get a sight' of Prince Eugene of Savoy, and Addison thus took an opportunity to praise the great general who was identified in the public mind with the continuance of the war and the Whig policy and for whose camp he had once been designated as secretary. The prince dined in state with Lord Sunderland and twice with Lord Halifax.[1] It is probable that Addison was at these banquets. Continuing in mildly political mood he published a *Spectator* in praise of the British Constitution, that is to say, the Revolution Settlement. It was a tea-table version of the doctrine of John Locke. Liberty was founded in wealth, wealth begat culture, and in England the division of power was the guarantee of liberty.[2] The noticeable increase in political content in the *Spectator* at this time perhaps reflected the acute political controversies then raging, and the disappearance of any hope that a moderate administration could be formed in that parliament.

At St. Stephen's Addison remained inactive, sitting on no committee more important than one upon a private bill, but behind the scenes, he was playing an important and highly secret part. This year the Hanoverian minister in London, Baron Grote, was conducting with Lord Halifax and other Whig leaders negotiations which were intended to secure the succession against a possible design by Jacobite elements. Open and frequent meetings between Grote and the Whig magnates would have offended the queen and the Government; and it was at the Baron's suggestion that Addison was selected for the purpose of intermediary. This

[1] *Post Boy*, 52; *Evening Post*; *British Mercury*.   [2] *S.* 287.

was a high tribute to his discretion and an encouragement to hope for favours to come. He was even employed, though (as he afterwards remembered) without payment, to assist the minister in drafting Hanoverian official documents for presentation to the British Government.[1] He was also still seated in the Irish Commons, though he was in doubt as to whether he remained on the Irish Privy Council, a matter of some moment to him since it would enable him to import wine free of duty. He asked anxiously of Dawson whether this privilege would extend to absent Members of the Irish Parliament, and strengthened his case by hinting that he would return to Ireland in the summer.

Amongst the events of the late winter were a play by Ambrose Philips, and a further series of Steele's concerts. For the play Budgell and Addison wrote an epilogue which appeared only in the name of the former. The *Distrest Mother*, like its author, was full of classical frigidity; but it was excellently acted, and succeeded on the stage, partly on that account, partly because the Kit-Cat supported it as meritorious, and partly because it fed the present appetite for virtue. The success of the play probably caused Addison to think once more of his own tragedy of *Cato*. Twice in his lifetime, once with the *Campaign* in poetry, once with the *Spectator* in prose writing, he had achieved the highest literary success. Once, with *Rosamond*, in opera, he had plumbed the depths of failure, perhaps undeservedly. To venture upon a fourth bid for success, in the drama, was to stake his now great reputation. Addison was cautious and ambitious, diffident yet highly esteeming his own abilities. It was a lifelong ambition to see *Cato* on the stage, and he had not abandoned the project even if he was not at present inclined to bring it forward.

Swift was ill in the early spring, but John Hughes, who had taken a principal part with Steele in the musico-literary ventures of the winter, staged a successful opera in May. Tickell wrote a poem on the 'Prospect of Peace', which Addison went out of his way to praise in a review, though disapproving of the policy.[2] Pope produced a divine poem, the 'Messiah', which the *Spectator* published in full, giving it

---

[1] Bohn, vi. 635. [2] S. 523.

a whole number. The power of literary patronage exercised by the authors of the paper was great, and nobody had been more highly favoured than Pope was upon this occasion. Addison may have been desirous of placating this rising genius, who now helped him with some of his own papers. Pope had submitted to him his *Rape of the Lock*, which had been written in 1711 and first appeared anonymously in this year.[1] 'Merum sal', commented Addison, 'a delicious little thing.' Consulted as to proposed additions to the text, he gave the excellent literary advice to leave a fine piece unaltered. He might well be pleased with Pope's poem, which was the adoption in verse of his own prose vein of gentle raillery upon women, a product hardly conceivable before the *Tatler*.

The literary world of London was now congregated in that famous group which, because of its intimate relationships and the interplay of genius, was so fertile in prose and verse masterpieces. Since the days of Dryden, London had not known a literary oracle. Congreve, who had the necessary distinction, was too gentlemanly and aloof to play the part. In the lives of his friends he seems to appear and disappear like a benevolent ghost. Addison, who had a great reputation, had hitherto been too busy in administration to preside over literary London. But the success of the *Spectator*, the centre of all that was polite and witty, the day-to-day nature of its publication, and his release from administrative cares, now made him the natural monarch of a literary kingdom. Dryden had congregated the wits around him at Will's, but with the death of the master and the passage of time, Will's had become commonplace. Now that he had time to spare for his friends, indeed now that he must live much in their society to replenish his stock of materials and to maintain that awareness of the currents of thought and fashion which was so important a feature of the *Spectator*, Addison needed a new meeting place. It was in this year that he obtained possession of a house near Dryden's old retreat in Russell Street, and there set up Daniel Button as coffeeman. Button had been in Lady Warwick's service for some years as steward, and in that of Addison in the summer of

[1] *Miscellaneous Poems and Translations*, published by Lintott.

1711. It has been observed from a study of his orthography in the Countess's household accounts that his literary attainments were certainly not one of the attractions of his coffee-house.[1] The advantages of 'Button's' were twofold. In the first place it excluded all Tories but a few moderates such as Tickell. That party frequented Will's, which now tended to become their exclusive property. Button's was the preserve of the literary Whigs. It was also inclusive; it created the atmosphere in which Addison's genius could expand without hindrance. Dick Steele had never pretended to rival his friend at any time; at Button's all the company sat at Addison's feet.

Amongst his company, besides Steele, were Tickell, Budgell, Edward Young, Garth, Hughes, Harrison, Henry Carey, and Colonel Brett. Like Dryden, he fell into something of a daily routine. He often had Budgell and a secretary living with him, and he would work all morning at home and often dine privately with his household. Then, going to the coffee-house, he would stay until somewhat earlier than Dryden's customary hour of retiring,[2] though still too late for the delicate Pope and occasionally far into the morning.[3] Button's was not a club, but a coffee-house; a place where one met to talk artistically, and Addison's conversation was carefully considered and disciplined.[4] A club at this time was a body of men often not domiciled in any particular place, but meeting semi-formally with certain set purposes. Apologies for absence were in order. Such was the Kit-Cat, which met in many places. But the Kit-Cat was essentially aristocratic and highly distinguished; it included two orders, whose portraits ultimately hung at different levels in the room built by Tonson at Barn Elms. The great magnates were at eye-level, and the first flight of literary men could be descried above. This society did not provide at all for the lesser fry of Whig pamphleteers and poets, who were the receivers of patronage, as the Kit-Cats were on the whole the givers. To fill the need for a less exalted yet congenial literary and political society the year 1712 probably saw the foundation of the Hanover Club. In this group

---

[1] A. L. Cooke, *PMLA*, vol. lxxii (1957), pp. 373–89.
[2] Spence, p. 114.   [3] Ibid., p. 155.   [4] *S.* 476.

Addison was a regular attender and exercised a powerful influence, and Ambrose Philips was at one time its secretary. It also had aristocratic members, such as the Duke of Newcastle, who lent it their patronage. Its work was highly political and its meetings sufficiently formal to require minutes kept by Philips with occasional help from Addison.

The *Spectator* had given a noticeable impetus to the club and coffee-house life of London. It popularized the idea of good conversation in the persons of Sir Roger and his associates. In the ninth number Addison had written upon the subject:

Man is said to be a Sociable Animal, and, as an Instance of it, we may observe, that we take all Occasions and Pretences of forming our selves into those little Nocturnal Assemblies, which are commonly known by the Name of *Clubs*. . . . When Men are thus knit together, by a Love of Society, not a Spirit of Faction, and don't meet to censure or annoy those that are absent, but to enjoy one another: When they are thus combined for their own Improvement, or for the Good of others, or at least to relax themselves from the Business of the Day, by an innocent and chearful Conversation, there may be something very useful in these little Institutions and Establishments.

The club was deliberate, the coffee-house spontaneous; and by contrast Addison thus described an imaginary conversation at the St. James's upon receipt of the news of the death of King Louis:

The Speculations were but very indifferent towards the Door, but grew finer as you advanced to the upper end of the Room, and were so very much improved by a Knot of Theorists, who sat in the inner Room, within the Steams of the Coffee Pot, that I there heard the whole *Spanish* monarchy disposed of, and all the Line of *Bourbon* provided for in less than a Quarter of an Hour.[1]

Addison yielded readily to this society which he now had leisure to enjoy. Perhaps aware of temptation, he had discoursed in the 195th *Spectator* upon the virtues of temperance. He had a genuine liking for plain food.[2] But the practice of temperance in wine had not come easily to the impecunious student who had none the less found money to note the good vintage of San Marino, the newness of that of Albano, the variability of that of Geneva, and the badness of that at Bologna,[1] who had learned to savour the soil in a good wine, who had drunk altogether too deeply of rhenish at Hamburg and had reported himself surfeited with society and champagne at The Hague, who had been at such pains to procure reasonable claret by way of Dublin and who in the *Tatler* had deplored the adulteration of wine. Temperance must now have come with all the more difficulty when he need not fear that if he chose to drink he might not eat, and now that so many men of means were willing to pay the reckoning if they might have it said that they drank a pint of wine with Mr. Spectator. Addison's physical health was indifferent, and his character was undergoing the test of much admiration. Temperance was doubly necessary to him if both body and mind were not to fall victims to the solvent of too much indulgence in wine.

He continued to press Dawson on the punctual remittance of his quarterly payments from Ireland, and was importunate for twenty pounds due to him in July 'to make up a small Sum which I have just now occasion for'. He was delighted to be assured that he continued a Privy Councillor in Ireland and thus qualified for an allowance. Yet in spite of, or perhaps because of, this eagerness to collect everything which might be due to him as punctually as possible, he had been able to write his bond for £1,000, he kept a coach and four, and he contemplated visits to the Bath, a house in Kensington Square, and a seat in Parliament with equanimity. Addison had once been very poor, and though no longer so he remained anxiously money-conscious and clung to habits of thrift. He certainly abandoned all thought of going to Ireland in the summer when he was reassured as to his financial interests there.

After Parliament rose on 8 July he stayed in London and worked on the *Spectator*. The series of papers in June on the Pleasures of the Imagination had been a major *tour de force*, and thereafter he had left the conduct of the paper to Steele for a fortnight. Possibly he accompanied Lord Sunderland

[1] See Addison's *Travels*.

to Tunbridge Wells.[1] In mid-July he exchanged visits with Swift, wrote in the *Spectator* on the usefulness of belief in a supreme Being,[2] and published his verse translation of the twenty-third psalm. But these journalistic reveries were rudely interrupted by the Government on 1 August, when a stamp duty of a halfpenny per half-sheet was imposed on all printed periodicals. To many of the lesser publications this was a mortal blow. As Addison expressed it in his last penny *Spectator*: 'This is the day on which many eminent authors will probably publish their last words' and, confident in the popularity of the paper, he agreed to assume the duty and added a halfpenny to the price thus doubling the total to the twopence usually charged for more elaborate publications in an expensive format. The circulation fell by at least half, but the *Spectator* continued to show a profit. With a sure instinct for publicity Addison made use of complaints of the price to raise the public estimation of his paper:

> I find by several Letters which I receive daily, that many of my Readers would be better pleased to pay Three-Half-Pence for my Paper than Two-Pence. The ingenious *T. W.* tells me that I have deprived him of the best Part of his Breakfast. . . . A large Family of Daughters have . . . offered . . . unanimously to 'bate . . . the Article of Bread and Butter in the Tea Table Account, provided the *Spectator* might be served up to them every Morning as usual.[3]

Addison continued thus for a whole paper, skilfully insinuating the great importance attached to the *Spectator* by its readers. He ended with an admonition to buy them 'in the lump', if all else failed, ten thousand sets of collected volumes three and four being ready for sale in September and a similar quantity of the first two having been already disposed of. The two new volumes were dedicated to Henry Boyle, the friend, and to the Duke of Marlborough, the hero, of both authors of the *Spectator*. At this point Addison surveyed the course of his paper, and reaffirmed the principles governing its conduct. He felt entitled to ascribe to himself a measure of success:

> If I have any other Merit in me, it is that I have new-pointed

---

[1] *Protestant Post-boy*, 122; *British Mercury*, 258.　　[2] *S.* 441.　　[3] *S.* 488.

all the Batteries of Ridicule. They have been generally planted against Persons who appeared Serious rather than Absurd; or at best, have aimed rather at what is Unfashionable than what is Vicious. For my own part, I have endeavoured to make nothing ridiculous that is not in some measure Criminal. I have set up the Immoral Man as the Object of Derision. In short, if I have not formed a new Weapon against Vice and Irreligion, I have at least shewn how that Weapon may be put to a right use, which has so often fought the Battels of Impiety and Profaneness.[1]

While these lofty aims were being treated in the *Spectator* the affairs of Gulston Addison made little progress in India. Desiring to send home some tangible wealth, no matter how small a fraction of the whole, Benyon had dispatched to Addison a consignment of diamonds purchased out of the funds of the estate. These Addison sold in London for £600 with the help of Governor Pitt, with whom he seems to have been at some pains to remain on friendly terms. It then appeared that Gulston had advanced money most imprudently to a local trader who had since died, and whose ventures had failed. At a first inspection the estate had seemed to be worth somewhere in the neighbourhood of 30,000 pagodas, which when transmitted in the form of diamonds might have yielded £18,000, a very substantial sum. It now seemed that a dividend would hardly be available even to the legatees for some time to come. "'Tis a world of trouble I have met with and more I must undergoe before I have concluded these unhappy Accounts', wrote Benyon. Amongst the English at Madras with him was Henry Jolley, brother-in-law to Gulston, who had gone there, like Lancelot, on the understanding that the Governor would establish him in some profitable situation. Jolley added to Joseph's perplexity by writing extremely lengthy and barely intelligible letters about the condition of the estate. Two things, however, emerged clearly from the Jolley correspondence; the first, satisfactory, that in Jolley's opinion Benyon was 'a man of an unspoted Carractor'; the second, not so, that 'things were very despectible' and that there had been 'darke doeings' which Benyon had arrived too late to prevent. Even the Rev. George Lewis referred to

[1] *S*. 445.

the estate as 'so ruin'd an affair'. At the English end things were little better. Addison had been granted letters of administration of Lancelot's estate on 9 January. He had employed an attorney, Mr. Higgins, to advise him, and had consulted Governor Pitt and George Morton Pitt, the heir of the deceased John. But George was still a minor and so unable to deal with his interests, which were deeply involved with Gulston's estate. This further complicated a situation already almost beyond repair. Thus when Addison proved Gulston's will on 20 October he had as yet no prospect of any considerable benefit from his brother's inheritance.

It was this autumn that two of Addison's friends had died. One of these was his riotous-living Kit-Cat friend, General Tidcomb,[1] who courted Mrs. Manley and was an object lesson in all the moral teachings of the *Spectator* ignored. Pope wrote that his 'beastly laughable life is at once nasty and diverting';[2] and is is possible that Tidcomb was the source of some literary material. Appropriately enough, the press reported him simultaneously as dying in France and at Bath,[3] but he appears to have lived to die again in both June 1713[4] and June 1718[5] if all the authorities are to be believed. The other death was that of Henry Maynwaring, who had been powerful in Whig literary circles and had been a principal dispenser of patronage to the lesser writers. After his death Addison became increasingly the arbiter of preferment, his approval conferring not merely a literary blessing but political support and the possibility of substantial reward.[6] Addison had disposed of much patronage to his own family, and his friends seem to have prospered surprisingly through the support of his superiors. In 1710 in an *Essay towards the history of the Last Ministry* the author suggested that Addison should 'dream' a dream in the *Tatler* on the subject of patronage. By its distribution the *Spectator* was a powerful and inexpensive means of offering rewards, not only by its reviews, which could make an author famous in a day, but also by its advertisements which were used to

---

[1] J. Caulfield, *Memoirs of the Kit-Cat Club*.   [2] E. & C. v. 78.
[3] *Weekly Packet*, 10; *Post Boy*, 2704.
[4] D.N.B.; Boyer, *Political State*, v. 399.   [5] Caulfield, op. cit.
[6] See Professor Sherburn's remarks on this subject in his *Early Career of Alexander Pope*.

sell the writings of Addison's friends. Ambrose Philips's
Distrest Mother, for example, was puffed in this way.[1]
Addison now continued to keep an eye upon young
Pope, to whom he had sent a friendly message through
Steele in August, and whose 'Temple of Fame' he read and
approved in November. He had also given high praise in
the *Spectator* to the miscellaneous poems published for Pope
in May 1712: 'I am always highly delighted with the Discovery of any rising Genius among my Countrymen.'[2] Yet
with an instinct for subtly rebuking the young poet, Addison
chose a phrase which could be taken to contrast the generosity of his own attitude towards other literary men with the
envy for which he had reproved Pope. He also unhappily
coupled his praise with that allotted to Tickell's 'Prospect
of Peace', an indifferently good poem, and with a commendation of Ambrose Philips's *Pastorals*. He complimented both
the latter poets upon omitting fables out of pagan theology
from their work, a matter in which Tickell had flattered
Addison by following the example of the *Campaign*. A few
days later Tickell was permitted by Steele to offer more in-
cense, by the publication of his poem 'To the Supposed
Author of the *Spectator*', in which Addison figures as
'*British* Virgil' and is complimented on the manner of instruction upon which he particularly prided himself:

> Nor harsh thy precepts, but infus'd by stealth,
> Please while they cure, and cheat us into health.

But Pope recognized that he was expected to praise the
powerful dispenser of benedictions who had just published
his first known prose fragments to go into print;[3] 'of every
one's esteem he must be assur'd already', he cooed to Steele.
Addison desired that Pope should remain on good terms
with the literary Whigs; Pope thought it convenient to have
the goodwill of the *Spectator*. But there was no familiar intercourse between the two men.

As Christmas drew near the *Spectator* approached its end.
The sustained draught upon Addison's intellectual resources
was beginning to dry the fountain of his wit. As he later
expressed it:

---

[1] *S.* 290.   [2] *S.* 523.   [3] Ault, *Prose Works of A. Pope*, xxiv.

It would be well for all Authors, if . . . they knew when to give over, and to desist from any further Pursuits after Fame, whilst they are in the full Possession of it. . . . The Author indeed often grows old before the Man, especially if he treats on Subjects of Invention, or such as arise from Reflections upon Humane nature : . . . We find . . . that Men, who write much without taking Breath, very often return to the same Phrases and Forms of Expression, as well as to the same Manner of Thinking. Authors, who have thus drawn off the Spirit of their Thoughts, should lie still for some Time, till their Minds have gathered fresh Strength, and by Reading, Reflection, and Conversation, laid in a new Stock of Elegancies, Sentiments, and Images of Nature.[1]

It seems likely that these thoughts were a reflection of his reasoning in the autumn of 1712. The *Spectator* had run for over 500 numbers, of which Addison had provided half. He may have contributed to, edited, or corrected many others. The paper had a fame and popularity unknown to any former periodical publication, and nothing which might now be written in it could add to its stature. On the other hand the stamp duty had considerably reduced the circulation and lessened the profit; while Steele was under pressure to re-enter the field of direct political controversy and was contemplating a new and mainly political periodical. Addison, for his part, may have been tempted to end the *Spectator* because he was at last considering a production of *Cato*. A further reason was that the anonymity which had been scrupulously preserved had worn so thin as to be almost wholly destroyed. In August Addison had remarked that 'the Papers I present the Publick are like Fairy Favours, which shall last no longer than while the Author is concealed'.[2] The secret originally shared by an inner circle of friends had become common property.

The decision to end the paper having been taken, its conclusion proceeded in the same orderly fashion as its beginning, in marked contrast with the haphazard growth and abrupt ending of the *Tatler*. On 23 October Addison announced to his readers 'Sir Roger de Coverley is dead', thus providing himself with the opportunity to write a moving description of the knight's decease, as from the pen of

Edward Biscuit, his butler. Budgell relates that Addison killed Sir Roger to prevent his 'murder'.[1] During the 'life' of the knight, he had had occasion to protest to Steele about rough handling of his character, when he had been made to stray from the paths of entertaining idiosyncrasy into those of downright vice. Recalling that other hands had taken up the *Tatler* after he and Steele had laid it down, Addison foresaw that the *Spectator* might suffer a similar fate; and by putting Sir Roger beyond the power of other pens to spoil he made their task the more difficult. On 7 November it was announced that Will Honeycomb, incorrigibly fashionable bachelor, had married a farmer's daughter. Meanwhile negotiations had been proceeding with the publishers for the publication of the whole of the paper in collected form, and with this in view Charles Lillie had dropped out of the production on 2 October and Jacob Tonson junior had been added. On 10 November, the rights in one half of the paper were sold to Tonson and in the other half to Buckley, for the sum of £575 in each case, with an undertaking on the part of the authors that it would continue to the end of November, thus making up material for a seventh collected volume. The transaction was completed over a glass of wine at the 'Fountain' tavern.[2] Thereafter the little 'club' dispersed rapidly. On 20 November the Templar announced his intention of retiring to devote himself to his practice; four days later Captain Sentry retired to the country to manage his estate; and on 29 November Sir Andrew Freeport, only remaining member of the club besides the Spectator, ceased to belong thereto on giving up business and, like many a successful Whig merchant, setting up for a squire in Tory fashion. The public was well aware that the *Spectator* was drawing to its end. On 4 December Addison wrote his last paper, in which he seemed to foreshadow a further periodical at a future date; and on 6 December Dick Steele, writing in his own name, wound up the publication with the 555th number.

[1] 'Mr *Addison* was so fond of this Character, that a little before he laid down the *Spectator* (foreseeing that some nimble Gentleman would catch up his Pen the Moment he had quitted it) he said to an intimate Friend, *I'll kill Sir Roger, that no body else may murder him.*' The Bee, i. 27.

[2] Bohn, vi. 630.

That Steele was still thought of by the public as the principal author there is no doubt. Tickell makes this clear in his poem 'To the supposed Author of the *Spectator*' where, after discussing the paper in general, he says of the more exalted speculations therein:

> Such hints alone could British Virgil lend,
> And thou alone deserve from such a friend:
> A debt so borrow'd is illustrious shame,
> And fame when shar'd with him is double fame.

'*British* Virgil', 'Maro' of the *New Atalantis*, was a name often applied to Addison, and the sense of the passage makes it clear that Steele was thought of as conducting the enterprise, even if Addison dictated its policy. Once again Dick paid high tribute as editor to the friend whom he was careful to identify without actually naming. In *Spectator* 532 he had told his readers: 'I claim to myself the merit of having extorted excellent productions from a person of the greatest abilities, who would not have let them appear by any other means.' He now added: 'All the papers marked with a C, an L, an I or an O, . . . were given me by the gentleman of whose assistance I formerly boasted in the preface and concluding leaf of my *Tatlers*', and continued in the strain of adulation which he adopted throughout most of his life when writing of Addison. By contrast with this curious combination of identification and anonymity, several other contributors, including Pope, Hughes, Carey, Tickell, and Eusden, were thanked by name. This continued insistence upon a formal anonymity when the secret of authorship had become well known could not be attributed to any doubts as to the reputation which the *Spectator* might carry with it. It is therefore worth remembering that Addison had observed of Cato that he acquired more fame the less he sought it.[1] And while he may have acted with an exaggerated modesty from a belief that such was the correct course by the highest standards, or merely because it was congenial to him to do so, he also undoubtedly thought that as virtue in general pays material dividends, so modesty in particular is an excellent publicity medium.

---

[1] *S.* 255 (the observation is drawn from Sallust).

The *Spectator* was already famous throughout Europe and its reputation continued to grow rapidly. As Addison himself put it:

the general Reception I have found, convinces me that the World is not so corrupt as we are apt to imagine; and that if those Men of Parts who have been employed in viciating the Age had endeavoured to rectify and amend it, they needed not have sacrificed their good Sense and Virtue to their Fame and Reputation.[1]

There had been adverse critics, though few and feeble. Even Mrs. Manley regretted only that he had been led away from poetry, for which she thought him pre-eminently gifted, to write in prose for the wealth which she thought the *Spectator* would bring him: 'Why did he prefer Gain to Glory? Why chuse to be an idle Spectator rather than a Celebrator of those Actions he well knows how to design and adorn?'[2] But the overwhelming approval of the British public, as much a moral as a literary judgement, needed no critic to give it a voice. With it more tangible marks of goodwill frequently came to the authors. 'Mr. Spectator gives his most humble service to Mr. R.M. of Chippenham in Wilts, and hath received the partridges', ran an advertisement in No. 156. A generation later, Johnson reported, it was still a title to distinction merely to have made a single contribution to the paper, which he found well known even on his tour of the 'Hebrides'.

On the continent the friendly notices of Jean le Clerc in the *Journal Littéraire* proclaimed the merits of the English original and of the French translation which soon appeared: 'The finest writers in England have executed, in the *Spectator*, all the force of their reflections, all the delicacy of style and all the fire of imagination that can be conceived.' Versions in German and Dutch followed. There were imitators in Holland, in Hamburg, and in Scotland, still hardly thought of as a home territory. In England itself a fashion of writing had been established and a standard had been laid down, while the modishness of vice had been supplanted by the intellectual superiority of virtue. Addison thought that his humour, his criticism, and his moral dissertations might

---

[1] *S.* 262.   [2] *New Atalantis* (1736), iii. 218–19.

survive three centuries, and in the retrospect of four years found the influence of his paper considerable:[1]

There are very good Effects which visibly arose from the above-mentioned Performances and others of the like Nature; as, in the first Place, They diverted Raillery from improper Objects, and gave a new Turn to Ridicule, which for many Years had been exerted on Persons and Things of a sacred and serious Nature. They endeavoured to make Mirth Instructive, and if they failed in this great End, they must be allowed at least to have made it Innocent.

The influence of the *Spectator* on English thought and manners demands a volume for its consideration. Its immediate effect was spectacular: its ultimate contribution in the eighteenth century might be found to exceed that of any other work except the Bible.

[1] F. 45.

VII

CATO IN THE WILDERNESS
1713-1714

IT is a misfortune, though perhaps it could not have been
otherwise, that the *Spectator* concluded its brilliant
course without the participation of Jonathan Swift's
singular genius. Shortly after its ending, he met Addison
and Philips in the Mall and walked with them: 'they both
looked terrible dry and cold, a Curse of Party.' He reflected
that: 'I set Addison so right at first that he might have been
employed; and I have partly secured him the place he has',
which was of most doubtful truth. Both men were at the
height of fame and success and neither owed anything of
importance to the other; nor had they shared their mutual
triumphs which had been achieved after the dissolution of
their brief period of intimate friendship. The two men met
again on 17 February 1713 at the funeral of Harrison, the continuator of the *Tatler*,[1] who had been a friend of both and
a member of the circle at Button's. Thereafter came something of a *rapprochement* consequential upon similar movement between Lords Oxford and Halifax. In March Lord
Oxford dined with a group of Whigs, and Lord Bolingbroke,
who was also present, toasted Lord Somers in Swift's company. Swift recorded a meeting at his lodgings: 'I deny myself to everybody except about half a dozen, and they were
all here, and Mr. Addison one.' George Berkeley was one
of the company: 'I breakfasted with Mr. Addison at Dr.
Swift's lodgings. His coming in while I was there, and the
good temper he showed, was construed by me as a sign of
an approaching coalition of parties.'[2] Thereafter Swift procured an invitation to Addison to dine with Lord Bolingbroke on Good Friday, 4 April, but it was a distasteful part
and he foretold correctly: 'I suppose we shall be mighty
mannerly.' They sat till midnight, talked civilly of party.

[1] *Wentworth Papers*, 319.   [2] H.M.C. vii. 237.

Addison proposed Lord Somers's health, whereupon Swift cautioned him against mentioning Lord Wharton's, with the comment to the accompaniment of a general laugh that he believed Addison loved that nobleman as little as he. The pen-portrait of 'Verres' was a political act of violence which could never be atoned, and the overtures came to nothing, either between the parties or between Swift and Addison. The *Examiner* was attacking Addison's last political chief with its accustomed fury, as an accompaniment to a hostile investigation of his administration by a committee of the House of Commons. Addison could not offer Swift friendship without disloyalty.

The House reassembled on 9 April and amongst political matters which claimed Addison's attention was an election at Malmesbury. His colleague, Thomas Farrington, had died and an election became necessary to fill his seat. Sir John Rushout, Lord of the Manor, who had recently come of age, was chosen. Addison's electoral machine, headed by the two 'surgeons', would be at the disposal of his late pupil's brother. On 13 May Addison's responsibilities were reduced by the dissolution of the Irish Parliament, of which he had remained a member.[1] Meanwhile in England, two days after the choice of a congenial colleague at Malmesbury, volumes v, vi, and vii of the collected *Spectator* were published, dedicated to Lords Wharton and Sunderland, and Paul Methuen, all prominent Whigs.

It was but a short time since the ex-Secretary had complained of his impecunious circumstances; but that such an attitude was one of banter, or the result of a distinction which he made between spendable income and capital for investment, is apparent from the fact that he now purchased a substantial country property. He set up for a squire in a part of England which lay two or three days' travel from the world of fashion and politics in which he was a considerable figure. Bilton Hall near Rugby could be of no use for occasional visits from London and was in no sense a country villa, but a substantial house, mainly in the style of the sixteenth century, built in the stone of the district and standing on the brow of a low ridge overlooking a stream and

[1] *Irish Commons Journals*, ii and iii.

meadows beyond. With its purchase, Addison became Lord of the Manor of Bilton. The church stood a few yards behind the Hall, and its bells could be heard in Rugby when the wind sat in the right quarter. Bilton was agreeable enough, but at first sight there seemed to be no particular reason to commend it to a busy man of letters whose interests lay in London, who had a parliamentary seat in Wiltshire, and who occasionally visited Bath. But an Act of Parliament of the year 1710 prescribed that, to be eligible as a burgess, a candidate must draw £300 per annum from landed property. This was a Tory measure directed at the Whig merchants and those of their supporters in Parliament, such as Addison, who had no land. To a man of apprehensive temperament this Act may have seemed a threat likely to be made good against himself personally. Lawyers soon devised fictitious qualifications and other means by which the law could be satisfied; but these were not yet in being. If Addison felt that he had thus to qualify himself, then it may be that land beyond the immediate neighbourhood of London would involve a smaller outlay of capital. He knew Warwickshire from a childhood spent in the neighbouring county and may have come to know Bilton when journeying to the Charter-house or to Oxford. His recollections may have been re-newed when making the journey as Secretary to Ireland, for he observed to Dawson that Bilton 'lies in your way'. His step-mother still lived at Lichfield, which was not far distant, and it is possible that he thought that when Lord Warwick came of age, Bilton might be acceptable to the countess dowager. There is no doubt that the purchase of Bilton would meet one of Addison's most insistent personal needs, and one which he proposed to satisfy in his ultimate retire-ment—that for communion with unreformed nature.

A love for the countryside was much in advance of an age which still looked upon it as crude and upon nature as something to be tamed. Addison's tastes in this matter originated in his early youth in the upper Avon valley. But he had never lived with country folk at any later time, and in those early days he was too young to savour them; con-sequently in his writings he treated them with undisguised contempt. He had ridiculed country gentlemen in both

Tatler and *Spectator*, he had laughed at country fashions[1] and country manners,[2] at country sports[3] and game preserving.[4] Yet he had a theoretical admiration for the country life, born perhaps of his reading of the *Georgics* and Pastorals,[5] and elaborated by a study of the *Criticon* and *Oraculo* of Gracian.[6] For the yeoman freeholder he had an unqualified respect founded in Whig political principles.[7] His ideas about the country-side were thus formed upon his boyhood recollections of wild nature, his reading of the poets, and his observations when travelling abroad and examining the gardens of palaces and great houses.

Superimposed on these slight foundations had been a rational curiosity about natural phenomena. Sea-shells,[8] wild flowers and trees,[9] birdsong, which he frequently praised and obviously delighted in, and birds which he found more lovable than the fruit which they destroyed, joined company with slightly ludicrous amateur experiments with volcanic gases, speculations about the bubbles in Lake Constance and the 'floating islands' near Rome,[10] and an analysis of the habits of the domestic hen.[11] He had read extensively in such works upon natural history as were then available,[12] and exalted the study of nature,[13] analysing its harmony,[14] and preferring its study, which he declared novel,[15] to that of metaphysics.[16] He had even sought to place man within a concept of the natural creation. He gave a religious turn to his speculations,[17] related the study of nature to that of the deity,[18] and suggested that it might reveal the ways of God to man.[19] A disciple of Locke and Newton, of Boileau and Bayle, he felt that the glory of an all-wise contriver could be revealed in the compilation of a natural encyclopaedia.[20] Yet for all his study of 'natural' philosophy and his enthusiasm for the branches of natural study, Addison had retained his contempt for what he considered to be students of minutiae. Collectors of butterflies,[21] minute students of insects, field work in general, and in particular the Royal Society, were ridiculed

[1] *S.* 129.   [2] *S.* 119, 122.   [3] *S.* 115.   [4] *S.* 131.
[5] *S.* 15, 155.   [6] 'Addison on Novelty', *P.M.L.A.* lii, 1937, p. 1126.
[7] *S.* 122.   [8] *Travels*: 'Monaco, Genoa.'   [9] *Letter from Italy*.
[10] *Travels*: 'Naples, Switzerland, Rome'.   [11] *S.* 120, 121.
[12] *S.* 69, 120, 212.   [13] *S.* 565.   [14] *S.* 120.   [15] *S.* 420.   [16] *S.* 519
[17] *T.* 100.   [18] *T.* 119.   [19] *S.* 393.   [20] *S.* 121.   [21] *T.* 221.

as preoccupied with unimportant hair-splitting unbecoming
to a rational man. He failed to perceive that broad generaliza-
tions can only be founded upon patient investigation in
small fields of knowledge.

But the purchase of Bilton Hall and manor with a thousand acres of land, which was completed on 27 February for
the sum of £8,000,[1] was neither entirely a political necessity,
nor a concession to a deeply felt, if curiously self-contra-
dictory, love of nature. Ownership of a country estate was a
confirmation of worldly success. Addison's wealthy friend,
Sir Gilbert Heathcote, Lord Mayor of London, like Sir
Andrew Freeport of the *Spectator* and many another Whig
merchant, purchased an estate in the country for his retirement. Successful administrators such as William Blaythwayt
did the same. In the purchase of Bilton, moreover, Addison
took a step nearer to his ideal of the Augustan statesman.
He provided himself with the country seat, the pleasant
solitude to which to retire from politics or the heats of
'Rome' in summer. This transaction therefore set the seal of
success upon his carefully poised scheme of life in a manner
easily recognizable by his contemporaries.

It was with the Roman concept of citizenship that Addison's second important project for the early months of the
year 1713 was concerned. He was now occupied once more
upon the manuscript of *Cato*. Drafted in Oxford and read by
Dryden, revised in Rome and shown to Tonson at The
Hague, shown to Cibber and Steele soon after Addison's
return to England in 1704 and later read by Swift, the play
reached the length of four acts. It embodied Addison's ideas
upon the nature and purpose of tragedy. The fact that he had
set his principles out in the *Spectator* doubtless had made him
reluctant to produce a play which might fall short of his own
precepts :[2]

As a perfect tragedy is the noblest production of human nature,
so it is capable of giving the mind one of the most delightful and
most improving entertainments. . . . Diversions of this kind wear

[1] Addison was described in the deed as a parishioner of St. Margaret's,
Westminster, which he would be in virtue of his membership of Parliament.
This probably indicates that he had no permanent abode in London.
[2] *S*. 39, 40, 42, and 44.

out of our thoughts every thing that is mean and little. They cherish and cultivate that humanity which is the ornament of our nature.[1]

Thereafter he had entered in detail into the design and production of tragedy, his thoughts being the product of much study and all of them being applicable to his own play. It was therefore probably with good reason that Steele observed to Cibber of *Cato* that: 'whatever spirit Mr. Addison had shown in his writing it, he doubted that he would never have courage enough to let his Cato stand the censure of an English audience', adding that it had only been the amusement of leisure hours and had occupied little labour, and, probably incorrectly, that it was never intended for the stage.[2] Pope, who had now seen the manuscript, echoed Dryden's earlier judgement, saying that the piece was not theatrical enough for presentation and that Addison would gain sufficient fame by printing it, an opinion with which the author inclined to agree.[3] Until this time there seems to have been a consensus of opinion on this point, for Arthur Maynwaring had also read *Cato* and had pronounced against its being acted. He embodied the opinion of the Kit-Cat Club, and his judgement had probably been decisive.

But the need for a change of literary occupation had begun to impress itself upon Addison long before he ended the *Spectator*; and *Cato* lay ready to hand. Furthermore, John Hughes's *Siege of Damascus* and the success of Philips's *Distrest Mother*, an edifying and correct tragedy first performed on 17 March 1712,[4] probably encouraged him to look once more at his own play. The political and social atmosphere, to which Addison was remarkably sensitive, was favourable to a piece which would exalt the virtues of public life, and in particular Addison's Whig friends in the Kit-Cat were looking for political plays. The story of *Cato* was applicable at many points by contrast with the present political scene. Steele was importunate with Addison, and, having successfully packed the house for Philips's play, did

---

[1] *S.* 39.   [2] Cibber, *Apology*, ch. xiv.
[3] Spence, p. 196. Though Pope later maintained that he predicted the success of *Cato* to Caryll after reading it with tears in his eyes.
[4] *Occasional Verse of Richard Steele*, ed. R. Blanchard, p. 93.

not doubt of putting *Cato* beyond the power of ignorant
censure by procuring an appreciative audience. Philips must
almost certainly have joined in persuading Addison to revive
the project; but it was Hughes who, if his own account be
true, succeeded in inducing Addison to agree to the manuscript being completed,[1] and whom Addison then invited to
finish the fifth act. Besides his tragedy, Hughes had been
successful in writing operatic libretti, and his *Ode to the
Creator* had been published this year by Tonson on Addison's advice. But having thus permitted Hughes to undertake the task, Addison was spurred into activity by the
argument of his friends that the spirit of liberty should be
vindicated on the stage, and by a reviving enthusiasm for
the project of so many years. He took up his pen and himself completed the fifth act[2] in a few days of intense labour.
Steele, who had intended to produce one of his own plays,
immediately postponed his project and gave his whole
attention to the staging of *Cato*.

News of a play from the pen of the Spectator was soon all
over town. George Berkeley, who had made Addison's
acquaintance through the intermediary of Steele,[3] wrote on
27 March: 'Cato, a most noble play of Mr. Addison . . . is to
be acted in Easter Week . . . .'[4] Berkeley had been immediately
captivated: 'Mr. Addison has the same talents [as Steele] in
a high degree, and is likewise a great philosopher, having
applied himself to the speculative studies more than any of
the wits that I know. . . .'[5] The two men plunged together
into metaphysics, and Addison, who deplored the materialism of Halley, arranged a meeting between Berkeley and
Samuel Clarke[6] to discuss the reality of the existence of
sensible objects. Clarke was celebrated for his unorthodox
brilliancy in religion and philosophy and was well known
to Addison through his folio *Caesar* for which, through the
agency of Leibniz, he had procured the double page illustration of the aurochs, and which he had reviewed favourably
in the *Spectator*.[7] Berkeley now entered with enthusiasm into

---

[1] Oldmixon, *Essay on Criticism*, 1729.
[2] Tickell, Preface to Addison's *Works*.
[3] H.M.C. vii. 238.   [4] Ibid. 237.   [5] Ibid.
[6] K. Stock, *Memoirs of Berkeley*, 2nd edn., 1784, p. 4.
[7] *S.* 367.

the *Cato* project. Swift reported the news to Stella a week later, and on the morning of 6 April attended a rehearsal at Drury Lane. Addison was present on the stage giving directions and receiving advice from a small group of friends, including Berkeley. Numerous corrections in the text had been made by Pope and accepted by Addison, including a new final line to the play.[1] Mrs. Oldfield, mistress of the dead Arthur Maynwaring, who through him had probably seen the play considerably before this time, also contributed suggestions from the fund of her theatrical experience. Edward Wortley had sent the manuscript down to his recently married wife, Lady Mary, now pregnant in the country, with a request for a critique. She had responded with a number of detailed alterations and suggestions, many of which Addison accepted while requesting with characteristic caution that her adverse criticisms be kept private. The most important of her contributions were an argument for more numerous lines on 'liberty' and for rhyming couplets at the ends of the acts. Both were accepted by the poet and contributed materially to the effectiveness of the play, though the latter point incurred the severe censure of Voltaire in later years.[2] Presumably Jacob Tonson was present at the rehearsal and liked the much corrected piece, for the next day he purchased the copyright for the sum of £107. 10*s.*, a considerable price, but probably one of the most remunerative that he ever paid, and one which bears tribute to the acuteness of his judgement of the English public.

It was on 14 April that the first performance took place. The cast was filled with the famous names of the stage. Anne Oldfield took the part of Cato's daughter, Cato was played by Booth, Juba by Wilks, and Syphax by Cibber. Mrs. Porter, Keen, Mills, Powell, Ryan, and Bowman took the remaining titles. The acting was beyond reproach except for that of Cibber who was criticized by Addison and Booth at the rehearsal and later by the public, on the ground that

[1] Spence, p. 151.
[2] Second Epistle Dedicatory to 'Zaïre'. For some interesting discoveries in this connexion see R. Halsband, 'Addison's Cato and Lady Mary Wortley Montagu', *P.M.L.A.*, vol. lxv (1950).

he exaggerated his part; while a French spectator likened his declamation to the dismal cry of a London watchman intoning 'Past twelve o'clock and a cloudy morning'.[1] But this was no more than a small blemish and Cibber hotly defended his playing. To encourage such a powerful company Addison waived his benefit money, thus permitting the managers to spend lavishly upon the production. Pope, now a fashionable poet, provided the prologue:

> To wake the soul by tender strokes of art,
> To raise the genius, and to mend the heart;
> To make mankind, in conscious virtue bold,
> Live o'er each scene, and be what they behold:
> For this the Tragic Muse first trod the stage,
> Commanding tears to stream thro' ev'ry age . . .
> Our scene precariously subsists too long
> On *French* translation, and *Italian* song.
> Dare to have sense your selves; assert the stage,
> Be justly warm'd with your own native rage.

Pope's lines were reminiscent of the crusading spirit of *Rosamond*; there was the same objection to foreign originals and translations, and the same appeal for native talent.

When the performance opened Addison was supported in a side box by George Berkeley and other friends, and burgundy and champagne were on hand. Berkeley reported that Addison was 'a very sober man', but he partook freely on this occasion. It was alleged that he was too nervous to appear in the front of the house, but that a succession of messengers to and from the box reported upon the state of the audience.[2] Parts of the prologue were hissed, because the public expected a highly political play, and read into the lines a meaning not intended. But Steele and the Kit-Cat had filled the house with a friendly audience,[3] or at least with one which it was hoped would do as Addison had enjoined upon theatre-goers in the *Tatler*: 'Every one should on these Occasions show his Attention, Understanding, and Virtue.'[4]

The play was received with thunderous applause. The Tory Lord Harley, in the next box to the author, was seen to

---

[1] Le Blanc, *Letters on the English and French Nations*, London, 1747.
[2] T. Cibber, *Lives*, iii. 313.
[3] Steele: Dedication to the *Drummer*, 1721.   [4] *T.* 122.

applaud heartily all of the lines which were thought to reflect
to the credit of the Whigs and to be designed against the
Government, thus setting a fashion in contention as to
which party should applaud the loudest.[1] As the prologue
was by Pope, who had some Tory connexions, so the
epilogue was by Dr. Garth, a strong Whig. Mainly for the
ladies, it was little apropos the play, and was the subject of
adverse comment on this account. But it carried some witty
couplets spoken by Mrs. Porter:

> The woes of wedlock with the joys we mix;
> 'Tis best repenting in a coach and six.

Addison evidently preferred Garth's lines to those offered
him by Lady Mary Wortley, who sought in this way to
express her admiration for the play.

The fame of *Cato* had run before and was immediately
multiplied many-fold by the mighty success of the first
night. On 23 April Gay wrote: 'Cato affords universal discourse, and is received with universal applause.'[2] On the last
day of the month Pope wrote to Caryll: 'The town is so fond
of it, that the orange wenches and fruit women in the Park
offer the books at the side of the coaches, and the Prologue
and Epilogue are cried about the streets by common
hawkers.'[3] Writing from Paris to thank Addison for a copy
sent to him by way of Simon Harcourt, Prior wrote, 'it can
certainly receive no greater compliment than that all parties
like it and everybody fancies his friend to be Cato.'[4] Cibber
recalled that it was played to constantly crowded houses and
was profitable to the company; and we have it on the
authority of Tickell that the run came to an end in May
only 'because one of the performers became incapable of
acting a principal part'.[5] Berkeley more interestingly tells
us that it would have run another month but 'Mrs. Oldfield
can not hold out any longer, having had for several nights
past, as I am inform'd, a midwife behind the scenes, which is
surely very unbecoming the character of Cato's daughter...'.[6]
Such was the success of the play, and so subtly ambiguous or

[1] H.M.C. vii. 238.   [2] Nichols, *Literary Anecdotes*, vi. 84.
[3] Sherburn, i. 175.   [4] C. K. Eves, *Matthew Prior* (1939).
[5] Preface to Addison's *Works*, 1721.   [6] H.M.C. vii. 239.

strictly non-party were the political innuendoes, that, as Lord
Castlecomer reported on 28 April, 'the Ministry has been
obliged to come into the applause. Now the word is given
that Cato must mean either the Lord Treasurer or Bolingbroke.'[1] With a famous gesture the latter had summoned
Booth to his box after a performance and presented him
with a purse of fifty guineas for 'defending the cause of
Liberty so well against a perpetual dictator', an allusion to
the fallen Duke of Marlborough, who had wished to accept
the post of Captain General for life. This, Peter Wentworth
rightly thought, 'was a home strock'.[2] But not to be thus
outdone, the Whigs also collected a purse and set about
devising an equally effective sentence, while both parties
flocked to the play. Astonished at its success, Pope wrote to
John Caryll on 30 April:

Cato was not so much the wonder of Rome itself in his days,
as he is of Britain in ours; and tho' all the foolish industry possible
had been used to make it a party play, yet what the author once
said of another may the most properly be applied to him on this
occasion.

> Envy it self is dumb, in wonder lost,
> And factions strive, who shall applaud him most.

The numerous and violent claps of the Whig party on the one side
the theatre, were echoed back by the Tories on the other, while the
author sweated behind the scenes with concern to find their
applause proceeding more from the hand than the head.

The controversy was soon transferred to the more discerning audience of the reading public. *Cato* ran into a third
edition by 29 April[3] and through eight by the end of the
year. It had also by then been printed at Edinburgh, Dublin,
and The Hague, and was translated into French in London
by Abel Boyer. Such was the demand that by 14 May when
the fourth edition was current there was also a pirated text
in circulation, against which Tonson cautioned the public
by advertisement.[4] Addison had intended to dedicate the
piece when published to an unidentified person, probably
Sarah, Duchess of Marlborough. He was embarrassed

[1] H.M.C. vii. 246.   [2] *Wentworth Papers*, 330.
[3] *Post Boy*, 2804.   [4] Ibid. 2810.

by those who made *Cato* a Tory play and such a dedication would have made his loyalty quite clear. The queen, probably on political advice, intimated that she would be pleased if asked to accept a dedication herself, a high but embarrassing honour.[1] Such a move would place Addison in a difficult position, for the two women, each formidable, had quarrelled beyond reconciliation, and a dedication to the queen would have confirmed Tory claims to the play and mortally offended the Marlboroughs to whom Addison was already deeply committed by the *Campaign* and *Rosamond*. Perhaps for this reason *Cato* appeared without a dedication, a step on Addison's part which in itself lent weight to his writing as suggesting that he was above the necessity to seek patronage.

Another and more agreeable source of embarrassment was the number of poets who sent verses to the author, either from a real admiration of his work or because they wished to enjoy for their own lines the circulation of which *Cato* was assured. One such with a just claim to have his lines printed was John Hughes; but even to him Addison wrote regretting that he could not print the proffered piece. His characteristic excuse was that: 'as my play has met with an unexpected Reception I must take particular care not to aggravate the Envy and Ill-Nature that will rise of course upon me.' He had, he added, received other poems and if he attached one to his play he would offend the writers of the others. Hughes replied protesting that he had no thought of publication and agreeing with Addison's opinion: 'I cannot but applaud . . . your chaste enjoyment of fame, which I think equally above envy and incapable of receiving any addition.'

Others who wrote lines to Addison were Steele, wittily:

> Forgive the fond ambition of a friend,
> Who hopes himself, not you, to recommend
> And join th'applause which all the Learn'd bestow
> On one, to whom a perfect work they owe.

Edward Young from All Souls, admiringly:

> To your renown all ages you subdue,
> And Caesar fought, and Cato bled for you.

[1] Tickell, Preface to Addison's *Works*.

Digby Cotes, a Fellow of the same Foundation, and a friend of Young and Tickell, who was associated with the editing of later editions of *Musarum Anglicanarum*, learnedly:

> How would old Rome rejoice, to hear you tell
> How just her Patriot liv'd, how great he fell!

and Lawrence Eusden, who wrote at length and with the public spirit becoming to a future laureate, beginning:

> 'Tis nobly done thus to enrich the stage,
> And raise the thoughts of a degenerate age,
> To show, how endless joys from freedom spring:
> How life in bondage is a worthless thing.

Remembering perhaps their common mortification at the hands of the Duke of Somerset, he extended himself to show how Addison had triumphed in turn in many branches of letters. Thomas Tickell, who in his lines to the author of *Rosamond* had been careful to flatter Addison upon the literary point and purpose of the piece, repeated this in his lines on *Cato*:

> France boasts no more, but, fearful to engage,
> Now first pays homage to her rival's stage,

a reference to the classical 'correctness' of the play as judged by the teaching of the French critics. Ambrose Philips struck the note of humourless virtue:

> The mind to virtue is by verse subdu'd;
> And the true Poet is a publick good.

There were other poems, some anonymous; but not until the seventh edition of *Cato* appeared on 27 June[1] did Addison permit some tributes to be published with his play.

After this rapturous welcome in London, *Cato* proceeded to Oxford where it was of particular interest because of its classical theme and scholarly background. Moreover the Oxford antecedents of the poet added to the attraction of the play. Once a don, he had attained the highest literary fame, administrative distinction, and political success, as well as material wealth; and his abstention from party polemics

---

[1] Advertised in *Guardian*, No. 92.

in the *Spectator* had caused his name to stand high in the predominantly Tory Common Rooms.[1] Speaking of Oxford's judgement of dramatists, Cibber recalled that: 'The only distinguish'd Merit allow'd to any modern Writer was to the Author of *Cato*. . . .' But the fame of the London performances had in any case ensured a full house:

> . . . on our first Day of acting it our House was, in a manner, invested; and Entrance demanded by twelve a Clock at Noon, and before one, it was not wide enough for many, who came too late for Places. The same Crowds continued for three Days together (an uncommon Curiosity in that Place) . . .[2]

Once more Addison allowed the whole of the first night's proceeds to the company, thus again ensuring that the excellence of the production did not suffer from lack of funds. On this occasion the prologue was by Tickell, handsomely complimenting author and university in some sprightly lines:

> Great Cato's self the glory of the Stage,
> Who charms, corrects, exalts, and fires the age,
> Begs here he may be try'd by Roman laws;
> To you, O fathers, he submits his cause;
> He rests not in the people's general voice
> Till you, the Senate, have confirm'd his choice.

Tickell's lines are interesting because they show that Addison had now come to be identified with the personality of Cato and to be referred to simply by that name. In the Oxford audience there must have been old friends from Magdalen and Christ Church who knew too well that the character of the poet in no way corresponded with that of the hero of the play. But the public could not be aware of this, and there was a younger Oxford literary group, Tickell, Edward Young, Digby Cotes, and, formerly, William Harrison, who were Addison's fervent admirers from a greater distance. Amongst the older men there was equal enthusiasm for the play. Dr. Smalridge sedately recorded: 'gave myself the pleasure of seeing Cato acted and heartily wish all Discourses from the Pulpit were as instructive and edifying, as pathetic and affecting, as that which the Audience was then enter-

---

[1] S. 560.   [2] Cibber, *Apology*, ch. xiv.

tained with from the Stage.'[1] Thus the play became a universal favourite. In the autumn it was revived for a further series of performances at Drury Lane and by the end of the year had cleared an unprecedented sum of £1,350 to each of the managers.

The success of Addison's play was not to be explained by any one reason and certainly not by its dramatic merits alone. As has been seen, the staging of the piece was so nicely judged that it caught the temper of politics and expressed the feelings of the best Englishmen of their day in both political parties more eloquently than they could do themselves. As Cibber put it:

let us call to mind the noble spirit of Patriotism which that play then infus'd into the breasts of a free people that crowded to it; . . . the sublime Sentiments of Liberty in that venerable Character rais'd in every sensible Hearer such conscious Admiration . . . as even demanded two almost irreconcileable Parties to embrace and join in their equal Applauses of it.[2]

But though extolling political virtues *Cato* was not intended by its author as a party but as a national appeal, and, as Pope hinted, Addison was mortified at the fate which befell it at the hands of partisans. He had striven to express noble political sentiments while avoiding party excitement, even inducing Pope to alter his 'Britons, arise' to the less inflammatory 'Britons, attend'. He probably therefore had his own play in mind when he wrote that 'An Author is very much disappointed to find the best Parts of his Productions received with Indifference, and to see the Audience discovering Beauties which he never intended'.[3]

But if the appeal to party rather than to national feeling was largely unintentional, the moral purpose of the play was a principal part of its author's design, and an important element in its success. It is interesting to recall that as a young man at Oxford Addison had complained of Spenser that 'the dull moral lies too plain below',[4] and had remarked that 'Precepts of morality . . . are so abstracted from Ideas of sense that they seldom give an opportunity for those

<hr>

[1] Graham, p. 484.   [2] Cibber, *Apology*, ch. xiv.
[3] F. 34.   [4] 'Account of the Greatest English Poets.'

beautiful descriptions and images which are the spirit and life of Poetry'.[1] But the middle-class element in the British character, dominant at the Commonwealth period, and subdued but never destroyed during the Restoration, was again stirring and was now ripe for the appeal to virtue, if not by precept, then at least in the example of a noble Roman. The elements which approved the more sombre *Spectators* also applauded *Cato*, which, though as a moral tragedy it was by no means a novelty, was the first such play to strike the imagination of the whole British people. It was therefore thought of as new. But the novelty in *Cato* lay not in its purpose, but in its literary quality. It was almost unique in an age when so many plays were influenced by Shakespeare or by the Restoration stage, in that it was not the product of either. Voltaire even suggests that the famous soliloquy which it contains challenged comparison with Shakespeare. Though the play was calculated to evoke the genius of contemporary England, and though its material was of orthodox classical stock, the critical theories of which it was the product, partly inherited from Dryden, were almost wholly of French origin. Addison thus set out, not merely to plant virtue in his hearers, but also to set a pattern of correctness to dramatists. His previous works contained many implications that the London theatre was full of ridiculous anomalies.[2] These it was his purpose to discredit by his example. Steele tells us that Addison seldom attended the theatre,[3] but formed his ideas of the stage from reading plays, including French plays, in the solitude of his study, there applying to them the writings of the critics. This probably accounts for the lack of dramatic quality in *Cato*, which must have been perceived and remedied by so sensitive an observer of human reactions, had he been really familiar with the theatre audience. Perhaps for the same reason *Cato* stands apart from English theatrical tradition and closer to that of France.

Because one of the governing principles of Addison's dramatic writing was an application of the neo-classical rules of correctness, and because of his own innate caution,

[1] *Essay on Virgil's* Georgics.
[2] e.g. *S.* 89, 195, 446.   [3] *Drummer*: Preface.

negative rather than positive influences dominate his greatest composition. Though dealing with the high passion of great events, it does so in philosophic calm; there is no poetic rage. Macaulay, an admirer of the play, remarked upon the uniform quality of the rhetoric throughout the speeches.[1] Its strength lies in the eloquence of its appeal to reason for virtue. Voltaire thought it 'faite pour un auditoire un peu philosophe et très-républicain'.[2] Reading it in the heat of Calcutta, Macaulay scribbled in the margin: 'There is plenty of fine declamation in the play, and one or two good dramatic touches. But it is even colder . . . and more turgid than I thought—in the love scenes quite unbearable.'[3] Voltaire, though an admirer of the poet, thought the same:

> Addison . . . .
> C'était le poëte des sâges,
> Mais il était trop concerté;
> Et dans son Caton si vanté,
> Les deux filles, en vérité,
> Sont d'insipides personnages.
> Imitez du grand Addison
> Seulement ce qu'il a de bon.[4]

Indeed according to Pope the love scenes, universally condemned by later critics, were an afterthought, added as a concession to the public. Voltaire crystallized his condemnation in a phrase: 'Le sage Addison eut la molle complaisance de plier la sévérité de son caractère aux mœurs de son temps, et gâta un chef-d'œuvre pour avoir voulu plaire.'[5] The love scenes, as Lady Mary had pointed out before the play was acted, were irrelevant to its main purpose, and *Cato* was later published without them and lost nothing thereby.[6] Not only are they irrelevant, but Addison, who pleased women so well in the *Spectator*, was unable to portray them on the stage and in particular to do so in circumstances where their action was to be revealed under the stress of great and heroic events, with which he was not familiar. In Cato he depicted virtue in public life, of which he had

---

[1] *Misc. Works*, 1st edn., p. 222.   [2] Voltaire, *De la Tragédie Anglaise.*
[3] See his copy of Addison's *Works* in the B.M.
[4] *Zaïre*: Epistle Dedicatory.   [5] *De la Tragédie Anglaise.*
[6] *Cato . . . without the love scenes*, London, 1764.

first-hand experience. His women possess a virtue which is not womanly, but that of men in women's clothes and subject to fainting. This is only the exaggeration of a defect noticeable in the principal characters. There is no person of either sex in *Cato* who lives like Sir Roger in the *Spectator*, and a heavy moral purpose dominates them all and leads them to act unnaturally. Moreover the application of artificial rules of drama led Addison to use the same scene throughout the piece, thus further reducing its dramatic quality by depriving his audience of the benefit of the considerable technical skill in scene construction which was a heritage from the Restoration stage; while the small number of characters yet further restricted the poet's scope. Thus the two principal defects of the play: its narrow range and the poorness of its character drawing, arise from its principal claims to merit, that is to say its neo-classical correctness, its refusal, except in the matter of the love scenes, to make concessions to the 'corrupt' taste of the London audience; and its powerful moral theme.

The brilliant success of *Cato* made it difficult for the critics to attack. Pope circulated a couple of coarse epigrams invited by the contrast between the character of Cato's daughter and the private life of Anne Oldfield, and by the political behaviour of the audience. But from a dramatic point of view *Cato* could only be assailed by one who had sufficient erudition to perceive its weakness and to discount its popularity and courage to defy public opinion. Of this species of critic, Dennis was the unique example. Meanwhile there were many prose eulogies. In line with government policy, the *Examiner* carried a laudatory review on 27 April. Many other periodicals and authors continued the strain and for some years there was a procession of commendatory pamphlets. Sir Richard Blackmore, whose *Creation* Addison had advertised and applauded in the *Spectator*,[1] was still praising the play several years later.[2] But Dennis lost no time in his attack, publishing his *Remarks upon Cato* in July 1713.[3] Like Addison, who was well acquainted with his scholarly writings, Dennis was a champion of the neo-

[1] S. 313, 339.   [2] *Essays upon Several Subjects.*
[3] Advertised in the *Examiner*, iv. 18.

classical movement in drama. He rightly perceived that the
success of this play was due to several causes other than
literary merit. This outraged his sense of propriety and the
passage of time and controversy converted his literary
indignation into personal rancour. He had perhaps not yet
associated Addison directly with his former quarrels with
Steele in the *Spectator*; and though he resented the papers of
criticism upon Milton as founded on an unacknowledged
debt to his own writings, he may not have attributed them
to Addison at this time.[1] But he bitterly resented the policy
both of the *Tatler* and of the *Spectator*, which had recently[2]
returned to the attack upon his theory of 'poetic justice' with
the argument that 'the best of Men may deserve Punishment,
but the worst of Men cannot deserve Happiness'. The Duke
of Buckingham had apparently advised Dennis against an
attack on *Cato* on the ground that Addison had not been the
author of the objectionable passages in the periodicals. But
the critic retorted that 'He went share in the Profits, and more
than share in the Reputation . . . the attacking me . . . was
not only an Assassination, but one of the blackest sort'.[3] He
therefore undertook an analysis of *Cato* and whether or not
he was encouraged thereto by Pope as he afterwards alleged,
he certainly had plenty of legitimate ground for his action,
and Lintott, Dennis's publisher, could expect profit from a
criticism of the great literary success of the year, besides
enjoying an attack upon the property of his rival, Tonson.

Dennis probably wrote from the text without seeing the
play acted. He thought it pretentious and hollow, and that
in its endeavour to observe the unities it lost its probability.
Cato, he pointed out, was unfitted to be the central figure of
tragedy because he was a Stoic, and the play for this reason
failed to move either pity or terror, a pertinent observation in which he had been anticipated by Lady Mary in her
advice to the poet. Addison himself had described the
character of Cato as 'rather awful than amiable',[4] thus excluding pity. Dennis's critical reasoning was sound, but his
writing was heavy and ill natured. He took the success of the

---

[1] J. Dennis, *Observations on the Paradise Lost*, provides an interesting
comparison.   [2] *S.* 548.
[3] J. Dennis, *Critical Works*, ed. Hooker, ii. 399.   [4] *S.* 169,

play as an immoral conspiracy between the author and the public, and in his opening attack inadvertently wrote an excellent puff for both:

I have maturely considered both the general and violent Applause with which that Tragedy has been receiv'd; That it was acted Twenty Days together; That Ten thousand of 'em have been sold since the Time it was printed; That ev'n Authors have publish'd their Approbation of it, who never before lik'd anything but themselves; That Squire Ironside,[1] that grave offspring of ludicrous Ancestors,[2] has appear'd at the Head of them; and, that things have been carry'd to that amazing Height, either by French Extravagance, or English Industry, that a French-man is now actually translating this Play into French, which is a thing beyond example. . . .

Such members of the public as could be brought to read this grim document were inclined, like Macaulay in later years, to agree that 'Dennis's criticisms have a good deal of truth in them,'[3] but also to admire the diction and sentiments of *Cato*. Matthew Prior, to whom Dennis sent a copy of his pamphlet, perhaps knowing that his dislike of Addison was shared in that quarter, answered evasively, speaking of 'the noble Errors of some English Poems and the great strength and judgment of the criticisms upon them.'[4] Had there been no dramatic sequel to Dennis's pamphlet it would have been forgotten in the general chorus of praise, such as George Sewell's *Observations upon Cato*, the anony-mous *Cato Examin'd*, the *Life and Character of Cato*, *Mr. Addison Turn'd Tory*, and an article carried in the *Flying Post*.[5] There was even a publication of Plato's 'Of the Immortality of the Soul' giving for its title-page excuse for appearance the fact that it was a work 'mentioned in the tragedy of Cato'. The public thus inclined to the robust view that much of Dennis's criticism arose from the failure of his own plays and the success of Addison's writing.[6]

---

[1] Steele in the *Guardian*.   [2] The *Tatler* and *Spectator*.
[3] See his notes in his copy of Addison's *Works* in B.M.
[4] C. K. Eves, *Matthew Prior* (1939).   [5] No. 3369.
[6] For example, in 1720 *A Critick No Wit: or, Remarks on Mr. Dennis' late play . . . In a letter from a Schoolboy to the Author* contained material appropriate to its title such as 'you neither have Genius or Judgment to be the Author of any Dramatick Piece whatsoever, vid. Your own Remarks on Cato'.

It is not proven that Pope was responsible for encouraging Dennis to attack the piece which he had corrected and for which he had provided a prologue. But whether or not he was involved at the earlier stage, on 28 July he published an attack upon Dennis, whose *Remarks* had appeared on 9 July. This was a revenge for Dennis's attack upon the *Essay on Criticism* two years before. In Pope's pamphlet a well-known practitioner in lunacy was made to report upon the 'strange and deplorable Frenzy of Mr. John Dennis'. It was coarse, brutal, and brilliant. Addison had been approached about the project before publication but had refused to be associated with it. He now read the pamphlet with strong disapproval. He respected Dennis's critical ability, and he probably agreed with much of his unreadable but solidly sensible work. He would thus wish to reassure Dennis that he had not taken part in Pope's attack, but to avoid being drawn into a lengthy and acrimonious exchange of letters with him. He was therefore careful to place not one but two literary buffers between himself and the outraged critic, when he caused Dick Steele to write to Lintott, the critic's publisher, on 4 August, in the following terms:

> Mr. Addison desir'd me to tell you, that he wholly disapproves the Manner of treating Mr. *Dennis*. . . . When he thinks fit to take Notice of Mr. Dennis's Objections to his Writings, he will do it in a way that Mr. *Dennis* shall have no Reason to Complain of.

It has been suggested that in disavowing Pope's pamphlet Addison was moved mainly by a desire to keep the peace in the ranks of Whig authors, of whom Dennis was one. This consideration was probably present to his mind. It has also been suggested that he intended a subtle rebuke to Steele, who was suspect of abetting Pope in this matter.[1] But such theories are unnecessary in explanation of an action wholly characteristic of the man who had sought every kind of protection for his name in connexion with the *Tatler* and *Spectator*. Indeed it was Pope himself who most succinctly expressed Addison's attitude in the face of critics: 'I think

[1] N. Hooker in his edition of Dennis's *Critical Works*.

you are best reveng'd . . . , as the Sun was in the fable upon those batts and beastly birds . . . , only by *Shining on.*'[1]

The fame of *Cato* grew unabated in subsequent years. Its influence on the English stage was profound and there were many imitations. As a French critic has put it: 'A partir du succès de "Caton", les tragédies qui ne mettent pas en scène des Grecs ou des Romains seront à l'état de rares exceptions.'[2] Yet *Cato* remained the only neo-classical tragedy to enjoy extensive revivals. In the six years following its first appearance it is recorded as having had many major performances and doubtless there were numerous provincial and minor ones. It continued popular throughout the century, with, for example, six performances on record at the great playhouses in the season of 1738-9. There was also burlesque on the play from time to time, by Gay, Fielding, and others. Its influence upon the reading public was yet greater than upon the theatre audience. As early as 14 May the Duchess of Marlborough, stern despiser of poetry, found a quotation to her purpose for use in a letter to a cousin:

> May some chosen Curse, some hidden thunder from the shores of Heaven, red with uncommon Wrath, blast the Men[3] that use their greatness to their Country's ruin . . .[4]

Two generations later, Horace Walpole was at pains to learn passages by heart for the political necessities of his day[5] and frequently used them.

Beyond the frontiers of England esteem of *Cato* was greater in the author's lifetime than in the case of any previous English play. It became popular in Dublin and remained so for many years. It was translated into Italian by Addison's Florentine friend, Mario Salvini, and was performed and twice printed at Florence. It was also played at Leghorn under the auspices of the British merchants. The editor of the second Italian edition wrote in his preface:

---

[1] Sherburn, i. 183.   [2] L. Morel, *James Thomson*, 1895.
[3] Her political opponents. It must have cost Addison some effort to reconcile his real admiration for the Duke and his views upon moderation in politics with the violence with which the Duchess habitually expressed herself.
[4] ex W. S. Churchill, *Marlborough*, iv. 582.
[5] *Walpole Corr.*, ed. Lewis, ix. 23.

La presenta Tragedia del Catone, parto felicissimo, del noble espirito del Sig. Addison, essendo per communà estimazione de' dotti dell' Inglese Idioma, si per la sublimità de' concetti, che per la finissima leggiadria dello stile, uno de più rari poetici componenti, che in simul genere abbia mai riportato il gradimento e l'applauso universale. . . .

In Venice another Italian version was performed, and yet a fourth was produced but not published. There were several French translations and adaptations, one of which found its way into an Italian paraphrase, with a lengthy preface. Voltaire was deeply interested in the play and admired it immensely:

M. Addison est le premier Anglais qui ait fait une tragédie raisonnable. . . . Caton est écrite d'un bout à l'autre avec cette élégance mâle et énergique dont Corneille le premier donna chez nous de si beaux exemples dans son style inégal. . . . Dans cette tragédie d'un patriote et d'un philosophe, le rôle de Caton me paraît surtout un des plus beaux personnages qui soient sur aucun théâtre. . . .[1]

Yet he thought the play highly irregular by the best French standards:

La barbarie et l'irrégularité du Théâtre de Londres ont percé jusque dans la sagesse d'Addison. Il me semble que je vois le Czar Pierre, qui, en réformant les Russes, tenait encore quelquechose de son éducation et des mœurs de son pays.[2]

The *Dictionnaire Historique* acidly concluded *Cato* to be 'la pièce la plus raisonnable des Anglais, qui ne réussirait pas cependant sur le théâtre français'. There were also two adaptations into German, and one into Polish, while the English Jesuits at St. Omer made a Latin version which was magnificently produced by them and a copy of the script sent to the author. Also in Latin was a partial translation by Dr. Bland, the Provost of Eton, presented to Addison through the intermediary of Robert Walpole.

It was *Cato* which in his own generation raised Addison to the highest fame, and which, with his *Spectators*, caused him to become the ark of the covenant of British letters. A hundred and twenty years later Macaulay still thought of

[1] *De la Tragédie Anglaise.*   [2] Ibid.

Cato as 'unquestionably the noblest production of Addison's genius'. In its own day it so far stirred the public as to revive interest in *Rosamond*, which was reprinted in this year. But with the passage of time public estimation of *Cato* declined until it has become of interest only to students, while the prestige of the *Spectator* has grown steadily. The latter is of far greater importance in English social history and letters. But it is indisputable that Addison had provided not merely the major literary events of the years 1711, 1712, and 1713, but one of the most important single contributions to English letters; and if after the Peace of Utrecht, which was signed in May 1713, he was the dominating figure of the English literary world, his stature had in no way lessened but had increased after the Battle of Waterloo a century later.

While Addison enjoyed one of the greatest literary triumphs ever accorded to an author in his lifetime, Swift had set out for Ireland to assume the deanery of St. Patrick's. This must have seemed a poor reward for his fervent partisanship, compared with the success and the laurels accorded to Addison by everybody—the Ministry included—a week before his departure. On 12 March Dick Steele had started a new daily paper to succeed the *Spectator*, calling it the *Guardian*. In this Addison had as yet taken no part, though Pope and George Berkeley were assisting the principal author. Without Addison's vigilance and restraint the new paper soon landed its authors in trouble. For several years Addison had encouraged Ambrose Philips to persevere as a writer of pastoral verse, a field in which he entered into competition with Pope. The coterie at Button's, where Philips was a leading figure, was inclined to partiality towards him. Pope, who was becoming the *enfant terrible* of the literary world, now wrote a *Guardian* in which he selected his own best lines and some of Philips's weakest, and drew a comparison between them, proclaiming Philips's to be by far superior. Unless Steele was a party to Pope's plan, he must have run his eye hastily over the paper, noticed nothing amiss, and sent it to press. The town was greatly diverted, and open war broke out between Philips and Pope in which the threat of bodily chastisement was freely used by the former. While the *Guardian* was thus in trouble the

Examiner attacked a noble lady whose father had recently been brought to desert the Tories for the Whigs, and Steele drew his pen in defence of beauty in distress and abused the *Examiner* in the roundest terms possible. A duel with that paper followed, in the course of which Swift was assailed as a conceivable author of the offending piece, and all Steele's anger at Swift's sustained malice to the Duke of Marlborough burst out in the literary war which followed. Thus, as Addison presided at Button's, the bolts flew briskly about his ears, and though they were not directed at him, he must have been acutely pained by the hostilities. Swift attempted to involve him in his sector of the battle by writing a letter of complaint about Steele, which Addison parried by passing it on to his friend. A savage epistolary duel then ensued, running parallel with that in the press, in the course of which the captain resigned his remaining place in order to free his hands to enter Parliament. There his friend the Member for Malmesbury was busy supporting the cause of Lord Wharton, still under attack for alleged financial irregularities. Addison was better acquainted with the facts than any other Member of the House, and signalized his loyalty by acting as a teller upon a motion which would have amended that under discussion in such a way as to indicate that Lord Wharton had not himself benefited by the alleged sale of an office for £1,000. On this he was soundly defeated, the House instead adding to the motion the words 'and receiving the same', while agreeing to take no further proceedings. In the midst of these various hostilities, the kindly Joseph Keally, who had been a friend of and bond between all the parties except Pope, died in Ireland on 21 May.

The little circle of the Republic of Letters was thus filled with quarrelling ill humoured poets, and the *Guardian* was hopelessly embroiled in political and personal quarrels, when, on 1 July, surprisingly, Addison took charge of the paper. One reason was that Dick Steele wished to give his whole attention to his approaching election contest at Stockbridge. Addison hoped to cut short the quarrels which frustrated all useful discussion, by giving the paper a different editorial policy. The two papers which he had himself contributed previously to this date were inoffensive enough. Furthermore, after the excitement and strain of *Cato* and the defence of Lord Wharton in the Commons, he had been out of town at the end of May for a short rest. His only recent literary undertaking had been to take a hand with Dick Steele in a prologue for D'Urfey's *A Fond Husband*, revived for the author's benefit at Drury Lane on 15 June.[1] Now coming refreshed to the *Guardian* he seized the paper in a masterful hand, and from his own pen supplied every one of the daily numbers until 3 August.[2] He was in excellent literary form, and Macaulay describes his first *Guardian* as 'an exquisite specimen of Addison's peculiar manner. It would be difficult to find in the works of any other writer such an instance of benevolence, delicately flavoured with contempt.' The purpose of this concentrated effort was probably to make sure that no quarrels were revived and to make it plain to the reading public that there had been a change in editorial policy. Steele's launching of the *Guardian* had been taken as a personal affront by Dennis, who saw in it a successor to the two previous periodicals which had attacked his theories. He had written angrily in protest.[3] Addison now sought to disarm the critics. His first paper in the new series had returned to a favourite and harmless subject, the usefulness of medals, and made a half-serious proposal for a new coinage. Evidently he had been turning over the manuscript of his unpublished *Dialogues* on this subject, and had discussed its printing with Tonson, to whom a week later he assigned the copyright for forty-four guineas. He had also evidently shown the manuscript to Pope, who began meditating complimentary verses on the subject probably against the day of an anticipated publication. Addison seems to have wished to make a few revisions, for delivery of the manuscript was to be deferred for one month; but these were not made and it appeared in imperfect form after his death.[4]

[1] For this attribution see *The Occasional Verses of Richard Steele*, ed. R. Blanchard, pp. 103–4.

[2] Norman Ault claims No. 106 for Pope. *Prose Works of Pope*, lxv.

[3] Dennis, *Original Letters*, 1721, p. 284.

[4] See R. E. Tickell, *Thomas Tickell and the 18th century Poets*, London, 1931, p. 74.

The following *Guardian* was equally inoffensive, beginning in Addison's lightest vein: '*Sir*, I was left a thousand Pounds by an Uncle, and being a man to My thinking very likely to get a rich Widow, I laid aside all Thoughts of making my Fortune any other way . . . .' In the next number he was ready to follow his *Spectator* precedent with a discussion of policy; and after implying that good nature would henceforth rule his pages, he proceeded to pick up a hint from one of his early papers and to develop it. In No. 71 he had written about 'lions': 'any one that is a great Man's Spy'; and recalled the lion figures outside the Doge's palace in Venice, into whose maw information of interest to the authorities might be thrust. He now proposed to set up at Button's a lion's head, later described for a sale catalogue as 'beautifully carved and gilt'. This bore the cryptic transcription of two unconnected lines from Martial:

> Cervantur
> Magnis isti Cervicibus
> Ungues, non nisi delecta
> Pascitur Ille Fera.[1]

Its purpose was to receive contributions for the *Guardian*, which probably indicates that, having withdrawn his paper from the current quarrels, Addison wished to ease his own burden in providing the whole of the material without taking the risk of calling in Pope and other contributors. Continuing impeccably, he praised the rule of law, the independence of the judiciary, and the tucker, that 'Slip of fine Linen or Muslin that used to run in a small kind of Ruffle around the uppermost Verge of the Womens Stays'. His interest in contemporary manners had led him to read the classic authors in that subject, and the *Guardian* has been thought to reveal a study of Giovanni della Casa. Thus when the appointed day for the conclusion of European Peace was due, Addison's paper was in suitably inoffensive mood. He opened his notebooks and skilfully avoided politics on this highly controversial issue by adapting some of his letters written from France fourteen years before. They were entertaining pieces and were well received; and thereafter he

---

[1] *Gents. Mag.* 1787, lvii. 311.

drew with success upon the same source, a fact which suggests the relative maturity of his writing in the year 1700.

Looking for further *Guardian* material, Addison's eye lit upon William Whiston. Whiston was a Cambridge man, an eminent mathematician and astronomer, an admirer of Locke and Newton, and well known for his courage and candour. He had been ordained a priest at Lichfield, Dean Addison and George Smalridge, then a prebendary of the cathedral, participating in the ceremony. He had applied his theories to the scriptural texts with disastrous consequences to himself, ending in deprivation of his professorship and expulsion from the university in the autumn of 1710. Arrived in London late in the following year, he published *Primitive Christianity Revived*, as a result of which he was now threatened with a prosecution by the orthodox. Addison was much interested in astronomy, was familiar with the work of Newton on the spectrum[1] and on comets[2] and with the discovery of the spots in the sun; and he apparently knew the observatory at Greenwich. On Whiston's arrival in London from Cambridge Addison and Steele arranged for him to deliver lectures in astronomy at Button's. This they did in consultation with Henry Newman, the Secretary of the Society for Promoting Christian Knowledge, from which the astronomer had recently resigned because of its Anglican affiliations. Newman regarded this as a useful way of occupying Whiston with science and of distracting him from dangerous religious speculation.[3] Whiston later gratefully recalled that the proceeds provided 'me and my family some comfortable support under my banishment'.[4] The influence of these lectures may be reflected in Addison's noble hymn upon the universe which he published in the *Spectator* on 23 August 1712 and which rather surprisingly found its way into the *Hymns Ancient and Modern*, the last verse running:

> What though, in solemn Silence, all
> Move round the dark terrestrial Ball?

[1] *T.* 218.   [2] *S.* 101.
[3] Rae Blanchard, 'Richard Steele and the Secretary of the S.P.C.K.', *Restoration and Eighteenth Century Literature*, ed. C. Camden (Houston, 1963). The date of the lectures is established as August 1713.
[4] Whiston, *Memoirs*, i. 302.

What tho' nor real Voice nor Sound
Amid their radiant Orbs be found?
In Reason's Ear they all rejoice,
And utter forth a glorious Voice,
For ever singing, as they shine,
'The Hand that made us is Divine.'

Whiston's speculations were of a nature to appeal to one interested in unorthodox religious theories, who had written verse in praise of Burnet's *Sacred Theory of the Earth*, and who was friendly with Benjamin Hoadly.[1] Indeed Hoadly's thesis that the greatest happiness is attained by those who use the highest parts of their nature was a pulpit version of Addison's teaching in the *Spectator*; and Addison's hymn was a development of the cartesianism of his early essay on ancient and modern philosophy. To this world of speculation and research the *Guardian* now made a contribution by printing a letter from Whiston advocating a new method of ascertaining data for astronomical navigation. Such a scheme was subsequently canvassed in Parliament, where Addison was one of a committee of nine members appointed to bring in a bill to provide a reward for the best proposals, which he doubtless hoped would be won by his friend. Addison with Stanhope, who also attended Whiston's lectures, was probably responsible for the bill.

The *Guardian* continued upon a variety of subjects, some grave such as that of foundling children, some flippant such as the art of flying: 'in the next Age it will be as usual for a Man to call for his Wings... as it is now to call for his Boots.'[2] By 22 July he felt confident that he had so far restored the paper to respectability as to be able to permit a reference to 'your predecessor, the Spectator'. Accordingly, when he handed over its conduct for ten days on 3 August it was in effect a different publication from that of which he had assumed control a month before. But the interval was now used by Dick Steele, who was in furious political mood, to write a series of attacks upon the Government and the *Examiner*, and Addison on his return to the paper was

---

[1] 'Little Ben' had been made Rector of Streatham under the Whig Government in 1710 probably as a reward for his attacks upon the theory of divine right as held by the Tory clergy.   [2] G. 112.

compelled to announce that the lion would refuse political contributions. Thereafter he contributed a further twenty-one papers, the last of them, No. 167, appearing on 22 September, and the publication came to an end at the hand of its originator with No. 175, in order that the *Englishman*, unreservedly political in purpose, might begin. To the *Guardian* Addison had contributed at least fifty-two papers.[1]

The Member for Malmesbury had been busy in the Commons as late as 9 July, when he served on a committee, and Parliament had been prorogued on 16 July, a general election being expected. It was with this in view that he laid aside the *Guardian* for ten days early in August to enable preparations to be made in his borough. The dissolution took place on 8 August and Addison again laid down his paper about 21 August and went down to Malmesbury for the contest. This resulted in the return of himself and Sir John Rushout on 29 August.[2] By 4 September he was back in London, where Dick Steele had now joined him as Member for Stockbridge. In the political world the tension, so often high during the queen's reign, was steadily rising as the parties prepared for the day when the Crown would fall by law to the Elector of Hanover. A confidential agent from the Elector was in London, with instructions to undertake no step without consulting Lord Halifax, whose attachment to the Hanoverian cause was undoubted and who was well known to the Electoral Court. This agent, Schutz, would be known to Addison and the two men undoubtedly met once more at this time. It appeared that if the Jacobite danger could be avoided, at the queen's death Addison and his friends would enjoy the royal favour.

In these circumstances nervousness prevailed in the Whig ranks lest the long-awaited fruits of the succession should be snatched from them by some violent turn of fortune. George Berkeley reported that 'Mr. Addison and Mr. Steele (and so far as I can find, the rest of that party) seem entirely persuaded there is a design for bringing in the Pretender',[3] in order that the Tory party might remain in power. Dick

---

[1] W. Graham, *English Literary Periodicals*, p. 81.
[2] *Evening Post*, 634.   [3] H.M.C. vii. 238.

Steele was now so violent in his politics that he was a constant embarrassment to his friend, who fully shared Lord Halifax's view that the moderate Tories must be brought to support any Ministry which might take office on the queen's death. Meanwhile, for all his political neutrality in periodical journalism, Addison had made his contribution on behalf of the Whig economic interest, by a pamphlet entitled *The Trial and Conviction of Count Tariff*. This anonymous piece attacked the commercial treaty negotiated by the Government as a part of the general pacification, on the ground that it was injurious to British commerce. Addison abandoned the calm reasoning of the *Present State of the War* and, as his title suggests, made use of an allegory, if such it may be called, reminiscent of the 'dreams' of the *Tatler*. In this he described indirectly the proceedings in Parliament where he had voted for and secured the rejection of the treaty. A pamphlet war had raged around the matter, and by adopting the device of an allegory Addison was able to protect himself from what he most disliked, a running controversy, and to indulge in what he greatly preferred, a series of *ex cathedra* statements setting forth the point of view of the Whig merchants and party and, in particular, praising Robert Walpole's speech in the Commons. The affectation of the piece makes it barely readable today; and although it was popular enough to secure re-publication, it can hardly have been effective political writing. Only those who had studied the issues would follow the allegory; and such readers would be well acquainted with the propositions put forward by the 'Count' and his accuser, 'goodman Fact'.

Amidst these political preoccupations, Addison found time to interest himself in the entry of young Lord Warwick into the university, corresponding with Dr. Smalridge at Christ Church, who arranged a meeting between Lady Warwick and the young man's prospective tutor. He may also have enjoyed the company of John Wyche, who had 'set his hand shaking' at Hamburg ten years before. Wyche was now in London, where he remained until the middle of September, and where he cannot have failed to be interested in the development of the opera under Handel, whose arrival in Hamburg ten years earlier had coincided with that of

Addison. He died unexpectedly in October,[1] and was succeeded in Hamburg by his son.[2] More than ever Addison was
the literary oracle, receiving, for example, a letter from one
John Morice, who forwarded a manuscript and diffidently
described himself as 'a young Gent. who does not pretend to
understand the Rules of the Stage so well as he ought' with
a request that the author of Cato would 'tell me impartially
whether you think pains might bring it to any tolerable
Perfection; and if so, which are the best methods to effect
it'. This was an age-long familiar request. A more serious
proposition came from John Hughes, who suggested a new
paper to replace the *Guardian*. This Addison politely declined. The effort of writing the *Tatler*, *Spectator*, and *Guardian* in succession had wearied him for periodicals for the time
being: 'to tell you truly, I have been so taken up with
thoughts of that nature for these two or three years last past,
that I must now take some time pour me délaisser, and lay in
fewel for a future work.' He encouraged Hughes to proceed
with the paper which ultimately appeared with Blackmore's
help as the *Lay Monk*. He then made a last attempt to
dissuade Dick Steele from the violent political course on
which he was embarked, but failed to make any impression:

I am in a thousand troubles for poor Dick, and wish that his
zeal for the public may not be ruinous to himself; but he has sent
me word that he is determined to go on, and that any advice I can
give him in this particular, will have no weight with him.

Addison then went down to Bilton where he had arrived by
12 October. His departure from town ended the short but
important period of intimacy which he had enjoyed with
George Berkeley, who left England next month and was not
again familiar with Addison for any length of time.

    This was in all probability Addison's first period of con-
siderable residence on his new estate. His sister Dorothy,
whose husband had died on 3 September,[3] was living there
with him. It is probable that she had seen much of her
brother in recent years, for the Sartre family had continued
to live in the close at Westminster near to the centre of his

---

[1] *Post Boy*, 2878; *Evening Post*, 612.
[2] *Evening Post*, 707.   [3] Boyer, *Political State*, v. 186.

activities. Addison thought of staying at Bilton a month or so, perhaps because Parliament was not to meet this autumn, and invited Hughes and Blackmore for a visit. Pope was also invited, to whom he wrote at the end of the month: 'I am at present wholly immersed in country business, and begin to take delight in it.' He was busy at work upon the house, which was largely rebuilt about this time and panelled and fitted in the interior. He took advantage of the autumn planting season and set himself 1,000 trees as his considerable first year's target. William Somerville, neighbour poet and foxhunter, wrote a set of welcoming verses 'To Mr. Addison occasioned by his purchasing an Estate in Warwickshire'; and the new squire amused himself 'killing hares and partridges' but continued to play the literary oracle by post. Pope had posed as his champion against Dennis, and, with Gay, had congratulated him upon incurring that critic's censure. The former now wrote outlining his proposals to translate the *Iliad*. Addison's reply was decorous and encouraging: 'I question not but your Translation will enrich our Tongue and do Honour to our Country': but Addison, possibly recalling his own retreat before Herodotus, seems to have doubted whether Pope had gauged the immensity of the task:

Excuse my impertinence . . . which proceeds from my zeal for your ease and happiness. The work wou'd cost you a great deal of time, and unless you undertake it will I am afraid never be executed by any other, at least I know of none in this age that is equal to it besides your self.

No man ever told another in politer terms that he thought his qualifications unequal to the task. As a politician Addison evidently despaired to recruiting Pope for the Whigs, but, still anxious to preserve him from surrender to the other camp, and acting in consistency with his own literary principles, he urged him 'not to content your self with one half of the Nation for your Admirers when you might command them all'. He observed that 'all your undertakings will turn to better account for it', a lesson just then being illustrated by the success of *Cato* which was revived in London during the autumn. It was mid-December by the time that Addison returned to the capital and resumed the premiership at Button's, which had been delegated in his absence to Steele and Philips. Despite all disappointments he evidently felt himself to be in fairly affluent circumstances and called upon to play the generous patron, subscribing amongst other current projects for a large paper copy of Thomas Broderick's *History of the Late War* and to Tickell's projected translation of Lucan. The hall at Bilton would hold more books than any previous lodging.

Dick Steele, now returned to Parliament, had anticipated the meeting of the House by a frontal attack on the Government. With all the skill at his command and with the help and advice of Benjamin Hoadly in Church matters, of his legal adviser Moore, of Nicholas Lechmere on the political side, and of Addison generally, he spent Christmas polishing and perfecting his pamphlet the *Crisis*. Addison had no objection to forthright political pamphleteering in its proper place, and Steele, having made it clear that he proposed going forward with his venture and being supported by the Whig leadership, received all the help that his friend could give him. Except for a few Jacobites, whose course was plain, everybody favoured the Hanoverian succession. But the Government was faced with an insoluble problem in trying to find a means of outbidding the Whigs for the favour of the Elector while still conducting the queen's business; and the *Crisis* touched them upon this tender spot. Its publication was widely advertised, and by the time it was on sale on 19 January 1714 there was great excitement. The press was full of articles or pamphlets on or around the document. The Government felt unable to allow an attack upon them in this form to pass and, urged by the advice of Defoe amongst others, when the House reassembled in March took steps to secure Steele's expulsion therefrom on the ground that his book was seditious and reflected upon the queen. This form of martyrdom with the maximum publicity was precisely what Steele hoped would befall him, providing a certain title to favour from the Whigs and the Elector after the queen's death. In this juncture Addison, who had been a relatively silent member of the Commons, was called upon to assist in drawing up his friend's defence, though he could not bring himself to speak thereto on the floor. For that purpose there was an able team of orators: Robert Walpole, General Stanhope, and Lord Hinchingbrooke, who were to take the brief prepared for them.[1] On 2 March Addison had been appointed to the Committee of Privileges, a powerful body in matters such as that now in hand. On 12 March Steele was ordered to attend the Commons and did so next day. On 18 March the debate upon his writings took place in a House cleared of the strangers who had crowded in to hear the proceedings. Steele made an eloquent defence lasting nearly three hours, and Addison sat beside him prompting from notes.[2] Steele was then ordered to withdraw while the debate took place, and Addison was sent after by his friends to restrain Dick from any rash further action until the result of the debate should be known. The expulsion was then carried.

Dick now ceased to be a source of immediate political worry and occupied his time with a couple of fleeting periodicals for which Addison supplied several papers. In one, the *Lover*, he advertised Budgell's translation of Theophrastus, and laughed politely at collectors of ornamental china: 'Did our Women take Delight in heaping up Piles of Earthen Platters, brown Jugs, and the like useful Products of our *British* Potteries, there would be some Sense in it.'[3] In another, the *Reader*, two papers on 'nonsense' have been attributed to his pen.[4] But if he was able thus to banter the times while *Cato* ran again at Drury Lane, Addison watched great events anxiously as they drew towards the climax of the queen's death: 'I hope Providence will dispose of all for the best', he wrote to Dawson, when sending his usual reminder for prompt forwarding of his quarterly moneys. Thrift and self-reliance were lessons which he had learned thoroughly, and which had been reinforced by the development of his interest in Gulston's estate. By January 1713 it

---

[1] Rapin, *History of England*, contd. Tindal, iv, 343.

[2] Boyer, *History of Queen Anne*, 675.

[3] *Lover*, No. 10.

[4] *Camb. Bibl. Eng. Lit.*, ii. 604. See also *Steele's Periodical Journalism, 1714–16*, ed. Rae Blanchard (Oxford, 1959), pp. 293–4. Miss Blanchard attributes these essays to Steele.

appeared that one Chitty had returned to England owing considerable sums to the trustees and thereafter had died. Addison had spent much pains in seeking to trace these funds in England, and had been before Sir Gilbert Heathcote, who had power to retain moneys in the hands of the company should a claim to them be made good. He contemplated bankruptcy proceedings against Chitty's estate in which Governor Pitt, also interested, was willing to join. He had secured the promise of about £400 due from the Pitt family upon a coffee venture. He had also taken legal proceedings against the widow of the captain of the *Lichfield*, although she was 'left in a very melancholy condition', to secure an inventory of goods left by her husband, in the belief that they included some of Gulston's merchandise. But it soon appeared that his litigation was being conducted for the benefit of other parties, particularly of George Morton Pitt, and he discontinued it. Though he was careful to take legal advice whenever it appeared necessary, Addison had more than the average Englishman's dislike of lawyers: '*Men* . . . that are more or less passionate according as they are paid for it.'[1] He may have been glad to be rid of a Chancery suit, the more so since successive letters from India unfolded a tale of disasters. As Henry Jolley put it comprehensively: 'at most Cullenys they do not understand the law nor gospel and if they do its but little practised.' He doubted whether 10,000 pagodas could now be rescued from the wreck.

Addison therefore decided upon a last attempt to terrify the men responsible for his disappointment. He wrote two letters to Governor Harrison, one to be shown to the offending parties, the other a reasoned analysis of his position, resting his interests in the Governor's discretion. 'It is very lucky for one or two of those infamous persons whom my Brother left as his Trustees that they have such an article as that of Pegu to throw their mismanagement upon', he wrote in the draft of the first letter. But upon reading it through he struck out 'infamous persons' and substituted 'honest gentlemen', revealing the wrath and scorn with which he regarded the financial trickery of which he was the victim,

[1] *S.* 21.

and displaying the accuracy with which he was able to barb his shafts when so minded.[1] Matters were aggravated when Edmund Montagu, one of the trustees, came home with the account, but delivered it discourteously and improperly to Governor Pitt. Addison wrote to Harrison that he had been cheated of a principal asset: 'there was such an unnecessary number of Directors, Subdirectors, Captains Carpenters &c. . . . that there is no wonder they have brought that part of the estate to nothing.' Detailing the frauds committed, he thundered: 'Raworth has acted after such a manner as very well deserves the Pillory and I long for an opportunity of letting him know so by word of mouth.' Only Harrison and Benyon retained his confidence, and beneath the cloak of his half-simulated anger he instructed them to negotiate a settlement which would recover as much as possible. He still expected to secure a good deal of the ruined estate by energetic piecemeal measures. Meanwhile, without any immediate literary preoccupation and perhaps impatient of the fleeting nature of Steele's papers, he restarted the *Spectator*, a curious decision. The first number resumed the series at 556 on 18 June 1714.

As he took up his pen Addison was once more at pains to declare his political neutrality: 'It is not my Intention to increase the Number either of *Whigs* or *Tories*, but of wise and good Men.'[2] Dick was at present an impossible colleague in an undertaking with such an object, and the new paper was a partnership of Addison and Budgell, who did the routine management. Budgell had deserved well of his famous relative for whom he had done much unobtrusive hard work. Besides his service in Ireland, he had written at least twenty-eight *Spectators*, helping particularly by supplying one paper each week at the time when Addison was much absorbed in his Milton series. If later comment suggested that Addison wrote or considerably corrected Budgell's work this merely reflects the fact that the two men wrote in a partnership in which one was dominant. But the absence of Steele's energy and resource was reflected in the fact that the revived publication appeared thrice weekly instead of daily. The range and tone were similar to that of

[1] B.M. Egerton MSS. 1972, ff. 83-84.   [2] S. 556.

the old series, but the new lacked zest. To write in his best vein Addison seemed to need the inspiration of his friend. He wrote a dozen papers in June and late July and helped Budgell with others. One was a considerable treatise on drunkenness:

> No Vices are so incurable as those which Men are apt to glory in . . . a drunken Man is a greater Monster than any that is to be found among all creatures which God has made; as indeed there is no Character which appears more despicable and deformed, in the Eyes of all reasonable Persons. . . .[1]

The paper had a reduced circulation, and, like so many revivals of great works, a limited success. The moment was not propitious for such writing. Public excitement was too great and current rumours more attractive. Pope told Swift: 'At Buttons it is reported you are gone to Hanover, and that Gay[2] goes on an Ambassy to you.'[3] The atmosphere was thick with rumour and apprehension.

Dick Steele gloried in the excitement in daily contact with the Whig leaders. Characteristically, Addison retired to Bilton in July leaving Budgell with sufficient material to keep the *Spectator* in publication. His experience in the writing of current English prose, added to his study of the literature of the past, of the critics and of Bayle, led him to contemplate the idea of compiling an English dictionary based upon extracts from the standard works of literature: and it is probable that he now amused himself with this project at Bilton.[4] As the month wore on the queen's health declined fast and the political situation moved to its climax. On 27 July the Lord Treasurer, with whom Lord Halifax had remained in contact to the last, resigned his staff. The position now seemed to be out of control as the extremist Bolingbroke assumed power. But in this as in every important crisis for many years, the Duke of Shrewsbury now intervened, accepting office as Lord Treasurer on 30 July, a presence almost more than royal, above the parties and behind the throne. On the same day the Privy Council met at Kensington; the militia and trained bands were called out to

---

[1] S. 569.
[3] Sherburn, i. 231.
[2] Who really went there.
[4] Cibber, *Lives*, iii. 316.

ensure order at the queen's death; and the Admiralty were instructed to make as many ships as possible ready for sea at short notice. On 1 August, early in the morning, the queen died, and until King George could arrive from Hanover the Government of England vested in a Regency. This was composed of persons nominated by the king in sealed papers lodged in advance with the Lord Chancellor, the Archbishop of Canterbury, and the Hanoverian Resident. When the lists were opened they were found to include Lord Halifax, besides the Dukes of Shrewsbury and Somerset.

Most of the regents were moderate men. The extremes of either party were excluded, probably upon Lord Halifax's advice. Halifax now occupied a central and influential position and it was on his proposition that Joseph Addison, experienced administrator and illustrious literary moderate, was unanimously chosen Secretary of the Regency.[1] This was now the highest administrative post in the land. Its acceptance meant for Addison the end of his four years in the political wilderness, and the end of a period of wonderful literary fertility. In the *Tatler* he had discovered the rich vein of prose satire and speculation which had been foreshadowed by touches in the Latin poetry and the early letters. In the *Spectator* he had exploited it to the full. In *Cato* he had achieved a success in the drama which had lifted him to the summit of international fame. In literary England he had become the oracle, the successor to Dryden, universally admired and respected. He was a squire in the country, a parliament man in town, the familiar companion of the great in society, the lion of the coffee-houses. With the highest honour both as a man of affairs and as a man of letters, he might feel that he personified the ideal of Roman citizenship which had been before his eyes since Oxford days. The wilderness of disfavour, so menacing at its outset, had proved fruitful.

[1] Boyer, *Political State*, vol. viii, pt. 2, p. 142; Budgell, *A Letter to Cleomenes*, 1731, pp. 209–10.

VIII

A YEAR OF BITTERNESS
1714–1715

IT now appeared that Addison was about to enter a political halcyon period which would crown his literary triumphs. He had filled his administrative posts of Under-Secretary of State and Secretary in Ireland with diligence and with general approval. During the four years of political exile he had made no enemies. No extremist excursion had marred his moderation. He remained closely associated with Lord Halifax, who represented the political centre, though the Whig section of it; and from the composition of the Regency it appeared that his patron's policy of seeking the support of moderates of all parties for the new establishment had found approval with the king. But he had been consistent in his support of the Whig pary, agreeably with his recognition of the value of consistency in politics which had occupied the hundred and sixty-second *Spectator*. The post to which he was now appointed, though of a temporary nature, was one of administrative power greater than that enjoyed by any official of government in normal circumstances. The jurisdiction of the Lords Justices, the representatives and custodians of royal authority, overrode that of every officer of State. Parliament was for the moment no rival. Addison thus found himself called upon to assume the central executive responsibility for, and to be the administrative instrument of, this supreme authority at a moment when there was an immediate need for action in every sphere of State. He hastened to take up his duties in St. James's Palace, where the regents were to meet to transact their business. As though to establish a home-like atmosphere, he hastened to appoint his old friend Jacob Tonson stationer to the Board.[1]

The accession of King George was proclaimed on 1 August

[1] *Cal. Treasury Books*, xxx. 479.

1714, and on the same day peers and members of the expiring House of Commons began to take the oaths to the new sovereign. In the lower House Addison was, as before, one of the Members appointed to tender the oaths. On 3 August his appointment as Secretary to the Lords Justices was announced and his arduous duties began. All correspondence for the Secretaries of State was directed to be sent to him, the regents thus securing immediate control of the Government. This was intended to prevent Lord Bolingbroke, the politically suspect Secretary of State and his colleague, Secretary Bromley, from any acts of political sabotage. It was a mortification to the former, who had so recently secured power, and who earlier in the year had sought an accommodation with leading Whigs, including Addison. Lord Bolingbroke was now 'oblig'd to wait with a Bag in the Hand at the Door of the Room where the Regents assembled'.[1] It is reported of Addison by Budgell that he admired the brilliance of the man with whom he was now called upon to work on these difficult terms, and that he regretted that politics had prevented their friendship. This is not inconsistent with Addison's pattern of life, for he enjoyed the company of several other debauchees, such as 'Rag' Smith and General Tidcomb, and he defended Lord Wharton; even at Oxford his earliest friend had been Henry Sacheverell, who at that time received a grave disciplinary reprimand from the college authorities.

The political difficulty of his position was matched by the immediate anxieties at home and abroad; but within a few days it was seen that there would be no serious trouble in England in the imminent future. There was no politically formidable opposition to King George sufficiently prepared for immediate action. Therefore on the first day of Addison's office, instructions were sent out to dismiss the militia. But in Europe the motions of the powers were narrowly watched, and a fleet was fitting out for sea,[2] with the double purpose of protecting the king on his voyage and of being in readiness for any emergency. Bolingbroke wrote to Swift, who had taken up residence in the country, a letter full of aggressive optimism for the Tory party. Erasmus Lewis also wrote, on

[1] *Hist. Reg.*, i. 22.   [2] *Evening Post*, 778.

the same day, reporting Addison's appointment.[1] To Swift, who had dreamed of great power but seen the reality elude him, who had allowed himself to condescend to his friend without ever having possessed the means of condescension, it must have been a time to exercise his philosophy. The alteration in political fortunes was a turning-point in the relationship of the two men. For his great political writings Swift lacked any adequate reward. The reason lay in his character, which had failed to commend itself first to the Whigs and then to the Tories. Lord Orrery penetrated and described those weaknesses which accompanied and vitiated his brilliance and strength:

... I am much inclined to believe that the temper of my friend Swift might occasion his English friends to wish him happily and properly promoted, at a distance. His spirit, for I would give it the softer name, was ever untractable. The motions of his genius were often irregular. He assumed more the air of a patron, than of a friend. He affected rather to dictate than advise. He was elated with the appearance of enjoying ministerial confidence. He enjoyed the shadow: the substance was detained from him. He was employed, not trusted; and at the same time that he imagined himself a subtle diver, who dextrously shot down into the profoundest regions of politics, he was suffered to sound only the shallows nearest the shore, and was scarce admitted to descend below the froth at the top. ... By reflections of this sort we may account for his disappointment in an English bishoprick.[2]

It is interesting to observe how this dissection of Swift's character shows to the world a man diametrically opposed in nature to Addison. 'The motions of his genius were often irregular': Steele it was who had described Addison, 'as regular in his Behaviour as a mere Machine'. 'He assumed more the air of a patron, than of a friend. He affected rather to dictate than advise', Orrery recalled of Swift; 'he chuses to be on a level with others, rather than oppress with the superiority of his genius. In friendship he is kind without profession', Steele reported of Addison, who had the gifts of character which make worldly success a practical proposition. Swift now went his way to Ireland, and though he

[1] Williams, ii. 98.
[2] Orrery, *Letters to his Son*, Letter V.

and Addison thought of one another with affection, their intimacy was never to be resumed.

As the political situation became clearer it seemed that the Government must seek to provide against foreign rather than domestic dangers. The first need was to secure a safe passage to England for King George. On his second day in office, therefore, Addison wrote to the commander-in-chief, his early patron the Duke of Ormonde, ordering sufficient half-pay officers to report immediately at Portsmouth for an emergency escort. At the same time he conveyed orders to the Admiralty for providing Lord Berkeley the necessities for the fleet which was fitting out for a convoy. On that day the Lords Justices spent much time examining the correspondence of the Secretaries of State, which Addison laid before them. Amongst other matters, Scotland was giving cause for anxiety because of the support which the Pretender might expect there, and Addison was called upon to meet a situation not dissimilar in some respects from that with which he was familiar from his work as Under-Secretary during the threatened Jacobite invasion of 1707. He sent orders from the regents for the castle at Edinburgh to be provisioned and ordered extra ships to sea. At the same time he scrutinized the measures being taken in the north of England against possible papist troubles. As a precaution, all holders of office were ordered to take the oaths and proceed to their posts.[1] Then he summoned the Lords of the Admiralty to meet the regents on 7 August to discuss naval defences and the king's voyage.

There was an accumulation of much routine business, some of it urgent, such as the complaints of merchants whose vessels had been seized by the Swedish Government. There were political prisoners to be dealt with, and the discretion of mercy to be exercised: Peter Hambleton 'not having made the discoveries he promised . . . is not to flatter himself with vain hopes of a reprieve', wrote the Secretary.[2] The prosecution of political libels also required attention and the law officers were consulted about the offences of the *Flying Post* and Defoe, against whom the Solicitor General advised that there was no evidence, but who was nevertheless arrested.[3] Addison was the repository even of the

[1] P.C. 2/85, f. 34.   [2] S.P. 35/1, f. 15.   [3] S.P. 35/1, f. 29.

military 'word' for the month.[1] The regents met daily, some-times thrice in a single day. In these circumstances it proved necessary to continue to use the services of Lord Boling-broke, who, under close supervision, was writing to the Lords Justices in Ireland about routine matters,[2] and who, together with the South Sea Company, was consulted by Addison about the complicated trade agreements with Spain.[3]

On 5 August, a busy day, the regents opened the residual session of Parliament and addressed the Houses. Addison, suddenly most prominent in the proceedings of the Com-mons where he occupied a semi-ministerial position, was one of the committee appointed to meet in the Speaker's cham-ber at five o'clock to draw up an address to the new king. All of this activity produced good results and at the end of the day *Dawks's News Letter* reported that 'Jacobitism, which was such an unruly beast some days ago, seems to be ty'd Neck and Heels, and no way able to help itself'. On the next day the States General came to a favourable resolution upon their treaty obligations to King George, who was also proclaimed in Dublin.[4] There was a strong Tory element in the Irish Government and the Irish Lords Justices were disposed to quarrel with the regents. In this delicate situa-tion Addison's experience and knowledge of personalities must have been of value, and the two most troublesome of the Irish Justices were quickly removed from office.[5]

Addison himself was still struggling to assume the many threads of policy from the Secretaries of State, in which task he was being assisted by Erasmus Lewis, whom he had reason to distrust politically though he knew him quite well as a colleague.[6] The Lords Justices now found time to turn their attention to settling affairs in the Colonies, and the Council of Plantations was accordingly summoned to appear before them on 6 August.[7] All of these activities made Addison's importance impressive. Peter Wentworth wrote to Lord Raby in Berlin: 'Mr. Addison being made secretary to the Lords Justices makes people fancy he'll be one of the

[1] W.O. 4/16, f. 249.   [2] S.P. 63/371.   [3] S.P. 35/1, f. 20.
[4] *Evening Post*, 782; ibid. 781.   [5] Graham, pp. 293-4.
[6] S.P. 44/115, ff. 269-70.   [7] C.O. 324/10, f. 50.

secretarys of State when the King comes.'[1] Next day the
newspapers took up the theme:

Mr. Addison is made Secretary of State; so that the present
Secretaries of State, however they retain the office and continue
to negotiate public business, yet are not in the same full power
and authority as before,[2]

which although an inaccurate account of the position indicates the impression received by the public. Amidst so much
business it must have been a relief when Parliament, having
discharged all its business, dispersed on 25 August and
released Addison from his duties in the Commons.

The diplomatic situation in Europe continued to cause
anxiety. The regents were hastily bringing British policy
into line with that of the new king, and this placed an immediate strain upon relations with France. Lord Peterborough arrived in London with assurances that the French
Government intended to abide by the Treaty of Utrecht,
particularly as regards the Hanoverian Succession; but the
regents took steps through Addison to arrange for a recon-
naissance of the French coast in case any expedition should
be preparing. At home Addison's relations with Lord
Bolingbroke continued delicate. He had written to that
nobleman on 7 August instructing him to attend the Lords
Justices, in all probability because it was suspected that
trouble now arising in Ireland was partly of his making.
He was accordingly introduced into their presence by
Addison at 9 o'clock on 9 August bringing with him all the
documents relating to that kingdom.[3] By this time Addison
was beginning to handle matters of considerable detail, and
was, for example, in correspondence with the War Office
reviewing the reliability of general officers, and demanding
a list of officers who had served the kings of France or
Spain.[4] Sound men were being chosen for places of trust
in the provinces, such as Lord Lieutenancies and Justiceships
of the Peace.[5] Much of this business was done at break-neck
speed; for example, a note from Addison ordered the Lords
of the Admiralty to attend the regents forthwith or other-

[1] *Wentworth Papers*, p. 411.   [2] *Flying Post*, vi.   [3] S.P. 44/116.
[4] W.O. 4/16, ff. 224, 260.   [5] S.P. 35/1, f. 13.

wise at 9 o'clock next morning. Lord Bolingbroke was no
longer trusted for business of any consequence, and this
increased Addison's burden; but Secretary Bromley, a lesser
figure more easily controlled, was carrying out instructions sent from the regents, particularly those relating to
diplomacy.[1]

The demolition of the port of Dunkirk, a principal
objective in the peace treaty, was causing much concern.[2]
By 11 August the suspicions of the regents as to the designs
of Lord Bolingbroke and his friends seem to have been increasing. Even Secretary Bromley was now warned by
Addison that he must lay before the regents all letters to
ministers abroad before their dispatch[3] and orders were sent
to the War Office by Addison that troops in Holland were to
stand by at the ports for embarkation.[4] Repeated rumours
were now reaching England of French preparations for an
invasion. On 12 August shipping was reported to be con-
centrating in French channel ports[5] though on the same day
the French Ambassador, in an effort to allay anxiety, announced that the King of France would respect the succession and would send a special envoy to congratulate King
George.[6] But next day produced a press rumour that the
Pretender had had a long interview with Louis in Paris and
two days later it was reported that he had gone to the channel
coast.[7] Still seeking to quiet anxiety the French Government
now sent a special messenger to London to repeat the
ambassador's assurances and to undertake that anybody
supporting the Pretender would be punished.[8] Yet the press
carried stories that he had sailed with an expedition from
Calais and that French troop movements were taking place
on the frontiers.[9]

In this perplexing situation Addison had written a stiff
reprimand to Matthew Prior, who was now ambassador in
Paris. He had been deep in the confidence of Tory ministers
and it is possible to discern in the unusual acerbity of Addison's Whig *Examiners* and of *Tatler* No. 239 a particular

---

[1] S.P. 35/1, f. 14.   [2] S.P. 41/34, Military, f. 36.   [3] S.P. 35/1, f. 16.
[4] W.O. 4/16, f. 228.   [5] *Flying Post*, viii.   [6] *Evening post*, 782.
[7] *Dawks's News Letter*, 24/8/1714.   [8] *Evening Post*, 784.
[9] *Flying Post*, 3532.

aversion to Prior's conduct and character. Addison now complained of the lack of correspondence and reports from him since the queen's death. He added a peremptory order to deliver to the same messenger, express, copies of all letters written to ministers, including Secretaries of State, since 8 August. This was a further step to prevent a subversive movement through the agency of Lord Bolingbroke, who, though suspended from activities of State, yet retained his office. Prior answered in due course to the effect that he had corresponded with the proper minister, though he had also written a letter 'jovial rather than serious' to Lord Oxford.[1] Addison read Prior's letter to the regents. The ambassador sent a further letter enclosing a bundle of transcripts of his correspondence and later a copy of the *Paris Gazette* in which King George was reassuringly referred to as King of Great Britain. This he followed up by a private audience with King Louis in which he received assurances in terms similar to those already given.[2] But any satisfaction thus caused was more than outweighed by the Pretender's declaration of his right put forth on 26 August;[3] and the Regency, losing patience, ordered Prior's recall.[4] It was now felt that Lord Bolingbroke's continuance in office could not be tolerated, and it was on 25 August that he wrote to the king apparently for the last time.[5] On 30 August his last entry appeared in the Secretary of State's entry book[6] and on that day he was deprived of the seals with ignominy and his office at the Cockpit, which Addison knew so well, was locked and sealed by the regents.[7] Bolingbroke's comment to Atterbury was merely that 'the manner of my removal shock'd me for at least two minutes'.[8] Meanwhile Addison pressed forward with defence preparations, requiring assurances from the Admiralty that they were satisfied with the number of ships available to cruise off the Scottish coast and corresponding with the War Office about the dispatch of regiments beyond the Tweed.[9] Finally on 15 September a draft proclamation offered a

---

[1] S.P. 78/159.   [2] *Evening Post*, 795.   [3] S.P. 35/1, f. 30.
[4] *Weekly Packet*, 114.   [5] S.P. 44/116.
[6] S.P. 44/358.   [7] *Hist. Reg.*, p. 39.
[8] S.P. 35/1, f. 314.   [9] W.O. 4/16, f. 275.

reward of £100,000, a vast sum in those days, to anybody seizing the Pretender.[1]

While these anxieties of State and current diplomatic negotiations in northern Europe, Spain, Italy, and Austria were being watched by the Regency, the Secretary was concerned with the royal funeral. This proved no simple matter. On 1 August the Lords Justices had ordered the body to be embalmed[2] and had appointed a committee to arrange the ceremonies. This committee reported on 11 August, but its proposals were rejected by the regents.[3] Addison then wrote to the Clerk of the Council instructing the committee to revise the arrangements so that the queen should be buried from Westminster instead of from Kensington, and so that the arrangements should conform as much as possible to those made by the queen for Prince George's interment.[4] The committee reported next day, their proposals were generally approved by the regents on 17 August[5] and were returned by Addison with a number of small amendments.[6] But the funeral plans were now interrupted from above, for on 19 August letters arrived from the king containing his own wishes as to the procedure to be adopted.[7] Addison entered into further correspondence with the Privy Council,[8] which continued up to the night of the funeral, that of 23–24 August, when the ceremony was performed by Addison's Christ Church acquaintance Francis Atterbury. Addison's feelings upon this occasion can not have been profoundly stirred. The accession of the queen had cost him his first chance of official employment; throughout her reign she had been coldly hostile to his friends and patrons; and he disapproved of the policies which she was seen to favour. Edward Young used this occasion to address him with a poem upon the queen's death; but this was a testimonial to the esteem with which he regarded the author of *Cato* and the *Spectator*, now translated to the highest administrative honours, rather than any indication of Addison's own affections for the dead sovereign.

The Secretary was much concerned with the more con-

[1] S.P. 35/1, f. 38.   [2] P.C. 2/18.
[3] P.C. 1/2, bundle 11.   [4] Ibid.   [5] Ibid.   [6] Ibid.
[7] *Hist. Reg.*, pp. 25–26.   [8] P.C. 1/2, bundle 11.

genial arrangements for bringing the new king to England. He was in constant correspondence with his old colleague, Burchett, who still reigned as Secretary of the Admiralty, and with the War Office, with regard to the movement of ships and troops. On 12 August he ordered the Officers of the Green Cloth to be in readiness to embark, and next day sent instructions for Lord Berkeley to sail for Holland with any ships ready in the Downs. Thereafter followed a series of additional instructions. Preparations were made by him with the War Office for a landing either at Greenwich or at Harwich.[1] Evidently doubting the adequacy of the naval force available in an increasingly perplexing international political situation, on 19 August Addison ordered a ship of at least fifty guns to join the squadron immediately. He then turned his attention to the ceremony to be observed in England, for which there were no exact precedents. The Clerk of the Council was instructed to produce the ceremonial used at the meeting of King William when he returned to England after the Peace of Ryswick, together with the ceremonies used at St. Paul's and elsewhere upon royal State occasions.[2] On the same day came an express from Hanover saying that the king expected to arrive shortly;[3] but it was 31 August before George left Hanover. He reached The Hague on 4 September.[4] On 6 September the carefully prepared ceremonial was published; on the 8th the Lords Justices thoughtfully prohibited the throwing of squibs during the rejoicings;[5] and on the 13th the proceedings were sufficiently in train for Addison to be able to attend to a detail very much to his liking, namely the design of a coronation medal. He instructed the Clerk of the Council that the Lords Justices agreed with Sir Isaac Newton's advice as to the reverse: there should be no motto but 'Inauguratus Oct—MDCCXIV'.

Addison was the centre of an increasingly complicated administrative situation in which matters of most trivial detail went side by side with others of great and historic importance. There were also the usual personal worries.

[1] W.O. 4/16.   [2] P.C. 1/2, bundle 11.
[3] *Weekly Packet*, 112.   [4] *Evening Post*, 795.
[5] Boyer, *Political State* (September 1714), p. 226.

The Archbishop of Canterbury, a principal figure, was of no assistance because unwell. He wrote to Addison to say that his attendance on the king was uncertain: 'My heart is with him, I wish my strength were equal to my will.'[1] As late as 15 September Addsion informed the Duke of Ormonde that it was still uncertain whether the king would land at Harwich, or at Greenwich, and that provision for guarding the roads in either event must be made. Next day crowds began to congregate at the latter place since a fresh easterly wind was blowing up the river.[2] Addison must have spent an exasperating day, for he was troubled with the rival claims of the great officers of State as to the privilege of fitting up Westminster Abbey for the coronation, a delicate controversy which he passed to the Coronation Committee for a report.[3] On the evening of 18 September the king arrived off the Nore.[4]

As the royal landing approached, Addison must have looked forward to the favour which would recognize his service to the nation and to the House of Hanover. His successful management of the difficult administrative problem of the Regency had been taken notice of by the Justices in a unanimous resolution to memorialize the king on his behalf.[5] It seemed likely that such a memorial would be well received and its subject rewarded.[6] He had been known to the Hanoverian Court since the year 1703, had been to Hanover on official business in 1706, had been prominently associated with the men who were the chief supporters of the

---

[1] Magd. Coll. MSS. B. II. 3, 9, ff. 22–23.
[2] *Dawks's News Letter* for that date.   [3] P.C. 1/14, A 2.
[4] *Evening Post*, 798.   [5] Graham, p. 301.
[6] There is no evidence amongst a mass of official documents to support the story that Addison was administratively clumsy in this office. The only hint of complaint is a reminder from the War Office with regard to an overdue document on 25 August (W.O. 4/16, f. 248). In the abnormal circumstances of the Regency with an interruption of the administrative machine and a change of policy accompanied by an unusual inflow of business, any weakness at the centre of business would have been immediately noticed and fatal. The administrative business of the Regency for which Addison was responsible was conducted remarkably smoothly and efficiently and to the satisfaction of the regents, themselves experienced administrators. Boyer, who was more likely than most reporters to be acquainted with the details, recorded that Addison discharged his duty 'with universal applause' (*Political State*, viii, part 2, p. 281).

Hanoverian cause in England, and had been engaged in secret negotiations with the elector's resident in London on their behalf. He was on reasonably friendly terms with the moderate Tories, and it appeared to be royal policy to take Lord Halifax's view of a future in which they were to play a part. Addison would therefore be acceptable in high office. Yet there were ominous signs. Lords Somers, Sunderland, and Wharton, whose claims to recognition were of the highest order, had been omitted from the Regency. New and younger men, as well as Germans, were replacing Addison's friends of the junto, while the king himself was preparing to undertake the central direction of affairs which had been left by the queen to her ministers. Addison perhaps knew that Lord Sunderland, with whom he might well have worked as a colleague, had approached the German ministers for the post of Secretary of State. But rumour ran that Lord Townshend would be appointed,[1] as indeed occurred.[2] Addison therefore also looked to the German ministers with more hopes because of his previous acquaintance with them; and he opened a correspondence with Robethon, King George's secretary, whom he reminded that at the express request of the Lords Justices he had drawn up the Prince of Wales's Latin patent. This service, he felt, was of a kind generally well rewarded.

When, therefore, on the misty morning of 19 September the regents went down to Greenwich to await the royal landing, Addison was in attendance with Budgell present as his secretary, in a mood of optimism tempered with misgivings. Afterwards Lord Halifax took both men to his library and discussed the expected appointments:

Well, Gentlemen, we have at length gained a compleat victory: The Hanover Succession takes place, the King is landed, and we shall soon have the pleasure to kiss his hand: You are so much my friends that I must tell you plainly I expect the White Staff.

Lord Halifax then went on to outline the policy of moderation which he had long advocated and which Addison had supported:

I resolve, by the help of God, to make King George the First

---

[1] *British Mercury*, 480.   [2] *Evening Post*, 798.

not the Head of a Party, but the King of a United Nation. . . . there shall be no Cruelties, no Barbarities committed. . . . As for you, Addison, as soon as I have got the Staff myself, I intend to recommend you to his Majesty, for one of his Secretaries of State.

Addison agreed with his patron's view that many honest Tories must be preferred to worthless Whigs, but protested that for his part he did not aim so high. But his oldest patron brushed this modesty aside:

Come, prithee *Addison*, . . . I made thee *Secretary* to the *Regency* with this very View: Thou hast now the best Right of any Man in *England* to be Secretary of State; Nay, 'twill be a sort of *displacing* thee not to make thee so. If thou coudst but get over that silly *Sheepishness* of thine, that makes thee sit in the *House*, and hear a Fellow *prate* for half an Hour together, who has not a tenth Part of thy good Sense, I should be glad to see it; but since I believe that's impossible, we must contrive as well as we can. Thy *Pen* has already been an Honour to thy Country, and, I dare say, will be a *Credit* to thy *King*.[1]

The logic was impeccable but Lord Halifax over-estimated his own power. Enmities remained from his quarrel with the Duke of Marlborough in 1707, and King George on his way to England had been advised that if he appointed a Lord Treasurer he would make a subject greater than himself.[2] Nevertheless it became clear at once that those personally known to or deserving well of the new court would be honoured. Lord Hertford, who had accompanied Addison to Hanover in 1706, became a Gentleman of the Bedchamber to the Prince of Wales,[3] and Benjamin Hoadly, Whig protagonist in the Church, a Chaplain in Ordinary to the King. The greater offices were distributed after the first council on 22 September, at which the regents relinquished their responsibilities and Addison ceased to be in employment. He was probably glad of a respite, for the weeks of incessant labour at high pressure and under a heavy responsibility had brought his health near to the breaking point.[4] All of his great friends were members of the new council: Lords Halifax, Manchester, Somers, Sunderland, and Wharton.[5] But Lord Townshend remained Secre-

[1] Budgell, *A Letter to Cleomenes*, 1731, p. 210.   [2] Ibid., p. 211.
[3] *Evening Post*, 799.   [4] Bohn, vi. 635.   [5] P.C. 2/85.

tary of State and General Stanhope was appointed his colleague,[1] thus disappointing both Lord Sunderland, whose impetuousness in party matters the king distrusted,[2] and Addison. The former was instead appointed Lord Lieutenant of Ireland[3] and he chose Addison for the post of Secretary.

After such brilliant expectations it was a bitter mortification to return to the same employment which he had held in 1708, before the literary glories of the *Spectator* and *Cato* and four years of political constancy in the wilderness; but no other opportunity offered. The king was hard put to it to find rewards for all those who thought themselves entitled to his favour. Addison himself reflected not long after this time that 'there are greater Numbers of Persons who solicit for Places, and perhaps are fit for them, in our own Country than in any other. . . . To use the Phrase of a late Statesman, who knew very well how to form a Party, *The Pasture is not large enough.*'[4] Dryly, in five lines which did not stoop to express even formal pleasure, he told Dawson of the news. Charles Delafaye, who had left the office of the *Gazette* to help run the *Guardian* and the revived *Spectator*, and whom Addison knew well enough to refer to as 'my friend', became private secretary to the Lord Lieutenant.[5]

Immediately after the queen's death Addison had become once more a centre of patronage and an intermediary with the great. He had even been offered a bribe by the South Sea Company, which he had refused. Hopeful poets, such as Young and Lawrence Eusden, addressed him in verse. Friends so far off as Governor Hunter in New York wrote to ask his intervention in personal matters.[6] The day before the queen's death he had written with the air of a man sure of success: 'a contented Mind is the greatest Blessing a Man can enjoy in this World'[7] and had followed this, on the day before assuming his secretaryship to the regents, with the reflection that 'Every wise Man . . . will consider this Life only as it may conduce to the Happiness of the other, and chearfully sacrifice the Pleasures of a few Years to those of an

[1] *Evening Post*, 800.   [2] Michael, *England Under George I*, i. 17.
[3] S.P. 44/358, f. 49 and 67/6, f. 28.   [4] F. 48.   [5] *Evening Post*, 801.
[6] B.M. Egerton MSS. 1971, f. 10.   [7] S. 574.

Eternity'.[1] Thereafter he wrote a further eleven papers, the last appearing on 29 September, when he divested himself of what must now have been a troublesome burden. The relative scarcity of the surviving original numbers, and the fewness of the advertisements, suggest that the paper was not financially successful, perhaps for lack of Steele's experienced management.[2] But before laying down his pen he condescended to a parting reference to Dennis, permitting himself a quite unusual freedom which perhaps reflected the change of mood from serene confidence to angry disappointment:

. . . it is a Rule among these gentlemen [critics] to fall upon a Play, not because it is ill written, but because it takes. Several of them lay it down as a Maxim, That whatever Dramatick Performance has a long Run, must of Necessity be good for nothing; as though the first Precept in Poetry were *not to please* . . . this Rule . . . tends very much to the Honour of those Gentlemen . . . few of their Pieces having been disgraced by a Run of three Days, and most of them being so exquisitely written, that the Town would never give them more than one Night's Hearing.[3]

The paper ran on for a further thirty-five numbers under the supervision of Tickell to complete an eighth volume.[4] Addison sold the copyright in this to Tonson next year for £53. 15s., the publisher having previously purchased Buckley's half of the preceding volumes and being thus the sole owner. As in the case of the ending of the *Tatler*, a continuation of the *Spectator* appeared almost immediately, written by William Bond and running twice weekly for fifty-nine numbers. It contained parodies of the *Campaign* and other matter which might be of interest to former readers of Addison's work. But the creator of the *Spectator* took a confident view of his imitators and Budgell recalls it as a favourite saying of his that their efforts resembled the attempts of Penelope's lovers to shoot with Ulysses' bow, and that they met with the same success.[5]

---

[1] *S.* 575.   [2] L. Lewis, *The Advertisements of the Spectator*, p. 75.   [3] *S.* 592.
[4] Budgell, who had acted as editor, left for Ireland on 8 October. He was replaced by Tickell, who, using Addison's accumulated material and writing a number of papers himself, brought the total to eighty numbers, sufficient to complete an eighth volume. M. J. C. Hodgart, 'The Eighth Volume of the *Spectator*', *R.E.S.* v (1954), pp. 367 et seq.   [5] *The Bee*, i. 27.

It was in this year that a new and enlarged edition of *Musarum Anglicanarum Analecta* was published, in which Addison had yet further revised his Latin poetry; and in the month of November he presented a copy of his *Cato* to the Princess of Wales with a new poem addressed to her. It was subsequently charged against him that, whereas under the Tory Government he had said that his play was not politically directed against the administration, he now claimed to have defended the Hanoverian cause. There is no substance in this charge. Addison had always explicitly supported the Hanoverian succession; in the *Spectator* he had praised the elector in his third paper and thereafter; and he had been a vigorous upholder of the British constitution as by law and custom established, and in particular of its implications for the monarchy. What he now claimed in an indifferent courtly piece was that 'boldly rising for Britannia's laws' the British muse had 'generous thoughts of liberty inspired' and had 'engaged great Cato in her country's cause'. This was quite correct. Moreover this tactic had probably been of greater service to the House of Hanover, which under the constitution was entitled to succeed to the British throne, than the more violent polemics of Dick Steele. If any offence is to be detected in these lines it is in the word 'boldly', which hardly conveys Addison's political caution in the staging of *Cato*. He may, however, have felt it a bold step to have launched a play which set the Government in the predicament of being compelled to claim its sentiments for their own, and which was the centre of political controversy for a considerable period during the year most critical to the Hanoverian cause.

Meanwhile, in Ireland Addison was confronted with a situation of complexity and danger, in which his former experience would be of much service to the new Lord Lieutenant. Archbishop King assured him that '. . . His Excellency's . . . pitching upon you to be the nearest concerned about his person and affairs is most gratefull to everybody'. There is no doubt that Addison was generally esteemed in Ireland. But Lord Wharton's carefully contrived balance of Protestant interests had been destroyed and Jacobites had secured numerous posts of authority in a

country recently ravaged by the Whiteboy troubles. Under
the Regency the necessary military measures had been taken
and no violence was now expected; but it remained to
rebuild a stable political position on which to found a
government. There was even trouble in Dublin Corporation[1] and in Trinity College. As a first step the old Privy
Council, from which Addison had never been removed,[2]
was dissolved, and a new one appointed of which he was
also a member.[3] Reliable men were then selected for the
chief posts of the judiciary.[4] To advise on these changes a
number of prominent Irish Whigs and moderates were in
London in consultation with Lord Sunderland and Addison,
to whom the bulk of the decisions probably fell. The
Secretary now dismissed Joshua Dawson and replaced him
as Clerk of the Council and Secretary of the Lords Justices
in Ireland by Eustace Budgell. Addison's cousin went to
Dublin early in October to assume his duties, in which he
received no help from his angry predecessor. That Addison
felt uneasy at displacing one who had occupied the office for
so many years, and who had served him for a considerable
time though without any evident signs of goodwill, is shown
by the fact that he made it clear that this was done 'at the
solicitation of those Irish gentlemen of whom I believe your
Grace [Archbishop King] had a good opinion and by the
particular direction of the Lord Lieutenant'. Addison understood how to shelter behind authority; and while it may
have been desired to replace Dawson by somebody less
involved in the recent Tory extremities, the lengthy past
correspondence between the two men scarcely conceals a
mutual irritation beneath the serenity of official courtesy.
Dawson must have been particularly angry at his super-
session by Addison's cousin.

It was generally assumed that Lord Sunderland and his
Secretary would go to Ireland to assume their duties, and
the press carried the news that they would arrive in Dublin
at the end of October.[5] Perhaps for this reason Addison
took for himself temporary lodgings in Cecil Street in the
Strand. But as far as it is possible to deduce from his writings

---

[1] Blenheim MSS. F.I. 23.   [2] Ibid. D.II. 10.
[3] S.P. 65/7.   [4] Gazette, 5264.   [5] Weekly Packet, 117.

he had no particular affection for the country in whose government he was once more a central administrative figure; and while the fruits of office were still being distributed in London neither he nor Lord Sunderland was anxious to leave the seat of patronage. The docquet of appointment for the Lord Lieutenant provided that the Lords Justices in Dublin should remain in charge until his arrival[1] and reliable men of high ability such as Archbishop King were now appointed to their number.[2] The trouble in Dublin Corporation was cleared up by firm handling;[3] and at the London end a thorough review of the finances of the Army was called for[4] and also an inquiry into Jacobite enlistment.[5] The business of displacing unreliable Tory office-holders was proceeding and by November had reached down to the county administrations; and Alan Brodrick submitted to Addison detailed recommendations for new appointments.[6] The Secretary was the main channel for the stream of patronage of which the Lord Lieutenant was the fountain, and he was the subject of many applications. Meanwhile Lord Sunderland drew £3,000 from the Irish Treasury for his 'equipage',[7] but as Christmas approached he seemed to be settling down to a routine of administering the Government of Ireland from London through the agency of his experienced Secretary, thus leaving his own hands free for national politics. It was even proposed to issue in England commissions which had formerly been handled in Ireland and which had paid fees to the Secretary. Addison avoided the loss of this emolument by arranging with Lord Townshend that his fees would be paid as usual.[8] He was transacting much business with Delafaye at Twickenham, where Lord Sunderland had a residence, and himself needed a secretary. Budgell was absent in Ireland, and Edward Addison busy up at Bilton. Casting around for a suitable man he considered his admirer from The Queen's College, Thomas Tickell. Tickell had acted as Professor of Poetry in Oxford University in the absence of Joseph Trapp, had a long history of poetical tribute offered to Addison's genius, had been of service in the *Spectator* and *Guardian*, and had

[1] S.P. 39/28.   [2] S.P. 63/371.   [3] Blenheim MSS. F.I. 23.
[4] Ibid.   [5] Ibid.   [6] Ibid.   [7] Ibid.   [8] S.P. 63/371.

himself been reported as running what Hearne called 'a silly weekly paper called the "Surprise" '. Although his politics as judged by his poem to the Lord Privy Seal in 1713 on the 'Prospect of Peace' were those of a moderate Tory, he was so inoffensive and politically insignificant that this evidently did not present an obstacle to his employment. Furthermore, Addison believed as a matter of principle that 'men of Learning who take to Business, discharge it generally with greater Honesty than Men of the World'.[1] So Tickell was engaged.

The autumn had been the most disappointing period of Addison's career. Even his accounts with Jacob Tonson as Secretary to the Regents had been disallowed.[2] The accumulation of brilliant prospects destroyed and of petty injuries caused him to feel and express a humiliation and bitterness not recorded in his earlier life. He would have done well to remember his own words in the *Spectator* that:

if we consider the little happiness that attends a great Character, and the multitude of disquietudes to which the desire of it subjects an ambitious Mind, one would be still the more surprized to see so many restless Candidates for Glory.[3]

But Addison did not regard literary glory, of which he already enjoyed more than any Englishman living, as the principal object of ambition, but thought first of his political distinction, with which he was wholly dissatisfied. At the end of September, when engaged in handing over the affairs of the northern department to Lord Townshend,[4] he had still regarded himself as commanding through Lord Halifax the disposal of very powerful English patronage, and solicited places at the request of Lord and Lady Warwick, and of others who might be thought much his social superiors. But it was now apparent that Lord Halifax was to be honoured in dignity rather than entrusted with power. Besides the Garter, a viscountcy, and an earldom,[5] and the honour of entertaining the king to dinner,[6] he had to content himself with the post of First Commissioner of the Treasury.[7] On his appointment Lord Halifax had tried to obtain for Addi-

[1] *S.* 469.   [2] *Cal. Treasury Books*, xx. 479.   [3] *S.* 256.   [4] S.P. 44/116.
[5] *Gazette*, 5268, 5269.   [6] *Weekly Packet*, 119.   [7] *Evening Post*, 804.

son the key post of Secretary of the Treasury, but he was unsuccessful even in this. Lady Cowper noted in her diary that he was in bad odour with the new ministers and with the German advisers who held the king's confidence, partly because of his former intimacy with Lord Oxford.[1] Perhaps not divining the greater disappointment which had thus befallen Charles Montagu amongst the glittering honours conferred upon him, Addison poured out his own discontent to his early and best loved patron:

> I fancy if I had a friend to represent to His Matie that I was sent abroad by King William and taken off from all other pursuits in order to be Employ'd in His Service, that I had the Honour to wait on your Lordship to Hanover, that the post I am now in is the gift of a particular Lord in whose service I have bin Employ'd formerly, that it is a great fall in point of Honour from being Secretary to the Regents, and that their request to His Majesty Still subsists in my Favour, with other Intimations that might perhaps be made to my advantage I fancy I say that His Matie upon such a Representation would be inclined to bestow on me some marke of his Favour. I protest to your Lordship I never gained to the value of five thousand pound by all the businesse I have yet been in, and of that very near a fourth part has bin laid out in my Elections. I should not insist on this subject so long were not it taken notice of by some of the late Lords Justices themselves as well as many others that His Matie nas yet done nothing for me tho it was once expected he woud have done something more considerable for me than I can at present have the confidence to mention.

Nor was he merely disappointed of financial reward and political power: Addison's considerable self-esteem was deeply wounded:

> I will humbly propose it to your Lordship's thoughts whether His Matie might not be inclined if I was mentioned to him to put me in the Commission of Trade or in some honorary post about the prince or by some other method to let the world see that I am not wholly disregarded by him. . . . I shall only beg leave to adde that I mention'd your Lordships kind Intentions towards me only to two persons. One of them was Philips whom I could not forbear acquainting in the fullness of my heart with the kindnesse you

[1] *Cowper Diary*, p. 29.

had designed both him and me, which I take notice of because I hope your Lordship will have him in your thoughts.

The last reference was no doubt to Lord Halifax's intention of securing the Secretaryship of the Treasury for Addison, and some subsidiary post for Philips. At the accession, the pastoral poet had been appointed tutor to the Prince of Wales's children, probably on Addison's recommendation. But he had been superseded soon afterwards. It is therefore probable that Addison was anxious to compensate his friend for such a disappointment, and the premature eagerness with which he conveyed the supposed good news of the kindness 'designed' him illustrates the special regard with which he returned the patient loyalty of his solemn admirer.

With these resentments Lord Halifax was disposed to sympathize. Both he and Addison belonged to the brilliant but brief period of alliances between poets and statesmen, which was now drawing to a close. Lord Halifax had himself raised Addison's hopes in his own hour of expectation; and he now strove against the tide of events to secure him substantial royal favours and in particular the place at the Board of Trade and Plantations. But at the end of November the names of the new Commission were announced and that of Addison was not amongst them. The places had gone by bribery and the favour of a royal mistress.[1] This was too much for disappointed Cato to endure and his wrath burst forth in the kind of letter which no man ought to write who values his reputation, but for which any man who had built his career by long years of patient hard work might be excused. Lord Halifax was again the recipient:

Finding that I have miscarried in my pretensions to the Board of Trade I shall not trouble your Lordship with my resentments of the unhandsome treatment I have met with from some of our new Great men in every circumstance of that affaire but must beg leave to expresse my Gratitude to your Lordship for the great favour you have shown me on this Occasion which I shall never forget. Young Cragges told me about a week ago that His M[ty], tho he did not think fit to gratifie me in this particular designed to give me a Recompense for my Service under the Lord Justices, in which Case your Lordship will probably be consulted. Since I

[1] *Cowper Diary*, p. 31.

find I am never to rise above the Station in which I first Entered upon public Businesse (for I now begin to look upon my self like an old sergeant or corporal) I would willingly turn my Secretary-Ships in which I have served five different Masters to the best advantage I can: and as your Lordship is the only patron I glory in and have a dependence on I hope you will honour me with your Countenance in this particular. If I am offer'd lesse than a Thousand pound I shall beg leave not to accept it since it will look more like a clerk's wages than a marke of His Majesty's favour. I verily believe that H.M. may think I had Fees and Perquisites belonging to me under the L^{ds} Justices, but tho I was Offer'd a present by the South-Sea Company I never took that nor any thing else for what I did, as knowing I had no Right to it. Were I of another temper my present place in Ireland might be as profitable to me as some have represented it. . . . I am informed Mr. Yard besides a place and an annual recompense for serving the L^{ds} Justices under King William had considerable Fees and was never at the charge of getting himself elected into the House of Commons.

The reference to 'our new Great men' and to 'Young Cragges' revealed a burden of resentment and Addison scribbled a savage postscript beneath his signature:

I beg your Lordship will give me leave to adde that I believe I am the first man that ever drew up a Prince of Wales's preamble without so much as a medal for my pains.

The hint to Robethon had evidently not borne fruit. It was a bleak Christmas, and looking back over the year Addison could only comfort himself that *Cato* had enjoyed a successful revival, being performed at least thrice at Drury Lane. One performance was by special command of the Prince and Princess of Wales when no doubt the lines to the latter were spoken.

The little society at Button's and its parallel institution, the Hanover Club, were now at the height of their fame and power, and in both Addison was undisputed arbiter of literary merit. Perhaps for these reasons they began to be uncongenial. Of all literary men in a brilliant age Addison seemed to be the most successful and distinguished, dwarfing all rivals in spite of his recent political disappointment. Jonathan Swift, compromised beyond hope of reconciliation,

held his peace and watched events. But Addison did not
wholly despair of securing Pope's support for the Whig
cause, though a recent meeting between the two men
arranged by Steele had gone off badly. He now dropped a
hint to Jervas, who was also working for a reconciliation,
which was duly reported, to the effect that he 'was afraid
Dr. Swift might have carried [Pope] too far among the
enemy, during the heat of the animosity; but now all is
safe, and you are escaped, even in his opinion'. This
encouragement, accompanied by the deprecation of familiarity with Swift, illustrates the lack of felicity with which
Addison seemed fated to handle Pope. Lord Halifax offered
a pension, which evidently proved no more attractive than
Addison's irritating advances.[1] The old resentments still
lingered, aggravated by the publication and success of the
Rape of the Lock in March this year, with the additions against
the inclusion of which Addison had advised the poet. Pope
seems to have felt that this advice had been malicious, while
Addison may well have had doubts as to the sincerity of the
young man who had prognosticated a failure for *Cato* on the
stage. Besides, Pope was in Oxford where the political
atmosphere was unfavourable to the new régime. He replied
stiffly to Jervas saying that the Whigs must give him leave to
be grateful to Dr. Swift, recalling his alleged ill usage at the
hands of Ambrose Philips, and promising Addison his 'real
friendship whenever he shall think fit to know me for what
I am'.[2]

Addison had in fact become, as Pope described him, the
'Lowndes of the learned world', without whose approval
'we . . . cannot think any scheme practicable or rational'.[3]
It was the situation which Swift had described at an earlier
date much aggravated:

> At Will's you hear a poem read,
> Where Battus from the table-head,
> Reclining on his elbow-chair,
> Gives judgment with decisive air,

---

[1] G. Sherburn, *Early Career of Alexander Pope*, p. 64.
[2] This reply is suspect of fabrication but substantially represents Pope's
attitude at this time.
[3] *S.* 457 attr. to Pope.

> To whom the tribe of circling wits
> As to an oracle submits;
> He gives directions to the town,
> To cry it up or run it down.

Some who would not submit to the oracle had withdrawn from Button's. This accentuated the already bad relations between Addison and Pope, which had secured enough publicity to be referred to in Gildon's *New Rehearsal* this year. As Professor Sherburn points out, each man was the victim of his own supporters.[1] The gossip of the Pope clique is preserved in the *Memoirs of Scriblerus*, published many years later; that of the Button's group can be judged from the pamphlets which came from thence. In *Peri Bathous* Pope selected many weak lines from Addison. Under the heading 'Macrology and Pleonasm' or 'the superfluity of words, and vacuity of sense', six lines are selected from the *Campaign* to prove the point. Then Pope adds, 'of all which the perfection is the Tautology', followed by three further lines from Addison, one being:

Divide—and *part*—the *sever'd* World—in *two*.

Admittedly this is not a strong piece of composition but it is maliciously chosen from a great deal of good verse. Then comes a general proposition: 'The expression is adequate, when it is proportionably low to the profundity of the thought. It must not be always grammatical, lest it appear pedantic and ungentlemanly; nor too clear, for fear it become vulgar....' A quotation is then given from Addison's *Account*, a poor production of early youth. A poet whose private circle was engaged in compiling and circulating matter which ultimately took this form was unlikely to enjoy cordial relations with his senior whose past rebuke he had earned and then resented, whose good faith he doubted, and in whom he divined the strain of jealousy which the effort of a lifetime had mastered but from which he deduced consequences appropriate only to the character of a lesser man.

But these personal relationships were the least of

---

[1] G. Sherburn, *Early Career of Alexander Pope*, ch. v and ch. vi, p. 149.

Addison's concerns in the winter of 1714. Bad news continued to come from India, where Henry Jolley lamented
that 'others reepes the benefitt of our relations labour'. But
while Gulston's estate at Madras fell into decay and his 'great
house' which had cost 7,000 pagodas was running into ruin
and thought to be worth less than a third of that sum,
Joseph's property at Bilton was flourishing under the care
of Edward Addison. The relative was a half-pay captain
in Wittewronge's regiment, a place probably obtained for
him by Joseph when formerly Secretary in Ireland.[1] He was
busy turfing 'your new Walke, . . . now very Handsom and
pleasant', while six or eight men were planting fruit trees
and shelter belts. 'You seem to dislike Sickamors, so non
you shall have', wrote Edward. Amongst the plantings was
'a Walk of trees out of the Towne up to your great-gate'
some of which, limes, still remain. With the unskilful
enthusiasm of a newcomer to the country Addison had
planted too many trees too hastily and probably too large;
most of them had died. A lake was under construction and
Edward was searching for a stock of perch, but, failing to
find any, put in roach and carp instead and, evidently not a
pisciculturist, pike as well. The pigeons were not prospering,
but it was hoped to send partridges to London every week
and sometimes hares, to be picked up at the 'Castle and
Falcon' by one of Addison's servants. Evidently his money
for investment was by no means exhausted and he planned
further purchases. Edward reported that 'Rugby Manor's
not to be had at present nor I am afraide never will . . .
Kendall's cottage nor Westley's close are not yet come-at-
able but I hope time will throw them into your Lapp'.
Addison was an enclosing landlord in the fashion of the
times: 'Your enclosure upon the heath will not yet plow a
2nd time, and that must be done before 'tis marled nor will
Rob: Winterbon part with any more this yeare, but the next
he will.' Addison's game had been destroyed and the Duke
of Montagu's keeper had now been persuaded to oversee it
for the future. Evidently the new self-made absentee squire
enclosing the heath and with a hunger for other men's land,
but who did not know how to plant a tree or to stock a

[1] *Cal. Treasury Books*, xxvii, 211.

pond, was himself fair game for his neighbours, for Edward
reported:

> I find upon enquiry that all the Neighbourhood has made
> Inroads upon you, by hunting, ffishing, shooting, setting, etc.
> without contradiction; 2 days after I came here I met a pack of
> Hounds in full cry just by the Bandylands, but I made bold to
> whip them off and promis'd the Huntsman to be at the Expence
> of a little Buck shott when he came next that way, and I'le be as
> good as my word.

In a postscript the captain added 'pray remember poor
Belisarius', presumably Addison's dog, who saw little of his
famous master but had the satisfaction of being named for
Justinian's general.

Addison's interest in planting and gardening was aesthetic
rather than practical. Edward plied his relative with a farmer's account of manuring and fencing; but Joseph stipulated in detail for the embellishment of his estate. In France
he had preferred the carefully studied negligence of Fontainebleau to the magnificent formalism of Versailles. 'The
King has Humoured the Genius of the place and only made
use of so much Art as is necessary to Help and regulate
Nature without reforming her too much.' He now sought
to humour the genius of Bilton Hall. The planting which he
carried out must be one of the earliest, if a relatively small
example, of the school which was to produce the grotto, the
wild garden, the water-garden, and the rockery. He had
already condemned current gardening fashions in the
Spectator: 'Our *British* Gardeners . . . instead of humouring
Nature, love to deviate from it as much as possible. Our
Trees rise in Cones, Globes, and Pyramids. We see the
Marks of the Scissors upon every Plant and Bush.'[1] He had
gone on to dream of the garden-estate which he designed to
fashion:

> I have several Acres about my House, which I call my Garden,
> and which a Skillful Gardener would not know what to call. It is
> a Confusion of Kitchin and Parterre, Orchard and Flower Garden,
> which lie so mixt and interwoven one with another, that if a
> Foreigner who had seen nothing of our Country, should be
> conveyed into my Garden at his first landing, he would look upon

[1] *S*. 414.

it as a natural Wilderness, and one of the uncultivated Parts of our Country. . . . I must not omit, that there is a Fountain rising in the upper Part of my Garden, which forms a little wandering Rill. I . . . have taken particular care to let it run in the same manner as it would do in an open Field, so that it generally passes through Banks of Violets and Primroses, Plats of Willow, or other Plants, that seem to be of its own producing.[1]

He projected a landscape designed on the grand scale: '. . . why may not a whole Estate be thrown into a kind of Garden' if 'helpt and improved by some small Additions of Art.'[2]

True to his lifelong affection for bird life and in particular for birdsong he had also made mental provision for its indulgence:

There is another Circumstance, in which I am very particular, or, as my Neighbours call me, very whimsical: As my Garden invites into it all the Birds of the Country. . . . I do not suffer any one to destroy their Nests in the Spring, or drive them from their usual Haunts in Fruit time. I value my Garden more for being full of Blackbirds than Cherries, and very frankly give them Fruit for their Songs. By this means I have always the Musick of the Season in its Perfection.[3]

At the lower end of his garden at Bilton, overlooking the stream, Addison constructed a handsome oak panelled and painted wooden summer-house in classical style, where he might sit to enjoy the company of his fruit-eating friends.[4]

His taste in gardening was not merely the companion of emotions evoked by the grandeur of alpine scenery at a time when neither was thought of in terms of the beauty of nature. He was well aware of the singularity of his views and had been at pains to rationalize them:

I think there are as many Kinds of Gardening, as of Poetry; Your Makers of Parterres and Flower-Gardens, are Epigrammatists and Sonneteers in this Art. Contrivers of Bowers and Grotto's, Treillages and cascades, are Romance Writers. . . . As for myself, . . . my Compositions in Gardening are altogether after the *Pindarick* manner, and run into the beautiful Wildness of Nature, without affecting the nicer Elegancies of Art.[5]

---

[1] S. 477.   [2] S. 414.   [3] S. 477.
[4] Destroyed by vandals since this book was first published.   [5] S. 477.

Characteristically he continued to consider the moral value of gardening. 'I cannot but think the very Complacency and Satisfaction which a Man takes in these Works of Nature, to be a laudable, if not a virtuous Habit of Mind.'[1] He singled out the planting of trees, his particular hobby, for the subject of one of the last *Spectators*, and, fortified by the example of Virgil, arrived at the conclusion that 'I can scarce forbear representing the Subject of this Paper as a kind of Moral Virtue'.[2] Thus Addison's estate at Bilton, upon which he was spending so much money in this autumn of disappointment, was not merely a mark of the distinction at which he had arrived, a social advance to the rank of country gentleman; it was also yet another respect in which he brought his pattern of life to conform with the Roman concept of virtuous citizenship.

The course of events in the New Year was not calculated to soothe Addison's wounded sense of desert. Dick Steele was licensed to conduct the Royal Company of Comedians, given a New Year's bounty of £500, made Surveyor of Stables at Hampton Court, and shortly afterwards was knighted. Vanbrugh, who, like Addison, had qualified by a visit to the Hanoverian Court, was made Comptroller of His Majesty's Works and Surveyor of Gardens and Water-works in the Royal Palaces with a salary of £400. It may be that Addison was offered and refused such minor solaces, but he remained without any mark of recognition from the king. In his private life he cannot have been pleased by the remarriage of his sister Dorothy to one Daniel Combes so soon after the death of her first husband, even if he was thereby relieved of some financial responsibility on her account.

On 17 January the proclamation was issued for a new Parliament, to which Addison was returned on 26 January, after a visit to Malmesbury for that purpose.[3] The new House met on 17 March and Addison was appointed as usual to tender oaths. On that night the king dined with Lord Halifax.[4] Four days later Lord Wharton took his seat in the House of Lords as a marquis and Lord Halifax as an

---

[1] Ibid.   [2] *S.* 583.   [3] *Post Man*, 11050.
[4] *Dawks's News Letter*, 19/3/1715.

earl.[1] After a short but violent debate in the Commons
Addison had been appointed with others to draw up an
address to the king in reply to his speech to the Houses,
and had again been appointed to the Committee of Privileges
and Elections. The political battle between the parties was
joined at Westminster and he seems to have been taking an
active part behind the scenes, serving as a teller upon an
election petition on 26 March, which indicates that he had
been prominently concerned in that matter. It having been
decided to appoint a Committee of Secrecy to investigate
the conduct of the late Ministry, Addison was a member of
the committee set up for the purpose of selecting that body.
In the midst of this political excitement Lord Wharton died
suddenly,[2] thus removing from the scene an influential if not
a favourite former master. Two days later, on 16 April, Lord
Sunderland was dangerously ill;[3] but on 19 April, after
having been reported past recovery, he began to mend.[4]
Early in May he left for Bath to recover his health,[5] while
Addison hastened to make light of the nature of the illness to
his Irish correspondents. Thus at this anxious time the main
conduct of Irish affairs in London rested with the Secretary.
In these circumstances it must have been a consolation that
Lord Halifax, in whom lay Addison's main hopes of royal
favour, was increasingly intimate with the king, with whom
he dined again at the end of April.[6] But a fortnight later
Lord Halifax was also taken ill,[7] and on 19 May the patron
who had lifted Addison out of the cloister and who for all
his vanity and failings had steadily supported his interests
through good times and bad, also died.[8] This was probably
the most grievous personal loss which Addison had suffered
since the death of his father, not excluding the decease of
two brothers. Not only was he genuinely grateful to Charles
Montagu, but he also greatly admired and indeed loved the
brilliant financier and ambitious politician who was somewhat repellent to the rest of the world. Addison's life had
been built around great men whose personal esteem and

[1] *British Mercury*, 518.   [2] *Gazette*, 5320.   [3] *Weekly Packet*, 145.
[4] *Dawks's News Letter*, 19/4/1715.   [5] Ibid. 7/5/1715.
[6] *Evening Post*, 895.   [7] Ibid. 902.
[8] Ibid.; *Dawks's News Letter*, 21/5/1715.

support he won by his literary gifts and administrative ability as well as by his personal character. One by one the pillars of his world were crumbling. Lords Wharton and Halifax were dead; Lord Somers was fast decaying; Lord Sunderland was still unwell, and the Duke of Shrewsbury, who might have befriended him, was again withdrawing from public life. Power now rested with new men who cared less for learning and letters and not at all for Addison's subtle genius. It was a vigorous but somewhat unfriendly environment, in which, with Swift in Ireland, Wortley married, and many friends dead, few of Addison's oldest associates remained.

Lord Halifax's funeral took place at Westminster on 26 May 1715.[1] Two days later Dick Steele gave an entertainment for two hundred people to celebrate the king's birthday.[2] This took place at the Censorium and emphasized experimental science: 'All works of Invention, All the Sciences, as well as mechanick Arts.' Its purpose was to present a reformed theatrical amusement, both pleasant and edifying. The epilogue for this occasion drew a witty but kindly picture of the manner in which Steele's enthusiasm had so often outrun his judgement:

> The Sage, whose Guests you are to Night, is known
> To watch the Publick Weal, tho' not his own . . .
> Early in Youth, his Enemies have shewn,
> How narrowly he miss'd the Chymic Stone . . .
> Still on his wide unwearied View extends,
> Which I may tell, since none are here but Friends:
> In a few Months he is not without Hope,
> But 'tis a Secret, to convert the Pope . . .

The lines have been attributed to Addison and certainly reflect the mixture of tolerance, amusement, and regret with which he had regarded his impetuous friend for many years.[3] Yet Dick Steele, the author of so many works of personal folly and literary genius, seemed to possess the drive and zest to keep pace with the new times and new men. Perhaps in an effort to establish himself politically with the new order which was essentially a House of Commons group,

[1] *Dawks's News Letter*, 28/5/1715.   [2] *Weekly Packet*, 152.
[3] J. Loftis, *Steele at Drury Lane*, p. 109.

Addison spent a great deal of time at Westminster and wrote correspondence from that palace. He did much committee work in such diverse matters as private bills, provision for Quakers to affirm instead of taking an oath, the payment of tithes, the provision of ministers for fifty new London churches rebuilt after the Great Fire, and the enforcement of law and order. In the House Addison doubtless gained authority as the representative of the Government of Ireland. He seems to have spent much time in the chamber during the important debates upon the impeachment of the late Ministry, reporting at considerable length to the Lord Lieutenant at Bath through the intermediary of Charles Delafaye. Finding the detailed work heavy, he took extra help, using Thomas Addison, a member of the Cumberland clan who sat for Whitehaven, as a kind of Parliamentary Private Secretary. In the House Addison had always been a staunch Whig and he prided himself upon never having voted against his 'friends'. When, however, it was proposed to impeach the Duke of Ormonde, he found himself in a delicate position. As Chancellor of Oxford University the duke had befriended him, and recently had been responsible for securing him in his place in Ireland during the Tory Ministry. 'I shall never pardon my self if I give a Vote that may have a tendency to the taking off his Head', he told Delafaye, and gave notice to Lord Sunderland that while he would not take his gratitude to the length of voting against the duke's impeachment, he would be conveniently absent from the premises should any such occasion arise.

In spite of his hard work in Parliament Addison still remained without any mark of royal favour. Yet his devotion to the person of King George never wavered, and in this year he addressed to Sir Godfrey Kneller a poem mainly designed to compliment the king. Calling forth all his funds of imagination and technique he produced a very sprightly piece taking for its theme Kneller's portrait of the new monarch. Perhaps he now felt that in the absence of Charles Montagu he had no means of bringing himself to royal notice except that of his pen. The poem proved popular with contemporaries and ran through four editions by the next year. Macaulay thought it 'Wonderfully ingenious—Neither Cowley nor Butler ever surpassed, I do not remember that they ever equalled it'.[1]

In poetry as in architecture, Addison admired the 'inherent Perfection of Simplicity of Thought'.[2] '*Homer*, *Virgil*, or *Milton*, . . . will please a Reader of plain common Sense, who would neither relish nor comprehend an Epigram of *Martial* or a Poem of *Cowley*.'[3] When commending the ballad of Chevy Chase, he had written that 'the Thoughts of this Poem, which naturally arise from the Subject, are always simple, and sometimes exquisitely noble; . . . the Language is often very sounding, and . . . the whole is written with a true poetical Spirit'.[4] Of Sappho he wrote that 'she followed Nature in all her Thoughts, without descending to those little Points, Conceits, and Turns of Wit with which many of our Modern Lyricks are so miserably infected'.[5] His dislike of 'Conceits' and 'Turns of Wit' was almost one of moral fervour, to which a whole *Tatler* had been devoted[6] and which recurred again and again in his writings as a parallel with his contempt for 'Gothick' architecture. All modern imitators of Pindar, producers of 'monstrous Compositions',[7] came within his general condemnation. So negative was his approach that he made no distinction in principle between the purposes of verse and prose: 'there are several ways of conveying the same truth to the mind of man; and to chuse the pleasantest of these ways, is that which chiefly distinguishes Poetry from Prose . . .'.[8] Such an attitude induced Johnson's comment: 'He thinks justly but he thinks faintly.' Of these thoughts upon the writing of verse Addison's poem to Sir Godfrey Kneller is a mature expression, the nature of the circumstances permitting the poet to produce a very elegant verse tribute to both artist and king.

Addison also drafted a prose petition to the king. This document set out at length his services to the Crown and to the House of Hanover, his lack of any reward, the unusual circumstances rendering his Irish office not particularly profitable, and ended with the complaint which remained

---

[1] MS. note in his copy of Addisons *Works* in B.M.
[2] *S*. 70.   [3] Ibid.   [4] *S*. 74.   [5] *S*. 223.   [6] *T*. 163.   [7] *S*. 160.
[8] *An Essay on Virgil's Georgics.*

his chief source of grievance: 'It is therefore an unspeakable mortification . . . to be regarded as one who has forfeited your majesty's favour.'[1] That he was thus regarded by the king is somewhat unlikely though not impossible. Lord Halifax had incurred much displeasure in the ruling political circle by his courtship of the moderate Tories, and Addison had been closely associated with him. Few Whigs would have cared to present 'a large silver cup' to Dr. Arbuthnot, as he did.[2] It is also not impossible that Addison's own advances to the Prince and Princess of Wales, who had incurred royal jealousy, had counted against him. But it is more likely that, like Wortley, who at first determined to accept no office below that of Secretary of State, Addison failed to understand the altered circumstances which had made him politically less rather than more significant than he had been in the reign of Queen Anne; while the king had found it quite impossible to gratify all of those who thought themselves entitled to consideration.

But in spite of disappointments Addison's duties as Secretary of the Irish Government proved less unsatisfactory to him than he had expected. So long as Lord Sunderland did not go to Dublin to take the oaths of office, Addison could not qualify for quite all of the benefits of his place. But with a principal absorbed in national politics, and who was unwell for a considerable period, Addison found himself virtually acting-Lord Lieutenant. It was, however, expected that Lord Sunderland would go to Ireland, and Budgell reported from Dublin that he was asked 'twenty times daily' when this would occur.[3] Doubtless he would have welcomed Addison's arrival, for the displaced Dawson was being 'very uneasy' to him and was withholding precedents and other necessary documents.[4] In London there was a heavy programme of Irish business, including the disbursing of Irish Secret Service funds. The regulation of the wool trade,[5] the raising of new regiments and the taking of security measures to meet a rumoured invasion by the Pretender at the head of French forces,[6] an overhaul of the

---

[1] Bohn, vi. 534-6.   [2] Ibid. 695.   [3] Blenheim MSS. D.I. 23.
[4] Ibid.   [5] S.P. 63/372; Blenheim MSS. F.I. 23.
[6] *Dawks's News Letter*, 15/3/1715 and Blenheim MSS. D.I. 23.

revenues,[1] the problems of the linen trade,[2] the revival of
the Dublin militia,[3] and the detailed allocation of patronage
on the Irish establishment, all required his attention. In the
last respect he was continually solicited,[4] and to afford him
some measure of protection it was now arranged that he
should not know the names included in the final draft of
offices. To take this important document to Ireland he
employed his Bilton agent, Captain Edward Addison.

During Lord Sunderland's illness formal business requiring the authority of a senior minister was conducted by
Stanhope, a Secretary of State, with whom Addison was at
this time in frequent contact. Addison also had occasion to
transact a certain amount of business with the Duke of
Marlborough, with whom he was apparently upon quite
familiar terms. At the Dublin end of government Archbishop King and the Brodrick family were correspondents
and principal supporters of the administration. The archbishop had many complaints, particularly of absentee officers.
He warned Addison of the fatal consequence of neglecting
Irish affairs, a complaint directed at the Westminster Government and perhaps at Lord Sunderland, but not at Addison
himself who seems to have been the only person in London
who took a really diligent interest therein.[5] Budgell's letters
bore out the archbishop's anxiety, as also did the views of
the Lords Justices and the judges.[6] The jails were full of
Tories; and in a land where there were six papists to one
protestant the Pretender's recruiting and preparations were
a serious matter.[7]

During this period Addison had had thoughts of a high
office at Trinity College, Dublin, probably of an honorary
nature. But on 18 March Alan Brodrick wrote that the
college was not in a temper to do itself the honour of choosing him.[8] It was seriously disaffected and on Budgell's
advice and that of the archbishop the elections then due for
vacant posts were deferred.[9] Peculiarly embarrassing was
the discovery in Dublin of documents[10] which disclosed a

[1] Blenheim MSS. D.I. 23.   [2] S.P. 63/372.   [3] Blenheim MSS. F.I. 23.
[4] Letter Archbishop King–Addison, 7/7/15 in Blenheim MSS. F.I. 23.
[5] Blenheim MSS. F.I. 21 and G.I. 19.   [6] S.P. 63/373.
[7] Blenheim MSS. D.I. 23.   [8] Ibid.
[9] Ibid. and F.I. 23; also S.P. 63/372 and 67/6, f. 86.   [10] S.P. 63/372.

treasonable or at least seditious correspondence addressed to Jonathan Swift by the Duchess of Ormonde's chaplain.[1] This must have doubly embarrassed Addison on account both of duke and dean, the more so because Lord Sunderland was eager to exploit the situation to good political advantage in the Westminster Parliament.[2] Upon a further examination, however, the case against Swift fell to the ground; he had remained passive and letters addressed to him had received no answer.[3]

Another personal incident of some interest in this period arose out of a letter written to Addison on 13 June by St. George Ashe recommending to his notice 'Major Dunbar, a very worthy honest Gentleman, . . . to befriend him in a very reasonable request he has to make to My Lord Lieutenant and which he will explain to you at large'.[4] David Dunbar offered Addison a substantial present for his intercession; firstly a bank bill for £300 and, on its rejection, a diamond ring of the same value.[5] This drew from the Secretary, who had so long prided himself upon taking all his due but no more, a rebuke in the grand manner:

And now Sir believe me[6] when I assure you, I never did, nor ever will, on any pretence whatsoever take more than the stated and customary Fees of my Office. I might keep the contrary practice concealed from the World, were I capable of it, but I could not from my self. And I hope I shall always fear the Reproaches of my own Heart more than those of all Mankind. In the mean Time, if I can serve a Gentleman of Merit, and such a Character as you bear in the World, the Satisfaction I meet with on such an Occasion is always a sufficient and the only Reward to . . . &c.[7]

Addison thus posed himself in the style of Cato, and his

---

[1] S.P. 63/372; Blenheim MSS. F.I. 23.   [2] S.P. 63/372.

[3] F. Elrington Ball, *The Correspondence of Jonathan Swift*, 1912, ii. 422.

[4] Blenheim MSS. D.I. 33.

[5] G. J., *Memoirs of the Rt. Hon. Joseph Addison Esq.* Curll, 2nd edn., 1724, and J. Ker, *Memoirs*, 1726, ii. 180–4.

[6] A favourite phrase of Addison's to the frequency of which Lady Mary had objected in *Cato* in its first draft.

[7] Some doubt has been thrown upon the authenticity of the foregoing letter, but my discovery of the introduction to Addison from St. George Ashe at Blenheim, published in Graham, p. 346, makes its contents too plausible to be rejected.

action was unusual by the standards of his age and wholly consistent with his philosophy of public duty and reward. It is somewhat remarkable that this private matter in which so secretive a man was the principal actor should have come to light; and it may indicate that his conduct in business was as steadfast and consistent as his adherence to his political principles.

The Lord Lieutenant, who was Addison's last remaining political patron in power, was not greatly interested in his office. As early as 5 March the press carried a rumour that he had asked to be relieved of his responsibilities[1] and that Lord Wharton would succeed him; but on 26 March a notice appeared that the earl 'with an intention to honour the Irish Nation, over which he is Ld. Lt.' was preparing a splendid equipage and had bought a set of eight 'curious coach mares' said to have cost £1,000.[2] On 14 April the same paper printed a notice that Lord Pembroke would be appointed to the post, while on 10 May there appeared an announcement that Lord Sunderland's equipage was getting ready and that he would set out in about a fortnight. But that nobleman, still at the Bath, was writing four days later to Stanhope that nothing short of certain death would prevent him from coming to London for the main business in Parliament, which makes it clear that he had no intention whatever of leaving for Ireland.[3] On the other hand, Addison, writing on 24 May, appeared to expect to be in Dublin with his chief quite soon. He had been in the habit of doing small acts of kindness for his friend and relative the Reverend Arthur Stevens. In 1709 the *Tatler* and *Gazette* had been sent down to him in the country from Addison's office in London.[4] Stevens now complained of loneliness and lack of occupation and asked to be allowed to accompany his relative to Ireland, paying his own expenses. It is therefore likely that Addison held himself out to correspondents as intending to go to Dublin, perhaps as part of the Lord Lieutenant's pretence of taking his duties seriously.

In fact Lord Sunderland returned to London towards the end of June[5] in excellent spirits, and on 2 July it was again

[1] *Weekly Packet*, 139.   [2] *Dawks's News Letter*, 26/3/1715.
[3] S.P. 63/372.   [4] Blenheim MSS. D.I. 32.   [5] *Flying Post*, 3663.

said in the press that he was about to set out for his Government.[1] But on 13 August there were rumours that he would
be appointed Lord Privy Seal,[2] and on the same day Addison
was writing to Archbishop King to say that the Government
of Ireland would, he believed, be put into commission, and
that he would lose his post of Secretary as a result. On
23 August Lord Sunderland resigned and Addison was
again without employment. Rumour had it that, greatly
disappointed with his preferment, he had never had any
intention of taking it seriously, but maintained a perpetual
air of being about to leave for Dublin if not prevented by
illness or circumstance, in order to retain royal favour. This
seems not unlikely in view of the fact that though the press
reported him desperately ill, Addison dismissed his ailment
as colic.

In the world of letters it had been a busy but difficult
period. In January 1715 there had appeared a spurious successor to the *Spectator* which expired in August. *Cato* had
been revived for three major performances at Drury Lane
and one at the Stationer's Hall. So deep was the impression
made by Addison on the public mind that the pseudonym
of *Cato* was adopted by anonymous letter-writers to the
Secretaries of State,[3] and a hawker was whipped for distributing a seditious paper entitled *Cato's Ghost*,[4] while there
appeared from the press a volume of anonymous *Translations from Bion, Ovid, Moschus, and Mr. Addison*. With this
aftermath of triumph there remained Addison's uneasy
friendship with Pope. The two men were in not infrequent
communication, exchanging manuscripts of poetry written
by friends, with conscious civility.[5] Pope says that he frequented Button's at this time,[6] and Swift evidently expected
him to be in touch with Addison, for, writing in June, he
sent his 'humble service' by that channel.[7] In January Pope
had published his *Temple of Fame*, which included the lines
in which he had rebutted Addison's charge of envy. There
could be no offence in this, for the verses were a plain
disclaimer and made no counter-charges; Addison had seen

[1] *Weekly Packet*, 159.   [2] Ibid. 162.   [3] *Gazette*, 5317.
[4] *Weekly Journal*, 14/7/1715.   [5] Sherburn, i. 284.
[6] Spence, p. 146.   [7] Williams, ii. 177.

them some years before without raising any objection. Addison went to some trouble to propitiate Pope at this time. As Thomas Burnet, who thought that Addison failed to support his pamphleteering projects, expressed it: '. . . I have seen Addison caressing Pope, whom at the same Time he hates worse than Beelzebub and by whom he has been more than once lampooned . . . .'[1] Addison never permitted himself to hate; but Burnet perceived and magnified the antipathy which it required the self-command of Cato to control.

Pope also evidently desired to remain on friendly terms. A product of this desire was the verse prologue to Addison's unpublished 'Dialogues upon Medals'. It is likely that Pope saw the manuscript about the time of its sale to Tonson, when Addison had this topic in mind and wrote thereon in the *Guardian*; and Mr. Norman Ault conjectures that a first draft of Pope's verses on the subject was written not later than this year. The matter certainly received some attention at this time for it was in 1715 that Curll published Addison's paper on the 'Error in Distributing Modern Medals' at the end of the *Knowledge of Medals* written by 'a Nobleman of France'. This had reached a second edition by August and quoted le Clerc's remarks, which had already been published in translation, urging Addison to print his study of the 'mystical meaning' of reverses. The praise of le Clerc and even of Curll's author, and the fact that when they were published the posthumous *Dialogues* were translated into French, Italian, and Spanish, suggest that Pope's good opinion was sincere. Mr. Ault conjectures that his lines of praise were developed in Pope's peculiar fashion from 1713 until 1717 or later. With such tenuous threads of goodwill between the two men, Jervas, who had been painting Addison in the spring, was still doing his best to effect a thorough reconciliation.[2] But Pope lacked the restraint to endure in silence the friction which temperamental differences generated. Furthermore there now occurred an event which made any real improvement of their relations, already unlikely, in future unthinkable.

[1] *Letters of T. Burnet to Geo. Duckett*, ed. Nichol Smith, letter of 1/6/1716.
[2] *Biographia Britannica*, 2nd edn., p. 88 n., letter Gay–Congreve 7/4/1715.

It will be recalled that Addison had written to Pope in October 1713 pointing out the difficulties of translating Homer but adding words which could be construed either as an encouragement to proceed, or as a delicately veiled hint to the contrary. Pope's interpretation of this enigmatic sentence was: 'Mr. Addison was the first whose advice determined me to undertake this task . . . .'[1] At that time Thomas Tickell was at work upon a translation of Lucan. To assist him 'to put out a fine, correct edition' the Master of University College had borrowed 'a Lucan in vellam, being a MS. about 400 years old, with a great many glosses', from Lord Treasurer Harley. This was seen by Hearne in December 1713.[2] In this work Pope and Jervas had encouraged Tickell. Meanwhile Pope had signed an agreement with Lintott for a translation of Homer and was raising a subscription to publish it. It was two months after this that Tickell signed a similar agreement with Lintott's rival, Tonson, to translate the whole of the *Iliad*. Addison then felt it necessary to invite Pope to dine privately so that he might explain the transaction, excusing himself from reading Pope's first book, on the ground that he had already looked over Tickell's, but consenting to criticize the second. This Pope sent him next morning.[3]

The precise details of these transactions and the motives behind them have been dealt with at length by Professor Sherburn and Mr. Norman Ault. The substance of them is that Pope, who already suspected Addison of jealousy of his rising reputation, could hardly think that Addison's literary and political protégé, Tickell, would embark upon a rival translation of Homer for a rival publisher without his patron's approval. He could not but resent the motive which he imputed to Addison and the possible financial loss to himself which might result from Tickell's action. But there is no evidence that Addison originated the project in which Tickell was now engaged; while Tonson, doubting Pope's scholarship, might well seek to promote a more successful translation from the hand of a poet of stronger academic qualifications, and is its more likely sponsor. It

---

[1] Preface to Pope's *Iliad*.
[2] Hearne, *Collections*, iv. 270, 289.   [3] Spence, p. 146.

would not have been consistent with Addison's detachment from other men's affairs to seek to dissuade Tickell from proceeding. He therefore viewed each translation with an impartial eye. He looked over Tickell's manuscript and suggested corrections, and before Lord Halifax's death he had listened to an extensive reading from the earlier books of Pope's version which he praised subsequently in print.[1] In his conversation at Button's he appears to have attempted a judicial attitude. Garth reported him saying that Tickell's first book was the best ever produced in any language, but that both were well done. His reason for preferring Tickell's version was that it had 'more of Homer'[2] which is true in one sense.

But the rival factions soon made sorry havoc of any attempt at impartiality by Addison. A brisk pamphlet war sprang up, in which Addison attempted to prevent attacks on Pope's person[3] and sought to moderate the heat of the battle. He thereby hopelessly embroiled himself in the hostilities, his good faith being mistrusted by Burnet, the author of an attack upon Pope entitled *Homerides*, and by his friend and collaborator, George Duckett. Thus good intentions involved Addison in distrust by both sides, and he found himself the recipient of a letter of remonstrance from the two last-mentioned authors, as a result of which they fancied that they had incurred his undying hostility.[4] The situation was further aggravated by the belief, which rapidly gained ground, that Addison and not Tickell was the substantial author of the latter's translation. A pamphlet entitled *Homer in a Nut-shell: or, the Iliad of Homer in Immortal Doggrel: By Nickydemus Ninnyhammer*, published in this year, mentioned 'the Odysseis design'd to be infinitely better Translated by Mr. Tickell, alias Jo. Addison'. This insinuated Addison's authorship of the earlier translation and also that the purpose of Tickell's *Iliad* was to discredit Pope's. In later years Steele, in the course of an attack on Tickell, made a similar insinuation as to authorship; but that singularly direct controversialist did not think fit to assert the fact. He merely challenged

[1] F. 40.   [2] Sherburn, i. 305.
[3] *Letters of T. Burnet to Geo. Duckett*, ed. Nichol Smith, p. 81.
[4] B.M. Add. MSS. 36772, f. 176.

Tickell to translate another book of the *Iliad* now that Addison was dead, a challenge not accepted. These circumstances lend colour to the belief that Tickell was indebted to Addison for considerable help in correction and revision, but also suggest that he was in fact the author of the translation which bears his name.

Lintott wrote to Pope on 10 June: 'the malice & juggle at Button's is the conversation of those who have spare moments from Politicks.'[1] The number of pamphlets published around the two translations probably arose from the rivalry of the two publishers, who had considerable financial interests involved. Tonson used the group at Button's to write in detraction of Lintott's book; and the conversation provoked amongst the Buttonians was, of course, reported to Pope. 'I am inform'd that at *Button*'s your character is made very free with as to morals *&c*' wrote Gay.[2] The position had been complicated by the production in February of John Gay's play *The What D'ye Call it*, with some hits at *Cato*, in which Pope had a share. The triumph of *Cato* continued and increased, and Addison evidently thought *The What D'ye Call it* a legitimate and good-humoured squib, which he could afford to ignore. He was at pains to show that he bore Gay no resentment by subscribing for ten copies of *Trivia* next year, an act of generosity which drew from the poet a warm acknowledgement of the 'Benefits you have done me'. But Pope had urged Gay to burlesque Ambrose Philips's *Pastorals* in his *Shepherd's Week*. This was a subject upon which Addison's deputy at Button's was particularly sensitive, and Philips, whose lack of humour had been aggravated by his elevation to the Commission of the Peace, was not the man to enjoy raillery at his own expense. Gay's piece was now attacked from Button's.

The controversy soon spread to Oxford, where the scholarly interest aroused by the translations was considerable and where Pope's was preferred. There seems to have been some canvassing by Tickell. Dr. Lancaster, for example, prudently but almost certainly inaccurately replied to his inquiries that: 'I hear very little in this place of any body's Homer'; while Edward Young reported the bad impression

---

[1] Sherburn, i. 294.   [2] Ibid. i. 305.

which the circumstances of publication of Tickell's version had made and the general prejudice against it as being maliciously intended. The whole episode redounded to the discredit of the Button's group and even of Addison himself; and from this time onwards the coffee-house circle of which Philips was the head came to be regarded more and more as a conspiracy of men of mediocre ability.

The impact upon Pope of this publishers' war and its accompanying unpleasantness was powerful. His attitude seems to have been quite clear by the summer of this year. He attributed to Addison the hostilities which had been aroused in part by his own conduct, in part by the activities of rival literary gangs, in part by the enterprise of rival publishers, and in part by the political feuds of the day. Surrounded by exploding literary fireworks on every hand, he crystallized his resentment around Addison's pretensions to authority in the world of letters. He recalled the quotation from Denham which Addison had used in the *Spectator* to reprove him for his attacks on contemporary poets, which had reminded him:

> Of Eastern kings, who, to secure their reign
> Must have their brothers, sons and kindred slain.

He now prepared this shaft against the man who had once used it to rebuke him, barbing it in so doing:

We have, it seems, a great *Turk* in Poetry, who can never bear a Brother on the throne; and has his Mutes too, a sett of Nodders, Winkers and Whisperers, whose business is to strangle all other offsprings of wit in their birth.[1]

Turning his mind to what appeared to him to be the central figure and defect of the literary world, he began to analyse the character of the man for whom he had a real admiration, but whom he hated with the bitterness of jealousy aggravated by a sense of personal injustice. Brilliantly he dissected the complex character of his great rival, selected the weaknesses of which Addison was perhaps aware but which he had overcome by a lifelong effort of self-discipline. He then cast his thoughts into a form which re-translated into verse his

[1] Sherburn, i. 306.

prose recollection of Addison's taunts from Denham, and flung it back in an expanded version. This recalled ironically the history of growing tension between the two men dating from the *Spectator* reproof. In his wrath he ground from his genius lines which have hardly been surpassed in the English language. Dismissing the poetasters with a gesture, he wrote verses which he ultimately perfected as the famous 'Atticus' lines:

> Peace to all such! but were there One whose fires
> True Genius kindles, and fair Fame inspires;
> Blest with each Talent, and each Art to please,
> And born to write, converse, and live with ease:
> Shou'd such a man, too fond to rule alone,
> Bear, like the *Turk*, no brother near the throne,
> View him with scornful, yet with jealous eyes,
> And hate for Arts that caus'd himself to rise;
> Damn with faint praise, assent with civil leer,
> And without sneering, teach the rest to sneer;
> Willing to wound, and yet afraid to strike,
> Just hint a fault, and hesitate dislike;
> Alike reserv'd to blame, or to commend,
> A tim'rous foe, and a suspicious friend,
> Dreading ev'n fools, by Flatterers besieg'd,
> And so obliging that he ne'er obliged;
> Like *Cato*, give his little Senate laws,
> And sit attentive to his own applause;
> While Wits and Templers ev'ry sentence raise,
> And wonder with a foolish face of praise.
> Who but must laugh, if such a man there be?
> Who could not weep, if Atticus were he!

The draft of these lines upon which Pope was now probably working differed in important details from the final text.[1] But it bears the marks of accuracy in describing the inner nature of the man whose conduct has been under consideration; the virtues dashed in in broad outline, the failings picked out with the minuteness of a medical illustration. The line about the 'little Senate' which referred to Addison's circle at Button's was doubly telling because, taken verbatim from Pope's prologue to *Cato*, it was thus intended to remind

---

[1] N. Ault, *New Light on Pope*, generally.

Addison of his indebtedness to Pope on that occasion. Cibber summed up the piece admirably in later years when he said: 'though I am charm'd at the poetry, my Imagination is hurt at the Severity of it';[1] and Congreve, when he saw it, is said to have sighed: 'from this time forth I number him [Pope] among the incurables.'[2] Yet in spite of so much pent-up anger, at least on Pope's part, the two men remained on civil speaking terms. Echoing his own lines, Pope noticed that 'we are each of us so civil and obliging, that neither thinks he is obliged. And I for my part treat with him, as we do with the *Grand Monarch*; who has too many great qualities not to be respected, tho' we know he watches any occasion to oppress us'.[3] Feeling himself thus menaced, Pope kept his lines by him unpublished, and probably uncommunicated, as a weapon of offence in case he needed and dared to use them.

[1] Cibber, *Apology*.   [2] *Ingratitude to Mr. Pope*, 1733, pp. 8–9.
[3] Sherburn, i. 306–7.

IX

A FORTY SHILLING FREEHOLDER
1715–1717

ADDISON was now without political employment, though seated in the Parliament at Westminster and a member of the Irish Privy Council. The Irish Parliament was not summoned to meet until the autumn of 1715 after he had ceased to hold office as Secretary and he was not a member of it. Archbishop King wrote regretting that he no longer had Addison's assistance: 'this is a real truth and no compliment'; and thanked him warmly for his care of Irish Affairs.[1] It had been a period when most of the legal and ecclesiastical appointments had been filled by Irishmen of merit. Lecky credited this to Lord Sunderland,[2] but it is not improbable that the Secretary, who knew the merits of his Irish friends, and who conducted most of the business of the Lord Lieutenant, was mainly responsible for this policy. A succeeding chief governor, the Duke of Grafton, reported that it had produced 'very mischievous consequences'; but had it been consistently followed the later history of Ireland might have been more fortunate.

Budgell had worked hard and won good opinions. He entered the Dublin Parliament and Addison was requested to permit him to remain in Ireland.[3] In Addison's place joint Secretaries were appointed, one of whom was Charles Delafaye.[4] Thus two men who had been of service to him were removed from his immediate circle of helpers. He can have had little to do at this time, and he contemplated a visit to Ireland to take the oaths of office in the new reign as Keeper of the Records. Perhaps with this in mind he sent friendly messages in advance to Jonathan Swift by way of St. George Ashe. Early in September he sat upon two

[1] Blenheim MSS. F.I. 23.   [2] *Ireland in the 18th century*, p. 445.
[3] Blenheim MSS. F.I. 23, Conolly–Addison letter of 30/8/1715.
[4] *Post Boy*, 4071.

unimportant committees at Westminster before the House ceased to sit. But thereafter he evidently abandoned his projected Irish visit. Meanwhile his friends prospered. Sir John Vanbrugh had been made King-at-Arms,[1] Lord Sunderland was rumoured for a Garter,[2] and Dick Steele for the Mastership of the Charterhouse[3] of which he was eventually disappointed. The eighth volume of the *Spectator* was published on 1 September, but looking round for a patron to whom to dedicate it, Addison could find none, and ordered it inscribed to Will Honeycomb Esq., perhaps feeling that it was no time to sound the note of gratitude. Rather humbly, he memorialized the king asking that his office of Keeper of the Irish Records be granted him for life, and for the salary to be increased from £400 to £500 per annum.[4] This was no more than had been promised him by Lord Godolphin in 1710 as a reward for his previous service in Ireland. On 4 October 1715 his request was granted as a reward for his much greater services to the Regency, and the previous debt of Government remained undischarged.

This year saw the publication in pamphlet form of Jean le Clerc's *Observations upon Mr. Addison's Travels through Italy*, translated into English by Theobald, with a dedication to Eustace Budgell:

All the writings of Mr. Addison have something in 'em so above the Pitch of modern compositions, that they are as easy to be distinguish'd from others, as they are impossible to be imitated. No wonder then, that he rais'd the Curiosity of Men of Taste to transfuse his Writings from one Language to another; and make them, even in his own days, by a respect of the same kind, equal to the Dead Classicks; from whom he may justly be said to differ, as our Milton does from their Homer, propter mille annos.

Addison received bad news of another friend. George Berkeley had revisited England for a brief period in August 1714, when Addison as Secretary of the Regency must have been too busy to spend much time in his company. He had then gone abroad again as tutor to a son of St. George Ashe. He can hardly have failed to discuss with Addison during their philosophical transactions in 1713 the occasion on

---

[1] *Weekly Packet*, 165.   [2] *Dawks's News Letter*, 17/9/1715.
[3] *Weekly Packet*, 169.   [4] Blenheim MSS. G.I. 19.

which the latter had visited Malebranche and had listened to his theory of colours. Berkeley now called upon Malebranche and found the philosopher unwell, engaged in infusing curative herbs in a pipkin. It is most probable that the name of Mr. Spectator and of *Cato* was mentioned. When, however, the conversation turned to philosophical subjects Malebranche became so greatly excited that his death, which occurred on 13 October, was thought to have been hastened thereby. Berkeley can hardly have failed to send Addison an account of this interview.[1]

In England *Cato* was again revived, being acted at Drury Lane on 21 October. Evidently the Princess of Wales again saw the play, and also occasionally saw Addison at her husband's court in this year, for early in November she wrote to Leibniz: 'Je n'ay pas vu Addison de quelques semaines. Sa tragédie est très-belle, et Caton luy-même ne se plaindroit pas des sentiments nobles et dignes d'un homme comme luy, qu'il luy a donnés.'[2] The political situation was now quite different from anything which Addison had previously experienced. He had succeeded in steering his way harmless between the enmities of the Duke of Marlborough and Lords Halifax and Sunderland. But the throne itself had remained above and beyond his daily cares. Now there was rivalry and jealousy between the royal court and that of the Prince of Wales, and it may be that during the summer he had incurred displeasure for his previous addresses to the princess and for his apparent attendance at her court, from which he now absented himself for a time. In the political field there was also a sharp division between Lord Sunderland on the one hand and Lord Townshend and Robert Walpole on the other. It behoved Addison to walk extremely warily, lest he should offend those who might help him; and his disappearance from the prince's court may have been connected with the fact that he was seeking once more, probably through the agency of Lord Sunderland, for a place at the Board of Trade. He was assisted by events, for the Jacobite rising of this autumn had impressed upon the Government the importance of securing moderate opinion in favour of

---

[1] K. Stock, *Memoirs of George Berkeley*, 2nd edn., 1784, has an account of Berkeley's visit.   [2] Klopp, *Leibniz Werke*, xi. 50.

the king, who was becoming dangerously unpopular. For this purpose a political periodical enjoying a wide circulation was required. On 20 December, therefore, Addison kissed the king's hand upon becoming one of the Commissioners of Trade and Plantations[1] at a salary of £1,000 per annum.[2] He thus redeemed his vow not to accept any office below that figure.[3] Three days later there appeared the first number of a new periodical to be published twice weekly, entitled the *Freeholder*.

Addison's paper was written entirely by himself without collaborators; and unlike any considerable previous periodical with which he had been associated, it was wholly political in its purpose. The *Freeholders* were essays which brought politics out of cabinets and parliamentary committees and the all-male society of the coffee-houses, and into the circle of the family tea-table. This was a political crusade parallel with the social crusade of the *Spectator* though on a smaller scale and designed to meet the emergency of the 1715 rebellion. He assumed the personality of the English freeholder of forty shillings' worth and based his arguments on that franchise: 'it is what I most glory in, and what most effectually calls to my Mind the Happiness of that Government under which I live. . . . The House of Commons is the Representative of Men in my Condition. I consider myself as one who gives my Consent to every Law which passes'.[4] Unlike Mr. Spectator, the Freeholder was a partisan rather than a detached observer. Loyalty was now the matter at issue, and Addison chided the political bystander: 'How . . . can any Man answer it to himself, if . . . he stands as a Looker-on when the Government is attack'd by an open Rebellion.'[5] But the vein of Addison's *Spectators* is often present, particularly in the humorous essays: parodies of memoirs, predictions, declarations, even royal histories as well as a mock club complete with mock lists and mock rules. Addison's feminine Order of the Garter reminded a contemporary of Pope's *Rape of the Lock*.[6]

Nevertheless the substance of the *Freeholder* was deeply

[1] *Dawks's News Letter*, 22/12/1715; *Post Boy*, 4119; *Gazette*, 5392.
[2] S.P. 38/30; *Weekly Packet*, 181.   [3] S.P. 44/458, f. 338 and 38/29.
[4] F. 1.   [5] F. 8.   [6] *Weekly Remarks*, i. 12.

serious politics. Faithfully following Locke, Addison based his political society upon the ownership of property, and identified the British Constitution, embodied in the Revolution settlement and subsequent legislation, with common sense and freedom. An examination of the sources of his political thinking has led some modern critics to conclude that 'Addison . . . provides the example of a surpassingly important English thinker whose significance lies in his genius for unification rather than for unique thought'.[1] Opposed to a consistent and attractive portrait of the British establishment, meriting the support of all intelligent people, he drew a picture of the Jacobite cause as that of popery, tyranny, poverty, and, above all, stupidity. Stating his purpose he wrote:

While many of my gallant Countrymen are employed in pursuing Rebels half discomfited through the Consciousness of their Guilt, I shall labour to improve those Victories to the Good of my Fellow-Subjects; by carrying on our Successes over the Minds of Men, and by reconciling them to the Cause of their King, their Country, and their Religion.[2]

His second paper was a panegyric upon constitutional monarchy as a principle and upon King George as an example thereof:

We have the Pleasure at this Time to see a King upon the Throne, who hath too much Goodness to wish for any Power, that does not enable him to promote the Welfare of His Subjects; and too much Wisdom to look upon those as his Friends, who would make their Court to Him by the Profession of an Obedience, which they never practised, and which has always proved fatal to those Princes who have put it to the Trial.[3]

This was a declaration of war upon all Tories holding the doctrines of passive obedience and non-resistance to a divinely appointed monarch. He went on to praise the bravery of the Royal House and their affection for their new country.

In his third paper he turned his batteries of ridicule upon the prisoners who had been taken from the rebels at Preston,

[1] Edward and Lillian Bloom, 'Addison and Eighteenth Century Liberalism', *Journal of the History of Ideas*, xii (1951), pp. 560–83.
[2] F. 1.   [3] F. 2.

by inventing the *Memoirs* of such a one; and he sought to identify the Tory and High Church party with popery and rebellion. In a fourth he turned to the ladies and, much in his element, pointed out that:

though a Husband is sometimes a stubborn Sort of a Creature, a Lover is always at the Devotion of his Mistress. By this means it lies in the Power of every fine Woman, to secure at least half a Dozen able-bodied Men to his Majesty's Service.

He went on to insinuate that prostitutes were notoriously Jacobite, and to point to the unfortunate lot of women in Catholic countries under absolute governments. In his fifth paper he analysed the nature of patriotism and demonstrated that it ought to be founded in reason as well as in sentiment. Thereafter, having mapped out the scope of his paper, he examined various topics bearing upon loyalty to the new establishment: the binding nature of oaths; the folly of rumours; an answer to the Pretender's declaration; the nature of rebellions in general and of the present one in particular; and the offence of indifference as being second only to that of rebellion. He returned repeatedly to the ladies, with such themes as the untrustworthiness of lovers who within a year have broken their oaths to the king, the unfashionableness of Tory ladies who were banished the court, Tory and Protestant fans, and a eulogy of the Princess of Wales following her birthday. Addison was thoroughly in his element, calling forth all his powers of entertaining ridicule, all of his learning, and his belief in the reasonableness of the constitution and the Protestant religion. He applied them with his own particular skill in stating conclusions in such a manner that they convince the reader without an elaborate supporting argument.

So important a new entry into the field of political controversy did not long go unnoticed.[1] By the time four numbers had appeared *A Supplement to the Weekly Journal* made observations at some length upon Addison's paper and continued to follow its writing with interest.[2] There were a number of attacks upon it, some in its own vein of banter: the *Freeholder* 'meets with Contempt among those whose . . .

[1] *A Supplement to the Weekly Journal*, 4/1/1716.
[2] e.g. issues of 28/1/1716, 18/2/1716, and 21/4/1716.

Favour and Esteem it courts, the most Beautiful of our British Ladies, I mean the Tories. For while some among the Whigs of that Sex must be own'd to be Raging Beauties, . . . we must own that . . . the Tory Ladies are the Reigning Belles of this Age . . .'.[1] By the end of March it was an open secret that Addison was the author of the *Freeholder*.[2] But although he may have undertaken rejoinders in pamphlet form he generally avoided them in his paper, while increasing the intensity of his political theme. Perhaps remembering the trespassing hounds at Bilton, he converted his benevolent ridicule of Sir Roger into a malicious study of an ignorant Tory fox-hunter. He wrote a mock history of the Pretender's reign. Then he applauded the Septennial Act, which would reduce the number of elections and therefore reduce public excitement. This was a key measure of the Administration and was instrumental in securing the Whigs in power; for the Bill applied to the present as well as to future Parliaments. Addison commended to his readers a pamphlet entitled *Arguments about the alteration of the triennial elections of parliament*. This was said to be 'generally fathered on the ingenious and judicious Joseph Addison Esq.',[3] perhaps as a result of the *Freeholder* references. But its awkward style proclaims it as certainly not his work, and it appears to have been claimed by Defoe.[4] Its arguments met with Addison's approval and he voted for the bill on 24 April.[5]

Addison now wrote upon the benefits of trade and upon the superiority of the commercial treaty negotiated by Whig ministers for the king in 1715 as compared with that obtained by their predecessors two years before. On this subject he could speak with authority as a member of the Board of Trade in daily contact with the merchant community. Another paper of particular interest was that addressed to the universities. Addison had spent twelve years at Oxford, where he had achieved considerable distinction; and it was not until twenty-four years after his entry into the university that he severed his connexion with Magdalen. His brother Lancelot had also been a prominent member of the college.

---

[1] *Weekly Remarks*, i. 12; see also ii. 21.   [2] H.M.C. *Stuart*, ii. 62.
[3] A. Boyer, *Political State*, 1716, p. 484.
[4] N. & Q. v. 577.   [5] *Parl. Hist.* vii. 367.

But though the *Spectator* is full of reminiscences of his travels, in all his writings about contemporary society references to Oxford, direct or indirect, are exceedingly rare. In one so observant, and taking into account the great importance of the university in matters of deep interest to Addison, it is almost certain that this turning away from so large a part of his past experience conceals from us a disagreement with authority or some cause of mortification. Since the Sacheverell trial Oxford had become progressively more Jacobite. This was particularly true of Magdalen which, during the rebellion of 1715, had been notably disloyal. Hearne recorded of the university on 28 May, King George's birthday, that:

the people ran up and down crying King James the third, the true king, no Usurper, the Duke of Ormond, etc. and healths were everywhere drunk suitable to the occasion, and everyone at the same time drank to a new Restoration, which I heartily wish may speedily happen.

George Smalridge, Addison's Christ Church and Lichfield friend, had recently refused to sign the declaration against the Pretender, but was nevertheless labelled a 'sneaker' by the implacable Hearne, because he celebrated the Pretender's birthday privately in his lodgings instead of openly. Magdalen had become a refuge for Jacobites fleeing from authority. It was therefore to a highly unsympathetic audience that Addison now addressed himself in a *Freeholder* devoted to this subject.

He began with a compliment to Trinity College, Dublin, which had recently chosen the Prince of Wales as Chancellor. Then he deplored the state of affairs 'when Arts and Sciences are so perverted as to dispose Men to act in contradiction to the rest of the Community, and to set up for a kind of separate Republick among themselves'.[1] Thereafter his argument pointed out that royal favour and preferment was unlikely to come to the disloyal. It was an unconvincing paper, likely to offend rather than to placate. Yet in the public mind Addison remained an Oxford man, and as Garth had put it:

> The gentle Isis claims the ivy crown,
> To bind th' immortal brows of Addison.[2]

[1] F. 33.   [2] 'Dispensary', iv. i. 207.

The king's birthday gave him an opportunity to return to the personal theme and to praise the virtues of his sovereign; and by the month of June the rebellion having been suppressed and no further danger being apprehended, the circumstances which called forth the *Freeholder* had passed away, and Addison had expended the heavy ammunition in his political arsenal. He therefore prepared to close the publication. In the fifty-fourth and penultimate number, he cast off some of the party zeal which had temporarily animated his pen, so far as to admit that a moderate position in politics is preferable to any other, though of the two extremes a Whig is the more to be commended. Examining history, he found that Queen Elizabeth had been a good Whig and King James I a Tory, and proceeded to wind up his argument on the merits of the two. On 29 June he wrote his last paper, to coincide with the rising of Parliament, the departure of the king for Hanover, and the easing of political controversies. Looking back over the *Freeholder* he restated his purpose in its production:

... the Design of the whole Work, has been to free the People's Minds from those Prejudices conveyed into them by the Enemies to the present Establishment, against the King and Royal Family, by opening and explaining their real Characters; to set forth His Majesty's Proceedings, which have been very grossly mis-represented, in a fair and impartial Light; to shew the Reasonableness and Necessity of our opposing the Pretender to his Dominions, if we have any Regard to our Religion and Liberties: And, in a word, to incline the Minds of the People to the Desire and Enjoyment of their own Happiness.

Anticipating that, as with the *Tatler*, *Spectator*, and *Guardian*, there would be others anxious to take up his vacant title, he added a public caution:

If any Writer shall do this Paper so much Honour, as to inscribe the Title of it to others, ... the whole Praise or Dispraise of such a Performance will belong to some other Author; this fifty-fifth being the last Paper that will come from the hand of the *Free-holder*.

The *Freeholders* were amongst his best prose works. Macaulay thought them 'As good as almost anything that

Addison ever wrote',[1] and No. 22 'delicious'. Addison was Dryden's pupil, and he now fully complied with his master's prescription for good English composition.[2] Fine writing must spring from a full life well lived; and his style was the product of his own life and achievements. It was not meticulously accurate; it was occasionaly prolix, and, in the circumstances of periodical writing, sometimes hasty. It contained few features which could be fairly called distortion, or which, on the other hand, were arresting methods of expression. There were some idiosyncrasies, such as a fondness for pairs of contrasting adjectives and nouns: 'agreeable Confusion',[3] 'agreeable Wildness',[4] 'agreeable Horror',[5] 'pleasing Horror',[6] 'prettiest confusion.'[7] It was a turn of phrase which he admired yet did not approve in Ovid and Claudian[8] and which he classified as 'mixt wit'. Claudian 'loves to set his epithet at variance with its substantive, and to surprise the reader with a seeming absurdity . . . some of his greatest beauties as well as faults arise from the frequent use of this particular figure'.[9] It was what Lucan called *concordia discors* and was much used by John Dennis. There were also minor blemishes in the frequent repetition of certain words and phrases. The idea and the word 'secret' have been observed to occur with disproportionate frequency in his writing, perhaps as a reflex of his own secretive nature. But these faults, and others which scholars have been at pains to discover, were small matters. The virtue of his prose writing was that it was easily familiar. As Johnson put it, 'his readers fancy that a wise and accomplished companion is talking to them'.[10] His style was a vehicle admirably suited to the purpose of his periodical essays, which was to persuade; and by the application of learning, reason, and moderation to English prose he succeeded in setting a standard which served for most English men and women for two centuries. Set forth in this familiar yet distinguished

[1] MS. notes in his copy.
[2] Ch. II, p. 32. [3] *T*. 218. [4] *T*. 111. [5] *T*. 90.
[6] *S*. 419.
[7] 'Dialogues on Ancient Medals', III.
[8] Notes upon Ovid's *Metamorphoses*.
[9] 'Dialogues on Ancient Medals', II.
[10] Boswell, *Life of Johnson*, ed. Hill, i. 244.

manner, the *Freeholders* were powerful political writing, designed to present Jacobitism as foolish, vicious, and unfashionable, and loyalty as plain common sense and virtue such as would distinguish any rational Briton.

The popularity of the *Freeholder* proved durable, for it contained much statement of political truth interesting to later generations. It passed through many collected editions and secured a French translation. Nevertheless Dick Steele, who had praised the *Freeholder* in his own writings,[1] is reported to have recalled the allegory of one of Addison's famous *Tatlers* saying that the Government had made use of a lute when they stood in need of a trumpet. But if reliance is to be placed on the report it goes to show how far Dick's judgement came to err when his friend's politics were in point. The *Freeholder* was valuable to the government; and if it is the only first-class pamphleteering to come from Addison's pen, it nevertheless shows him highly successful in yet another branch of literature.

Addison's political duties pressed hard upon him throughout the period when he was writing the *Freeholder*. His appointment to the Board of Trade necessitated his reelection at Malmesbury. Accordingly a writ was issued on 9 January and by the end of the month he was returned once more for the borough where his political position was now well entrenched. Meanwhile on 5 January his warrant of appointment to the Board had been passed[2] and his fee, probably £70,[3] was paid. On 17 January he took his place with his colleagues. Traditionally a Whig stronghold, the Board had been reformed by Lord Somers in 1696, and Jacob Tonson was its stationer. In the public mind Addison's appointment was thought to be a reward for two popular courtly poems:

---

[1] Vide *Town Talk*, No. 4 of 6/1/1715–16: 'I send you all the *Freeholders* that are come out; they are very Entertaining, Honest and Instructive', and also No. 7, 'This Paper comes out in the midst of Confusion and Animosity, which are fomented by Pamphlets and other loose Papers, like a Man of Sense in a Multitude, whose Appearance among them suppresses their Noise, and gains him an Authority to be heard with Attention for the common Service.' *Steele's Periodical Journalism, 1714–16* (Oxford, 1959), pp. 213, 234.   [2] C.O. 389/37, pp. 88–115.

[3] The amount paid by Stepney on a similar occasion: Jacobsen, *Blaythwayt*, p. 433.

Mr. Addison, who has an admirable talent, and a peculiar vein
at *versification*, and who has of late, by adding to several other
memorable operations of the brain in that kind, two late instances
of his panegyricks on King George and the Princess, given us
new demonstrations of his being a very good poet, and a particular
great genius in *that way* of Writing, is now appointed a *Commissioner of Trade*.[1]

That he thought the employment would prove congenial is
evident from the pains with which he had sought it. True,
his only trading venture to come to our notice, the dealing
in shoes in Ireland, had ended disastrously; and Addison
had no reason to love the merchant community in Madras.
But all his life as a true Whig he had been a zealous exponent
of trade and finance, and from his friend Charles Montagu
he learned the significance of money and coinage. On his
travels in Europe he had been careful to study the causes of
prosperity or poverty in the communities which he visited.
His views of the nature of wealth and credit, and the value
of bullion in commerce, were those fashionable in the age,
but were cast into popular form in his periodicals. He
thought commerce to be the foundation of British power:
'Trade, without enlarging the *British* Territories, has given
us a kind of additional Empire.'[2] There are many references
to the virtues of trade in the *Freeholder* and, in May 1716,
Addison devoted two complete issues to the subject. The
first (*F.* 41) is a brief history of English trade agreements
from Edward III to George I in which it is pointed out that
'the Care of our National Commerce redounds more to the
Riches and Prosperity of the Publick than any other Act of
Government' and that English historians had neglected its
importance. The following issue argues that 'Trade . . . is
absolutely necessary and essential to the Safety, Strength, and
Prosperity of our . . . Nation'. But perhaps more effective
than either of these secular sermons was his satire on the
Tory fox-hunter in the twenty-second *Freeholder*. While
enjoying a bowl of his favourite punch, the garrulous country
gentleman asserts that 'Trade would be the Ruine of *England*'; to which the Freeholder retorts: 'I took this Occasion
to insinuate the Advantages of Trade, by observing to him,

---

[1] *Weekly Remarks*, i. 5.   [2] *S.* 69.

that Water was the only Native of *England* that could be made use of on this Occasion: But that the Lemons, the Brandy, the Sugar, and the Nutmeg, were all Foreigners.'

But the Board of Trade, though Whig, was like many Whig institutions, aristocratic. It was presided over by the Earl of Suffolk, consisted of about eight members who attended with some regularity, and was responsible for the day-to-day management of commercial and plantations business. Addison was an assiduous Commissioner,[1] being usually in attendance at the meetings which took place according to the amount of business to be transacted and averaged about a dozen monthly. It is interesting to notice that he brought to plantations affairs an attitude of mind towards the negro much in advance of that of his contemporaries:

> What might not that Savage Greatness of Soul, which appears in these poor Wretches on many Occasions, be raised to, were it rightly cultivated? And what Colour of Excuse can there be for the Contempt with which we treat this Part of our Species; That we should not put them upon the common foot of Humanity....[2]

In his new office he would have many opportunities to temper the primitive harshness of the negro's treatment, for the duties of the Board ran into much detail. As Under-Secretary of State Addison had a good introduction to a special and important field of administration in which he would now widen his knowledge.

At the time that he was conducting a political periodical and taking up his duties at the Board, Addison was also preparing to stage a comedy, the *Drummer*. The circumstances were far different from those attending the production of *Cato*, but the motives were analogous in some respects. Addison's tragedy was enjoying a revival at Drury Lane, where it was produced twice in February and once each in March, April, and May of 1716. By way of inverted compliment, the 'Tory' house at Lincoln's Inn Fields produced Ozell's version of des Champs's adaptation of the play. This was soon published by the enterprising Curll, with 'a parallel

---

[1] *Journal of the Commissioners of Trade and Plantations*, vol. 1714-18.
[2] *S*. 215.

between this play and that written by Mr. Addison'. Controversy still raged around *Cato* and the fame which Addison derived therefrom continued to grow. In this year George Sewell made Addison's play the foundation for his *Vindication of the English Stage*. Addison had triumphed successively with Latin poetry, English poetry, prose essays, and a tragedy. He had been successful with a political periodical. His attempt at opera had been attended with credit if not with success. Regarding as he did every form of literature as a means to the improvement of mankind, it was natural that he should seek to set an example in the writing of comedy, to use it to correct and improve manners as he had used his tragedy to inspire the great virtues.

Dick Steele was now in charge of the king's company of comedians, and an intelligent woman such as Lady Cowper was expressing the hope that under his direction 'our stage . . . will mend'.[1] It was natural that Dick should look to his versatile friend for a comedy, and not surprising that one should be forthcoming. The initiative, however, seems to have come from Addison, who sent for Steele, 'which he could always do from his natural power over me, as much as he could send for any of his clerks when he was Secretary of State'.[2] When Steele arrived at the interview, Addison told him cryptically that 'a gentleman then in the room' had written a play that he was sure to like, but the authorship of which was to be secret. Addison believed that 'few works of genius come out at first with the author's name'.[3] Unlike *Cato*, the *Drummer* was not generally known to exist, and Steele seems to have gone away bearing the play with him, for on 12 March he sold it to Tonson on the author's behalf for fifty guineas.[4]

That Addison had kept the manuscript of the *Drummer* by him for many years, we are told on the authority of his friend who was now to produce it. He implies that it was written before its author had any considerable acquaintance with the theatre. There is also a hint in the prologue to the play that it was a 'first attempt to write'. This may have been camouflage under the licence of anonymity, but it may also

[1] *Cowper Diary*, pp. 46-47.   [2] Steele, Dedication to the *Drummer*.
[3] *S.* 451.   [4] Steele, Dedication to the *Drummer*, 1721.

mean that the first drafts of the *Drummer* antedated *Cato*. If this was the case, it is certain that they had been the subject of the application of much scholarship at a later date. But the ghostly drummer from which the play takes its name evidently had an origin in the haunting of the Mompesson house at Tidworth, near Addison's childhood home. He thought it foolish to be terrified of ghosts, but unreasonable to disbelieve in their existence in view of the almost universal testimony of mankind.[1] His *Drummer* was not therefore ridiculous in his own eyes, but reflected the reality of a story which he heard in childhood. It had been in the year 1661 that a mendicant drummer, perhaps an old Commonwealth soldier, had been detected travelling on forged papers by Squire Mompesson, who took away his drum and handed him over to the Constable. Thereafter the Mompesson house was disturbed by drummings and thumpings, the furniture was unaccountably thrown about, and the bible found in the ashes of the fire. The drummer was sentenced to transportation at Gloucester, but evaded that fate by 'raising storms and affrighting the seamen', who refused to carry him. In 1663 he was therefore prosecuted as a witch at Salisbury on evidence of having said of Mompesson: 'I have plagued him, and he shall never be quiet until he hath made me satisfaction for taking away my drum.' The Grand Jury indicted the drummer, but he was subsequently acquitted upon his trial, and the drummings and thumpings eventually subsided.[2] This country tale of mystery provided the central figure of Addison's plot.

It is alleged that he had passed the idea of a play woven around a ghostly drummer to William Harrison, who roughed out a draft under his direction.[3] On the other hand it appears from Steele's preface to the piece finally published in Addison's name that Tickell had some pretensions to a share in the authorship. In this Curll at first supported him.[4] But when Steele declared Tickell's part to be not much more than that of an amanuensis, he withdrew his allegation.[5]

---

[1] *S.* 110.

[2] For an account of the foregoing see W. E. A. Axon, *Literary History of the 'Drummer'*.   [3] Ibid.

[4] G. J., *Memoirs of the Life of the Rt. Hon. Joseph Addison, Esq.*, 1719.

[5] Ibid., 2nd edn., 1724; see also Charles Wilson, *Memoirs of the Life of W. Congreve Esq.*

Tickell, who was closely associated with Addison at this time, probably worked upon the preparation of the manuscript while Addison was busy with administrative matters. But Steele's evidence as to the authorship must be conclusive in view of his close association with the play : and Macaulay scribbled in the margin of his copy before he was halfway through Act I: 'I have no doubt this was Addison's . . . as if I had seen him write it.'[1] Thus, although the *Drummer* may have had a long history of development from early origins, and may have passed through other hands, it was substantially Addison's work, and Tonson was informed of this authorship under bond of secrecy.

The extraordinary precautions taken to conceal the authorship of the play were probably attributable to other motives beside Addison's belief in the principle of anonymity; there were considerable doubts as to the fate of the piece on the stage, and he had too much reputation as a dramatist to feel inclined to risk any portion of it. Even Steele and his partners in the theatre had doubts as to the likelihood of success :

> I own I was very highly pleased with it, and lik'd it the better, for the want of those studyed Similes and Repartees, which we, who have writ before him, have thrown into our Plays, to indulge and gain upon a false Taste that has prevailed for many Years in the *British* Theatre. . . . I was confirmed in my Thoughts of the Play by the Opinion of better Judges to whom it was Communicated, who observed that the Scenes were drawn after *Moliere's* Manner, and that an easie and natural Vein of Humour ran through the whole. . . . My Brother-Sharers were of Opinion, at the first reading of it, that it was like a Picture in which the Strokes were not strong enough to appear at a Distance. . . .[2]

The merits which commended the play to critics were those points in which its author declined to gratify popular taste. Colley Cibber recalled in his *Apology* that Addison, sitting next him at Hamlet, had 'asked with some surprise, if I thought Hamlet should be in so violent a Passion with the Ghost, which, tho' it might, have astonish'd him, it had not provok'd him?' Addison's nicety of taste, of which his comedy was the product, was beyond the capacity of the

---

[1] See his copy of Addison's *Works* in B.M.   [2] *Drummer*: Preface.

majority of the audience. He had also applied the rules of contemporary French drama to his comedy as thoroughly as he had done to *Cato*. It was 'correct' and decorous, and inevitably negative in its virtues, properties which had contributed least to the stage success of his tragedy. It was, like *Cato*, heavy with moral purpose. In the prologue of the *Tender Husband* in 1705 Addison had written of the barrenness of subjects for comedy:

> Our modern wits are forced to pick and cull,
> And here and there by chance glean up a fool:
> Long ere they find the necessary spark,
> They search the town, and beat about the Park.

He used the stock-in-trade of comedy; the ingredients of his play were a husband and wife, a lover, a 'ghost', and four domestics: but he disposed them in a new order. The fool, who had so often been the faithful husband of comedy, was in this case the lover. The hero, who had usually been the fashionable and witty lover, was the husband. The wife, instead of conspiring to deceive her husband, contrived to expose the lover. Thus the purpose of the play was to present the joys of married life, its pathos, and its tenderness, by contrast with the folly of infidelity. For good measure the fool was made an atheist. Thus the *Drummer* was a comedy of sentiment and virtue which would have been acceptable to the public a century later. Directed to the middle class, it was even more interesting and unusual than *Cato*. As Steele described it:

there is not an expression in the whole piece which has not in it the most nice propriety and aptitude to the character which utters it; there is that smiling mirth, that delicate satire, and genteel raillery which appear'd in Mr. Addison when he was free among Intimates.[1]

As with the *Tatler* and *Spectator* so in the production of the *Drummer*, Dick was the business manager of the operation. It was he who apparently succeeded in convincing the managers of the Theatre Royal of the play's merits. The only new play presented at Drury Lane in the 1715–16 season, it was produced for the first time on 10 March, when, as Steele

---

[1] *Drummer*: Dedication.

tells us, it was 'exquisitely well acted'. He had given it a
good puff in his current paper *Town Talk* on 13 February,
and had provided a discerning audience by the means used
with success at the launching of *Cato*. Mills, Wilks, Cibber,
and Anne Oldfield were from the cast of Addison's tragedy,
with Pinkethman, famous comedian, added to them.

Steele evidently used the group at Button's to push the
play, and an offensive epilogue attacking Pope came from
that source, but was not permitted to be spoken.[1] The
prologue used at the performance proclaims the purpose of
the poet in the manner of a *Spectator* upon the motives of the
authors:

> Long have your Ears been filled with Tragick Parts,
> Blood and Blank-Verse have harden'd all your Hearts;
> If e'er you smile, 'tis at some party Stroaks,
> *Round-Heads* and *Wooden-Shooes* are standing Jokes;
> The same Conceit gives Claps and Hisses Birth,
> You're grown such Politicians in your Mirth!
> For once we try (tho' 'tis, I own, unsafe)
> To please you All, and make both Parties laugh.

The lesson of *Cato* had evidently made a deep impression
upon Addison, who was determined that his comedy should
not become a political battleground. The epilogues, spoken
by Anne Oldfield, had some good bantering lines:

> To Night the Poet's Advocate I stand,
> And he deserves the Favour at my hand,
> Who in my Equipage their Cause debating,
> Has plac'd two Lovers, and a third in waiting . . .

It was also big with moral teaching:

> Too long has Marriage, in this tasteless Age,
> With ill-bred Raillery supplyed the Stage;
> No little Scribler is of Wit so bare,
> But has his fling at the poor Wedded Pair.
> Our Author deals not in Conceits so stale,
> For shou'd th' Examples of his Play prevail,
> No Man need blush, tho' true to Marriage-Vows,
> Nor be a Jest, tho' he should love his Spouse.

[1] Sherburn, *Early Career of Alexander Pope*, p. 160.

In the circumstances of secrecy attaching to the play, and in lines which reveal so clearly the drift of Addison's and Steele's writings upon social topics, the prologue and epilogue were probably written by one or other of the two men, and their sprightly turn and particular cadence seem to indicate Steele as their author.

At the second performance on 13 March, Dudley Ryder, later Attorney-General, was in the audience. He recorded in his diary:

At past 5 went to the play called *The Drummer*. There is a good deal of mirth in it and something pleasant and entertaining. The prince was at the play. An epilogue was spoken to recommend the cause of religion and liberty and loyalty to the care of the ladies, some part of which was very good. . . . I was very well pleased to hear it clapped by a full house and a general approbation of the sentiments. The Duke of Argyll stood with the prince talking with him.[1]

But in spite of excellent acting and perhaps because of the remarkable qualities of the play, the fears of the promoters proved justified:

. . . the touches being too delicate for every taste in a popular assembly. . . . As it is not in the common way of writing, the approbation was at first doubtful, but has risen every time it has been acted, and has given an opportunity in several of its parts for as just and good action as ever I saw on the stage.

Thus thought Dick Steele; but after performances on 10, 13, and 17 March there were no further presentations of the *Drummer* in Addison's lifetime.

Steele, however, was prepared to back his judgement; and on 21 March the play was published by Tonson without the author's name, but with an introduction by the patentee in which he conjectured: 'I do not question but the reader will . . . see many beauties that escaped the audience;' and in a later edition he added a further recommendation:

The Drummer made no great figure on the stage . . . but when I observe this I say a much harder thing of the stage, than of the Comedy. When I say the Stage in this place, I am understood to mean in general the present Taste of Theatrical Representations,

[1] *Diary of Dudley Ryder*, ed. W. Matthews (1939), p. 195.

where nothing that is not violent, and, as I may say, grossly delightful, can come on without hazard of being condemn'd, or slighted. It is here republished, and recommended as a Closet piece, to recreate an intelligent mind in a vacant Hour; for vacant the Reader must be from every strong Prepossession, in order to relish an entertainment . . . which cannot be enjoy'd to the degree it deserves, but by those of the most polite taste among scholars, the best breeding among gentlemen, and the least acquainted with sensual pleasure among ladies.

Steele's judgement was vindicated; for when published posthumously under Addison's name, the *Drummer* was acted frequently, not entirely because of the reputation of the author, but because the public taste had moved in the direction which Addison had indicated. There were nine English editions by the end of the century, two French and two German adaptations of the theme, and an Italian verse paraphrase taken from the French of Destouches, which was condemned preface and play by the authorities of the Catholic Church.[1] Fittingly this general acclaim was confirmed by Macaulay, who wrote at the end of his copy:

I admire this Comedy extremely. It is Addison all over, full of delicate humour and amiable feeling. The fun is never coarse [illegible passage] I am convinced that if he had cultivated his talent for the drama he would have surpassed any [illegible] writer since the days of James the First. I like this play better than any of Congreve's, Sheridan's, Farquhar's or Vanbrugh's. An odd taste perhaps but so it is.[2]

In *Cato* Addison had shown how a man of noble character ought to act in a crisis of great events. The *Drummer* is the embodiment of his teaching about human conduct in the ordinary circumstances of life. He had given detailed and systematic study to human nature. This is apparent from his analysis, for example, of jealousy,[3] ambition,[4] and mirth.[5] He thought that man had a natural tendency to folly,[6] hypocrisy,[7] and many other failings,[8] each with its attendant griefs. He urged others to study the nature of man, as 'the

---

[1] See a manuscript in the flyleaf of *Il Tamburo*, Florence, 1750, the copy in the London Library.
[2] See his copy of Addison's *Works* in B.M.
[3] *S.* 171, 172.   [4] *S.* 255, 256.   [5] *S.* 249, 598.
[6] *S.* 169.   [7] *T.* 237.   [8] *T.* 220, 146.

best Means . . . to recover our Souls out of Vice, Ignorance, and Prejudice, which naturally cleave to them.'[1] But he rejected the low view of human nature expressed in current French writing and exemplified in de la Rochefoucauld,[2] and upheld the 'natural greatness and dignity' of man[3] whom he thought 'too virtuous to be miserable and too vicious to be happy'.[4] It was upon this view of the conflict in man's nature that his teaching in manners and morals was founded. He sought to prune away the exaggerated and the unreasonable in the conduct of mankind, as he had done in his own life and character. Many of the details of human behaviour had caught his censure: preoccupation with the news and politics to the prejudice of the business of life,[5] exaggerated fondness for domestic animals,[6] affected management of the fan,[7] gaming,[8] tulip-mania,[9] fortune-hunting,[10] fashionable impudence,[11] and fashionable riding-habits.[12] These were the petty transgressions, the minor deformities of society; yet they were condemned as a waste of effort in harmless folly.[13]

But Addison's satire was effective even in these details of behaviour, partly because beneath it there was a deeper moral undertone. He had little esteem for birth or privilege: 'All Superiority . . . that one Man can have over another . . . is either that of Fortune, Body, or Mind.'[14] His teaching of human conduct was designed to improve all three. He exalted the basic virtues of thrift and industry, esteemed the merchant classes, and, like John Locke, he linked all of these with a chain of reasoning ending in the ownership of property.[15] He advocated temperance and exercise, though not himself conspicuous for their practice. He urged his contemporaries to acquire self-command, the distinguishing virtue of a wise man,[16] which he had himself nearly perfected. Thus like Collier, the pioneer of the reformed stage, he sought to exalt classical virtue; but where Collier chastised, Addison laughed, and where Collier lectured, Addison demonstrated. Rejecting alike the ridiculous insolence of the cavalier tradition, and the ridiculous gloom of the puritan, he reduced manners to a code of behaviour which all could

---

[1] S. 215.   [2] T. 108   [3] Ibid.   [4] S. 183.   [5] S. 10.   [6] T. 121.
[7] S. 102.   [8] S. 93.   [9] S. 218.   [10] S. 311.   [11] S. 231.
[12] T. 116.   [13] S. 173.   [14] S. 219.   [15] F. 1.   [16] S. 225.

understand and obey. For this purpose satire was his chosen weapon: 'there is nothing so difficult as the art of making advice agreeable: and indeed all the writers, both ancient and modern, have distinguished themselves among one another, according to the perfection at which they have arrived in this art.'[1] In the *Spectator* he had sought with much success to overcome this difficulty in prose essays, but the *Drummer*, a sentimental comedy presenting the beauty of the familiar virtues of affection, fidelity, courage, and sense, and the ugliness of affectation, vanity, cowardice, and folly, was the supreme example of this aspect of his art.

The production of the *Drummer* was to prove the last occasion upon which Addison and Steele worked together upon a joint venture. On 16 March, the day before the last performance, Addison published the twenty-fifth *Freeholder*, which contained some slighting remarks about English fickleness and instability as an argument favouring the repeal of the Triennial Act. This seems to have irritated Steele, who drafted a reply dated the next day: 'I am called forth . . . by a subtle destructive Paper called the Freeholder. I have read it often with as great approbation as any of its Readers, but the pleasure . . . is destroyed by some intimations now and then which I think have a pernicious tendency . . .'.[2] Though this was apparently never published, it may well show the beginning of the coolness which marked the last years of the two men's friendship. If this was so, it was not the only instance of friction in the world of letters which troubled Addison at this time.

While he was occupied with the *Freeholder* and the *Drummer*, and with duties at the Board of Trade, Addison was troubled by friction between Pope and the Button's group. This was becoming a serious nuisance which a statesman would gladly be rid of. Fortunately events now worked towards a crisis. John Dennis had joined the attack on Pope's *Homer* with *A true Character of Mr. Pope and his Writings*. This was believed at the time to be by Gildon, a Whig hack-writer dependent upon the Hanover Club for patronage and

---

[1] S. 512.
[2] Steele's whole essay is published in Rae Blanchard's *Steele's Periodical Journalism, 1716-18* (Oxford, 1959), pp. 330-2.

thus associated with Addison. This proved too much for Pope, who, believing his rival to be involved in the publication of the *True Character*, drew from his desk the verse character of Atticus already noticed, added a biting couplet dealing with Gildon, and sent it to Addison with a letter of protest.[1]

It is interesting to consider that when first offended by Addison's criticism of his *Essay*, Pope had written lines of rebuttal but, though he did not publish them at once, after an interval had showed them to Steele knowing that Addison would see them. Eventually these lines were published in the *Temple of Fame* after a period of working-up lasting for three years. Pope had written the 'Atticus' lines when angered at the *Homer* controversy, but had not published or transmitted them until further offended by the *True Character*. He understood Addison's extreme sensitiveness to criticism, as the lines themselves show; and the implication of his sending them to Addison was that he would publish them in due time if so minded. The effect of this communication upon Addison can be conjectured. He was anxious to calm the warring factions of the literary world, as is evident from his intervention with Burnet seeking a modification of attacks on Pope in his pamphlet *Homerides*. Such an attitude was only consistent with his invariable course of conduct in similar situations. So sensitive a man would certainly wish to avoid the publication or circulation of Pope's devastating lines. Whether the two men now met it is impossible to say; but it is certain that a truce was arranged. This was substantial enough to survive the pirated publication by Curll of Pope's lines *To Mr. John Moore, author of the celebrated Worm-Powder*, one of the dangerous squibs with which the poet amused himself. *Worms* contained a venomous couplet upon Button's, and its publication was Curll's second attempt this year to keep the Homer quarrel going. No reply was forthcoming from Addison's satellites, as it would undoubtedly have been if he had not exerted pressure to restrain them. Further, on 7 May he published a *Freeholder* in which he reproved the minor combatants with all the majesty at his command: 'How often do we see a Person,

---

[1] In the version so transmitted the name 'Addison' would stand in place of 'Atticus', as it did in early printed versions of the text.

whose Intentions are visibly to do Good by the Works which he publishes, treated in as scurrilous a Manner, as if he were an Enemy to Mankind?' After developing that theme, so obviously applicable to the author of the translation of Homer, Addison paid, as he thought, a handsome compliment to the work itself by comparing it with Dryden's *Virgil*. But with an unhappy facility for angering the younger poet in a manner to which no direct objection could be made, he coupled his commendation with equal praise of Rowe's *Lucan*. It is conceivable that this compliment was even more irritating. For an anecdote survives in which Pope is made to intercede with Addison in favour of Rowe, who was grieved by Addison's displeasure towards him in connexion with a particular matter. In the anecdote Addison is made to say of Rowe's contrite mood: 'I do not suspect that he feigned; but the levity of his heart is such, that he is struck with any new adventure; and it would affect him just in the same manner, if he heard I was going to be hanged.'[1] In so far as Pope knew Addison's opinion of Rowe's character, and recalled that his own had been under censure from the same source, his association in praise with the light-hearted poet would seem unpleasantly pointed.

Nevertheless the *Freeholder* declaration, perhaps reinforced by a personal command, had been effective in stopping the hostilities from Button's, for on 1 June Burnet noticed that: 'Mr. Addison and the rest of the rhiming gang have dropt their resentment against the Lordlike Man [Pope].' Burnet was now thoroughly distrustful of Addison's motives, yet even he was persuaded to insert in a new pamphlet[2] a compliment to Pope more generous than that in the *Freeholder*. On his part Pope certainly used every endeavour to suppress his verses, and he more than reciprocated Addison's advances by the lines in praise of the 'Medals' and by the noble couplets in the *Epistle to Augustus*, both of which were published after Addison's death. Thus an uneasy truce now prevailed.

This controversial incident, here only described in out-

---

[1] Spence, p. 258 n.

[2] *Homerides: Or Homer's First Book Moderniz'd*. By Sir Iliad Doggrell. See G. Sherburn, *Early Career of Alexander Pope*, p. 176.

line, has been represented as a threat by Pope to publish
his verses, to which Addison bowed as to blackmail.
There is no evidence that this is what occurred, although
such may have been Pope's intention. But the most likely
explanation of what subsequently took place, as well as
that most honourable to the two poets, is that their
relationship having drawn to a crisis, common sense and
generosity, in which neither was lacking, dictated that the
controversy should be laid to rest. Pope alleged that he
was used 'very civilly' by Addison after this time; but
cordiality between the two men was impossible. Young
Lord Warwick, who knew both poets well, divined the
strength of their antipathy, and told Pope that it was in vain
to think of a 'settled friendship' between them. Addison's
attitude towards Pope, based upon several years of trouble,
is doubtless accurately expressed in his advice to Lady
Mary Wortley Montagu: 'Leave him as soon as you can; he
will certainly play you some devilish trick else; he has an
appetite to satire.'[1]

The late winter and spring of the year 1715-16 was a
time when Addison was watching the development of high
politics with special interest and particularly the part played
by Lord Sunderland, the only magnate now likely to help
him to further advancement. This nobleman, hitherto
defeated by the rival Whigs in bidding for royal favour,
was now manœuvring to overreach them. At the end of
February he gave a 'magnificent' banquet to 'several noble
lords' at his house in Piccadilly.[2] Early in March rumours
ran that he would succeed Lord Somers, who was now
politically negligible, as President of the Council.[3] He was
appointed to a lucrative sinecure in Ireland,[4] a mark of royal
favour, and Addison was one of those who sat on a Commons committee considering a bill enabling him to take in
England the oath necessary for qualification. Doubtless he
watched Lord Sunderland's interest in that matter. Then
Lady Sunderland was brought to town dangerously ill,[5] and
shortly after died.[6] There was a momentary lull in political

---

[1] Spence, p. 237.   [2] *Weekly Packet*, 191.
[3] *St. James's Evening Post*, 175.   [4] *Post Man*, 11250.
[5] *Evening General Post*, 12.   [6] *Evening Post*, 1045.

intrigue.[1] Addison meanwhile had reappeared at the Prince of Wales's Court and had published a laudatory *Freeholder* on the princess's birthday. He also amused himself by drafting a Latin letter for the summons of Sir Thomas Parker, the Lord Chief Justice of the King's Bench, to the House of Lords. Then Lord Somers died.[2] He had been one of the earliest of Addison's patrons but had not been intimate with him for some years. His place in Addison's affections had never been comparable with that of 'My dear and ever-lamented Ld Halifax'. But Addison had a deep admiration for and gratitude towards the great lawyer who had done more than any other Englishman to shape the modern constitution; and on 4 May, the morning following Lord Somers's memorial service, he drew his portrait at full length in the *Freeholder*,[3] in one of the finest pen pictures in the English language.

In the redistribution of offices which now took place, Lord Sunderland had to content himself with his Privy Seal, though there were again rumours that he would become Lord President,[4] and with succeeding Lord Somers as a Governor of the Charterhouse.[5] But he was deeply involved in the growing quarrel between the king and the Prince of Wales, and in the split amongst the Whigs, both of which merged in a single complex political problem. Determined to benefit from fishing in these troubled waters, Lord Sunderland decided to leave England in August to follow the king, who left for Hanover on 7 July. In preparation for his departure, the press announced on 28 July, Joseph Addison, Esq. and Mr. Charlton were to be appointed Commissioners of the Privy Seal, that is to say they were to be jointly empowered to discharge the formal functions which attached to the office, in the absence of its holder.[6] But other counsels prevailed and Charlton was given a different colleague.[7]

Addison had been occupied in Parliament until the prorogation on 26 June but it had not been a particularly busy

[1] *Post Boy*, 4169.   [2] *British Weekly Mercury*, 565.
[3] *F*. 39.   [4] *Whitehall Courant*, xxv.   [5] *St. James's Post*, 204.
[6] *Weekly Packet*, 212; *Dawks's News Letter*, 28/7/1716.
[7] *Weekly Packet*, 213.

sitting; he was a member of a few minor committees, such as that for the naturalization of Fräulein von Schulenberg, one of the king's mistresses. He was present at all of the meetings of the Board of Trade in the latter half of July until it adjourned for a week's holiday on the last day of the month. But no ripple of unusual excitement appeared upon the surface of his official life as recorded in the available documents. On 30 July, however, the *Whitehall Courant*[1] and the *General Post*[2] carried a report that 'Joseph Addison, Esq., is to be married to the Countess of Warwick'. On 4 August the *Weekly Packet* printed an announcement that 'the discourse still continues' that such a marriage would take place and on the same day the *EveningPost*[3] reported it (wrongly) as having been celebrated. Then on 8 August the Board of Trade began to meet again and Addison attended it as usual. But on 9 August he was absent from his place, and for that day the register of St. Edmund the King and Martyr, Lombard Street, carries the inscription:

Joseph Addison of Bilton in the county of Warwick Esq, was married unto Charlotte Countess Dowager of Warwick and Holland of the Parish of Kensington in the County of Middlesex . . . by Mr. Nathaniel Heugh.[4]

Addison had thought and written much about women and marriage before sampling his own advice at the age of 44. His intentions towards women were chivalrous, and he deplored Boileau's satire upon the sex in general, which ignored 'the valuable Part of it'.[5] But he could not conceal a kindly contempt for their intellect, while deploring their lack of education.[6] He observed that:

when in ordinary Discourse we say a Man has a fine Head, a long Head, or a good Head, we express our selves metaphorically and speak in relation to his Understanding; whereas when we say of a Woman, she has a fine, a long, or a good Head, we speak only in relation to her Commode.[7]

Yet more frankly:

I . . . fancied I might receive great Benefit from Female Conversation, and that I should have a Convenience of talking with the

---

[1] No. xxxix.   [2] No. lx.   [3] No. 1092.
[4] The *Historical Register* wrongly reports the date of the marriage as Aug. 2.
[5] S. 209.   [6] S. 10.   [7] S. 265.

CHARLOTTE MYDDELTON OF CHIRK
by Van der Mijn

In the possession of Colonel R. Myddelton at Chirk Castle

greater Freedom when I was not under any Impediment of thinking: I therefore threw my self into an Assembly of Ladies. . . .[1]

He thought women incapable of logic and not amenable to
reason.[2] That these opinions were sincere seems to be borne
out by the fact that when he wished to address himself
specifically to women, Addison usually assumed the weapons
of raillery and banter rather than the methods of logic. He
distrusted women, and seemed to wish them all frumps,
being apparently quite unaware of the qualities of wisdom
to be found in the worldly members of the sex. There is in
fact every evidence in Addison's writing that, intimate as
he was with men and acute as he was in perception of their
character, his knowledge and ideas about women were
drawn from reading and from polite conversation, rather
than from their intimate friendship. Had this been otherwise
his great talents of observation could hardly have failed to
draw forth for literary use some echoes of a woman's deeper
thoughts.

Beginning a *Spectator* on courtship and marriage he wrote
of an imaginary wooing:

> I was in my younger Years engaged . . . in the Courtship of
> a Person who had a great deal of Beauty . . . but as my Natural
> Taciturnity hindered me from showing my self to the best Advan-
> tage, she by degrees began to look upon me as a very silly Fellow,
> and being resolved to regard Merit more than any thing else . . .
> she married a Captain of Dragoon who happened to be beating
> up for Recruits in those Parts.[3]

He had already recorded his thoughts upon the 'numberless
Evils that befall the Sex from this light fantastical Disposition' of being 'smitten with every thing that is showy and
superficial'.[4] 'In short, they consider only the Drapery of the
Species, and never cast away a Thought upon those Ornaments of the Mind that make Persons Illustrious in themselves and useful to others.'[5] Beneath this raillery there is an
ever-present though carefully controlled distrust of the sex.
Yet in spite of his apparently distant behaviour to, and poor
opinion of, women, Addison judged courtship to be the
happiest period of life,[6] and of marriage itself he was the

[1] S. 556.   [2] F. 32.   [3] S. 261.   [4] S. 15.   [5] Ibid.   [6] S. 261.

avowed champion in *Rosamond*, in *Cato*, anonymously in the *Drummer*, and in a hundred places in the *Tatler* and the *Spectator*. He thought the institution founded in a difference of temperament:

As Vivacity is the gift of Women, Gravity is that of Men . . . we may conclude that Men and Women were made as Counterparts to one another, that the Pains and Anxieties of the Husband might be relieved by the Sprightliness and good Humour of the Wife.[1]

It is by no means certain that Lady Warwick possessed these qualities. Addison himself was heavily laden with cares, and might well recall that he had caused Sir Trusty to complain in *Rosamond*:

> Hard is our fate,
> Who serve in the state,
> And should lay out our cares,
> On publick affairs;
> When conjugal toils,
> And family broils
> Make all our great labours miscarry!

On the choice of a wife he had given much other advice, mostly of a cautionary nature:

I should prefer a Woman that is agreeable in my own Eye, and not deformed in that of the World, to a Celebrated Beauty. . . .

Before Marriage, we cannot be too inquisitive and discerning in the Faults of the Person beloved, nor after it too dim-sighted and superficial.[2]

He had certainly known Lady Warwick long enough to understand her good qualities and defects. She was a handsome woman in early middle age, certainly not deformed in the eye of the world, who must have been beautiful in youth. On the subject of marriage itself he had surmised that:

A Marriage of Love is pleasant; a Marriage of Interest easie; and a Marriage where both meet, happy.[3]

Love being of an intangible nature he doubtless assured himself that happiness ought to ensue upon his marriage with Lady Warwick, which certainly did not lack interest.

[1] *S.* 128.   [2] *S.* 261.   [3] Ibid.

In that view he was reinforced by his reflections upon the length of courtship:

Those Marriages generally abound most with Love and Constancy that are preceded by a long Courtship. The Passion should strike Root, and gather Strength before Marriage be grafted on it. A long Course of Hopes and Expectations fixes the Idea in our Minds, and habituates us to a Fondness of the Person beloved.[1]

Such had evidently been his own case. He had even gone so far as to prescribe a woman's conduct on receiving a proposal:

A Virtuous Woman should reject the first Offer of Marriage, as a good Man does that of a Bishoprick; but I would advise neither the one nor the other to persist in refusing what they secretly approve.[2]

Therefore whatever the limits of his experience, it is certain that Addison had devoted a great deal of thought to the subject of matrimony, and almost equally certain that in conformity with the pattern of his life he now embarked thereupon as a considered act of wisdom.

Of Addison's closest friends, Dick Steele probably attended the wedding, for he was in London on the day. Edward Wortley, who had been appointed ambassador to the Porte,[3] had left town on 2 August.[4] Lord Sunderland had not yet gone abroad and returned to town on 7 August.[5] He may have been present but it was evidently a very quiet ceremony. It was not performed in Kensington Parish Church, which stood almost in the shadow of Holland House, and where the Warwicks were all-powerful. Possibly it was not desired to celebrate a second marriage of a countess of the house of Rich in that place. The church selected was St. Edmund King and Martyr, one of Wren's new city churches, a model of that elegant simplicity of style which Addison had never doubted to be 'the right way' in architecture. Mr Heugh was not the priest who normally officiated at marriages in this church at the period in question, and it is therefore probable that he was a friend of Lady Warwick's. There was also a remote connexion with Addison, in that his

---

[1] Ibid. [2] *S. 89.* [3] *Dawks's News Letter*, 7/4/16.
[4] *Post Boy*, 4214. [5] *Evening Post*, 1094.

fellow Demy, Grandorge, who had proceeded step by step with him and Richard West in the college hierarchy, was incumbent of the nearby and closely associated St. Dion Backchurch for a short period at about this time.

So carefully did Addison and, apparently, Lady Warwick destroy the least evidence of their affection for each other, that almost nothing is known of it. An anecdote is preserved to the effect that he had sounded the countess by reading to her printed matter bearing upon matrimony; it may well have been some of the *Spectator* extracts noticed above. But few hints of the progress of their relationship have come down to us from contemporaries, who would certainly have been highly interested in the amours of Mr. Spectator or *Cato* had they been a matter of common knowledge. Nicholas Rowe had written a set of verses *To Lady Warwick on Mr. Addison's going to Ireland*. These were probably upon his appointment as Secretary in the winter of 1714 when it was generally believed that he would go to Dublin, or in the autumn of 1715 when he had thoughts of a visit. They envisage that this had been the only important affection of Addison's life, and seem to imply some degree of mutual obligation at this date:

> And since his love does thine alone pursue,
>   In arts unpractis'd and unused to range;
> I charge thee be by his example true
>   And shun thy sex's inclination, change.
>
> When crowds of youthful lovers round thee wait,
>   And tender thoughts in sweetest words impart;
> When thou art woo'd by titles, wealth and state.
>   Then think on Lycidas, and guard thy heart.

Long after the event, Jacob Tonson recorded his belief that Addison had intended to marry Lady Warwick from his first introduction to her. There are the letters to the young earl which display an interest in the family at Holland House much beyond normal courtesy, eight years before this time. There is the complaint to his intimate friend, Wortley, of the loss of a 'mistress' in the days of political adversity. All of this considered together suggests a long-standing attachment.

Addison's political fortunes had revived sufficiently for him to carry himself with confidence as a suitor. Previously without any dignified post, he now held a Commissionership at the Board of Trade of which any gentleman might be proud. His financial circumstances were also quite good. A week after the marriage it was reported that he was able to pay his bride £4,000 in compensation for loss of jointure upon her marriage.[1] A bachelor moving from lodging to lodging as circumstances dictated, he had for many years taken pleasure in the entrée to a family life at Holland House as well as the aristocratic pomp of that establishment. If he harboured any intentions of matrimony his circumstances may well have deterred him from pressing them. But the years were now advancing upon him, and his old companions were dying fast, had married, or were leaving England. He had re-established himself in the world of politics and was financially beyond the hand of fortune or the fear of dependence upon a wife's inheritance. Physically he was none too healthy and a woman's care would be welcome. To marry seemed the rational and sensible thing to do.

Mr. Willard Connely, studying her portrait, describes her as 'good-looking enough to wait years for ... the single thing which marked off Lady Warwick's handsomeness of feature as that of a woman different from the rest was her straight upper lip, very straight, but determined, not without humour, and charming'. Her birth and first marriage made her automatically of consequence in society; but before her remarriage little notice was taken of her either by men of letters or by politicians. A good deal of verse was poured to her thereafter, and it is noticeable that poets casting around for compliments to pay do not seem to have found a wealth of material. In a poem attributed to Tickell addressed to Lady Warwick on her marriage to Addison, the author is mainly concerned with complimenting the bride upon marrying a virtuous and brilliant husband. A similar piece came from the pen of Leonard Welsted, who had known Addison for several years, perhaps through a relative at Magdalen, or because of his marriage with Harry Purcell's daughter in

---

[1] *Gents. Mag.* xlix (1779), p. 550.

1707, or because of a place subsequently obtained in the office of a Secretary of State. Welsted merely complimented Lady Warwick upon selecting for her second husband a man of such distinguished intellect. Both poems are addressed to the praise of Addison and ignore Lady Warwick except as a lay figure on which to drape the verse. Pope wrote incorrectly to Lady Mary Wortley, herself not the most charitable judge of other women, that: 'Mr Addison has not had One Epithalamium that I can hear of, and must e'en be reduced, like a poorer & a better Poet, Spencer, to make his owne.'[1] The impression given is that a highly distinguished man had married a woman of aristocratic birth whose qualities of character, though nothing positive is known to their detriment, certainly did not entitle her to notice. The immediate consequence of the marriage was that Lady Warwick was able to offer Addison the shelter of one of the most princely roofs near London, at Holland House. At his disposal were a chapel, a great library, and extensive grounds with a 'green lane' reminiscent of the Magdalen water-walks, in which he might indulge his love of nature and solitude.

If contemporaries were able to throw little light upon the character of the mistress of this splendid establishment, a detailed and delightful examination of her household papers by Professor Arthur L. Cooke has enabled him to arrive at some conclusions based upon the evidence of her household accounts:

'The available facts do not appear to support the traditional view of the Countess of Warwick's character or of her supposedly haughty attitude toward Addison. . . . Actually the available evidence seems to show that she was far from being a haughty woman. Instead, one is struck by the many ways in which her character is similar to Addison's. She was conscientious in her duties, careful with her money, shunned publicity, never caused a scandal, avoided great social entertainments, loved the countryside at Bilton, and was interested in literature and politics. It is no wonder that Addison fell in love with her when he first met her in

---

[1] Sherburn, i. 385. There is also a letter from Lady Mary to Pope in which she speaks disparagingly of the countess as a wife for Addison. Its authenticity is doubtful and Dr. Robert Halsband, the editor of Lady Mary's *Letters*, does not reprint it.

1704, or that she accepted him as her suitor. The only wonder is that she did not marry him until 1716. Perhaps the reason is that her first marriage had been such a disaster. Apparently the second one was far more successful.'[1]

Her accounts show that she spent very little on wine but substantial sums on books and newspapers, including *Tatlers* and *Spectators*. She was on friendly terms with her household staff and frequently gave money to the poor. For example, Daniel Button, who was in her service in 1707, paid out the following sums for her:

my Ladys garters	7–0
to apor man in covent garden	0–3
for my Ladys cloggs	3–6
to apore woman	0–2

She signed every bill and reduced many, including, for example, an account of Jacob Tonson's for £8. 12*s*. 0*d*. which she reduced by two shillings and which he receipted as payment 'in full'. In her will, Lady Warwick left an annuity of £50 per annum to Mrs. Dorothy Combes, 'sister of my late dear Husband', and directed that her funeral should be 'without Escutcheons or any other Pomp' and limited the expense to be incurred to 'not above One Hundred Pounds and if possible not above Eighty Pounds', an attitude which seems very much of a piece with her character as a whole.

Marriage and translation to truly lordly surroundings seem to have made little interruption in Addison's immediate occupations. He attended all the Board of Trade meetings in August except those of the day of his wedding and of the day immediately following it. The first meeting of the Board which he attended after the ceremony was on 14 August, so that he took not more than five days respite from duty. But from 21 August until 31 October he was absent for the only considerable period this year. During that time he went on a honeymoon trip with his wife and Lord Warwick, who is reported to have set out 'on his travels oversea' on 8 September,[2] probably the date of the family's departure.

[1] 'Addison's Aristocratic Wife', *PMLA*, lxxii (1957), p. 389.
[2] *Weekly Journal*, 8/9/1716.

James Craggs, a rising young Whig politician, was with them in Paris on 23 September and reported that the weather had turned to rain 'which makes Mr. Addison, my Lady Warwick, and Lord Warwick very peevish'.[1] But the amiable physician, Garth, was also there so that good company did not lack; and Jacobite circles thought that conversations took place between the travelling Whigs and Lord Bolingbroke.[2] If this was so, Addison, who belonged to that wing of the party which had formerly been most inclined to friendship with the Tories, who had had conversations at dinner with Bolingbroke during the abortive negotiations of 1713, and who was reported to think highly of his abilities, would be an obvious contact. It is difficult to believe that a man immersed in politics since 1705 could easily discard them even on his honeymoon at this critical moment, when his only remaining patron stood so near supreme power.

Addison attended the Board of Trade on 31 October, and as the return of Lord Warwick was reported in a paper covering the period 27 October to 3 November, the party probably arrived in London between 27 and 30 October. The return of the bridegroom to London was awaited with some curiosity. His friends wondered whether he would be transported with his aristocratic marriage. Tom Burnet proposed to make a heavy jest by purchasing a dark glass from 'honest Senex', a maker of optical commodities, through which to view Addison if he had not condescended to drink a glass with him within a week of the end of the honeymoon.[3] Burnet need have had no fear, for on 4 November, after attending the Board, Addison repaired to the *Trumpet* with Dick Steele and Benjamin Hoadly, now Bishop of Bangor, and other Whigs, to celebrate King William's birthday and perhaps his own restoration to his friends.

Sir Richard, in his zeal, rather exposed himself, having the double duty of the day upon him, as well to celebrate the immortal memory of King William . . . as to drink his friend Addison up to the conversation pitch. . . .[4]

[1] Bohn, vi. 744.   [2] H.M.C. *Stuart*, ii. 469.
[3] *Letters of T. Burnet to Geo. Duckett*, ed. Nichol Smith, p. 109 n.
[4] Blanchard, *Correspondence of Richard Steel*, p. 118.

Evidently the occasion was sufficiently convivial for Steele to feel obliged to apologize to the bishop next day, when he wrote:

> Virtue with so much ease on Bangor sits
> All faults he pardons, though he none commits.

For Addison the year now drawing to a close had been an eventful one in literary matters. Besides the *Freeholder*, his lines to Lady Manchester, written in 1703 on a toasting glass of the Kit-Cat Club, were first published, along with other of his earlier poetry in a reprint of Tonson's *Miscellany Poems*, vol. v. His poem to Sir Godfrey Kneller on the king's portrait had reached a fourth edition and that to the Princess of Wales had been printed. *Cato* had been reprinted, and the *Drummer* had been staged, and was published anonymously with Steele's commendatory preface. 'Proelium inter Pygmaeos et Grues' had been translated by Newcomb and the 'Machinae Gesticulantes' by George Sewell, both for publication by Curll. The 'Sphaeristerium' also appeared in translation.

In his private affairs this year saw the troublesome matter of Gulston's estate finally laid to rest. George Morton Pitt, no longer a minor and now able to come to terms with Gulston's trustees and the various other estates concerned, himself went to Madras to conclude matters. Addison's friend Benyon had now died, but Governor Harrison was acting on his behalf. In October 1715, pursuant to Addison's instructions, the trustees sold the 'great house' at auction for 3,455 pagodas. Next month arbitrators were appointed to wind up the disputed inheritance, and in December they agreed a balance sheet showing 11,340 pagodas owing to George Pitt. It is difficult to determine how much, if anything, was in the end received by Addison, who on balance may have remained a debtor to the estate as a result of the interim payments made to him which could not later be justified. The legatees, who took precedence of his residuary interest, are shown in a balance sheet of 10 June 1716 as being paid only a dividend of 68 per cent. of their bequests. But at least a settlement had been arrived at when George Pitt signed a release to the trustees on 3 January 1716,[1] and

---

[1] For these transactions see B.M. Egerton MSS. 1972.

Addison must have felt justified in his earlier decision not to prosecute actions at law in a matter in which Pitt turned out to be the principal beneficiary.

About the middle of November 1716 Lord Sunderland returned to London and political intrigues rose to a high pitch of intensity. Paul Methuen, the experienced diplomat to whom a volume of the *Spectator* had been dedicated, now a Secretary of State, was miserable in politics and wrote to Stanhope protesting that he had accepted office unwillingly, that he understood nothing of it, that the fatigue was great, and hoping that the king would relieve him of his burdens;[1] but he evidently had to continue in harness with Stanhope. Lord Sunderland, who now went to The Hague on diplomatic business,[2] resigned the Privy Seal, and Methuen again wrote, this time to the king, asking to be excused his duties unless he could be permitted to exercise only those which did not concern the House of Commons.[3] As the New Year came in the political position was fluid and likely to be resolved only when Parliament met, when the greatest gamble of Addison's life, that upon the power and political skill of Lord Sunderland, would be drawn.

Parliament met on 17 January, Addison being appointed to tender oaths; but it was immediately prorogued, the political situation not yet being ripe, and negotiation and intrigue continuing on every hand. Sunderland and Stanhope returned to England in company with the king in the middle of January[4] and on the 24th of that month Parliament met again and was again prorogued. As a correspondent put it, 'the prime minister is the king, and they are only his favourites who can go help themselves. . . . Lord Sunderland is thought to be at the head of all Councils, but with no distinguishing . . . yet at least.'[5] From his stately mansion at Holland House Addison watched as the political chess-board took shape and Lord Sunderland moved into the key position. He had no literary ventures near to maturity with which to divert himself; only *Cato* continued, with a per-

[1] S.P. 44/267.   [2] *Weekly Journal*, 12/1/1717.
[3] Quai d'Orsay MSS.: Corr. Pol. Ang. 287, f. 73.
[4] *Weekly Journal*, 26/1/1717.
[5] Ellis, *Orig. Letters*, ser. ii, vol. iv, White-Kennet–Blackwell, 2/2/1717.

formance in January at Drury Lane and another in March. On 13 February there was an important meeting of the Privy Council[1] at which Lord Sunderland appears to have been the most powerful figure present. Parliament met again on 20 February and Addison was appointed as usual to the Committee of Privileges. On 30 March there was a special meeting of the Kit-Cat with the Duke of Newcastle in the chair, at which it may be that an attempt was made to reunite the two quarrelling factions of the Whig party. But under the strain of rival personalities and of the difficulties created by the unpopularity of the king's northern policy and of his German ministers, this was impossible. On 9 April, after a series of violent parliamentary scenes, the Government broke up with the dismissal of Lord Townshend and the resignation of Robert Walpole, followed by other ministers. Paul Methuen was now allowed to go and was succeeded as Secretary of State by Lord Sunderland.

The news broke in the press on 12 April,[2] the day on which the new Secretary took the seals and at nine o'clock at night resumed authority at the Cockpit.[3] At the same time Stanhope moved from his own post as Secretary of State to become First Lord of the Treasury; thus leaving one Secretaryship vacant. The loss of talent to the party as a result of the resignations had considerably increased Stanhope's difficulties in forming a government. An experienced administrator and moderate Whig, known for his probity and of celebrated distinction, was available for employment in high office. Two days previously, on 10 April, Dick Steele, writing to Prue in the country, had reported that Mr. Addison was to be Secretary of State, dryly and without comment, for in this hour of greatest triumph Joseph was drifting away from his lifelong friendship. Only a few weeks before, there had died Dr. Lancaster, Provost of The Queen's, College kindly tutor and forwarder of the fortunes of young men, just too soon to see the Latin poet whose career he had set in motion with a first step to preferment attain the summit of power and authority.[4]

---

[1] P.C. 2/86, f. 105.
[3] *Original Weekly Journal*, 13-20/4/1717.
[2] *Gazette*, 5528.
[4] *Evening Post*, 1172.

X

AMBITION FULFILLED
1717–1718

The Condition of a Minister of State is only suited to Persons, who, out of a Love to their King and Country, desire rather to be useful to the Publick, than easie to themselves.

THUS wrote Addison in the *Freeholder* less than a year before he accepted the most arduous administrative post in Britain, with the duties and vexations of which he was closely acquainted from his service as Under-Secretary. Writing to Davenport, British Resident at Genoa and a close personal friend, a few days after his appointment, he spoke of 'my new station, which you may believe I did not enter upon without much reluctancy'. Jacob Tonson, who quarrelled with Addison, suggested in later years that he now accepted the appointment at the desire of his wife 'to qualify himself to be owned for her husband'.[1] But it will be recalled that Addison had hoped for preferment in 1714, and that he had been most bitterly disappointed at his failure. It must be remembered that he had throughout life adopted a code of conduct in which public service was an essential part of virtue, and that it was precisely to fit himself for such an office that he had undertaken a lifelong preparation. It is likely that he now accepted the Secretaryship of State as the crowning achievement of his life, but not without apprehension of the burden which it must place upon his indifferent health. If these were his thoughts, they were also those of Lady Mary Wortley:

I received the news of Mr. Addison's being declared Secretary of State with the less surprize, in that I know that the post was almost offered to him before. At that time he declined it, and I really believe that he would have done well to have declined it now. Such a post as that, and such a Wife as the Countess, do not seem

---

[1] Spence, p. 47.

to be, in prudence, eligible for a man that is asthmatick; and we may see the day when he will be heartily glad to resign them both.[1]

The Secretaryship which Addison now assumed was an exceptionally arduous post, far different from what it had been in Queen Anne's day. In her reign a Lord Treasurer had conducted the major policy and politics of government with the Secretaries of State as his principal executive ministers. Now, with no Lord Treasurer, and the king himself absorbed in the complex politics of Europe, though insisting upon being consulted on most other issues, the two Secretaries of State were the principal ministers. Furthermore, executive business tended to increase in their hands, a process which ultimately gave rise to the multiple subdivision of the Secretaryships of State into specialized departments.

On his accession to power Lord Sunderland reversed the arrangement of his predecessors, himself taking from Methuen what was generally considered the junior Secretaryship, that of the Northern Department, while Addison succeeded Stanhope in the senior or Southern Department. Many reasons must have suggested this alteration. The king was passionately interested in the politics of northern Europe; therefore by selecting the Northern Department Lord Sunderland was enabled to identify himself particularly with the royal wishes. He also desired to devote much attention to the management of the political situation in England in order to make sure of retaining power. He therefore did not wish to be troubled with more administration than was necessary, and preferred that Addison should carry the major burden of day-to-day work. Of the two Secretaryships, the Northern was by far the lighter administrative commitment. Furthermore, Addison was peculiarly fitted to deal with the Southern Department. He had served in it as Under-Secretary, he was well acquainted with France, Switzerland, and Italy, which, with Spain, Portugal, and the other Mediterranean countries, comprised the

---

[1] Sherburn, i. 423. The apparent contradiction in the statements that the post was 'almost offered' to Addison before and that at 'that time he declined it' is one of several defects which make the letter suspect, but it probably represents the substance of Lady Mary's thoughts.

foreign responsibility of the Southern Secretary. He had served twice with success as Secretary of the Irish Government, and Ireland fell within the ambit of the south. He had also served upon the Board of Trade and Plantations, and the business of the Board came within the responsibilities of the Southern Secretary. The historian who calendared the colonial papers which Addison put out as Secretary of State, many of them in his own hand, commented that they 'exhibit just that lucidity and simplicity and that easy adoption of official directness, without any attempt at literary ornament, which one would naturally expect from such a master of style'.[1] Addison's lucidity was that, not merely of a man who had a fine command of English prose, but of one who also thoroughly understood the subject matter with which he dealt and the machinery of government through which action must be taken. It was just such administrative qualities, which Addison possessed in abundance, that Lord Sunderland required in a colleague who would relieve him of the bulk of administrative duty.[2] The arrangement must have seemed a particularly satisfactory one. It was rendered more so by the fact that Stanhope was First Lord of the Treasury. He was married to a daughter of Governor Pitt and was well known to Addison whom he had met in Holland in 1703. He had been an occasional visitor at Button's, where he had attended Whiston's lectures,[3] and had been associated with Addison in Steele's defence in Parliament in 1714 as well as upon many other occasions. Stanhope was mainly concerned with and interested in major European policy, and had been instrumental in negotiating the Triple Alliance between England, France, and Holland in January of this year. He was now entrusted with the strategy of foreign policy which resulted in the formation of the Quadruple Alliance next year. He was therefore performing some of the more important policy functions which would otherwise have fallen to the Secretaries of State. The structure of the three major offices thus

[1] Headlam, *Cal. S.P. Col. A. & W.I.* 1716–17, p. vi.

[2] The evidence of the documents in the Public Record Office disposes of Pope's allegation that Addison had 'too beautiful an imagination for a man of business'.

[3] W. Whiston, *Memoirs*, i. 302.

tended to concentrate in Addison's hands a mass of administrative business of a day-to-day nature. He was not therefore called upon to initiate major European policy, which
was laid down in broad outline by the king and Stanhope.
It was his task to conduct the diplomacy of Britain within
the framework which they fixed, and in the area which fell
to his control, as well as to assume responsibility for Irish
affairs in conjunction with the Lord Lieutenant, for Plantation matters in conjunction with the Board of Trade and
Plantations, for trade matters with the same body, and for his
share of home affairs.

Addison's appointment was received with some surprise
by those not acquainted with the inner working of the
political machine. Thomas Burnet wrote to George Duckett:
'who would have expected to have seen the Head of the
Poets a Secretary of State? However, he has the character
of an incorrupt man, which is no little matter now a days.'[1]
The French Ambassador, the Marquis d'Iberville, who had
accurately forecast Addison's appointment,[2] commented in
a dispatch: 'Mr. Addisson un homme d'esprit es tres poli
mais imaginés vous ce qu'on auroit dit en France si l'on eut
fait Mr. Racine Secretaire d'Etat.'[3] Pucci, the Florentine
minister, upon the same occasion, described Addison as
'persona litterata . . . di soavi maniere, e creatura del prefato
Mylord Sunderland . . .'.[4] He recalled Salvini's Florentine
translation of *Cato* and later discussed it with the Secretary
as a suitable lead into a somewhat disagreeable negotiation.[5]
The world of letters was complimented by the appointment
particularly the group at Button's, who anticipated halcyon
days. Even Tory and Jacobite Oxford thought the appointment a good one.[6] Only in political circles can there have
been considerable misgivings. As Secretary of State sitting
in the lower house, with his colleague absent in the Lords,
Addison would be answerable on behalf of the Government

---

[1] B.M. Add. MSS. 36772, f. 150b.
[2] Quai d'Orsay MSS.: Corr. Pol. Ang. 299, f. 203.
[3] Ibid. 293, f. 43 (cipher).
[4] Archivo di Stato di Firenze, Md. P. f. 4222.   [5] Ibid. f. 4223.
[6] e.g. *A congratulatory Epistle to the Rt. Hon. Joseph Addison Esq., Occasioned
by his being made one of H.M. principal Secretaries of State*. By a Student of
Oxford.

upon a wide range of topics. The importance of this duty had been reflected in the obvious misgivings which Lord Halifax had expressed when himself considering Addison's appointment as Secretary of State in 1714.[1] Addison himself had written that: 'It is impossible that a person should exert himself to advantage in an assembly . . . who lies under too great oppressions of modesty.' He must now overcome that obstacle as best he might, in a House of Commons where the Whig party was sharply and bitterly divided and where the ablest debating skill was ranged against the Government.

The news of Addison's appointment was not carried in the press until 13 April,[2] when it was unofficially rumoured along with the announcement of Lord Sunderland's appointment. On 15 April Royal Letters Patent issued appointing Addison and Sunderland Secretaries of State.[3] On 16 April the *Gazette* announced the news.[4] The warrants for both appointments had been dated 12 April and were consecutive documents.[5] Addison had sworn the oath of a Secretary of State even earlier, on 6 April,[6] probably because, as the French Ambassador reported, the resigning ministers had refused to stay long enough to give the king time to find successors,[7] and it was desirable that somebody should be immediately empowered to sign formal documents. By a curious turn of fate the precedent used for the oath was that of the case of Henry Boyle in 1705, who had climbed to the Haymarket garret to invite Addison to take a first step in a political career.[8] By 10 April the new Secretary was signing office documents such as messenger's bills,[9] and he seems to have signed some letters ante-dated which were awaiting signature, such as those in Latin to the Republic of Venice and to Genoa.[10] It was therefore in an atmosphere of administrative urgency that Addison assumed his duties.

On 13 April he received the royal warrant enabling him to disburse Secret Service funds, and on the night of 15

[1] *Supra*, p. 306.
[2] *Weekly Journal*, 13/4/1717; *Weekly Packet*, 249; *Evening Post*, 4200; *Post Man*, 11520.   [3] *Cal. Treasury Books*, xxxi. 270.
[4] No. 5530.   [5] S.P. 44/359, ff. 266 (Addison) and 267 (Sunderland).
[6] S.P. 35/8, f. 114.   [7] Quai d'Orsay MSS.: Corr. Pol. Ang. 299, f. 208.
[8] S.P. Dom. 34/9, f. 73.   [9] S.P. 44/360, f. 33.   [10] S.P. 45/21, f. 80.

April he visited the king to kiss hands and receive the seals of office.[1] Next day he dined with Dick Steele, who reported the event very dryly and again without comment. He then proceeded to the Privy Council at St. James's where he was sworn a member and took his seat amongst the greatest in the land in the presence of the king.[2] On 17 April he took possession of the office at the Cockpit which he knew so well as Under-Secretary.[3] It now became necessary to tell a large number of officials who depended directly upon or corresponded with him that he had assumed responsibility. These included all ambassadors, ministers, and consuls in the territories of the south[4] and all governors of colonies in America and the West Indies.[5] Amongst them were many friends. Abraham Stanyan at Vienna as ambassador fell within Addison's sphere for certain negotiations and was an old friend and mentor in diplomacy; Alexander Cunningham, resident at Venice, was well known to Addison, also George Bubb, ambassador in Madrid, Davenant, the resident at Genoa, James Dayrolles at Geneva, Edward Wortley at the Porte, Manning at Berne, Lord Polwarth at Copenhagen, Governor Hunter in New York and others, who knew the qualities of the new Secretary. Lord Polwarth was strictly outside Addison's territory, but hastened to offer himself 'either for your service or diversion'.[6] It was also necessary to circularize the foreign diplomatic corps in London, who would now look to Addison for the conduct of relations if their governments fell within the territory of his department. Such formalities were completed by the attendance of the new Secretary of State at court on Sunday 28 April when there was 'a great appearance of the nobility'.[7]

The office to which Addison succeeded was one which would enable him to live according to his dignity even were he not now a prosperous man and married to a woman who in virtue of her son, not yet of age, enjoyed a princely heritage. A 'Mem. of What a Secretary of State receives

---

[1] Blanchard, 340.
[2] S.P. 35/8, f. 4; P.C. 2/86, f. 11.
[3] Quai d'Orsay MSS.: Corr. Pol. Ang. 297, f. 347.
[4] S.P. 104/96, 104/36, and 104/29.
[5] C.O. 324/33, f. 76.
[6] H.M.C. *Polwarth*, i. 253.   [7] *Weekly Journal*, 21.

yearly'[1] which relates to this period, computed the sum as follows:

	£
Patent Fee	100
Salary	1,850[2]
Secret Service	3,000[3]
Board Wages	730
Total	£5,680

to which would have to be added a half share in the proceeds of the *Gazette*, which might amount to a further £200 if the figures for 1717–19 are a correct average. But in addition to the foregoing there were also the fees of the office, paid for the passing of certain types of document. In this respect the Southern Department was much the more lucrative of the two, because it contained the Irish and Plantation business. In the latter part of Queen Anne's reign these fees had amounted to between £3,000 and £5,000 per annum, since when there had been a tendency for the Secretary of State to gain at the expense of the Irish establishment. So that if a rough estimate of his official income is made, it must be in the region of £10,000 per annum, out of which he would have to pay salaries and expenses, but which would still leave him a rich man. An additional perquisite was an allowance of 1,013 ounces of silver plate from the Jewel Office, to be made into such vessels and after such fashion as he shall direct,[4] valued at £337. 17s., together with the expenses of engraving his arms thereon.[5] This was an agreeable windfall for an ex-bachelor who a dozen years before had parted with a covered cup to pay his debt for school fees. He thus found it convenient and possible to maintain a house in Albemarle Street, three minutes' walk from the seat of government at St. James's, in addition to his wife's establishment at Holland House, which was somewhat too remote for a very busy administrator.[6]

The office staff consisted of two Under-Secretaries and six or seven clerks. Addison took as his senior Under-Secretary

---

[1] Blenheim MSS. D.I. 36.   [2] *Cal. Treasury Books*, xxxi. 274.
[3] S.P. 38/30; *Cal. Treasury Books*, xxxi. 274.
[4] *Cal. Treasury Books*, xxxi. 300.
[5] *Original Weekly Journal*, 27/4/1717.
[6] B.M. Egerton MSS. 1971, f. 20.

Temple Stanyan, whom he had probably known at Oxford, and who was a brother of his friend the ambassador in Vienna. Stanyan was an experienced administrator with service under Lords Townshend and Stanhope, and was on friendly terms with his chief. Their relationship was, however, ruffled by financial transactions. It appears that Stanyan borrowed a sum of money from his superior, and immediately thereafter became acquiescent in everything proposed to him, finally causing Addison to protest: 'Sir, either contradict me or pay me my money', a salvo of which Johnson himself might have been proud.[1] He replaced Stanyan's colleague, Micklethwaite, by Thomas Tickell.[2] This appointment we are told on the authority of Steele, who was jealous of Tickell, 'incurred the warmest resentments of other gentlemen'.[3] Of these resentments Addison was evidently well aware.[4] Presumably there were junior administrators in office who thought they had prior claims or Whigs who felt the same and who thought Tickell's former moderate Toryism to be objectionable. But Addison was invariably anxious to promote his relatives, for whom he seems to have felt it a duty to provide; and second only to them came his dependants. Tickell is not known to have been a relative, though coming from the same north-country stock as Addison. But he was a loyal supporter, and having taken him from the university Addison probably felt bound to provide for him much as Charles Montagu had done in his own case. Besides which Tickell was by no means unqualified, having served as Under-Secretary to Addison during his recent Irish administration. Like Addison, he now sought a dispensation from the necessity of taking orders at Oxford, and this was obtained by royal grant, perhaps at Addison's intercession; it would probably have been in vain for him to petition the Queen's College authorities as Charles Montagu had approached the President of Magdalen eighteen years before, Oxford being bitterly hostile to the Government.

Tickell's duties were the collection of news for the *Gazette*

---

[1] *Biographia Britannica*, 2nd edn., I. 'Addison'.

[2] *Original Weekly Journal*, 20/4/1717.   [3] *Drummer*: Dedication.

[4] See his letter bequeathing his works to James Craggs, in which he commends Tickell to Craggs's protection, of which he 'will stand very much in need'.

as well as routine matters.[1] As time progressed Addison required extra confidential aid, and he also took on the services of Richard Tickell, elder brother of his Under-Secretary.[2] Charles Delafaye became Under-Secretary to Lord Sunderland, thus establishing a good inter-office liaison at the lower level, and he and Thomas Tickell were, of course, added to the Commission of the Peace.[3] In addition to the regular staff it was the custom of the Secretaries of State to engage extra staff over and above that carried on their wage allowance. Such was Woodward, a cousin of Alexander Denton, Addison's colleague in Ireland and in the House of Commons, probably recommended to him through that channel.[4] Besides his immediate staff, a relatively small item, the Secretary for the South had a voice in innumerable appointments. He had a considerable part in the nominating of British diplomatic staffs abroad. He also had decisive influence in the plantations, and an intimate correspondence with the Lord Lieutenant of Ireland, with some influence over appointments on that establishment. He had, in fact, unrivalled access to every department of government, for the Secretaries of State were more than ever before the clearing house through which all business must pass, and were in frequent contact with the king himself.

In home affairs the Secretary's duties undertaken by Addison were of the most diverse character. There was the whole range of Secret Service work[5] which in his term of office as Under-Secretary had engendered in him a particular dislike of spies and informers.[6] Such was Daniel Defoe, now working for the Government. The management of jails,[7] the committal of individuals thereto after their arrest on a Secretary's warrant, and their delivery upon demand[8] were Addison's responsibility. Many petitions from all kinds of persons and bodies public and private were decided with the advice of the appropriate departments of government.[9] The prerogative of reprieve and pardon was his to exercise.[10]

---

[1] e.g. S.P. 97/24, f. 120. [2] S.P. 44/147.
[3] *Original Weekly Journal*, 5/10/1717. [4] S.P. 35/10, f. 72.
[5] e.g. S.P. 35/10, f. 93. [6] *S.* 439.
[7] S.P. 44/119, f. 42. [8] S.P. 44/80, numerous entries.
[9] Many refs. in S.P. 44/250, 33/77, 35/9, and 35/10.
[10] S.P. 44/360, 44/119; C.O. 324/33.

JOSEPH ADDISON IN HIS MATURITY
from a portrait signed and dated by Kneller in 1716
In the Collection of Dr. James M. Osborn of Yale University

Staffs of foreign diplomatic missions had to be registered
and notified to the local authorities.[1] The advice of the law
officers was required from time to time on behalf of the
Government and the Secretaries of State were responsible
for obtaining it.[2] There was the examination of inventions
and projects, such as a power-operated saw,[3] or the erection
of a lighthouse on St. Bees Head. The maintenance of
the Royal Armorial bearings,[5] the granting of Crown lands,[6]
appointments to a wide range of posts outside regular administration, such as Master Bailiff of the Thames,[7] Regarder
of Windsor Forest,[8] or Captain of Carisbrooke Castle,[9] fell
to the Secretary. The affairs of the Ballast Office,[10] the
obtaining of warrants for offices of State,[11] and the procurement of documents for the House of Commons from government departments and agencies came within his field of
activity.[12] There was also a considerable number of documents passed under the signet which required the counter-
signature of a Secretary of State, such as royal letters and
letters creating titles of nobility.[13]

These were the trivia of secretarial duty which were
handled for the most part by the Under-Secretaries, if
necessary over Addison's signature. But almost immediately
after assuming office he was forced to intervene personally
in one of those tiresome diplomatic incidents which require
to be handled by a minister. On 20 April he was requested
by the Venetian Ambassador, Signor Tron, to arrest Nicolas
Manni, one of the embassy domestics, on suspicion of steal-
ing the ambassadress's jewels.[14] Addison immediately set the
machinery of government in motion, and Manni was
arrested at Dover,[15] attempting to escape from the country.
Meanwhile the ambassadress had complicated the situation
by alleging under examination, first that Manni stole the
diamonds, then that she gave them to him to show to a

---

[1] S.P. 104/251, 93/32, 104/268, and 44/118.
[2] e.g. S.P. 44/119, f. 63; 24/218.   [3] S.P. 44/250, f. 110.
[4] S.P. 44/360, f. 72.   [5] S.P. 44/119, f. 121.   [6] Ibid., f. 69.
[7] S.P. 44/360, 35/77.   [8] S.P. 44/360, f. 53.
[9] S.P. 44/178.   [10] S.P. 35/10, f. 85.
[11] e.g. S.P. 44/359, f. 278, Chancellor of the Duchy of Lancaster.
[12] S.P. 44/119, 44/218, numerous entries.
[13] S.O. 1/16, numerous entries.   [14] S.P. 100/30.   [15] S.P. 44/149.

lady, and finally that she gave them to him to pawn. 'Qui ne voit pas que Madame a desiré de sacrifier un honnête homme pour le soustraire à la fureur d'un Mary naturellement violent, et animé par sa mauvaise conduite', commented Manni, and he alleged that the ambassador had offered him money to keep his mouth shut.[1] Addison endorsed Manni's statement on 27 April and next night had the secretary to the ambassador and a woman brought before him for examination.[2] The ambassador was now offering grateful thanks to Addison, while Manni in custody protested his innocence, prayed to be released, and to be protected from his master. After three weeks' imprisonment, during which the ambassador demanded the return of allegedly stolen documents and Manni denied having any in his possession, means were used to extract from him a confession that there were papers hidden elsewhere and he agreed to write for them. He now denied that he was a domestic of the ambassador and referred Addison to the register of diplomatic staffs. Meanwhile Manni's counsel found that he had to deal with a dangerous client, who wrote to Addison saying that his adviser had sought to procure his escape by bribing the guard, had alleged that he did so by the direction of Addison and Madame Kielmansegge, the king's mistress, and had promised him employment in Hanover. Manni claimed through Addison £150 due to him, of which the ambassador sent £50 through the same channel. It was June before Addison was rid of this troublesome domestic controversy. Manni relapsed into the obscurity of a debtor's jail,[3] the ambassador recovered his papers and, presumably, redeemed his wife's jewels.

Meanwhile Addison was occupied with greater matters, and on 21 April he attended his first Cabinet Council. His scribbled manuscript note of the business which he had to perform as a result of the meeting is fortunately preserved as the first of such a series:[4]

Copy of the Manifesto published at Paris for the K of F, directed to procure.

[1] S.P. 100/30 *et al.* for the case generally.
[2] *Original Weekly Journal*, 4/5/1717.
[3] Quai d'Orsay MSS.: Corr. Pol. Ang. 297, f. 44.   [4] S.P. 35/10, f. 1064.

To speak to the Count de la Perouse, Monsr (illegible) of the protestants in the valley of Pragelas.

D'ayrolles may compliment the King of Sicily at P— &c.

If the Bp. comes with a small retinue to Col. Stanhope show him civilities & watch his motions.

Mr. Bubb to have his letters of revocation but desired not to make use of them.

Ld. Stair to observe the motions of the Court.

Mr. Tunstall in the Marshalsea to be put into the hands of Squire the Messenger at Ld. Parker's request.

Carnegy at Duke of Roxburghe's.

Then followed the date, and a list of those 'present':

A. B. of Canterbury	E. of Berkeley
D of Bolton	
D of Roxburghe	
Ld. Parker	
Mr. Stanhope	E. of Sunderland

Another matter engaging the attention of the Cabinet was the situation in the University of Oxford, which continued most unsatisfactory. Addison's friend George Smalridge had been instrumental in an attempt to prevent the presentation of a loyal address to the king. There was a considerable public demand for reform, and the matter was discussed in Council, where it was resolved that the king had power to visit the universities. This was necessary because the Duke of Ormonde, now in exile, was the Chancellor of Oxford University and no effective visitation could take place. A Bill for University Reform was drafted, which if enacted would deprive Oxford of all patronage for a period of eight years, during which the university would be governed by Royal Commission and the Chancellor would be removable at pleasure. The threat proved of some effect, and the measure was never passed into law.

To the Cabinet on 11 May he took a carefully prepared agenda.[1] He was now reporting to his colleagues upon the matters within his province, and was taking their advice thereupon. He scribbled the decisions given by the Cabinet against the various heads of his paper, as he put them forward. The Dukes of Marlborough, Newcastle, and Kent

[1] S.P. 35/9, f. 4.

were present at this meeting as well as most of the members from the previous one. Since Queen Anne's day the methods of government had altered considerably. Striving to master the new procedure, Addison had a 'List of the Cabinet Council' drawn up, with a note attached thereto that it is summoned in the form '. . . are to attend His Majesty at St. James' etc.', unless it was a Committee at the Office, in which case the form should be '. . . are desired to meet at the Earl of Sunderlands office in the Cockpit . . .'.[1] Such documents show the methodical side of Addison's nature, and the manner in which his administrative experience had taught him the ease with which business may be handled by subordinates if it is reduced to formulae. A meeting at the Cockpit took place on 31 May, and from Addison's agenda and notes it appears that the Cockpit meetings dealt with commercial and plantation matters,[2] while in the meetings at St. James's foreign affairs were the main subject. The king understood French but not English; therefore Addison's command of the former language must have been valuable. He was present as Secretary of State at four Cabinets in the month of May, besides meetings of the Privy Council. This latter was a more formal body, of which Addison was now a member, but for the proceedings of which he was not administratively responsible. The Privy Council had its own secretariat and dealt with many matters beyond the purview of the Secretaries of State.[3]

The political situation in which Addison had assumed office was full of trouble. Lord Townshend and Robert Walpole had gone to their country seats in dudgeon, doubtless thinking, like Addison's Cato, that when 'impious men bear sway the post of honour is a private station'.[4] Addison found himself responsible in Parliament as a principal Minister of the Crown with these redoubtable ex-colleagues absent, but present in spirit. His appointment had meant that he must be re-elected. But the Wharton influence continued to predominate at Malmesbury, where the young marquis had been chosen Lord High Steward to succeed his

[1] S.P. 35/9, f. 12.   [2] e.g. S.P. 35/9, ff. 11, 35.
[3] Addison's attendances at the Privy Council and agenda are to be found in P.C. 2/86.   [4] *Original Weekly Packet*, 20/4/1717.

father.[1] Addison was again returned unopposed, the writ
being issued on 16 April and the result reported in the press
on his birthday, May Day.[2]

It has been reported that upon the one occasion when
Addison rose to speak in the Commons, he was so abashed
by the cries of 'Hear him! Hear him!' which rose on every
hand, that he subsided on to the bench speechless and never
to rise again. There is no doubt that he was a diffident
speaker and no parliamentarian. But that he was literally
silent in the House is disproven by the *Journals* which record
him from time to time declaring His Majesty's pleasure upon
a number of points, some of them important. This must have
required at least a few words of explanation,[3] as for example
when he set before the House a complicated set of memorials
and documents relating to trade with the West Indies. He
was not, however, particularly prominent in Parliament
even in his new ministerial capacity. That he was well aware
of the importance of oratory, and had studied the subject
with some care, is evident from his writings;[4] and it was
undoubtedly a mortification to him to realize how much his
inability in this respect circumscribed his effectiveness in
high office. He had, however, a large variety of responsibilities of a parliamentary nature outside the chamber, such
as summoning private meetings of members at his office to
discuss the parliamentary aspect of matters of State. He
called a meeting of this kind to consider the impeachment
of Lord Oxford.[5] In that particular matter the absence of
Walpole and others who had conducted the proceedings of
the committee now considering the proposal proved a
serious difficulty. Addison joined that body on 14 June, on
which day he summoned it to meet at his office,[6] and it
was ordered to sit daily to expedite these proceedings.[7] He
was a member of a committee drafting a proposal for a bill
in connexion with the king's pardon and of another to
prepare an address to the king excepting Lord Oxford from
the general act. In the autumn, when Parliament met again,

---

[1] *Flying Post*, 3974.
[2] *Daily Courant* of that date; *Post Man*, 11520.
[3] *Hist. Reg.*, ii. 250.
[4] e.g. *S.* 407.
[5] S.P. 35/9, f. 19.
[6] Bohn, vi. 671.
[7] *Collection of Parliamentary Debates*, vi. 482.

he was engaged in the major committee work of the house, such as drafting a reply to the king's speech. It was not a distinguished ministerial part which he played, but he seems to have discharged the essential parliamentary duties of a Secretary of State.

In the House of Peers Lord Oxford was presenting a petition demanding a speedy trial, which could not now be easily refused but which would be almost impossible to conduct. The Government was consequently at pains amidst its manifold troubles to gain popular support. Addison had written in 1707 that 'There is not a more disagreeable thought to the people of *Great Britain* than a standing army'.[1] Now, during his term of Cabinet office, it was possible to please the people by substantially reducing it. The king, on the advice of his ministers, was also making a great personal effort to achieve popularity. There was a course of entertaining at court such as had not been seen since the last century. This required the presence of ministers who would doubtless have preferred to attend to their duties. On the king's birthday, 28 May, there was a monster celebration which Addison attended with his colleagues.[2] He was in the royal presence a great deal, for not only did it fall to his lot as Secretary of State to explain to the king the business of his department, but it was also his duty to present formal addresses from colonial governments, to introduce ambassadors, and to intervene wherever necessary as the correct means of communication between the throne and certain classes of persons and bodies.

On assuming an office to which the Board of Trade and Plantations was answerable Addison ceased to be a member of that body. He attended his last meeting on 12 April and on 16 April the Board addressed him as Secretary of State. The work which he was called upon to perform as Secretary in this field of responsibility was diverse and large in volume. It was a particularly busy time in the affairs of the American and West Indian colonies. The woes of every colonial government were poured into his ear, as were those of the chartered trading corporations. The appointment of Governors and other important colonial officials was a continual

[1] *Present State of the War.*   [2] *Flying Post*, 3964.

source of controversy. One or two of Lord Bolingbroke's friends who remained in office, such as Governor Moody at Placentia, were a source of anxiety, and their replacement was not a matter which could be rapidly completed.[1] There was also trouble with foreign colonial powers, particularly with the Danes who had interests in the West Indies and with whose minister in London Addison was in frequent correspondence.[2] The cutting of logwood for dye by British squatters in the Gulf of Campeche and the Bay of Honduras was a continual source of controversy with Spain.[3] Piracy was a frequent subject of complaint by British merchants,[4] by the French Ambassador,[5] and by the local communities.[6] Addison secured a royal proclamation for its suppression,[7] authority for the setting up of commissions to try piracy cases in the colonies,[8] and the dispatch of three extra ships to the Jamaica seas.[9]

Colonial work tended to be heavy because of territories recently acquired under the Treaty of Utrecht. Such a one was Nova Scotia where lands were now being granted to settlers and merchants.[10] Elsewhere relations with the French colonies remained uneasy and it was necessary for Addison to restrain the British communities from attacking their old opponents when favourable opportunities offered.[11] On the other hand the Spaniards were taking an aggressive attitude towards British shipping and continual protests were required. Certain colonies gave particular trouble. The garrisons of Placentia and Annapolis Royal required constant attention[12] and in Carolina there was an Indian war in which the Lords Proprietors required help from the central government. Addison's friend, Governor Hunter, was having difficulties in New Jersey, where he opposed the separatist ambitions of New York and where there was an intrigue to replace him with Charles Delafaye. As Ambrose Philips was Hunter's agent in England, while Delafaye had

[1] C.O. 194/23, f. 26.
[2] e.g. S.P. 44/119, f. 52, and many other references.   [3] S.P. 94/231.
[4] S.P. 44/119, ff. 61–62; C.O. 324/10, pp. 117–20.
[5] Quai d'Orsay MSS.: Corr. Pol. Ang. 293, ff. 46–47.
[6] S.P. 44/250.   [7] S.P. 44/119, f. 71.
[8] S.P. 38/30, many documents.   [9] S.P. 44/218.
[10] e.g. S.P. 44/250, f. 98.   [11] C.O. 324/33, f. 88.
[12] C.O. 324/33; S.P. 44/218, 44/147, 42/16, 44/111, 41/5, many references.

been intimately associated and friendly with Addison for a number of years, the position was delicate.[1] But Addison instructed the Board of Trade rather tartly that the king was well satisfied with the Governor and that they were to signify as much to his critics.[2] In Jamaica Addison's fellow Whig Member of Parliament and partner in litigation, ex-Governor Pitt of Fort St. George, had been appointed Governor and Captain General at a moment when a firm hand was badly needed. But he then succeeded in selling his fabulous diamond to the Regent of France for a great price and thereafter declined office. A successor therefore had to be found.[3] The Bahamas were also in bad condition and a plan was approved for their surrender by the Lords Proprietors. Captain Woodes Rogers was made Governor with a programme of development.[4]

Amongst more general matters the chaotic Plantation Laws required revision and were to be printed.[5] It was in fact also necessary to keep a watchful eye upon colonial legislatures which had a tendency to encroach upon the functions of the Government of London. As a result of a discussion in the Privy Council, Addison sent orders to all Governors that no acts should be passed affecting trade and shipping unless containing a clause to the effect that they would not come into force until they had received the royal assent.[6] Probably for similar reasons he sent instructions to Governors to make a regular return of revenues.[7] Of the numerous private petitions coming to the office from the colonies, such as that of Anne Low to be allowed the sole privilege of curing sturgeon in America,[8] almost all were referred for advice to the appropriate department. Addison's period at the Secretary of State's office was one in which a considerable restaffing of the colonies took place, and in which a number of administrative reforms were carried out. It is noticeable that most of these schemes were implemented during the earlier portion of his term when he was in fair health and personally in charge of business.

[1] *Cal. S.P. Col. A. & W.I.* 1716–17, xxviii.
[2] S.P. 44/119, ff. 80–81.   [3] S.P. 38/30.
[4] S.P. 44/119, f. 86, and many other references.   [5] Ibid.
[6] P.C. 2/86, f. 23; C.O. 324/33, f. 102; S.P. 44/119, f. 105.
[7] S.P. 44/119, f. 71.   [8] S.P. 44/250, f. 121.

In Irish matters the Secretary of State for the South was the minister with whom the Lord Lieutenant transacted his business. Addison's appointment must have meant that it would be easy for the Dublin Government to make its point of view understood by one who had twice been Secretary of the Irish administration. Furthermore, Addison's relative, Eustace Budgell, who had been in England during the winter, was now in Dublin again and was prominent in Irish affairs. He was advanced to the lucrative post of Accountant General of the Revenue in August of this year, and Addison could count upon him as a loyal supporter and informant. Nevertheless, Addison's position in the Government of Ireland, where the Lord Lieutenant, a great officer of State, was the executive authority, was not comparable with that in the colonies, where he was himself the person of greatest influence beneath the king.

From Dublin Archbishop King sent him a warm letter of welcome to office:

I hope I need not bespeak your favours to that poor Kingdom of Ireland, you have so many that esteem and love you there, that I persuade my self you will not come short of the confidence they have in you or expectations they have from you.

The new Lord Lieutenant was the Duke of Bolton to whom Addison immediately began to pass a large volume of business in parts of which he acted only as a post box. A certain number of elevations to the Irish peerage and Privy Council, in which Addison would have a voice, were now being made.[1] The duke went to his government in August and on arrival stipulated for exchange of news with Addison's office by every post. Addison meanwhile began to lay the duke's proposals and correspondence before the king,[2] whose consent he obtained for, amongst other things, a grant of £5,000 for the extension of Trinity College Library. The affairs of the college had been satisfactorily regulated on the appointment of Provost Baldwin. Addison evidently did not disappoint Archbishop King, for the Lord Lieutenant thanked him for his expedition in getting the Irish Bills passed in London, an achievement the importance of which

[1] S.O. 1/16.   [2] S.P. 67/7.

would not be lost on the one-time Secretary in Dublin.
Apart from the local political issues the Irish administration
was conducting an inquiry into the faulty nature of 10,000
arms sent from Holland during the rebellion of 1715. A test
and report showed that out of six arms chosen at random,
two were good, two burst, and two blew the breeches off.
Addison sent the report on to the Treasury for action.[1] On
the whole it appears to have been a routine administration,
much of the work being done by Stanyan and Tickell, and
by Webster, the Secretary in Dublin.[2]

In the field of his foreign responsibilities Addison's
views were those of a good Whig. He had always believed
that England's power depended upon her wealth, her
wealth upon her commerce, and her commerce upon the
freedom of the seas and the checking of the power of France
and Spain. Since he first expounded these thoughts in his
Poem to His Majesty in 1695, they had been vindicated by
events. Yet he took no narrow view of Christendom, but
understood the community of all mankind: 'Nature seems
to have taken a particular Care to disseminate her Blessings
among the different Regions of the World, . . . that the
Natives of the several Parts of the Globe might have a
kind of Dependence upon one another, and be united
together by their common Interest.'[3] He was now much
occupied with Spain. The policy of the Government aimed
at friendship with one of Britain's best customers, but
conflicted with the expansionist designs which were being
secretly prepared by Alberoni, the minister of King Philip V.
Addison was in frequent contact with the Marques de
Monteleone, Spanish Ambassador in London; and he had a
heavy correspondence with George Bubb the British
Ambassador in Madrid and with several British consuls in
Spanish ports. The expulsion of the Jews from Gibraltar,
recently ceded to Britain, had been stipulated in article 10 of
the Treaty of Utrecht, and was giving rise to much difficulty.[4]
There was also continual trouble about the treatment of
British merchants in Spain, and a prolonged negotiation
about the tariff rates which they should pay. King George

---

[1] S.P. 44/119, ff. 103–4.   [2] S.P. 67/7, 63/375.
[3] *S.* 69.   [4] S.P. 104/255, 94/86.

was at this time offering to mediate between Spain and the emperor, who had serious differences in Italy, and Addison was evidently entrusted with this matter which was kept secret from those usually informed of government policy in foreign affairs.[1] There was trouble about the appointment of consuls, Addison instructing Bubb that the Spanish ones at Gibraltar and Mahon[2] would not be received until the British were correctly treated in Spanish ports.[3] From Cadiz and elsewhere came reports of intense naval preparations.[4] These were being anxiously watched by all Europe and their purpose remained unknown. On 24 June Bubb correctly forecast the destination of the fleet to Addison[5] to whom news of the preparations now poured in from every consulate.[6] The emperor became thoroughly alarmed and at the request of his ambassador in London a dispatch from Addison to Bubb asked the latter to draw Alberoni's attention to the fact that Britain was pledged to assist the emperor in the event of a violation of his territories in Italy. If Alberoni did not reply satisfactorily Bubb was to memorialize the King of Spain. So important was this document thought to be that Addison and Sunderland together received the imperial ambassador before it was dispatched[7] by express courier.[8]

At this critical juncture it was decided to send Colonel William Stanhope, a cousin of the minister, as ambassador to Madrid to relieve Bubb, who was anxious to return home. He was authorized to promise certain concessions in an attempt to keep the peace between Spain and the emperor and had instructions to offer a large cash bribe to Alberoni.[9] This was a delicate and elaborate transaction, and Addison's office was even busier than usual. The rush of work kept Temple Stanyan busy far into the night.[10] So urgent was the matter that Colonel Stanhope could not wait for a yacht and Addison's office ordered a special packet to carry him to France on the first stage of his journey.[11] Meanwhile news was

[1] S.P. 104/218.   [2] S.P. 104/55.   [3] S.P. 104/136.
[4] e.g. S.P. 94/213, 94/214.   [5] S.P. 49/87.
[6] e.g. S.P. 94/213, letter of 8/7/1717, Alicante.
[7] S.P. 94/87.   [8] S.P. 44/147.
[9] S.P. 104/137, document of 17/8/1717.   [10] S.P. 35/9, f. 94.
[11] S.P. 44/147.

received that the Spanish expedition had sailed to Sardinia, imperial territory, where a landing had been made and the conquest of the island begun, precisely as Bubb had forecast. When Stanhope arrived at Madrid he found the Spanish Government so far from acceding to his requests for restraint that he reported to Addison the possibility of a Spanish invasion of Portugal.[1] Shortly thereafter matters took a yet more dangerous turn, Stanhope warning Addison that the Spanish Ambassador in London was to threaten to leave England unless he received an assurance that the British fleet now fitting out as rapidly as possible was not destined for the Mediterranean.[2] Consul Herne reported that British trade in Alicante was at a standstill, ships seized and crews imprisoned.[3] The commercial negotiations with the Spanish Government had likewise broken down. Thus Addison's colleagues in charge of high policy had misjudged the character and intentions of the Spanish Government, and much detailed and careful direction of diplomacy on his part was thrown away. Even his representations to Sir Martin Wescombe, the consul at Cadiz, to recover what he might of £12,000 of land tax moneys with which a collector, Bowdidge, had absconded from England, bore little fruit.[4]

In Portugal the principal concern of the Government was to protect British trade and to prevent British merchants from being expelled from Brazil. The ambassador at Lisbon, Worsley, was also endeavouring to assist the Portuguese Government in recovering 600,000 pieces of eight due from Spain under the Treaty of Utrecht. Poyntz, the consul, was trying to obtain a plot of ground for an English cemetery.[5] Bubb at Madrid thought the Portuguese Ambassador there to be badly served and incompetent, and Addison did much business through Worsley which might more properly have been transacted through the faulty channel. He also instructed Bubb to memorialize the Spanish Court for payment of the 600,000 8/8 on the ground that King George was guarantor of the Spanish–Portuguese treaty and a mediator.[6] Meanwhile Spain was pressing a counter-claim aganst the Portuguese arising out of shipping on the River Plate, and

---

[1] S.P. 94/88.   [2] Ibid.   [3] S.P. 94/213.
[4] S.P. 104/136.   [5] S.P. 89/25.   [6] S.P. 104/136.

Bubb reported that the large sum due to Portugal would not be paid whatever King George might urge.[1] There was trouble in the local British factory upon which Addison took the king's instructions and there was an incident in which naval clothing for Admiral Cornwall's squadron in the Mediterranean was seized in Lisbon and duty demanded, while the admiral complained that his men were nearly naked. It was thus a forlorn collection of diplomatic assets which Addison had to administer in the Iberian Peninsula.

Relations with France, where Lord Stair was an able ambassador, centred upon negotiations to enlarge the Triple into a Quadruple Alliance. This would include the emperor; and would be the means of avoiding a war between Spain and the empire, which would probably become general, by the kind of solution in compromise for which Colonel Stanhope was working in Madrid. Much of Stair's correspondence with Addison was devoted to the movements of the Pretender's supporters, including Addison's former patron the Duke of Ormonde, and their relationships with their friends in England. Jacobite activity centred in the 'Court' at St. Germains, and Jacobite hope in the King of Sweden whose unstable policy gave some expectation that he might attack Britain and whose corsairs did much harm to British trade. Efforts were therefore being made by Addison through Stair to prevent the Swedes from receiving any sympathy or encouragement from France, and Crawford, the Secretary of Embassy, reported that the Jacobites began to despair, the king was so long a-coming.[2] It is likely that Addison had used his honeymoon visit to Paris to inform himself on this subject and to renew his acquaintance with French politics. He now had much opportunity to use his knowledge.

A particularly difficult controversy centred in the demolition of the sluices which the French Government had built at Mardyck, thus infringing the spirit if not the letter of the Peace Treaty.[3] Under Addison's administration commissioners were supervising the demolition as the only means of securing any progress in that respect. Another source of

---

[1] S.P. 94/87.   [2] S.P. 78/161.
[3] S.P. 76/2, 44/147, and 90/13 refer.

anxiety was the movements of the czar, then travelling in western Europe, whose plans had an important bearing upon King George's northern policy. Although the north lay beyond the scope of Addison's administrative responsibility, the czar was now in his territories and he was careful to obtain through the Paris Embassy detailed accounts of the Russian movements and conversation. When Peter arrived in Paris Stair reported to Addison his own attempts to obtain a promise that Russian troops would leave Mecklenburg, a particular desire of King George.[1] In this Stair received surprisingly satisfactory assurances, and Addison was authorized by the king to send his thanks and to offer to send a minister to the czar to conclude an agreement immediately.[2]

In the delicate situation following the arrest in England of Swedish diplomats detected plotting against the establishment, the Regent of France was acting as mediator for their return in exchange for the British minister at Stockholm. Addison corresponded with Stair in arranging the mediation,[3] and received the French Ambassador in London at least twice in connexion with this matter.[4] He also had lengthy correspondence with Stair upon the admission of Prussia to the Triple Alliance, which was desired by the French but which King George thought would antagonize the emperor. Addison therefore instructed Stair to seek to persuade the French to use all means of bringing the empire into the alliance before seeking to include Prussia.[5] On his way to Madrid Colonel Stanhope had been instructed to call at Paris to explain his mission to the regent and to seek to obtain French agreement in attempting to arrive at a settlement between Spain and the emperor;[6] in this he was successful.[7]

At home in Britain an Act of Grace was projected, from which certain persons were excepted for political reasons. Addison now wrote to Stair instructing him to insinuate to the regent that Lord Bolingbroke was under His Majesty's

---

[1] S.P. 78/161.   [2] S.P. 104/29.   [3] Ibid.
[4] Quai d'Orsay MSS.: Corr. Pol. Ang. 287, ff. 128, 295 several refs.
[5] S.P. 78/161, f. 120 and many previous references.
[6] F.O. 90/60b, f. 41 et seq.   [7] S.P. 78/161, ff. 133, 134.

protection because of the good disposition which he had shown towards the Government.[1] This may have been a following up of the conversations alleged to have taken place between Bolingbroke and the visiting Whigs in Paris the previous autumn. These concessions, Stair told Addison, were gratefully received by the exiled Harry St. John, who now obtained permission to send his secretary, Brinsden, to London to explore the possibility of his own return to England.[2] The secretary, on his arrival in October,[3] was interviewed by Lord Sunderland, probably because this was a matter of high internal policy; but he would meet and negotiate with Addison, who was responsible for handling the correspondence with Lord Stair which had made his journey possible. The Government favoured permitting Lord Bolingbroke to return to England, a course probably advised by Addison in the discharge of his duty; but such clemency did not prove acceptable to the bulk of the Whig party at this time.

There was a tendency for the centre of European diplomacy to shift to London. Forecasting the visit to England of the Abbé Dubois and of Pendtenriedter the imperial envoy, to undertake negotiations for a Quadruple Alliance, Lord Stair remarked to Addison that he was glad to see how Europe's business was now done in the British capital. This was a handsome tribute to the active diplomacy of George I and his ministers. In London the French Ambassador, the Marquis d'Iberville, was on good terms with Addison, with whom he had numerous interviews upon various topics.[4] For example, on 25 June Addison wrote to him:

Si vous passés prés de mon Bureau vers les 11 heures, je serai bien aise vous y voir, or s'il vous est plus commode de vous trouver a l'escalier secret a St. James, je ne manquerai pas de m'y rendre.[5]

But until the arrival of Dubois in London in September most of the diplomacy between England and France was conducted by Stair with the regent on instructions

---

[1] S.P. 104/218.   [2] S.P. 78/161, f. 133.
[3] Weekly Packet, 278; Original Weekly Journal, 2/11/1717.
[4] Quai d'Orsay MSS.: Corr. Pol. Ang. 287, ff. 128, 295 several refs.
[5] S.P. 104/246.

forwarded by Addison. Thereafter negotiations for the
Quadruple Alliance passed into secret channels and were
conducted between the abbé, Lord Stanhope, and the king.
Addison saw a good deal of the brilliant French diplomat
and accompanied him upon social occasions such as to
dinner with the Duke of Newcastle on 12 October.[1] And
whereas the relations which Addison conducted with Spain
within the framework of King George's foreign policy saw
failure as their result, his similar work with Lord Stair upon
Paris matters, in conjunction with that of Dubois and Lord
Stanhope in London and elsewhere, was rewarded in the
following year with brilliant success in the conclusion of
the Quadruple Alliance. This marked the highest point in
British prestige and the greatest advance of British diplomacy up to that time.

Addison was not responsible for any direct diplomacy
with the empire; but he had four important interests in
events in Vienna from the point of view of his own department. One was to bring about an accommodation between
the emperor and Spain, whose troublesome court was his
direct responsibility. Another was through Lord Stair in
Paris to seek to include the Empire in the alliance. He also
had an interest in Vienna in that he was responsible for
relations with the Sublime Porte at a time when King
George with the States General was to mediate in the war
between the Turks and the emperor. A fourth interest arose
from his responsibility for relations with the Swiss Cantons,
in view of the fact that King George as a part of his many-
sided diplomacy was seeking to obtain through the emperor
a satisfactory settlement of differences between the Cantons
and the Abbot of St. Gall.

Negotiations for a peace in the east had been much helped
by Prince Eugene's victory over the Turks at Belgrade.
This, as Bubb reported to Addison from Madrid, had a
general good effect in discouraging trouble makers from
attacking imperial territories. But the proposed mediation
had alarmed the Venetians, for relations with whom Addison was responsible. They feared that the Turks were seeking to make a separate peace with Vienna which would leave

[1] *Original Weekly Journal,* 12/10/1717.

them exposed.[1] Matters were somewhat complicated by the fact that Wortley, who as ambassador to the Porte was imploring Addison to urge that the opportunity to make peace be seized immediately, was thought by the emperor to be so favourable to the Turks that his recall was pressed for and obtained.[2] Wortley was hampered by lack of a cipher, by the fierce opposition of the French Ambassador and the corruption of the Dutch, and by not being an experienced diplomat. For the last-mentioned reason he failed to appreciate the opposite side of the case to that of the court to which he was accredited, nor did he know how to defend his point of view with his own government, where Addison was powerless to help him in the face of the emperor's representations.

The new ambassador to the Porte was Abraham Stanyan, who was as pro-Imperialist as Wortley was pro-Turk, but who had a long experience of diplomacy. Addison wrote a personal letter to Wortley 'not as the Secretary to the Ambassador, but as an humble servant to his friend', in which he endeavoured to soften the blow. Reciting the certainty that Wortley would shortly obtain a place as an Auditor of Imprest, he continued:

> Our great men are of opinion that . . . it would be agreeable to your inclinations, as well as for the king's service, which you are so able to promote in parliament, rather to return to your own country than to live at Constantinople. For this reason, they have thoughts of relieving you by Mr. Stanyan, who is now at the Imperial court, and of joining Sir Robert Sutton with him in the mediation of a peace between the Emperor and the Turks. . . . I find by his Majesty's way of speaking of you, that you are much in his favour and esteem, and I fancy you would find your ease and advantage more in being nearer his person. . . .

On the letter Wortley endorsed: 'Mr. Addison . . . Reason for my being recalled', but was not pleased, having hoped for the honour of making peace. His friend in London ordered a ship to Constantinople to bring him and Lady Mary home,[3] an action which would be agreeable to Pope, who paralleled Addison's official correspondence with

---

[1] S.P. 80/34.
[2] See his letters in S.P. 97/24; also S.P. 80/34.   [3] S.P. 44/218.

Wortley, by a gallant one with Lady Mary. The recall which thus took place was probably hastened by the fact that Wortley on the one hand, and Sir Robert Sutton and Stanyan at Vienna on the other, were now mutually offended and not corresponding, and it was high time to end such a situation. Stanyan was writing to Addison, into whose sphere of responsibility he was now passing. The Secretary evidently tried to calm his warring subordinates in a series of private letters not preserved. The correspondence with the mediatory commission now fell mainly into Addison's department[1] though the negotiations were not concluded during his term of office. He was also dealing with Stanyan upon a number of other matters, such, for example, as the needs of British commerce in the Levant.[2]

Addison received a copious correspondence from residents Dayrolles at Geneva and Manning at Berne.[3] He was well equipped to follow the complex diplomacy of the Confederation, which he had studied in 1702, and where he had since maintained some contacts. Switzerland was a focal point from which a great deal of news of movements of refugees, including the Pretender and his followers, and also intelligence from Europe generally, could be obtained and forwarded. With the intelligence there also came a good many wild rumours and some wry humour. Manning reported that the Pretender had seen the Pope and that 'the interview is said to have been very mournful, and plenty of tears was shed between them'. Dayrolles was particularly asked to watch the movements of the King of Sicily, whose erratic behaviour was one of the minor hazards of European diplomacy. He was later promoted to The Hague and replaced by Baron de Marsay, a friend of Addison's, who resumed the correspondence. At the request of Geneva Addison was seeking to protect the Protestants of the valleys of Pragelas and Cezanne from persecution, by representations to Count de la Perouse, the Sicilian minister in London. He was endeavouring to dissuade the emperor from rash designs, of which he was suspect, upon the Grizons. He was intervening, again with de la Perouse at the instance of Geneva, in favour of the pretensions of that Canton to the

[1] S.P. 97/24.   [2] S.P. 97/56.   [3] See S.P. 96/17-18.

tithes of Fonsenex. Through the two British ministers in Switzerland he was also treating with the emperor in the dispute between the Cantons of Zurich and Berne and the Abbot of St. Gall, whose territories he had visited in 1703 and described in his *Travels*. This ended in a conference at Baden. Finally he was keeping a watchful eye upon the proceedings of the Diet at Soleurre. The extraordinary intensity of British diplomacy in Switzerland reveals the attention to detail and the fertility of initiative which enabled King George and his ministers to make Britain the foremost diplomatic power in Europe. In a traditionally French diplomatic preserve it is not surprising that Manning complained to Addison that he was ignored by the French Ambassador and had to use great diligence to avoid a quarrel.[1]

Alexander Cunningham, the resident in Venice, and Neil Brown, the consul, were busy reporting news of the Pretender and his followers to Addison, and also stopping their credit.[2] Jacobite officers were encouraged to enter the service of the republic against the Turk, a course which kept them occupied harmlessly and might result in a lessening of their numbers. The only diplomatic move of importance by Addison in Venetian affairs was, at Stanyan's suggestion, to propose that King George should mediate between the Republic and the Porte as well as between the empire and the latter power. This offer was readily accepted as a safeguard against a separate peace being made by the emperor. In Genoa Davenant, the resident, and consul Henshaw,[3] were also occupied in reporting the activities of the Pretender and were at one in advising that no opportunity be lost to reduce the power of the King of Sicily who was inclined to support Spanish pretensions in Italy. Davenant was an old friend and wrote to Addison informally. He was trying to secure a set of statues for Blenheim Palace, sent cordial messages from Addison's friend and translator Salvini at Florence, also copies of an Italian translation of the 'Letter to Lord Halifax', and begged now and then for the advice of a friend as well as the commands of a Secretary. At Leghorn

[1] S.P. 104/96.
[2] S.P. 99/61, 104/96 contain correspondence with Addison.   [3] S.P. 79/8.

a new consul, Fuller, was appointed by Addison on the advice of an old acquaintance, Daniel Gould.[1] In Naples Consul Fleetwood was Addison's correspondent,[2] but most business was handled direct with de la Perouse in London. Fleetwood, like every other British representative in Italy, was pressing upon Addison the desirability of sending a fleet to the Mediterranean where its presence would have a restraining effect. He had some trouble with British seamen enlisting with foreign powers and Addison sent instructions that they should be persuaded to desert, together with a royal proclamation against foreign enlistment.[3]

At Minorca Lord Forbes, the Governor and commander-in-chief, corresponded with Addison about the holding of the new base at Port Mahon.[4] He was convinced that Spain was preparing to retake the island[5] and received a bad fright when a large Spanish fleet, on its way to capture Sardinia, put in to water. He thought that the Spaniards noticed and tried to increase his alarm.[6] Reinforcements were, however, on their way.[7] The religious situation in the island was delicate and Addison found himself involved in negotiating a settlement which would safeguard the beliefs of the inhabitants while providing for the spiritual needs of the garrison.[8] At Gibraltar the colony was in bad condition, and most English statesmen were prepared to consider its cession if that should prove advantageous in diplomatic negotiations.[9] But Addison had understood the importance of the Rock to a trading nation so long ago as 1707 when he wrote: 'The Straits mouth is the key to the Levant . . . .'[10] He now had much trouble with Gibraltarian matters. Colonel Cotton, the acting Governor, was conducting the evacuation of the Jews in pursuance of British treaty obligations,[11] but this presented problems, particularly in the case of those who owed money locally, and there were numerous diplomatic exchanges with Spain in this connexion. Addison was particularly interested in the Jews, especially those of Barbary described by his father, and he had devoted a

[1] S.P. 98/23.   [2] S.P. 93/4.   [3] S.P. 104/96.
[4] S.P. 94/87.   [5] B.M. Egerton MSS. 2174, f. 295.
[6] Ibid., f. 176.   [7] B.M. Egerton MSS. 2175, f. 50.
[8] C.O. 174/15.   [9] See S. Conn, *Gibraltar in British Diplomacy.*
[10] *Present State of the War.*   [11] S.P. 42/69.

Spectator to their affairs. But though he regarded them sympathetically and thought them useful in the community, there was little that he could do in this case where their fate was prescribed by treaty. Admiral Cornwall, the naval officer commanding a squadron based at Gibraltar, had projects for making the colony more useful to the Crown and for remedying abuses in its administration,[1] but was hampered in his good intentions by quarrels with the military authorities.

Addison doubtless took particular pleasure in conducting relations with the Barbary States, recalling his father's experiences in Tangier and his writings, which had given him a taste for oriental fable revealed upon many occasions in the *Spectator*. An important diplomatic problem presented itself in the fate of British captives taken by the Barbary corsairs. Of 198 captives at Meknez, when Addison assumed office 41 had died, 4 had turned mohammedan, and 153 were alive.[2] Admiral Cornwall had instructions to exact reparation from the Emperor of Morocco for losses sustained by British shipping at the hands of the Sallee rovers. He was instructed to negotiate a treaty with the emperor, but if unsuccessful was to make a truce for as long as possible and to exchange Moors held by Britain for British captives. He was authorized to offer a present to the emperor which was not to be delivered until satisfaction was obtained. Finding nobody empowered to treat with him the admiral wrote direct to the emperor who sent a plenipotentiary to Gibraltar where a year's truce and exchange of captives was arranged. But no confirmation being forthcoming and the Bassa through whom Cornwall had arranged the meeting demanding $10,000 as due from the last British minister, the admiral feared that his correspondence had in fact never reached the emperor at all. The captives at Meknez meanwhile were imploring that a minister be sent there, but although the Bassa supported the suggestion, the admiral advised that it would be useless. Instead, he put a stop to all commerce, told the Bassa that captured Moorish ships would be sold at the pleasure of the captors, and begged Addison, who now assumed responsibility as

[1] B.M. Egerton MSS. 2174, f. 256.   [2] S.P. 71/16, f. 499.

Secretary, to say whether he might seize the Moors and Jews in Gibraltar in reprisal. This forthright naval diplomacy had had its effect upon the Bassa, and further reactions from Meknez were awaited.[1] Addison acknowledged five of the admiral's letters, approved his conduct, but warned him to bear in mind the commercial needs of Gibraltar.[2] Evidently his interest in these matters drew his attention to the fact that Mr. Beard, embellisher of letters to the eastern princes, had not been properly rewarded for 'extraordinary services', and a request was put to the Treasury on his behalf.[3]

The admiral now altered his view and was pressing Addison for a representative to be sent to Meknez to take advantage of the results of his pressure, but deplored the choice of Consul Hatfield for Tetuan against his advice, stating that he was a broken merchant who fled christendom to escape his debtors.[4] On 31 May Addison read to the Cabinet a summary of the 'State of the Barbary Affair'. He pointed out that although much success had been secured at sea and promises had been made by the ministers of Muley Ishmael, they dared not tell him of his reverses or of their undertakings, as he believed himself supreme by land and sea. His daily barbarities showed how little he cared for his subjects, and it was unlikely that any hurt done to them would be of weight. First setting out the arguments against sending an emissary to Meknez, the danger of the undertaking, the expense, and the little value attaching to a treaty, Addison answered them one by one. He urged that the enterprise was worth risking on the grounds of the saving to commerce which would follow an agreement, of the necessity to secure the market for woollen goods which was passing to the French, and of obtaining the release of the captives.[5] He succeeded in making the admiral's case, and noted on his agenda 'one to be sent to Mequinez'.[6] But communications were slow and in September the admiral complained to Bubb that he had heard nothing from Addison for two months and added that he was heartily sick of so treacherous a people as those he was to deal with.[7]

[1] S.P. 71/16, f. 467.   [2] Ibid., f. 489.   [3] S.P. 44/119, f. 56.
[4] S.P. 94/87.   [5] S.P. 71/16, f. 507.   [6] S.P. 35/9, f. 11.
[7] B.M. Egerton MSS. 2175, f. 174.

Meanwhile he urged the need for a handsome present to bribe the Bassas, Álcalde Hamet, and other dignitaries. If a minister were to be sent without means the admiral thought he would merely be detained, and he suggested one Anthony Corbiere for the post.[1] As Consul Hatfield had put it to Addison from Tetuan, an ambassador at court would be cheaper than keeping ten men-of-war on the station.[2] Possibly this argument helped Addison to obtain from Stanhope at the Treasury the necessary credits in Gibraltar.[3] He ordered eight ships of the line of 50–70 guns and two bomb vessels to the station to strengthen the squadron,[4] doubtless with objectives other than Morocco in mind, but probably reflecting that their presence would have a good effect in the Barbary States.

Unfortunately the admiral now quarrelled with Colonel Cotton at Gibraltar. He had been pressing the Governor to expel the remaining Jews in order to clear the field for his negotiations with the emperor at Meknez. He now somewhat fiercely reminded Cotton that when the Rock was taken the latter had said on the day of capture that he would expel the Jews and had posted a notice to that effect on the gates of the town. Only one Englishman, the admiral alleged, still had a debt due to him from a Jew, so that objections on that score were invalid. This was resented by Cotton as interference, particularly as it was rounded off with a threat to write to Secretary Addison advising the expulsion of the Jews before the conclusion of a peace with Barbary.[5] Cotton forbade his officers to communicate with the admiral, an action characterized by the latter as 'not for His Majesty's service'.[6] Meanwhile the emperor had released some captured sailors and had proposed to Cornwall that he should come in person to his court to treat for peace.[7] He sent a safe conduct to Cadiz addressed to Russell, the acting consul.[8] The admiral unfortunately continued to quarrel furiously with Colonel Cotton. Garrison guns were trained on a vessel to prevent her sailing, and the words 'vile fellow'

[1] S.P. 71/16, f. 535.
[2] Ibid., f. 557.
[3] S.P. 44/119, f. 86; 35/9, f. 150.
[4] S.P. 44/218.
[5] S.P. 42/69.
[6] Ibid.
[7] S.P. 71/16, f. 549.
[8] S.P. 94/213.

entered into the exchanges.[1] Cornwall even threatened to write to the Speaker asking for the recall of both of them. By the end of the year, however, one of Cornwall's captains, Coningsby Norbury, who had been transporting Jews back to Barbary, signed a three months' truce with the emperor in Tetuan[2] and matters were put in a state of preparedness for further negotiations, for which purpose Admiral Cornwall was appointed plenipotentiary.

While the affairs of Morocco were thus confused, those of Algiers were only less difficult. Consul Thomson was in touch with the Dey and reported to Addison upon the release of captives and the suppression of piracy. Articles of peace had been agreed and the Dey pressed for a document signed with the king's hand.[3] The unfortunate consul then had to report that one Israel, a British subject, had insulted a Bulga-Bassa, and that the Dey had sent for Thomson to explain. Asking what he was expected to do, the consul was told that the draft treaty provided for English subjects to receive the same treatment as Turkish, which in this case would be the bastinado and expulsion.[4] In the face of this threat Israel then made his escape, leaving the consul to pay for the slaves which he had taken with him.[5] There was an endless story poured into Addison's ear about other troubles, mostly connected with the seizure of shipping, liberation of captives, and finally a plot to assassinate the Dey. There was but one bright passage, when Thomson related to Addison that he had been struck by a drunken Moor and had complained to the Dey. The man was promptly seized and given 700 strokes one night and 300 more next morning, and only escaped hanging at Thomson's particular request. This, said the consul, would show Addison what 'immediate justice we have from the Dey'.[6] There remained the consular post at Tunis, but this caused Addison little concern during his term of office.[7] The present occupant was Consul Lawrence, whose most serious worry seems to have been the ghost of a former consul, Loddington, at Tripoli. This man had absconded in debt and a brisk passage of memorials was in

---

[1] S.P. 42/69.   [2] Du Mont, *Corps Univ. Diplomatique*, viii, pt. i.
[3] S.P. 71/5, f. 425.   [4] Ibid., f. 429.   [5] Ibid., f. 441.
[6] Ibid., f. 433.   [7] S.P. 71/27.

progress with his former French colleague.¹ The unorthodox diplomacy of the Barbary States thus afforded Addison
a diversion from the elegant and highly important negotiations surrounding the Quadruple Alliance.

Across the whole scene of foreign affairs at this time there
flitted the erratic figure of Lord Peterborough, the unpredictable self-important peer who had captured the fort at
Barcelona in Queen Anne's reign and who was never for
long out of the public prints. Shortly after Addison took
office the earl, then in Rome, had scandalized politicians by
his abuse of the emperor, at whose hands he considered
himself to have been wronged; and had equally shocked
society by taking his mistress to religious functions of a
public nature.² One of Addison's first, and, as a commoner,
most delicate duties, was to write him a severe royal repri-
mand.³ Peterborough was now on his way to England and
his movements were reported to Addison from British
ministers along his line of travel. In Paris he replied to
Addison's letter, characteristically at very great length, paying him the compliment that 'It is a satisfaction to receive it
[the king's reprimand] from your hands, being confident
my answer will be fairly represented'. He arrived in London
shortly thereafter,⁴ called upon Addison, restored himself to
royal favour,⁵ and almost immediately returned to Europe.
Passing from Paris back to Italy, he assumed an air of
mystery, which gave rise to the belief that he was the king's
special envoy come to settle the affairs of the nations of the
peninsula.⁶ Alarming reports were made to the Pope, as a
consequence of which Lord Peterborough was arrested at
his house in Bologna in papal territory, and kept under
guard of the archers of the Cardinal Legate.

Accounts of this event poured in to Addison from every
diplomatic post from Switzerland to Naples.⁷ The greatest
excitement, interest, and amusement, heightened by the
earl's declaration at the time of his arrest that he was married
to the lady living in his house,⁸ ran throughout the diplomatic world. Davenant, at Genoa, was greatly angered,

¹ S.P. 71/22, f. 69.   ² S.P. 99/61.   ³ S.P. 104/218.
⁴ *Flying Post*, 3980.   ⁵ *Evening Post*, 1242.   ⁶ S.P. 79/9.
⁷ e.g. S.P. 96/17.   ⁸ S.P. 79/9.

suggesting that the fleet should burn Civita Vecchia in reprisal, and fearing that Peterborough might disappear and never
be heard of again. In a private note to Addison he emphasized
that the whole affair was devised by the Papacy to bring
discredit on the king.[1] He talked of poison, and a Jacobite
conspiracy, and doubted the reality of the earl's marriage.
Cunningham in Venice waited more calmly for instructions.
Meanwhile Addison showed the correspondence to the King
and sought his commands in an embarrassing situation.
George was exceedingly angry, not so much on Peterborough's account as because of allegations made by the
papal court of a plot by him against the Pretender's life, in
which the Crown might be thought implicated. Addison
accordingly wrote to the earl stating that the king proposed
to exact satisfaction. Davenant continued to fume from
Genoa: 'I hope such resolutions will be taken by His
Majesty, as will make these Priests tremble for what they
have done', and now doubted whether the burning of
a papal port would be sufficient punishment. Addison on
instruction took advantage of the occasion to protest to the
emperor through Count Gallas, asking for imperial intervention on Peterborough's behalf and widening the issue
to a complaint against the whole Papal attitude in Italy with
regard to the Pretender. He demanded satisfaction and
assurances for the future under five heads, failing which the
king would seek his remedy in a suitable manner. He added
that orders had already been given for a squadron to sail to
the coasts of Papal territory 'laquelle Escadre doit aller à
Civita-Vecchia ou autres Lieux de ses Etats, où Elle trouvera
occasion de donner des marques du juste Ressentiment de sa
Majesté'. It would be expected that the Pope would pay the
cost of the expedition, and the officers in charge would be
given instructions to that effect. But before this thunderous
diplomacy could be brought to bear, the Pope had already
begun to think second thoughts, setting Lord Peterborough
at liberty and letting him know that he felt he had paid too
much attention to the fears of his advisers.[2] At the same time
Dubois in London was counselling moderation to Addison
in an interview which he sought for that purpose.[3]

[1] S.P. 79/9.   [2] Ibid.   [3] Quai d'Orsay MSS.: Corr. Pol. Ang. 295, f. 222.

The burden of an immense amount of detailed and important administration, of parliamentary work and of attendance at court, often involving the most unseasonable hours, soon began to tell upon Addison. By 10 June he was indisposed. He retired to Holland House where his secretaries attended him.[1] Tickell was writing letters on his behalf and with his instructions. His illness was evidently of short duration for he was at the Cabinet on 9 June[2] and was at court again on 14 June presenting an address[3] and introducing the Venetian secretary in London to the king.[4] But he was away from work again on 20 June.[5] It was a desperately busy time and Temple Stanyan remarked to the ambassador in Madrid: 'There are so many other things upon the Tapis at present that you can't expect any regular correspondence from the office.'[6] Addison is recorded as remaining busy in the royal circle and in the Council until the king moved to Hampton Court at the end of July. The change caused a further dislocation of the work of the Secretaries of State, Addison being unable to obtain the king's instructions while the move was proceeding.[7] By 26 July, however, he was acting in his usual capacity at the newly established court in the country,[8] presenting an address from the island of Nevis and another from Bermuda. A post ran twice daily between Whitehall and the palace at Hampton,[9] and the Secretaries of State were constantly back and forth from their offices in London. It was not for long that Addison's health stood up to this furious pace and on 8 August he was indisposed and Lord Sunderland was writing to the Duke of Bolton, Lord Lieutenant of Ireland, in his absence.[10]

This time the illness was more serious. The press of 17 August carried a notice that Addison had been dangerously ill of a fever at his seat but was in a fair way of recovery.[11] On 24 August, however, Tickell was writing urgent letters from Holland House and the press reported Addison still

[1] *Original Weekly Journal*, 15/6/1717.
[2] S.P. 35/9, f. 16.   [3] *Gazette*, 5546.   [4] Ibid. 5547.
[5] R. E. Tickell, *Thomas Tickell*, p. 59.
[6] B.M. Egerton MSS. 2174, f. 308.
[7] S.P. 104/29 to 22/7/1717.   [8] *Gazette*, 5550.
[9] *St. James's Evening Post*, 339.   [10] S.P. 67/7, f. 30.
[11] *Original Weekly Journal*, 17/8/1717.

sick,[1] while two days previously he had not been well enough to present the French Ambassador upon his audience of leave, which he would certainly have wished to do had his condition permitted.[2] Tickell nevertheless thought he would be able to go to Hampton Court very shortly,[3] and on the last day of the month the press printed a notice that the Secretary was perfectly recovered and in charge of the affairs of his office.[4] He was at court again on 1 September[5] and Vincent Bourne celebrated his recovery in Latin verses. But it was evident that Addison was fighting against illness with the determination of a man of principle who will not abandon himself to infirmity. His duties again proved too much for him and on 9 September the press carried a notice that he was dangerously ill.[6] The moment was one of great importance, for the Abbé Dubois was expected in London to begin the crucial negotiations at Hampton Court for the enlargement of the Triple into a Quadruple Alliance. His staff was due on 13 September. On 11 September the press announced that through the means of some eminent physicians who attended him—doubtless Dr. Garth was amongst them—the Secretary had been well enough to appear at his office where there were a number of foreign ministers to call upon him, particularly those of Spain and Sicily, who would be alarmed at the proposed conference.[7]

Dubois arrived on 16 September and Addison was much at court where he presented addresses to the king from the City and County of New York, Massachusetts Bay, and Connecticut.[8] He was involved in a round of banquets and important courts,[9] and was travelling frequently between his office, Hampton Court, and Holland House. On 1 October, for example, Tickell reported the Secretary too busy to write to Ambassador Worsley in Lisbon.[10] Then, perhaps because the imperial delegation had failed to arrive, the king left for Newmarket followed by Lord Sunderland. Addison was left in London for a few days to make up arrears

[1] *Weekly Journal*, 37.   [2] *Gazette*, 5566.
[3] S.P. 35/9, f. 117.   [4] *Original Weekly Journal*, 31/8/1717.
[5] *St. James's Evening Post*, 355.
[6] *Original Weekly Journal*, 14/9/1717.
[7] Ibid.   [8] *Gazette*, 5574.
[9] e.g. *St. James's Evening Post*, 364.   [10] S.P. 104/113.

of routine work,[1] before following to the same place. Then he was suddenly ordered to remain in London as a Great Council was to be held at Hampton Court,[2] whither the king was returning, and on 13 October Addison instructed the Officers of the Ordnance to be ready to fire the guns, the Princess of Wales being expectant.[3] In the midst of the excitement Lord Sunderland became engaged to marry a girl in her teens,[4] but that did not prevent him from joining Addison and Dubois at dinner with the Duke of Newcastle at Claremont.[5] October 20th was the anniversary of the coronation and there was another large court with a great celebration and illuminations.[6] Tickell wrote to Webster, the Secretary of Ireland, four days later, that Addison had been detained late at Hampton and could not write.[7] There were serious riots in Devonshire at this moment, and urgent measures were taken by Addison and Craggs, the Secretary at War; the Council was consulted and the Law Officers asked to give advice in the greatest haste.[8] On 28 October Addison had an important interview with Dubois;[9] on 30 October came another large court and illuminations;[10] and next day Addison was heavily engaged in Council.[11] In the course of many journeys back and forth to Hampton he had suffered a mishap disconcerting to a man of dignity and poor health. His coach met with an accident and overturned on the road near Isleworth, two of his servants receiving injuries, but Addison himself fortunately escaping unhurt.[12] Then on 2 November the princess gave birth to a prince. Addison evidently waited at Hampton Court late that night. On his return to London at 3 a.m. he received a note from the Duchess of St. Albans, lady-in-waiting to the princess, requesting the customary respite for condemned criminals preparatory to a pardon. Before going to bed the Secretary set messengers upon the road to the king and obtained the necessary permission by 5 a.m. He then sent out the

[1] *Gazette* for 3/10/1717.   [2] S.P. 35/10.
[3] S.P. 44/119, f. 106.   [4] *Weekly Packet*, 276.
[5] *Original Weekly Journal*, 12/10/1717.   [6] *Gazette*, 5583.
[7] S.P. 67/7, f. 39.   [8] S.P. 35/10, ff. 35, 37.
[9] Quai d'Orsay MSS.: Corr. Pol. Ang. 295, f. 222.
[10] *Gazette*, 5586.   [11] S.P. 67/7, f. 44.
[12] *Original Weekly Journal*, 2/11/1717.

appropriate orders and retired.[1] Two days later there was a
great ball in celebration of the birth at Hampton Court.

On 13 November the king returned to St. James's[2] and
on the 18th Dubois left for Paris.[3] Lord Sunderland's
wedding was approaching and so was the christening of the
prince. In this desperate rush of business and festivity
Addison was seeking to ease himself of every burden he could
spare, taking, for instance, the opinion of the Law Officers as
to whether he need go to Ireland to qualify himself for his
post of Keeper of the Records for life. Fortunately he was
assured by Sir Edward Northey that it would be sufficient
if he took the oath of abjuration in England.[4] But the burden
of business, already nearly intolerable, was now much aggravated by the violence of the royal quarrel. There were in
effect two separate courts, and such was the jealousy and
hostility of father and son that the king had announced that
those frequenting the establishment of the prince would not
be received at his own. Addison, who hated faction and
strife in any circumstances, was in a painful position, having
made his advances to the princess so soon after the arrival
of the family in 1714, having praised her in the most glowing
terms in the *Freeholder* next year,[5] and having been acquainted
with all the parties since 1703. He was even exposed to some
risk of ridicule, having so recently written in praise of the
prince for 'that submissive Deference . . . both from Duty
and Inclination to all the Measures of his Royal Father'.[6] So
violent did the quarrel become as Christmas approached,
that it was found necessary for an official version of events
to be drafted and circulated to allay the rumours which ran
in diplomatic circles throughout Europe. This was sent
with a covering letter from Addison to all British diplomatic posts. A similar document was circulated to all
diplomatic missions of foreign powers in London.[7] As
Addison put it to Stair with evident feeling:

I heartily wish it were possible to conceal this disagreeable
story; but, as it must be public, it is fit your Excellency should

[1] S.P. 4/119, f. 134.
[2] *Gazette*, 5590.   [3] *Flying Post*, 4037.
[4] B.M. Egerton MSS. 1931, f. 19.   [5] F. 21.
[6] F. 24.   [7] S.P. 104/255, document of 4/12/1717.

know the truth of it, both for your own information, and that you may set others right who shall happen to ask about it.

To de Marsay at Geneva he remarked that the quarrel remained unchanged and 'suivant ce qui en paroit à present, on doit plutôt souhaiter leur Reconciliation, que l'attendre'.

The strain of carrying on business of State under such circumstances was more than Addison could hope to support and his health was again sinking under it. Early in October the French Ambassador had commented: 'Je vis hier . . . Mr. Addison qui ne me paroist pas bien guery. Sa poitrine menace d'une prompte ruine.'[1] On 10 October his chargé d'affaires, Chammorel, who knew Addison well, had told his court that thus soon after his appointment the Secretary had requested to be relieved of his office:

> Mr. Adison n'ayant pas assez de santé pour soutenir la fatigue de son employ demande à Se retirer. Il y auroit plutot lieu de croire que son caractere d'esprit doux et tranquile le rendant peu propre au manege de la Chambre Basse la Cour Seroit bein aise de s'asseurer d'un Ministre plus alerte et plus capable de faire jouer les ressorts dont on est persuadé qu'elle aura besoin dans le séance prochaine. . . .[2]

The astute Frenchman thus penetrated simultaneously the physical weakness and the lack of robustness of character which unfitted Addison for the fatigue of office and the rough and tumble of the Commons. His deficiencies in the latter respect must have been the more acutely felt after July, when General Stanhope was raised to the peerage and his talents were lost to the Government in the lower house. Addison had so lately poked fun at the transience of English ministers: 'We are told, that the famous Prince of *Conde* used to ask the *English* Ambassador, upon the Arrival of a Mail, *Who was Secretary of State in* England *by that Post*?'[3] Now after six months' tenure to resign himself to abandoning his great office, attained after a lifetime of hard and brilliant endeavour, must have called forth all the reserves of his character and philosophy. But it was not desired to disturb

[1] Quai d'Orsay MSS.: Corr. Pol. Ang. 294, f. 220
[2] Ibid. 296, f. 24 (cipher).
[3] F. 25.

the ministry for the present and he did not secure the release for which he asked.[1]

The rumour was soon current. On 28 October James Hamilton had written to the Duke of Mar that Addison would retire.[2] Again on 2 November, this time in print, it was said that Addison would be made a Teller of the Exchequer, and that Craggs would succeed him.[3] On 9 November Hearne heard a report that Addison had in fact resigned and noted that it was commonly said that he was unfitted for business, in particular because of his inability to speak. All of this was before his most recent illness. Now on 7 November the press had reported him again much indisposed,[4] and dangerously ill.[5] Chammorel told the French Court that even if he recovered he would be replaced by Craggs.[6] After 22 November the rugged Sunderland, victorious over his enemies and newly married to a young girl, was discharging the duties of the Southern Department in so far as they could not be carried out by the Under-Secretaries or by Addison signing papers at Holland House.[7] In that great mansion it was a battle with death, the sick man, fortified by Sir Samuel Garth, fighting grimly for life.

The course of the illness is evident from the correspondence and newspapers. On 3 December Addison wrote to the Duke of Bolton that the bad state of his health had confined him for some time to his chamber. On 5 December the press reported him 'much indispos'd',[8] but he was still conducting business from Holland House.[9] On 13 December George Tilson wrote to Lord Polwarth: 'Mr. Secretary Addison lyes extremely ill, and the doctors seemed to have given him over, but this morning he was a little better. However his recovery is very uncertain.'[10] On the next day Matthew Prior wrote to Lord Oxford: 'The news of the day is that the Prince and Princess are better as to their health, and Mr. Addison is at the point of death.'[11] On the same day

[1] Quai d'Orsay MSS.: Corr. Pol. Ang. 296, f. 159.
[2] H.M.C. *Stuart*, v. 187.   [3] *Weekly Journal*, 47.
[4] *St. James's Evening Post*, 396.
[5] *Original Weekly Journal*, 7/12/1717.
[6] Quai d'Orsay MSS.: Corr. Pol. Ang. 296, f. 159.
[7] S.P. 104/113, 44/250.   [8] *Post Boy*, 1244.   [9] S.P. 67/7, f. 58.
[10] H.M.C. *Polwarth*, i. 407.   [11] H.M.C. *Bath*, iii. 451.

the press reported three physicians in constant attendance at Holland House, and Addison given over after a relapse, his life despaired of.[1] Another paper described his illness, corroborating the French Ambassador, as an 'asthma'.[2] A private news letter more precisely and hopefully said that:

> Mr. Secretary Addison has been ill long, and had lately an apoplectic fit, but on bleeding was relieved, and is better, this day, though reported to be dead; but his life is still despaired of, his will made, and affairs settled.[3]

Thus stood matters sixteen months after Addison's brilliant marriage and eight months from his equally brilliant appointment to high office.

But the illness seemed to pass for a time. Though never physically strong Addison had the stamina which belongs to men of high moral courage and deep convictions. This probably explains a remark by his intimate friend Wortley in 1711: 'The strength of your constitution would make you happier than all who are not equal to you in that.'[4] Thus on 17 December against all expectation Addison was well enough to sign a number of formal documents, and the press reported that there were now hopes of his recovery.[5] On the same day George Tilson scribbled to Lord Polwarth on the back of the Court Circular that 'Mr. Secretary Addison is much mended since last post and the physicians begin to conceive hopes of him'.[6] Meanwhile there were expressions of anxiety from all over Europe. Stanyan had evidently warned some ministers abroad of the seriousness of his master's condition, for Manning wrote from Berne: 'Should we lose a man of his extraordinary merit, how would the publick, as well as his friends suffer', adding, 'I find the gazettes give him Mr. Craggs for a successor.'[7] Lord Stair, himself ill, sent a message to Tickell through Crawford, his Secretary of Embassy, that he 'express'd a great deal of concern as every honest man that has the honour to know him must doe'.[8] A London paper permitted itself to say that:

> Mr. Secretary Addison whose late indisposition has given so

[1] *Weekly Journal*, 14/12/17; *Post Boy*, 4428.   [2] *Evening Post*, 1305.
[3] H.M.C. *Portland*, v. 548.   [4] *Addisoniana*, i. 236.
[5] *Evening Post*, 1306.   [6] H.M.C. *Polwarth*, i. 410.
[7] S.P. 96/18.   [8] S.P. 78/161, f. 165.

much concern to all who have a value for the greatest sense with the greatest integrity, and who has been reported to have been dead, is now said to be in a hopeful way of recovery.[1]

But a private news letter predicted: 'Mr. Addison is out of present danger but not likely to recover ever perfectly.'[2] It seems likely that in the crisis of his illness he had suffered a slight stroke.

Meanwhile events in the world of politics had been moving fast. The royal quarrel had reached the proportion of an open international scandal and the prince was a semi-prisoner in Lord Grantham's house, close to Addison's town residence in Albemarle Street. Dubois was about to return from France to complete the negotiation of the Quadruple Alliance, which he did on 4 January of the new year. Up to that day Lord Sunderland was still discharging many of Addison's duties. The press meanwhile was full of rumours of his immediate resignation on grounds of health and of his replacement by Craggs.[3] By 6 January, however, he was able to discharge a considerable number of duties, though not to leave Holland House. By 21 January he was picking up the threads of business, but was not dealing with Irish affairs, or indeed with a considerable number of matters which he formerly handled. Addison knew himself to be still very ill. To Archbishop Wake he wrote: 'My recovery is still uncertain and at the best will be very slow.' He was more than ever anxious to resign,[4] although his mind remained absorbed in the business in his charge; but it is probable that he had agreed to continue until the moment was convenient for him to be replaced, on the understanding that in the meanwhile his burden would be lightened. On 1 February the press carried a report of the position, which was probably accurate except in so far as it concerned Addison's health:

Mr. Secretary Addison is perfectly well recovered from his late indisposition; but for fear of impairing his health by the fatigue of that employment, has desired His Majesty's leave to resign, who

---

[1] *St. James's Evening Post*, 454.   [2] H.M.C. *Portland*, v. 549.
[3] Numerous press references.
[4] Dispatch of Pucci, Florentine Resident in London, of 10/1/18: Archivo di Stato di Firenze Md.P., f. 4223.

has been graciously pleased to comply therewith; and in consideration of his faithful services and known abilities, has made him one
of the Tellers of the Exchequer, in the room of the late Lord
Onslow: And Mr. Craggs, the present Secretary at War, will
succeed Mr. Addison, and not that good-natur'd, sweet-temper'd,
courteous, affable, obliging, complaisant, meek, humble worthy
gentleman Mr. L——e, as has been groundlessly reported.[1]

The date upon which Addison had written to the king is
not certain, but a draft is preserved of a letter dictated to
Temple Stanyan[2] and dated tentatively 14 March in which
it is stated that his health will not permit him to discharge
his duties and that he therefore wishes to resign his office.
Tickell, who also made a draft,[3] afterwards wrote that it was
asthma which compelled Addison to this step, thus confirming the two sources already noticed; and in spite of the newspaper optimism quoted above, he was still extremely ill and
not able to leave his house. That Addison excused himself to
the king on grounds of health is put beyond doubt on the
evidence of his successor, Craggs, who stated the fact in an
official document.[4] Nevertheless he did not immediately
vacate his office. Until 13 March he signed messengers' and
stationers' bills. On that day, after Addison had resigned the
seals, James Craggs was appointed Secretary in his place.
It was part of a general change of posts in which Addison's
political chief, Lord Sunderland, became President of the
Council and First Lord of the Treasury, thus tightening his
grip upon the administration, while his colleague Stanhope
moved back to a Secretaryship of State in partnership with
Craggs, who was more robust in health for daily work, and
in character for parliamentary knock-about, than his highly
distinguished predecessor. There is no doubt that Addison
would have resigned his post long before this date had he
been permitted to do so, in which case he might well have
been spared a terrible illness and might have prolonged his
life considerably. His only recorded sentiment at this time
was his feeling of gratitude and admiration for the king:

though I shall hereby lose the honour and pleasure of serving the

---

[1] *Weekly Journal*, 60. The adjectivally wealthy alternative was probably
Lechmere.   [2] Sotheby Sale Cat. of 3–5/4/1939, item 341.
[3] Graham, p. 399.   [4] S.P. 76/2 of 17/3/1718.

greatest and best of Masters in that high station with which your
Matie has been pleased to honour me, I shall embrace every
opportunity to the last moment of my life to promote Y.M's
service, which is only promoting that of your people, as all who
have had the honour to lay business before Y.M^ty ought in
justice to acquaint the world. . . .

Among the cares and responsibilities of a year in great
office, Addison must have found a good many moments of
satisfaction in assisting his friends. From Trinity College,
Cambridge, Dr. Colbatch, fellow victim of the Duke of
Somerset in 1703, wrote asking for the visitatorial powers
of the bishop to be defined so that they might be made use of.[1]
From The Queen's College, Oxford, came a suggestion forwarded by Tickell, that he might subscribe to the new
buildings:

A Queen's College Secretary of State laid the foundation, and
who can tell how far another may carry it on. . . . I must own I have
no little ambition to see the Honble Mr. Addison's arms over
against Sir Jos. Williamson's in our new Chapel, and to hear him
annually celebrated in our Founder's speech, as a Benefactor, as he
has constantly been one of the brightest ornaments of our College.[2]

Addison licensed the printing of Tickell's friend Trapp's
translation of the *Aeneis*,[3] and forwarded for Sir Isaac
Newton's consideration the project first commended to him
by Whiston for finding the longitude. He signed the ducal
patent of the brilliant but unstable son of his former patron
Lord Wharton,[4] perhaps recalling with amusement the day
at Winchendon when the boy had lured him into climbing a
gate and then set it swinging, carrying the author of so
many masterpieces back and forth at pleasure.[5] He saw
Budgell appointed to a lucrative post in Ireland[6] and Dr.
Hough, who in 1715 had refused the primacy, translated to
the bishopric of Worcester;[7] while for University College,
Oxford, he secured a licence to hold Dr. Radcliffe's bequest
in mortmain.[8] A man controlling such resources of patronage must have performed many other deeds of kindness
which his reticent habits have concealed from us.

[1] S.P. 25/9, f. 3.   [2] L. Aikin, *Life of Addison*.   [3] S.P. 44/360, f. 41.
[4] S.P. 44/360.   [5] Spence, p. 350.   [6] S.O. 1/16, f. 185.
[7] *Evening Post*, 1262.   [8] S.P. 44/360, f. 46; 38/30; 44/250, f. 68.

In the literary world it had been a barren period. Such time as remained from official duty was consumed in the family circle, and there is no record of any literary activity at Holland House. There was a new edition of the *Travels* at The Hague. Sir Samuel Garth printed Books II and III of Addison's translations in his edition of Ovid's *Metamorphoses*, and *Cato* continued to hold the stage triumphantly, being revived 'with new scenery taken from the Opera' in the autumn and again about the time of Addison's resignation. The circumstances of the revival led to some criticism of Dick Steele who staged it and may have meant to compliment his friend at a time of sickness and disappointment.[1] The play was still a subject of universal interest, but Addison had arranged a truce with its principal critic, Dennis, as with Pope. Dennis had proposed to follow up his attack upon the structure of the play with a criticism of its sentiments. This he had prepared at some date previous to 5 December 1716, and had sent his draft to Blackmore, who admired the play.[2] It is probable that through Blackmore the document came to Addison's knowledge. What then occurred is not known, but Dennis alleged that he was deprived of his manuscript by a 'poor artifice'.[3] He was too sincere and courageous a critic to be bought off by the subscription which Addison made to the publication of his *Select Works* in 1717:[4] but Gildon relates that at an interview at which Rowe was present he promised Addison to attack *Cato* no further. Though it was Addison's practice to ignore criticism when it was published, he did not spare himself trouble in suppressing it if he could before it became generally known. Thomas Burnet reports that when Addison heard of some satirical lines upon *Cato* which he had written, the service of a third party was engaged to secure their destruction.[5] Gildon's story is therefore not improbable. After Addison's death Dennis justified his views on the sentiments of *Cato* but commended its author as a 'learned and very Ingenious Man' and spoke patronizingly of the *Tatler* and *Spectator*.[6] But while busy

[1] *Weekly Journal*, 1/3/1718.   [2] Dennis, *Original Letters*, 1721, p. 1.
[3] Ibid., p. 304; C. Wilson, *Life of W. Congreve*, ii. 36.
[4] Wilson, *Life of W. Congreve*, pp. 140–1.
[5] H.M.C. *Egmont*, i. 105.   [6] *Original Letters*, Preface, 1721.

correcting faults, which undoubtedly existed, in a drama which is now forgotten except by scholars, the critic failed to recognize the greatness of Addison's genius in prose satire.

In the world of art, Sir Godfrey Kneller had painted Addison for the series of Kit-Cat portraits, his being one of the last four to be completed.[1] In the famous room at Barn Elms, where the portraits were finally housed, a man standing in front of the fire would see Addison on the middle of the wall on his left-hand side. He was not in the lower row with the aristocratic Kit-Cats, but above, between Garth, his physician, and Congreve, one of his earliest friends and mentors, in company with Dick Steele, Vanbrugh, and old Jacob. This wall seems to have been devoted to the more literary members of the club, the more political facing them from the opposite side.[2] This was not unfitting, for it was upon literary foundations that Addison had built his political greatness.

There had been an interesting visitor to London on diplomatic business, in the person of Philippe Néricault Destouches, a writer of comedy. He met Addison and, much influenced by him, in 1727 wrote the first French sentimental comedy, *Le Philosophe Marié*, inspired by the *Drummer*, which he also later adapted to the French stage. A humble supplicant had been Oldmixon: 'did you know, sir, how I have been used by the faction in the country and then persecuted here by their procurement, I flatter my self your humanity would extend to an old servant of yours, and you would grant me your protection . . . .'[3] For his relative, Arthur Stevens, Addison wrote to the Archbishop of Canterbury. Lord Warwick had presented Stevens to a city living, and the assistance of the archbishop was required in order to secure the exchange of this living for a prebend of Worcester Cathedral. This was no doubt also available through Addison's influence, in this case the channel being Bishop Hough. In return for a promise of help, the archbishop desired Addison to assist Laurence Echard, the historian, by increasing the royal grant towards his history

---

[1] Tonson Papers at the National Portrait Gallery.
[2] Ibid., where there is a plan of the hanging.   [3] S.P. 79/8 of 1/6/1717.

of England from £200 to £300. This Addison promised to try to procure.

For Ambrose Philips provision was also made during Addison's term of office. Besides his earlier dignity of Justice of the Peace, he became a Commissioner of the Lottery at £500 per annum. This was quite a rich reward. Philips was not a man to everybody's taste, and Swift finally wrote him off with the word 'puppy'. Addison had sent Swift a 'kind remembrance' by St. George Ashe, now Bishop of Derry, who had remained the friend of both men through prosperity and adversity. Swift was stirred to write a belated but affectionate letter of congratulation to the Secretary:

I should be much concerned if I did not think you were a little angry with me for not congratulating you upon being Secretary but I chuse my Time as I would to visit you when all your company is gone. I am confident you have given ease of Mind to many thousand People, who will never believe any ill can be intended to the Constitution in Church and State while you are in so high a Trust, and I should have been of the same Opinion tho I had not the Happynesse to know you . . .

I examine my Heart, and can find no other Reason why I write to you now, beside that great Love and Esteem I have always had for you. I have nothing to ask you either for any Friend or for myself. When I conversed among Ministers I boasted your Acquaintance, but I feel no Vanity from being known to a Secretary of State. I am a little concerned to see you stand single, for it is a prodigious singularity in any Court to owe ones Rise entirely to Merit. I will venture to tell you a Secret, that three or four more such Choices would gain more hearts in three weeks than all the methods hitherto practiced, have been able to do in as many years.

It is now time for me to recollect that I am writing to a Secretary of State, who has little time allowed him for Trifles.[1]

In the circle of private life it must have been a painful year, in which the burden of office and sickness wholly excluded the communion with friends in which Addison particularly excelled and delighted; 'the most open, instructive and unreserved Discourse, is that which passes between two Persons who are familiar and intimate Friends'.[2] Such had been Dick Steele and Jonathan Swift. But with Dick he was upon bad terms, evident in the latter's remark to his

<hr>

[1] Williams, ii. 276–7.   [2] S. 68.

wife in May: 'I do not ask Mr. Secretary Addison anything.'
All his life Dick had been profusely generous. The talents
which he had to offer to his friend he had freely given, often
postponing his own literary interests or peace of mind.
But Tickell, who knew Addison better than any other man
during these latter years, committed him to posterity as:
'A candid censor, and a friend severe.'[1] Steele found it hard
to comprehend that in the height of power and patronage
he should put the principle of friendship quite low down
amongst the priorities of public duty. It is interesting thus
to observe that over many years the friendship with Dick
had crumbled, though based in common political conviction
and confirmed by so many successful joint ventures, the
character of the man not being sound enough to sustain it;
but that for all the bitter differences of politics and wide
divergences of fate, that with Jonathan Swift remained in-
violate. The passage of events had put it beyond the wish of
the dean to seek favours of a Whig Government, and beyond
the power of a Whig Secretary to grant them. Neither now
sought any preferment, and no stain of jealousy remained
upon their friendship.

From the family at Holland House nothing emerges upon
which a picture of Addison's life can be based. The first year
of his marriage had been so full of documents and sickness
that he can have had little time to cultivate his home life.
There was some but probably not much entertaining, such
as the occasion upon a September evening when Madame
Kielmansegge, one of the king's two principal German
mistresses, dined with 'Mr. Secretary Addison and his lady'.[2]
But there can have been little real relief from work, and
from the sickness which had broken his political career.
That career had grown from humble beginnings into a considerable edifice by the consistent and unwavering application of principles of belief and conduct. Of the English
people to whom these principles were directed he thought
highly, but he was not blinded by prejudice to their faults.
For the aristocracy he had little respect[3] and for the claims
of birth as such, none at all.[4] As early as 1695 he had cast

---

[1] Verse dedication of Addison's *Works*, 1721.
[2] *Original Weekly Journal*, 25/9/1717.   [3] *S.* 219.   [4] *S.* 299.

doubt upon the martial ardour of the peerage.[1] But for the bulk of the people, particularly the yeoman and merchant classes, he had a deep respect and admiration formed early in life:

One may generally observe that the body of a people has juster views for the public good, and pursues them with greater uprightness than the nobility and gentry, who have so many private expectations and particular interests, which hang like a false bias upon their judgments, and may possibly dispose them to sacrifice the good of their country to the advancement of their own fortunes.[2]

On the other hand he regarded politics as beyond the understanding of the masses, whom he counselled to ignore such matters.[3] He thought of them not as a science which could be taught or studied,[4] but as a practical part of the wisdom of a good citizen, who was essentially an educated bourgeois. He looked to the middle class which happened to be the emergent part of society. Judging the English in the lump, he found them modest, good natured, polite, and hospitable,[5] but inclined to be morose and gloomy: 'Melancholy is a kind of Demon that haunts our Island.'[6] They were therefore in need of humour as a counter-agent. In politics he thought them inconstant[7] and somewhat dangerously speculative: 'There is scarce any Man in *England* of what Denomination soever, that is not a Free-thinker in Politicks, and hath not some peculiar Notions of his own . . . .'[8] The business of governing such a people, in which he chose to engage, must of necessity be adventurous:

a *British* Ministry . . . ought to be satisfied, if, allowing to every particular Man that his private Scheme is wisest, they can perswade him that next to his own Plan that of the Government is the most eligible.[9]

The peculiar importance of the press to government, upon which Addison had insisted in his early poetry, was therefore evident to him from several points of view, and he had come to regard prose as a more powerful vehicle than

---

[1] 'A Poem to his Majesty.'   [2] *Travels*.   [3] F. 5.
[4] S. 305.   [5] 'Dialogues on Medals', II, book iv; S. 407, 435.
[6] S. 387.   [7] F. 25.   [8] F. 53.   [9] F. 48.

verse for political writing. This reflected the development of an organized public opinion on political matters, begun in Lord Shaftesbury's day and making much progress in Addison's lifetime. Thus the *Freeholder* superseded the *Campaign* as an instrument for rallying support to the Government. He thought political writing beneficent when conducted 'with candour',[1] but believed it to be responsible for the universal interest in politics which, paradoxically, he deplored,[2] and he did not hesitate to advocate government control to prevent its abuse.[3]

In constitutional matters his views were those of John Locke and the moderate Whig party and they are evident from his actions as well as from his writings. Not a republican, he hated the Commonwealth[4] yet was suspicious of monarchy and thought a prince a burden to any but a wealthy state.[5] But he held King William and King George in an almost passionate admiration, their personal virtues as he understood them being magnified many-fold in the context of the royal office. In his eyes the British constitution as it existed in 1714 was incomparably well suited to the government of a free people: 'the Bulk of the People virtually give their Consent to every thing they are bound to obey, and prescribe to themselves those Rules by which they are to walk.'[6] 'Liberty', which he never failed to commend in all its consequences, political, social, and, especially, economic, he defined as that 'which exempts one man from subjection to another, so far as the order and economy of government will permit',[7] and without inquiring too nicely into the extent of the proviso, he took the love of liberty naturally planted in the breast of man to be the principal safeguard against tyranny. He thought religion and morality indispensable to good government and prosperity.[8] Looking at the matter in reverse and posing to himself the question as to what is the purpose of civil institutions, his answer was: 'the perfection of human nature.'[9] This illustrates the intimate relationship between his political career and his writings, almost all of which were designed to improve

---

[1] F. 40.   [2] F. 53.   [3] F. 35.   [4] T. 161.
[5] *Travels*: 'Bolonia, etc.'
[6] F. 1.   [7] S. 287.   [8] F. 29.   [9] S. 287.

mankind and were therefore at one in purpose with his endeavours in public life. Had he been asked to specify the best existing polity, he would probably have answered that the excellence of British institutions was vitiated by party violence, and would have indicated the Helvetic Union.[1]

Addison wrote and acted moderation. To what he thought to be moderate as exemplified in the Whig party he adhered with unswerving loyalty and prided himself thereupon. He did not reject all party organization, though he sometimes echoed the seventeenth-century dislike of it as such. Indeed his whole cast of thought is reminiscent of the great 'Trimmer' of the previous age. His reason was shocked at expressions and actions which denied the existence of other legitimate points of view. 'A Man must be excessively stupid, as well as uncharitable, who believes that there is no Virtue but on his own Side, and that there are not Men as honest as himself who may differ from him in political Principles.'[2] Consequently: 'There cannot be a greater Judgment befall a Country than such a dreadful Spirit of Division as rends a Government into two distinct People, and makes them greater Strangers and more averse to one another, than if they were actually two different Nations.'[3] And if Addison found such sentiments reprehensible in men he found them wholly outrageous in women: 'This is, in its Nature, a Male Vice, and made up of many angry and cruel Passions that are altogether repugnant to the Softness, the Modesty, and those other endearing Qualities which are natural to the Fair Sex.'[4] By a strange irony the man who held these views on the subject of party was the creature and sincere admirer of the men who, more than any others, laid the foundations of party politics in England, the Whig Junto; and his life and writings, if not his administration, contributed powerfully to the consolidation of their work.

[1] *Travels*: 'Fribourg, etc.'   [2] *S*. 243.   [3] *S*. 125.   [4] *S*. 57.

XI

A RAPID DECLINE
1718–1719

A LIFE of hard work and no undue abstinence had reduced Addison's indifferent physique to a point where it was quite unable to sustain the burden of worry, and of long, irregular hours of work, which a further pursuit of ambition would entail. It was therefore necessary for a man of such deliberate habits and powerful guiding principles to devise for himself a new attitude towards his daily life and future prospects. A further inducement to do so was the dwindling of his circle of friends; St. George Ashe died in February of this year, a grievous loss. For immediate necessities he had no reason to feel concern. Besides his own fortune and his wife's resources, on 19 March 1718 he received a pension of £1,600 retrospective to Christmas 1717, settled upon him for life and charged on the Irish establishment.[1] On 8 May he received a discharge permitting him to retain the silver plate which had been issued to him as Secretary of State out of the Jewel Office.[2] He also retained the income from his place in Ireland. In the world of politics he remained a member of the Privy Council both in England and in Ireland, and of the House of Commons, honourable positions in which he need not exert himself more than his health would permit. There were therefore no important external limitations to the readjustment of his life to new circumstances in the light of his own philosophy.

'True Happiness', he wrote in the fifteenth *Spectator*, 'is of a retired Nature and an Enemy to Pomp and Noise; it arises in the first place from the Enjoyment of one's Self; and, in the next, from the Friendship and Conversation of a few select Companions. . . .' It was to such a life that Addison now addressed himself. Yet he did not believe full hap-

---

[1] Not £1,500 as stated in the press and *Historical Register*, see S.O. 1/16, f. 226. [2] Bohn, vi. 642.

piness as he understood it, in the sense of a complete development of the individuality, to be attainable on earth, and he qualified his prescription by adding that: 'The utmost that we can hope for in this World is Contentment.'[1] This state of mind was best attained by a conduct which he distinguished as cheerful rather than gay: 'I have always preferred Chearfulness to Mirth. The latter I consider as an Act, the former as a Habit of Mind . . . Chearfulness keeps up a kind of Day-light in the Mind, and fills it with a steady and perpetual Serenity.'[2]

Cheerfulness in its turn could be achieved only by a life founded in virtue and right reason. It was therefore an indicator of morality if not in itself a moral virtue.[3] By virtue, as has been noticed, Addison understood not merely the conventional qualities passing under that name, but the enlargement of the faculties of the mind to their fullest extent. Such an enlargement, for example, included the polite hobbies: 'A Man that has a Taste of Musick, Painting, or Architecture, is like one that has another Sense, when compared with such as have no Relish of those Arts.'[4] This process of enlargement when applied to the speculative faculties of the mind he termed 'imagination'. It was the crucial point in his philosophy of living, and he had devoted a series of eleven consecutive *Spectators* to its analysis. He summed up his observations by saying that one who enjoyed an absolute command of his 'imagination' might 'so exquisitely ravish or torture the Soul through this single Faculty, as might suffice to make up the whole Heaven or Hell of any finite Being.'[5] It was at this point, the expansion of the imagination, that there appeared in Addison's thought that strain of mysticism which, though apparently anomalous, yet indicated a side of his character which was strongly developed if carefully controlled, and which was divined and appreciated by a later generation. It followed logically that idleness or vacuity of the mind was second only in reprehensibleness to the thinking of positive evil,[6] and that self-command was a first essential to virtue and the principal distinguishing characteristic between the wise

[1] *S.* 163.   [2] *S.* 381.   [3] Ibid.   [4] *S.* 93.   [5] *S.* 421.
[6] *S.* 93, 471; *T.* 110.

man and the fool.[1] This requirement of rigid self-discipline and intense mental activity Addison was always careful to temper by a stipulation for 'urbanity', 'politeness', and 'good breeding' without which the basic virtue of a man's nature could not appear and operate to full advantage.[2] He allocated to 'fortune' but a small share in the life of man, declaring that what passed under that name was 'often the Reward of Vertue, and as often the Effect of Prudence'.[3]

Of human nature Addison made a low estimate. He thought Hobbes's *Discourse* upon that subject 'much the best of all his Works'[4] and himself sometimes talked like a Hobbist: 'Give a Man Power of doing what he pleases with Impunity, you extinguish his Fear, and consequently over-turn in him one of the great Pillars of Morality.'[5] But the tenor of his thought was formed by the study of Plato, the Cartesians, and Locke. The theories of Locke, in particular his political teaching, had been presented to Addison con-vincingly in the lives and policy of his patrons; but his understanding of philosophical subjects, which he defined very loosely, had been clarified and precipitated by his friendship and conversation with Berkeley and Whiston in 1713, too late to influence his principal philosophical writ-ings. Furthermore, the achievement at this later date of the highest recognition had lent magnanimity to his philo-sophy. Even the author of a lampoon published on 21 April 1718 confirmed the impression of tranquillity of mind which dwelt around him when, addressing Tickell, he told:

> How A—on, thy Friend, withdrew
> From Cock-Pit cares to Holland House;
> From State-Intrigues, to chear his Spouse;
> To all Things Elegant and Quiet,
> His Chambers, Co—ss, and his Diet.[6]

The accuracy of this picture is confirmed by Tom Burnet's report that it left Addison 'damnably stung'.[7] He thus faced his retirement with gifts of philosophy as splendid as those with which he had built his career.

---

[1] S. 225.   [2] S. 557.   [3] F. 2.   [4] S. 47.   [5] S. 287.
[6] *The Tickler Tickell'd*, 1718.
[7] *Letters of T. Burnet to G. Duckett*, ed. Nichol Smith, p. 284 n.

One of Addison's first actions in his new circumstances was to write to Jonathan Swift:

> Multiplicity of Businesse and a long dangerous fit of sicknesse have prevented me from answering the obliging letter you honoured me with some time since, but God be thanked I can not make use of either of these Excuses at present, being entirely free both of my office and my Asthma. I dare not however venture myself abroad yet. . . .

It was a friendly letter, though it hardly breathed the warm generosity of that to which it was a reply. It ended with an invitation to Holland House, and showed Addison by no means disinterested in the world of affairs. He then wrote to Archbishop King a letter designed to secure payment of his new pension, which was charged on the establishment wherein King was so powerful. The spring must have been quite agreeably passed at Holland House.

In April Lord Warwick became a Gentleman of the Bed-chamber to the Prince of Wales.[1] Addison's adherents, Temple Stanyan and Thomas Tickell, had both been continued as Under-Secretaries by Craggs.[2] Eustace Budgell, however, had indulged in a foolish quarrel with Webster, the Secretary of the Irish Government. The Lord Lieutenant had backed his Secretary and Budgell lost his place. Thereafter he set about conducting a lone pamphlet war against high authority, a hopeless undertaking at that period. At some time during the summer,[3] Addison interceded personally on his behalf with Webster and with the Duke of Bolton and, according to Budgell, was fully convinced 'that I have done *nothing* unworthy the *Honour* I have to be his *Kinsman*, and to have been made choice of for his *Friend* and *Companion* for *seven Years* together.'[4] But it was beyond the power of any patron to help a man who was his own enemy, and he had lost his place irretrievably by December. He was endeavouring to enter Parliament for Wallingford during the summer of this year, but without success. Budgell was already showing that unbalance of mind which

---

[1] *Flying Post*, 4095; *Post Boy*, 4649.
[2] *St. James's Evening Post*, 441.   [3] Previous to 3 Oct.
[4] Budgell, *Letter to the Lord . . .*, 1718, p. 24.

ended in suicide, and his folly must have been a mortification to the patron who had been at pains to promote him.

Cato was being revived again at Drury Lane in the spring
of 1718; but there was as yet no question of Addison
recovering sufficiently to think of any serious literary projects. By July he was well enough to attend the Privy
Council where he sat with the Bishop of London, the Vice-
Chamberlain, and the Master of the Rolls on the committee
to hear appeals from the colonies, the precursor of the
Judicial Committee.[1] About the middle of August he was
well enough to think of going away for convalescence. For
this purpose he and Lady Warwick decided to take a course
of the waters at Bristol where George Smalridge was now
bishop. As Addison put it to Swift, since the death of St.
George Ashe, Dr. Smalridge was 'to me the most candid and
agreeable of the Bishops, I would say clergymen, were not
Deans comprehended under that Title'. He found that his
Jacobite-inclined friend, mollified with a mitre, gave him
'the greatest pleasure I have met with for some months'.
Young Lord Warwick, with whose entry into Christ Church
the bishop had been of help, did not accompany the party,
but remained in London. He was somewhat given to esca-
pades, though taking his duties as heir to a great peerage
seriously enough. Tickell evidently kept an eye upon him
and reported to Bristol, whence Addison thanked him for
'finding out the young Lord so frequently'. Addison's
letters to Tickell were full of a literary enthusiasm for which
he can have had little time during the previous two years
and which his health would not have permitted earlier in
the season. It seems that he was preparing the *Travels* for the
new edition which Jacob Tonson published this year. He
asked Tickell to visit Mr. Ball with the sheet relating to
Leghorn, 'where he lived more years than I did Hours', to
obtain corrections of his account of that place. There was
a kind of easy greatness about the freedom with which
Addison now felt able to accept criticism, somewhat different from the timorous anxiety with which he sought it in
years gone by. A few days later he sent some more corrections and asked Tickell to compare them with criticism in

[1] P.C. 2/86, f. 162.

the preface to Dr. Trapp's *Virgil*, which he had licensed when Secretary of State and may therefore have had an opportunity to read. Apparently he thought there was no substance in Trapp's remarks, and he instructed Tickell, who had been the doctor's deputy as Reader in Poetry at Oxford some years before, to insert in his text: 'If the late ingenious Translator of Virgil gives the foregoing Passage a second Reading he will find that he had either mistaken or forgot it in the Preface to his Translation.'

It appears that the cure did not proceed as quickly as might have been hoped. Addison had planned to stay about a month, and on 20 September was writing to Tickell for some money to be sent to him, having locked up his cash and bills at Holland House where they could not easily be reached. He found time to read Tickell's latest piece of verse, to make a suggestion for an alteration, and to say that 'Without a Compliment it is perfectly good according to my Taste in Poetry'. Tickell, following the example of his master, had turned his hand to political pamphleteering, writing in the previous year *An Epistle from a Lady in England to a Gentleman at Avignon* which had run through five editions and had been serviceable to the Government. But the present piece was a verse prologue written by command of the Lord Chamberlain, to be spoken at the opening of a series of plays for performance before the king at Hampton Court. Steele, in virtue of his office, was in charge of the production and, not knowing of the Lord Chamberlain's command, had written a prologue which Wilks had learned by heart, before he heard of the existence of Tickell's lines. Protesting indignantly, he suggested that his own lines be used at least for an epilogue; but in the event it appears that they were not spoken at all. Tickell was generally regarded as Addison's creature, and Addison himself had corrected the text. This episode therefore further estranged him from his boyhood friend.

There seems to have been plenty of conversation on political matters over the Bristol waters, for Addison noticed that 'we have many Critics and Statesmen in this Place'. He was careful to commend his successor for a masterly reply to the slanders of the retiring Spanish Ambassador, the spelling of whose name he evidently did not very well remember although he had been in correspondence with him for some months. He was beginning to show some of the traits of an old man. It irritated him disproportionately that a letter from Tickell came unsealed, and he recommended his late Under-Secretary to his own practice of having a chamber-keeper seal the letters in his presence. He was evidently enjoying criticizing Tickell's poetry with George Smalridge. But by 1 October the course of waters was drawing to its close, and Addison wrote to Swift that he hoped it had 'pretty well recover'd me from the Leavings of my last Winter's Sicknesse'. He urged the dean to visit him at Bilton, and would 'strain hard' to meet him there if it might be for some days.

But Addison was not the only member of his family who required medical care, for the countess was now pregnant. On 25 October the press announced, somewhat prematurely, that the 'Countess of Warwick was far gone with child and that great preparations were making at Holland House for her lying in'.[1] That the family called at Bilton on their return journey, as the hint to Swift seems to suggest that they had thoughts of doing, appears unlikely. Addison had made little use of his country property which he had planted at such expense. During his term of office as Secretary to Lord Sunderland's Irish Government he had found time to assist the Shuckburgh family, who were neighbours at Bilton, and to whom the place had belonged at the end of Queen Elizabeth's reign. They in turn advised him in stocking his pond. William Somervile of Edstone, foxhunter and poet, continued his warm admirer. But there are few instances of neighbourly relationships other than the dealings of his agents. After his marriage he had continued to develop the house and garden. From seed brought back by his friend Craggs from Spain he had grown a number of Ilexes, amongst the first established in England. Yew hedges were taking shape, though still quite small. The Bilton Taxodium had been planted, and, as it was then an exceedingly rare tree in England, it seems probable that seed had been sent by a friend in America. Addison erected a

[1] *Original Weekly Journal* for that date.

handsome wrought iron double gate and caused the cipher
of 'J.A.' and 'C.W.' to be placed thereupon, the whole work
costing £50.[1] With the house renovated and the garden
taking shape after six years of careful development, Bilton
was an elegant country seat.

On the return of the family to Holland House rumours
were current of a marriage between Lord Warwick and the
second daughter of Lord Cadogan, to take place when the
young man came of age in January.[2] Addison had returned
to the republic of letters, but in the capacity of an elder
statesman; he had been at pains to withdraw from literary
conflicts more than two years ago. Possibly it was at this
time that he was visited at Holland House by Milton's
daughter, remarking as she entered the room that she
needed no other introduction but her likeness to the poet.
He gave himself the pleasure of collecting a hundred
guineas from friends to relieve her poverty.[3] He also recon-
sidered his project for an English dictionary in which Swift
had encouraged him in days gone by when they had discussed the structure of the language. He is reported to have
taken Tillotson as a standard of English writing, and to have
annotated his sermons.[4] Johnson was shown some drafts
which he had begun. He understood the fluid state of the
English language in the previous century, but failed to
divine its new stability, and the logic of his thought led to
the conclusion that in the years to come his own writings
would seem as archaic as those of Chaucer.[5] He resented the
current importation of words of French origin,[6] many of
which have since taken a respectable place in the English
language, though he had nothing against its earlier modifications and positively approved of the Hebrew content. It was
in fact to current English as spoken by his unsophisticated
countrymen that his loyalty attached. He praised the English
monosyllables. 'The Sounds of our English Words are commonly like those of String Musick, short and transient,

[1] Now standing in 'Addison's Walk', Magdalen College, Oxford.
[2] *Original Weekly Journal*, 8/11/1718.
[3] Budgell, *A Letter to Cleomenes*, 1731, p. 265.
[4] *Addisoniana*, ii. 55; T. Tyers, *Historical Essay on Mr. Addison*, 1783, p. 39.
[5] *S*. 101.
[6] *S*. 165.

which rise and perish upon a single Touch.'[1] He noted the
recent disappearance of the sounded last syllables : 'drown'd'
for 'drowned', for example : and the substitution of 's' for
'eth' in a similar manner : 'drowns' for 'drowneth'. He by no
means disapproved of the changes which had been so
marked during the past century but he thought that an
authority was required to 'settle all controversies between
grammar and idiom' and to rule upon the standards of the
tongue. He suggested an 'academy',[2] to which his dictionary
may have been intended as a contribution. It is probable,
however, that he had now turned the detailed work on this
project over to Ambrose Philips. Lady Mary had heard of
it but reports that Addison laid it aside before his death;[3]
while shortly thereafter Philips put out an elegant advertisement for a dictionary to be completed in two volumes folio.[4]

Addison also contemplated a tragedy upon the death of
Socrates, for whom he had so often expressed admiration
in his writings.[5] He also set to work upon a book defending
the fundamentals of Christianity. This was the product of
a resolve to spend the years of retirement in the study of
religion and, as Tickell reports, in writing divine poetry.
Perhaps Addison was influenced by the example of Locke,
whom he had followed in two offices as well as in doctrine.[6]
When out of office in Queen Anne's reign he had collected
materials from the fathers, and he had written a number of
Spectators upon religious topics. He had also begun studies
for a book upon the Christian religion.[7] He now set to
work with great application to develop his former project,
Whiston reporting him as engaged in reading Justin Martyr.
But the published text of his book *Of the Christian Religion* is
unsatisfactory. It is incomplete, and lacks, amongst other
things, the Hebrew evidences which Addison intended to

---

[1] *S.* 135.   [2] Ibid.
[3] *Letters*, ed. Wharncliffe, ii. 136.
[4] Starnes and Noyes, *The English Dictionary*, p. 148, There is a copy of
Philips's Prospectus in the British Museum, reproduced in *Poems of Ambrose
Philips*, ed. M. Segar.
[5] Tickell, Preface to Addison's *Works*. A fragment of yet another tragedy,
alleged to be by Addison but doubtfully so, was found amongst the Steele
papers. *Steele Correspondence*, ed. Aitken, i. 55.
[6] Fox-Bourne, *Life of Locke*, ii. 495–501.
[7] Tickell, Preface to Addison's *Works*.

adduce towards proving the truth of Christian belief.[1] It is also obviously uncorrected even so far as it extends. Indeed the whole nature of the draft suggests that it is but a preliminary assembly of arguments and materials. The numbered paragraphs appear to be no more than headings jotted down for discussion, and it may have been Addison's intention to publish his work in dialogue form or as a collection of letters, for either of which purposes the draft seems to be suitably laid out. The opening sentence, so often the most difficult and pondered, seems to suggest the latter: 'That I may lay before you a full state of the subject under our consideration, and methodize the several particulars that I touched upon in discourse with you: I shall first take notice . . . .' It is most improbable that Addison would have used the first and second persons in a work intended to appear as a treatise; yet the conversational form is soon displaced by mere statement of propositions. It is conceivable that he had a periodical in mind, in which his work would appear in series, perhaps weekly, as had been the case with the graver papers in the *Spectator*. But whatever form Addison ultimately intended to give to his book, its motive is quite clear. Analogous with the improving purpose of *Rosamond*, the *Spectator*, *Cato*, the *Drummer*, and the *Freeholder*, it is intended to reform mankind, in this instance by seeking to reclaim an average reader from scepticism. It seeks to make readily accessible and palatable to one of little learning matters which were generally expressed in abstruse or lugubrious terms. There is no doubt that further papers appearing weekly would have been popular with the readers who purchased Addison's *Spectators* upon religious topics, which had included such items as his verse paraphrase of the 23rd Psalm and his hymns. In a work of this kind the shortcomings of his scholarship would not have been of much importance, since its main appeal would have lain in a good purpose and a popular style of writing. Edmund Gibson, Bishop of London, thought sufficiently highly of the work to order its separate publication in 1731.

In the surviving text Addison begins by giving reasons why it was improbable that any of the evidences of Christianity

[1] Ibid.

would be preserved. He then sets out those facts in the life of Christ which might have come to the notice of pagan authors, and compares them with those which were so noticed, adduces the evidence of Aristides, and proceeds to verify from the fathers the authenticity of the four gospels. Examining the Christian era he points out that it was not a dark age but one of culture and philosophy, and that, in spite of the penalties attaching to Christian belief, men of learning were convinced of the truth of the gospels. The manner in which the Christian truths were handed down during the first three centuries, a time when pagan philosophers were relatively well able to examine and refute them had they wished to do so, is set forth, and he explains the strength of the auricular tradition, and stresses the importance of St. John and of the conduct of Simeon. Passing from the external evidences he examines the recorded relationship between Christians and pagans in the early centuries of the Church, and begins to speak of the important influence of the Old Testament upon the fathers. At this point the work breaks off. It is doubtful whether as much as half of the project is preserved. Whiston, who was much interested in Addison's religious studies, searched for but failed to find the materials upon which he had based his writings.[1]

Macaulay, however, poured contempt upon Addison's scholarship:

it is melancholy to see how helplessly he gropes his way from blunder to blunder. He assigns as grounds for his religious belief, stories as absurd as that of the Cock Lane Ghost and forgeries as rank as Ireland's 'Vortigern'; puts faith in the lie about the thundering legion; is convinced that Tiberius moved the senate to admit Jews among the gods; and pronounces the letter of Abgarus, King of Edessa, to be a record of great authority. . . . The truth is, that he was writing about what he did not understand.

But Addison had been attracted to religious speculation all his life and, peculiarly modern in his outlook, drew no hard line of distinction between religion, philosophy, and scientific inquiry. His regular mode of life and restrained manners

[1] Whiston, *Memoirs*, i. 299.

led contemporaries to believe that in his last years he thought
of taking Orders; and this belief was strengthened by his
religious studies. He drew to himself the dislike which
belongs to a man who is obviously virtuous and obviously
intends to be. He was called a 'parson in a tye-wig', that is to
say, disguised by the Ramillies wig worn by the laity; and old
Jacob Tonson, who was a hard-headed bookseller before all
else, disliked Addison's religious vein. The irritation was
evidently mutual, Addison finding Tonson's preoccupation
with business oppressive. Jacob's importunities to be made
stationer to the War Office when Addison was Secretary of
State had become so irritating that Tickell was instructed
to write that he might 'Spare both Mr. Craggs and your
self any further trouble of Solicitation'. When, therefore,
Tonson growled that he had always thought Addison 'a
priest at heart',[1] and that it would not surprise him to see
Cato in lawn sleeves, he need not be taken too seriously.
Not only was Addison still interested in politics, but his
Christianity had always been of so doubtful an orthodoxy
that entry into Orders would not have been easy for him.
A lifelong admiration for the views of Dr. Burnet, Benjamin
Hoadly, Whiston, and, later, George Berkeley, and friendship with Ambrose Philips and Hugh Boulter, his fellow
Demy, who were now writing the *Free Thinker*,[2] was not the
background of a man who would wish for Orders late in life
or be readily acceptable in them. Their assumption would
have immediately restricted his audience, which had been
willing to hear from a layman what it would not attend to
from the pulpit.

Addison's ideas upon religion appear more fully in his
periodicals than in his unfinished book upon the subject.
His approach to the problems of belief and its consequences
was, like so much of his criticism, largely negative. He
thought that Roman Catholicism was irrational and therefore
unworthy an intelligent man, that it was politically inimical
to a free people, and that socially it was a cause of poverty.
These were the results of his study of Locke and of his

[1] Spence, p. 200.
[2] A more orthodox Christian periodical than its name suggests today, but
nevertheless unconventional.

visit to Italy, superimposed upon an upbringing in an age which had narrowly escaped from a royal tyranny associated with Rome. For Puritanism he had an almost equal dislike and contempt:

About an Age ago it was the Fashion in *England*, for every one that would be thought religious, to throw as much Sanctity as possible into his Face, and in particular to abstain from all Appearances of Mirth and Pleasantry, which were looked upon as the Marks of a Carnal Mind. The Saint was of a sorrowful Countenance, and generally eaten up with Spleen and Melancholly.[1]

For his own part he insisted repeatedly that it was possible to *'serve God and be chearful'*.[2] A knowledge of the world was necessary to the full development of virtue,[3] and he thought saints who live in society and do charitable works much preferable to those who practise 'a sour retreat from Mankind'. Of religious[4] zeal he thought that 'where it is once laudable and prudential, it is an hundred times criminal and erroneous'; and he prescribed reason as the sovereign corrective.[5] The religion of the Quakers he dismissed as 'nothing but a new fashioned Grammar, or an Art of abridging ordinary Discourse',[6] and the Presbyterians, though in many respects laudable, he thought 'Splenatick'.[7] In human conduct Addison was more concerned with 'virtue' than with 'godliness'. He interpreted virtue as the civic quality of a good citizen, and thought of belief as an indispensable element therein:

Reason directs us, to promote our own Interest above all things. It can never be for the Interest of a Believer to do me a Mischief, because he is sure upon the Ballance of Accompts to find himself a Loser by it. . . . An Unbeliever does not act like a reasonable Creature, if he favours me contrary to his present Interest, or does not distress me when it turns to his present Advantage.[8]

For all forms of unbelief Addison entertained a contempt which exceeded by far his disapproval of erring belief. The Kit-Cat and Button's were both attacked for ungodliness, and the Whig party in general was suspect of atheism in the eyes of its High Church opponents. But to Addison the

---

[1] *S*. 494. [2] *F*. 45. [3] *S*. 245. [4] *Travels*: 'Pavia, etc.'
[5] *S*. 185, 201. [6] *T*. 257. [7] Ibid. [8] *S*. 186.

notion of disbelief in a Deity was manifestly absurd, and
wherever he speaks of atheists it is to expose them to ridicule
without the least flavour of compassion. Lady Truman in the
Drummer puts his view of the matter succinctly in a retort
to Tinsel the atheist:

Tin. Oh, I shall then have time to read you such Lectures of
Motions, Atoms, and Nature—that you shall learn to
think as Freely as the best of us, and be convinced in less
than a Month, that all about us is Chance-work.

Lady. You are a very complaisant Person indeed; and so you
would make your Court to me, by persuading me that I
was made by Chance.[1]

He was irritated not merely by the evident ridiculousness of
unbelief, but yet more by its presumption, and made Tinsel
continue to expose his own folly:

To tell you the Truth, I have not Time to look into these
dry Matters myself, but I am convinced by four or five learned
Men, whom I sometimes overhear at a Coffee-House I frequent,
that our Forefathers were a Pack of Asses, that the World has
been in an Error for some thousands of Years, and that all the
People upon Earth, excepting those two or three worthy Gentlemen, are impos'd upon, cheated, bubbled, abus'd, bamboozled.

This belief that atheism was the product of ignorance, and
his assumption that the complexity of nature was in itself
evidence of the existence of a creator, had its logical consequence when he urged upon the Royal Society the undertaking of an encyclopaedic study of natural history. This
would, he believed, reveal the orderliness of the creation
and 'not a little redound to the Glory of the All-wise
Contriver'.[2]

Characteristically, he thought that if anything could be
more ridiculous than atheism, it was a zeal for propagating
this doctrine which, by its very nature, could have no
useful consequences.[3] His zeal against unbelief led him to
pursue the atheist into what he considered to be intellectual
refuges such as deism.[4] His own faith was a mixture of belief
in the gospels and deduction of the existence of a supreme
being from the orderly nature of the universe. This position

[1] Act I   [2] *S.* 121.   [3] *S.* 185.   [4] *S.* 196.

was admirably illustrated by his hymn already quoted, and is expressed more categorically, if less convincingly, in prose in the *Spectator*: 'I think the Being of a God is so little to be doubted, that it is almost the only Truth we are sure of, and such a truth as we meet with in every Object, in every Occurrence, and in every Thought.'[1] Thus he adduced the evidence of an analysis of the bills of mortality,[2] of the starlit sky, of the works of Sir Isaac Newton,[3] of the revelations of anatomy[4] and of the nature of 'eternity' to prove the existence of God. He found the same significance in the stirrings of his soul when he contemplated the vastness of the ocean:

Such an Object naturally raises in my Thoughts the Idea of an Almighty Being, and convinces me of his Existence as much as a Metaphisical Demonstration. The Imagination prompts the Understanding, and, by the Greatness of the sensible Object, produces in it the Idea of a Being who is neither circumscribed by Time nor Space.[5]

God, therefore, was revealed to man by Christ, but was also coextensive with and deducible from 'nature'.[6]

If it was thus comfortable, useful, and logical to believe in a creator, it was equally so to believe in an after life. A principal argument for such a belief was that it engendered cheerfulness, while the atheist must live in gloomy apprehension of annihilation if he were right and of torment if he were mistaken.[7] The after life in which Addison expected to partake would, he thought, be an enlargement of the faculties of the mind and character, or indeed the reverse process. This was merely a projection of his own philosophy in heaven. 'The Business of Mankind in this Life being rather to act than to know, their Portion of Knowledge is dealt to them accordingly.'[8] It was the business of man on earth so to act that he might equip his soul to enjoy the hereafter. 'The State of Bliss we call Heaven will not be capable of affecting those Minds, which are not thus qualified for it',[9] or, stated in the opposite form: 'our whole Eternity is to take its Colour from those Hours which we employ in Virtue or in Vice.'[10] The soul, he thought, contained 'hidden

[1] *S.* 381.   [2] *S.* 289.   [3] *S.* 453   [4] Ibid.   [5] *S.* 489.
[6] *S.* 565.   [7] *S.* 381.   [8] *S.* 237.   [9] *S.* 447.   [10] *S.* 93.

Stores of Virtue and Knowledge, . . . unexhausted Sources of Perfection'. To draw upon these reserves was to continue in heaven the process of self-development advocated by the *Spectator* for those dwelling upon earth; and having experienced cheerfulness in this life to ensure happiness in the next.

When he examined his own countrymen Addison found them sadly irreligious:

> It is a melancholy Reflection, that our Country, which in Times of Popery was called the Nation of Saints, should now have less Appearance of Religion in it, than any other neighbouring State or Kingdom; . . . This is a Truth that is obvious to every one, who has been conversant in foreign Parts.[1]

The irreligion of England he ascribed partly to the excesses of the Puritans, which had rendered Christianity first odious and then ridiculous.[2] Herein lay sufficient reason to try to adapt the missionary technique of the *Spectator*, so efficacious in the reform of manners, to the propagating of the Christian faith and life. Addison appealed to his contemporaries in the name of a reason which came near to being no more than self-interest. The belief in an after life improved behaviour in this one.[3] A behaviour pleasing to God in this life is prudent since he is the only just rewarder in the next.[4] The observance of Sunday is an evidently beneficial practice.[5] To put the matter broadly:

> the Practice of Religion will not only be attended with that Pleasure, which naturally accompanies those Actions to which we are habituated, but with those Supernumerary Joys of Heart, that rise from the Consciousness of such a Pleasure, from the Satisfaction of acting up to the Dictates of Reason, and from the Prospect of an happy Immortality.[6]

Addison thus related religion, as he did all his teaching, to the intimate affairs of daily life. In so doing, it may be said, he endowed it with a worldly quality and a material appeal. Yet he gave it fresh interest by adducing an orderly creation in its support, just at the moment when the examination of the universe was beginning to capture the imagination of man.

[1] F. 37.   [2] Ibid.   [3] S. 186.   [4] S. 257.   [5] S. 112.   [6] S. 447.

In such a system of belief the priesthood could not enjoy exalted spiritual authority, though it might be of great social importance. Benjamin Hoadly, by implying this in his teaching, had precipitated the Bangorian controversy still raging. Throughout life Addison was firmly convinced that the Church of England offered a blend of reason and authority best suited to an enlightened people; but for the clergy, particularly the country clergy, he had little respect. He thought them too numerous[1] and insufficiently educated.[2] His ideal country parson was 'a good Scholar, though he does not show it', and above everything else a social worker:[3]

Nothing is so glorious in the Eyes of Mankind, and ornamental to Human Nature, setting aside the infinite Advantages which arise from it, as a strong steady masculine Piety; but Enthusiasm and Superstition are the Weaknesses of Human Reason, that expose us to the Scorn and Derision of Infidels, and sink us even below the Beasts that perish.[4]

In the light of this belief he thought the High Church clergy too friendly to Popery[5] and so purely political in inspiration that they discredited the Church. The cry of 'High Church' or 'Church in danger' was merely a means of raising a disorderly rabble.[6] The true position lay between 'superstition' and 'enthusiasm'. The Church was an integral part of the State, indissolubly linked with the Crown, which in turn must be in religious harmony with its subjects,[7] as the squire must be at one with the parson.[8]

While Addison worked upon his *Evidences* in the library at Holland House he was not unmindful of other men's projects. On Wycherley's death he had promised to subscribe to a memorial pamphlet by Gildon. This was now a source of some embarrassment, for in it Gildon attacked Pope. Consequently when he sent Addison a present of the work he received no acknowledgement and wrote again in deep distress disclaiming any intention of giving offence. He was now blind and poor.[9] During his Secretaryship of State Addison had been far removed from the atmosphere of literary quarrels. Indeed, he had never allowed them to

[1] S. 21.   [2] S. 107.   [3] Ibid.   [4] S. 201.   [5] F. 28.
[6] F. 52.   [7] F. 49.   [8] S. 112.   [9] B.M. Egerton MSS. 1971.

engross his attention, as most of his brother poets did at one time or another. He had little sympathy with the Grub Street writers:

> Would a Government set an everlasting Mark of their Displeasure upon one of those infamous Writers, who makes his Court to them by tearing to Pieces the Reputation of a Competitor, we should quickly see an End put to this race of Vermin.[1]

Gildon might well qualify for such a description. Nevertheless we have it on the authority of Lord Warwick that Addison afforded him ten guineas in charity, perhaps on this occasion. But he was now more than ever withdrawn from such matters. He did not frequent Button's as of old. The society there was declining into a factious group, and within a few years Button was drawing relief from the parish.[2] There is a story that after his marriage Addison used to escape from the stately régime at home to a neighbouring refuge in Holland House Lane.[3] This is not likely to be true if it is presented as a picture of Addison desiring to regain the company of convivial companions. During his period as Secretary of State he had been too busy or too ill for any such excursions to be possible. Then followed his convalescence and his absence in Bristol. It is only to the present winter that such stories could apply, and they appear most unlikely in view of his preoccupation with his book and his delicate health. Furthermore, Pope tells us that after his marriage he dropped the company of his coffee-house familiars.[4] Stories to the effect that Addison drank himself to the grave also purport to belong to this period. He certainly thought drinking a likely pastime for such as live 'in a moist air and moderate climate, and have no such diversions as bowling, hunting, walking, riding and the like exercises to employ them without doors'.[5] But though all his life Addison had loved wine and drank at least as heavily

---

[1] S. 451.

[2] H. J. Jesse, *Literary Historical Memorials of London*, 1847. In this year 'Critical Remarks upon the four taking plays of this season; . . . dedicated to the Wits at Button's Coffee-House. By Corinna, a Country Parson's Wife' assured them scathingly: 'your reputation is spread near 50 miles from Covent Garden.'   [3] *N. & Q.* vii. 1859, p. 275.

[4] Pope spoke to Spence about Addison's companions 'before he married Lady Warwick'.   [5] *Travels*: 'Venice.'

as the age, there is no firm evidence that he drank to excess in his latter years, and much of the gossip about alcoholism is traceable to Pope or Horace Walpole.

Cato had been revived again in October with two performances at Lincoln's Inn Fields and one at Drury Lane. Addison's Latin poem on the Magdalen altarpiece had been translated by Nicholas Amhurst and passed through three editions this year; and his *Odes* to Burnet and Hannes had been rendered by Thomas Newcomb. Both were published by Curll, apparently without authority. There was also an eight-volume reprint of the *Spectator*. Parliament met early in November when Addison was a member of the committee to draft the address in reply to the king's speech, and sat on the Committee of Privileges and Elections. In early December he attended the Privy Council to consider the dispute between the Vice-Chancellor of Cambridge University and Dr. Bentley, at which the right of the king to visit both universities was again asserted.[1] During the autumn Budgell had finally lost his places in Ireland[2] and Nicholas Rowe, the Poet Laureate, Addison's confirmed admirer, died on 6 December. As editor of Tonson's *Miscellanies* after the death of Dryden,[3] he had been connected with the publication of some of Addison's minor poetical pieces. His successor as Laureate was Lawrence Eusden; and it is likely that he was appointed on the advice of Addison, whom he venerated.

As January approached, the Earl of Warwick's peer's robes were reported making,[4] and there were great preparations at Holland House both for the coming of age and also for the birth of Addison's child. Dick Steele gave *Cato* at Drury Lane on Boxing Day, and the day following his wife died unexpectedly. She was buried in Westminster Abbey on 30 December.[5] Lady Steele, aged forty, had been pregnant, and this circumstance doubtless increased the anxiety felt by Addison with regard to his own wife, who was thirty-nine. However, on 7 January he went down to the Commons to support Lord Guernsey's motion for a clause to be added to the Schism Act. This would oblige those taking the oath

[1] P.C. 2/86, f. 193.   [2] *Weekly Packet*, 332.
[3] N. Ault, *New Light on Pope*, p. 130.
[4] *Original Weekly Journal*, 20/12/1718.   [5] Ibid. 3/1/1719.

of abjuration of the Pretender to acknowledge the divine
inspiration of the bible and the doctrine of the Trinity.[1]
Guernsey was defeated by ninety votes and Addison did
not support a further amendment moved by him. Three
days later the press reported that the Countess of Warwick was now 'looking every hour'.[2] Meanwhile Addison's friend and physician who had tended him since
1709, if not before, who had recently saved him from
death, who had been the companion of many a literary
venture, and whom Addison had defended warmly against
the attacks of the *Examiner*, himself lay dying. Addison
visited Garth on his death-bed[3] and, it is related, exhorted
that kindly sceptic to prepare for the end by acknowledging
the truths of Christian belief. Garth had told Addison in
previous discussion that the infidelity of a famous mathematician was a principal reason of his unbelief.[4] He now
asserted that Halley assured him that the doctrines of Christianity were incomprehensible and religion an imposture.
Samuel Garth died on 18 January, as Pope put it: 'the best
good Christian he although he knows it not.' On 20 January
Lord Warwick came of age and took his seat in the House of
Lords.[5] He had evidently profited from the instruction of
his stepfather over the years and now repaid him. On 28
January he was appointed to his first committee, and thereafter was singularly assiduous and active in his attendance
at Parliament.

On 30 January Lady Warwick at last gave birth to a
daughter,[6] who on 26 February was christened at St. Martin-
in-the-Fields and named Charlotte.[7] In his lifetime, Addison
had reflected in prose upon many subjects and had embodied
his conclusions in his own person as statesman, writer, and
husband. Now a father, it was late indeed to practise the
principles of fatherhood which he had stated in his writings,
and Charlotte Addison knew him only as a figure loved and
revered by others. Many years later, she requested that she
be buried 'by my dear father (if there be room in the vault)'

[1] *Parl. Hist.*, vii. 586.   [2] *Original Weekly Journal*, 10/1/1719.
[3] Spence, p. 2 n.   [4] G. Berkeley, *Works*, 1871, iii. 305.
[5] *Post Boy*, 4599, 4602,   [6] Ibid. 5605.
[7] St. Martin-in-the-Fields Baptismal Register.

and only, if that were not possible, by her mother. Thus the affection of Addison's child fed only upon the image of her father reflected in the memory of others.

In February *Cato* was revived yet again at Drury Lane and another complaint from New Jersey against Governor Hunter was hearing before the Plantations Appeals Committee of the Privy Council, which Addison attended.[1] He was now himself preparing to enter the field of political controversy once more upon a matter of first class importance. It was the Duke of Somerset who on 28 February introduced into the House of Lords a Peerage Bill designed to prevent the abuse of the royal prerogative of creating peerages and to limit it upon the accession of the Prince of Wales. This procedure had the approval of the king, but the inspiration was that of Lord Sunderland, who wished to retain control of the Government after the death of his present sovereign. The Bill therefore proposed, amongst other things, to permit the creation of six new peerages, after which only the extinction of an existing title would permit the creation of a fresh one. Though supported by the peerage in general, this measure was hotly opposed by the Tory party and the dissident Whigs, and such discussion as took place revealed that there would be difficulty in its passage through the Commons. In these circumstances a pamphlet war inevitably broke out, and on 14 March number one of a paper entitled the *Plebeian* attacked the Bill on the ground that it would give too much power to the House of Lords; the author was Sir Richard Steele.

The Peerage Bill had been Lord Sunderland's particular care and he had been to immense pains with it. His draft contains numerous corrections and notes in his own hand.[2] It now fell to Addison to support the Government of which he had so lately been a member by writing in reply to Steele. Accordingly on 19 March there appeared the first number of the *Old Whig*.[3] Addison took his stand upon the doctrines of John Locke, asserting the theory of mixed government and the division of powers. He then argued that it was a

---

[1] P.C. 2/86, ff. 224–5.   [2] Blenheim MSS. D. II. 10.
[3] Advertised in the *Daily Courant* 5430 of 18/3/1719 as an answer to the *Plebeian*.

defect of the constitution as at present established that the King might control two of the three organs of the state. He admitted that it was proposed to lop a branch of the royal prerogative, but asserted that it was a pernicious one, the absence of which would not impair the functions of the Crown, and that in any case the King had offered to forgo it if that should be the wish of Parliament. He then set out further alleged advantages of the Bill, such as that it would keep rich and able men in the lower House and would thus strengthen it. He argued the case at length and in detail in the unadorned logical style which he had used twelve years before in the *Present State of the War*. After twenty-four paragraphs he arrived at a consideration of the *Plebeian* and immediately declared war:

> As for the introduction, the digression upon the Ephori, and the concluding paragraph, they are only arguments ad conflandam invidiam, and such as are not to be answered by reason, but by the same angry strain in which they are written, and which would discredit a cause that is able to support itself without such assistance.

He then completed a detailed refutation of Steele's pamphlet which was logical and lengthy. By his thirty-sixth paragraph Addison had dealt with the *Plebeian* and turned to the *Thoughts of a Member of the Lower House*, which he answered quite shortly. The *Old Whig* was a pamphlet for those deeply versed in the controversy and written in a mood of restraint except for the reproof quoted above.

On 24 March Steele published a second *Plebeian*. He ran rapidly over various pamphlets published on the Government side of the controversy and then came to the *Old Whig*: 'The next that follows these two combatants for this bill is somebody or other that is used to masquerading, as I suppose; indeed he is so well disguised, that it is impossible to know him.' This was a subtle and biting reproof to Addison in support of whose anonymity Steele had borne the brunt of many a literary combat. At the same time it implied that Addison was not himself in his writing, while by its assumption of ignorance as to the identity of his opponent it excused Steele to his readers from the charge of barbarity to his friend. It was thus a masterpiece of compressed innuendo. He accused Addison of betraying Whig principles by seeking to increase the power of the Lords to a point where the Commons would be helpless. 'I am afraid he is so old a Whig, that he has quite forgot his principles.' Recognizing Addison's pamphlet as the official Government case, he answered its objections to the first *Plebeian* and then dissected its argument. For Dick it was a restrained performance. He merely permitted himself to hint at bribery by the Government to support its case; thought that Addison 'wilfully or ignorantly' mistook his point; and suggested that he lacked spirit to act as he thought right on this occasion. Possibly what annoyed Addison most was Steele's interpretation of the allegations which had been made in the *Old Whig* about the purchase of peerages, as a charge against the King, for whom he had a deep admiration. This was perhaps the more telling because the sale of peerages was in fact a scandal, though it was German favourites and not George himself who benefited thereby. In his last paragraph Steele suggested that by saying that the King had signified his assent to the project Addison was arguing that he had improperly taken the decision before the Commons had considered the matter. Both of these were deliberately unfair presentations of what Addison had said and of what the King had done, but Steele's pamphlet was a good piece of political polemic, subtly designed to cause as much hurt and annoyance to the author personally as its writer knew how to devise. After its publication there followed a pause of some days, and, no second *Old Whig* appearing, Steele published another *Plebeian*, passing on to other matters with the remark that 'age is apt to be slow'.

But the innuendoes in the second *Plebeian* had sunk deep. Addison was not accustomed to the rough and tumble of pamphleteering and particularly resented the thrusts of his former friend, to whom he published a reply on 2 April.[1] Thoroughly angry, he began:

The author of the Plebeian, to show himself a perfect master in the vocation of pamphlet-writing, begins like a son of Grub

[1] Advertised in *Daily Courant* 5442 of 1/4/1719.

Street, with declaring the great esteem he has for himself, and the contempt he entertains for the scribblers of the age. One would think, by his way of presenting it, that the unexpected appearance of his pamphlet was as great a surprise upon the world as that of the late meteor, or indeed something more terrible, if you will believe the author's magnificent description of his own performance.

Then, warming to his task, he accused Steele of having 'with much ado' gone through his pamphlet without really attempting to answer it. 'Having routed Baronius and confounded Bellarmine, pass we on to the next, said the country curate to his admiring audience.' He then answered Steele's complaint of his taking the title of *Old Whig* by reproving him for taking that of the *Plebeian*, 'a title which he is by no means fond of retaining, if we may give credit to many shrewd guessers', an insinuation that Steele himself coveted a peerage. In the succeeding paragraphs he fell upon Steele's pamphlet in a manner which reveals that if he had refrained all his life from verbal fisticuffs, it was not for lack of ability to contrive them. There was even an oblique and rather offensive reference to 'Little Dickey'. If he could have permitted himself to be angry oftener, Addison might have written some excellent political pieces. He then continued with a mixture of logic and ridicule to attack the remainder of the *Plebeian*, winding up with the following paragraph:

I should not have given myself, or the public, all this trouble, had I not been so peremptorily called to it by the last Plebeian. I do assure him my silence hitherto was not the effect of old age, as it has made me slow, but to tell him the truth, as it has made me a little testy, and consequently impatient of contradiction, when I find myself in the right. I must own, however, that the writer of the Plebeian has made the most of a weak cause, and do believe that a good one would shine in his hands; for which reason, I shall advise him, as a friend, if he goes on in his new vocation, to take care that he be as happy in the choice of his subject as he is in the talents of a pamphleteer.

This was doubtless a reply to the personal imputation which had been most wounding in Steele's pamphlet, namely that Addison had written at the desire of the Government in a cause which he knew to be a poor one.

Steele replied, but his paper contained nothing substantial

except the last paragraph, which was a personal reproof. He quoted a sentence from the *Old Whig* which ran: 'The rest of this paragraph is very mean; and this author's menaces in this place are as vain, as his compassion in another part of his pamphlet is insolent.' Steele then commented:

Authors in these cases are named upon *Suspicion*; and if it is right as to the *Old Whig*, I leave the world to judge of *this cause* by comparison of this *performance* to his *other writings*. And I shall say no more of what is writ *in support of vassalage*, but end this paper, by firing every free breast with that noble exhortation of the tragedian: . . .

and thereafter he quoted six appropriate lines from *Cato*, a rich treasury which had already been drawn upon for phrases with which to rebuke its author.

Numerous other pamphlets appeared in the Peerage Bill controversy, some referring to Addison's writing. Budgell is said to have taken part, as did Robert Walpole who, writing of Addison's *Old Whig*, referred angrily to 'those who set him to work', doubtless meaning Lord Sunderland, and assailed the rest of the pamphlet presuming that the author had 'more wit than money' and concluding that he had said 'not only all that the subject will admit of but a great deal more'. But Addison wrote no more *Old Whigs*, although his papers were published in a second edition on 10 April,[1] and again on 30 November.[2] Steele's quotation from *Cato* thus closed the controversy between the two men. It would have been an entertaining little tiff had it not taken place between two lifelong friends. Addison had been provoked by the strength of his resentment to abandon the reserve which he had adhered to throughout his life. In fact an important political controversy had become much more a personal paying of scores, the accumulation of several years of growing mutual offence, than a direct argument upon merits. The fact that the *Old Whig* was not printed with Addison's collected works probably indicates that he regretted his action. In any case it had been in vain, for on 14 April the Government, alarmed at the extent of opposition to the Bill, postponed further progress therewith.

[1] Advertised in *Daily Courant* 5450 of 10/4/1719.
[2] Ibid. 5650 of 30/11/1719.

Back at Holland House Addison's portrait was being painted by Michael Dahl, fashionable Swedish rival and successor to Sir Godfrey Kneller. Steele's latest biographer points out that Dahl found a man much changed from the one painted by Kneller, two years before.[1] Dahl, who fulfilled Addison's requirement of an artist, that he should 'vie with nature',[2] saw a man:

puffy over his eyelids, puffy of cheek, with the creases which age draws from the nose to mouth-corners marked deep. The veins and the tendons on the hands stood out, like ranges on relief-maps. Dahl did not, probably with truth, paint happiness on the face of his subject, for the fine eyes had grown dullish, and the light from them was gone. A brick-red velveteen jacket hardly brightened the likeness, but the elaborate cuffs, almost to the elbow, did recapture one's attention to the hands, slenderly beautiful still.[3]

It was now a period of inactivity in Addison's life, and it is difficult to penetrate the family circle in which he lived. That Lady Warwick was fond of her husband, but not to the exclusion of her son, is evident from her will. She directed that she be buried near her son in Kensington Church, failing that, 'where my dear husband Mr. Addison is buried'.[4] There were other choices open to her had she not felt so inclined. She even left a conditional annuity of £50 to Dorothy Combes, 'sister of my late dear Husband', probably in an endeavour to discharge his responsibilities and indicating that the two women were upon good terms. Charles Lillie recalled of Lady Warwick that she 'always passed for a woman of small sense, but it is not known that she gave him (Addison) any domestic chagrin'. This is probably a near approximation to the truth; and writing for Curll immediately after Addison's death a pamphleteer described the marriage as a happy one, which, while it may mean little from such a source, probably indicates that it was not notoriously the contrary.[5] Lord Warwick, Addison's stepson, was intelligent and promising. That he was frequently in the

[1] Willard Connely, *Sir Richard Steele*, p. 361.
[2] *Poem to Sir Godfrey Kneller on his Portrait of the King.*
[3] W. Connely, op. cit.   [4] *N. & Q.* x. 513.
[5] G. J., *Memoirs of the Life of the Rt. Hon. Joseph Addison Esq.*, 1719, p. 8.

company of Pope may perhaps suggest that he was impatient of his decorous stepfather. But had there been any dislike or hostility between them it is most improbable that Tickell would have addressed his 'Elegy' on Addison to this young man. At this time, Addison had few preoccupations. *Cato* was again on the boards at Drury Lane: and a collection of his eight Latin poems with English translations and of his 'Dissertation' upon the Roman poets was preparing for the press. Life at Holland House in the company of his wife and young Warwick was probably quite agreeable.

On 14 May the young earl was made a Gentleman of the Bedchamber to the King,[1] possibly as a reward for Addison's championship of the Peerage Bill, and because of Warwick's assiduity in the Lords. There was no reward for which Addison could now ask upon his own account, and on the same day he made his will. It was quite a short document. It bequeathed all of his possessions to his wife, with a legacy of five hundred pounds to his sister Dorothy and an annuity of fifty pounds to his 'mother', still living at Coventry. This was his step-mother, who seems to have played little part in his life. To his daughter Charlotte he left nothing, but expressed confidence that his wife, who was executrix of the will, would 'take due care of her education and maintenance and provide for her in case she live to be married'. He evidently felt too weary of the world to remember old friends with small gifts, or even to include the young earl in his plans. Possibly he had already made private provision for such matters. As for the rest, he trusted 'my dear and loving wife' to use her discretion.

The will itself does not recite, as is sometimes the case, that it was made in the expectation of death, but it was certainly made in the belief that death could not long be delayed. 'I Joseph Addison now of the Parish of Kensington . . . being of sound and disposing mind and memory yet considering the uncertainty of this mortal life, do think it necessary to make and ordain this my last will and testament . . .' might be but a form of words were it not for the actions surrounding the document. Addison was at this time negotiating the sale of his place as Keeper of the Records in

---

[1] *Post Boy*, 4649.

Dublin. This was approved on 21 May by Craggs, who told the Lord Lieutenant that the purchaser 'gives a good round price'. Addison's undoubted intention was to convert into cash an asset which would be of no value after his death. At the same time at Lichfield an outstanding obligation of a different kind was being discharged. A monument to Dean Addison was in process of erection inside the west wall of the cathedral at the expense of his son, surmounted by the arms which both men bore but to which neither of them seems to have been entitled. It also stands as a monument to the purity and excellence of Joseph's taste in architectural matters at the end of a life much of which had been devoted to polite studies. On 4 June a further step directly in anti-cipation of death was the letter which Addison addressed to James Craggs constituting him his literary executor and commending Thomas Tickell to him for carrying out his instructions. This has always seemed to posterity, and un-doubtedly was, a curious choice. Craggs was a young man of charm and ability, who had gained wealth in the South Sea Company, and who won good opinions everywhere. He had been associated with Addison in politics since the accession of King George and, though well known to him before that time, became increasingly intimate in Addison's later years.[1] Addison had invested in South Sea Stock, perhaps under his guidance; and since resigning from the Secretaryship of State he had been at peculiar pains on every occasion to emphasize his affection for his successor. That there was such an affection there is no reason to doubt, even if Pope had not borne witness thereto.[2] That Addison was so anxious to demonstrate its existence may have been some reflex of disappointment, the wish that the world should know that he relinquished the Secretaryship, at a time when he might justly have claimed twenty years of power and fame, without bitterness, or envy of the man who succeeded him. He had certainly been careful to make this clear in his letter to Swift, whose esteem he valued. He now exaggerated in his desire to prove a small if important point:

I cannot wish that any of my Writings should last longer than

[1] Tickell, Preface to Addison's *Works*.
[2] *Verses Occasioned by Mr. Addison's Treatise of Medals.*

the Memory of our Friendship, and therefore I thus publickly bequeathe them to you, in return for the many valuable Instances of your Affection.

But it was Steele who had been above all other friends in intimacy during the period of Addison's life when most of his works had been written. That he did not bequeath the literary executorship of his works to the joint author of so many of them marks in part the estrangement between the two men and in part Addison's estimate of Steele in the capacity of a painstaking editor and trustee.

Of Tickell, on whom the burden of editing now fell, Addison went on to say: '. . . I have left the care of them [his writings] to one whom, by the experience of some years, I know well qualified to answer my intentions.' This was quite true; for where Dick Steele was brilliant and unpredictable, Thomas Tickell was competent and obedient. It was a convenient arrangement, for Tickell was Under-Secretary to Craggs. Evidently in expectation of death, Addison continued: 'I have no time to lay out in forming such Compliments as would but ill suit that Familiarity between us, which was once my greatest pleasure and will be my greatest Honour hereafter.' What Addison's instructions to Tickell were we cannot be sure except that they are presented to us in the form of the four quarto volumes of his collected works, including the *Dialogues upon Medals*, *Of the Christian Religion*, and some minor unpublished pieces the ascription of which caused surprise, as Dick Steele had hitherto been thought their author. The *Drummer* was a notable omission, possibly because the author of *Cato* did not wish that triumph lessened by the stage failure of another piece. Addison had evidently spent some time in revising his works for publication. A collation of texts of the *Campaign* and the *Spectator*, for example, shows that in each case considerable textual alterations were made at various times.[1] Many of these modifications took the form of toning down expressions which might by any stretch of imagination be thought to overstate or distort a meaning. He thus applied the principle of restraint to his own works in their

[1] See R. D. Horn, *Studies in Bibliography*, iii (1950), and Jan Lannering, *Studies in the Prose Style of Joseph Addison*, Uppsala, 1951.

latest revision, and verified Budgell's remark that 'That great man is well known to have been so extreamly jealous of his reputation that no consideration could have made him say any thing in print, for which he apprehended his judgment might be call'd in question'.[1] Addison did not forget a dying compliment to 'the most gracious and amiable Monarch that ever filled a Throne', thus carrying to the grave his admiration for the cold-hearted but extremely capable king whose establishment upon the throne had been one of the major themes of his life work. Though this admiration sprang from sources different from those which normally give rise to human affection it was undoubtedly sincere.

Two days after making his literary testament Addison wrote to the Secretary of the South Sea Company instructing him to accept transfers of South Sea Stock to Lady Warwick. On 15 June his resignation of his Irish place became effective. Thereafter, having settled all of his worldly affairs in a methodical fashion, it remained to compose himself for death by applying those precepts of philosophy which he had advocated in his lifetime.

The first onset of Addison's illness seems not to have been noticed in the press, or perhaps he had been sick so often during the past year that it was no longer heeded. Thomas Burnet the previous autumn had written to George Duckett in words characteristic of the man:

Addison is now spending his last hours at the Bristol waters, nobody imagines he will live long; considering to how little purpose he has lived, I think he cannot [here a well-wisher of Burnet's erased what appear to have been the words] dy too soon.[2]

On 6 June the press reported that Addison was again dangerously ill.[3] Tickell records that after his release from office his health improved so considerably that his friends had hoped that he would live for many years. His last illness was, he thought, precipitated by too much application to his book upon the Christian religion and perhaps by his sedentary mode of life. He records that it was 'a long and

[1] Budgell, Bee, ii. 856.
[2] B.M. Add. MS. 36772, f. 193b and his letters ed. Nichol Smith, p. 156 n.
[3] Original Weekly Journal of that date.

painful relapse into an asthma and dropsy'. Addison, though he read William Hervey with pleasure,[1] was not in the least hypochondriac. But he was profoundly suspicious of the medical profession:

> This Body of Men, in our own Country, may be described like the *British* Army in *Caesar*'s time: Some of them slay in Chariots, and some on Foot. If the Infantry do less execution than the Charioteers, it is because they cannot be carried so soon into all Quarters of the Town, and dispatch so much business in so short a Time.[2]

Now bereft of the kindly ministrations of Samuel Garth, Addison was content to die. He wished no molestation, and Young tells us that, given over by his physicians, he sent them away. His friend Whiston, who begged to see him, was refused entry.[3] That he saw Dick Steele is most improbable. Dick, who in retrospect felt uncomfortable about their quarrel, tried to make light of it, and in the year following wrote thus:

> these two men lived for some years last past, shunning each other, but still preserving the most passionate concern for their mutual welfare. But when they met they were as unreserved as boys, and talked of the greatest affairs, upon which they saw where they differed, without pressing (what they knew impossible) to convert each other.[4]

But if in fact Addison had felt any such 'passionate concern', it is likely that he would have sent for Steele on his deathbed, for which he was making such careful preparations; and had he done so, it is certain that Steele would have proclaimed the fact to the world. It is only possible to conclude that Addison in the course of years had arrived at one of those characteristic moral judgements which no consideration of sentiment would be permitted to disturb, and that this judgement was adverse to his friend.

Budgell reported of Addison that he 'used frequently to say that there was no such thing as real conversation between more than two persons'.[5] But the man who had excelled in friendship, to whose magnetic personality so

---

[1] T. 119.   [2] S. 21.   [3] Whiston, *Memoirs*, i. 303.
[4] *Theatre*, No. 12, 1720.
[5] E. Budgell, *Memoirs of the Boyles*, 1732, ix.

many of his contemporaries have borne witness, seems to
have made no effort to take leave of his friends. But he
sent for John Gay through the agency of Lord Warwick.
The poet found himself kindly received and Addison proceeded to beg his pardon for some injury which he felt he
had done and the nature of which Gay could not conjecture.[1]
It may have been some event in the tangled relationship
between the Button's senate and Pope's friends.[2] If Addison
was setting his mind at rest by removing therefrom the last
outstanding causes of uneasiness he needed to feel no concern
about Gay's friend Pope. Pope seems to have purged his
emotions of his dislike of Addison, perhaps by transferring
it all to Philips, whom he hated cordially as long as they both
lived, and whom he held responsible for their quarrel.
Edward Young, who was particularly close to Addison in his
last years, was probably the person to whom Swift referred
when he wrote to Pope that 'our friend Addison had a
Young fellow (now of figure in your Court) whom he made
to dangle after him, to go where, and to do whatever he
was bid'.[3] Young seems to have taken to himself the grave
melancholy of Addison's last year of life. He recalled that:

more than once I have heard the famous Mr. Addison say that it
was his wish—if it so pleased God—to die in the summer, because
then, walking abroad, he frequently contemplated the works of
God, which gave such a serious turn and awful composure to the
mind as best qualified it to enter the Divine presence.

It was now such a time, with the beauty of Holland House's
stately surroundings in its freshness and prime. Addison
had remarked that:

Death only closes a Man's Reputation, and determines it as
good or bad. . . . As there is not a more melancholy Consideration
to a good Man than his being obnoxious to such a Change, so there
is nothing more glorious than to keep up an Uniformity in his
Actions, and to preserve the Beauty of his Character to the last.[4]

[1] Spence, p. 150.
[2] See J. Gay, *A Letter to a Buttonian Knight*. Addison had also been severe
upon Gay's *Three Hours after Marriage*, to such an extent as to sting the
author into a defence (Spence, p. 202). But it is unlikely that this troubled
him now.
[3] Williams, iii. 458.   [4] *S.* 349.

He had studied attentively the deaths of Augustus,[1] Socrates,[2] Petronius Arbiter, Seneca, Cato,[3] and Sir Thomas More. He decided that 'The End of a Man's Life is often compared to the winding up of a well-written Play, where the principal Persons still act in Character, whatever the Fate is which they undergo.'[4] He particularly admired Sir Thomas More because 'His Death was of a piece with his Life. There was nothing in it new, forced or affected.'[5] His conviction that death might be borne with cheerfulness by those equipped with philosophy to endure it is recorded in innumerable places in his writings.[6] Furthermore, he attached much beyond a personal significance to a proper behaviour in that hour:

The truth of it is, there is nothing in history which is so improving to the reader, as those accounts which we meet with of the deaths of eminent persons, and of their behaviour in that dreadful season. . . .

Addison had used every intellectual weapon in a crusade for the improvement of mankind, and the most remarkable feature of his life had been, what he so admired in Lord Somers,[7] its awe-inspiring consistency. It now remained for him to die as he had lived, according to his philosophy; that is to say, cheerfully, in the calm self-possession of faith and in a manner exemplary to his fellow men. All of these requisites he prepared to fulfil when on 17 June he sent for young Warwick to come to him. Entering the room on the first floor leading off the great library, the young man, after a considerable silence, reminded Addison of his presence by saying that he believed he had sent for him, and presumed that he had some commands to lay upon him. Addison then grasped the young man's hand and said in a low voice: 'See in what peace a Christian can die.' These words uttered, he died shortly thereafter[8] in the weeping presence of Thomas Tickell.[9]

[1] *S.* 317.   [2] *S.* 183.   [3] *S.* 349.   [4] Ibid.
[5] Ibid.   [6] e.g. *S.* 381.   [7] *F.* 39.
[8] E. Young, *Conjectures on Original Composition*.
[9] Miss Aikin thought this scene so theatrical that it owed much to the embellishments of the narrator, though she recognized that the couplet in Tickell's elegy quoted below indicated that Addison had died in an exemplary Christian manner. The present writer is not in agreement with her. The whole

The body of Joseph Addison lay in state in the Jerusalem Chamber of Westminster Abbey on 26 June. On that night he was buried in King Henry VII's Chapel in the Albemarle vault, next to Charles Montagu. This would undoubtedly be by his own expressed wish. Francis Atterbury, a lifelong friend though a political opponent, whose eloquence was commended in the sixty-sixth *Tatler*, performed the rites;[1] and Westminster boys noticed the tenderness with which he read the service upon this occasion.[2] Addison is thus buried in the building in which he had strolled as he meditated the twenty-sixth *Spectator*:

for my own Part, though I am always serious, I do not know what it is to be melancholy; and can therefore take a View of Nature in her deep and solemn Scenes, with the same Pleasure as in her most gay and delightful ones. . . . When I look upon the Tombs of the Great, every Emotion of Envy dies in me; when I read the Epitaphs of the Beautiful, every inordinate Desire goes out; when I meet with the Grief of Parents upon a Tomb-stone, my Heart melts with Compassion; when I see the Tomb of the Parents themselves, I consider the Vanity of grieving for those whom we must quickly follow. . . . When I read the several Dates of the Tombs, of some that dy'd Yesterday, and some six hundred Years ago, I consider that great Day when we shall all of us be Contemporaries, and make our Appearance together.[3]

It fell to Thomas Tickell to write the lines which commemorate his patron, and in so doing to prove to posterity the real depth of his affection for the dead man. A competent but not an inspired poet, he was transported by his sorrow

of Addison's life in its consistency pointed to such a studied ending. The words uttered would be sincere, and in keeping with all of Addison's teaching; and it is inconceivable that such a man, who had written so much on the subject of death, should not have prepared himself therefor. Young is a reliable witness concerning Addison; and Horace Walpole's comment on his account: 'unluckily he died of brandy—nothing makes a Christian die in peace like being maudlin' (Letter of 16/5/1759) is not supported by evidence. Not himself a witness of the event, Young tells us that he was told the story by Tickell with the tears still undried in his eyes. This is also a probable circumstance. Both men had been Addison's secretaries and they were close friends. Tickell we know was at Holland House and witnessed Addison's death. All of these considerations seem to point to the likelihood of this famous story being true and I entertain no doubt upon the point.

[1] *Evening Post*, 1545.
[2] Macaulay, *Misc. Works*, ii. 220.   [3] *S.* 26.

to speak in words which will live as long as the English
tongue:

> Can I forget the dismal might that gave
> My soul's best part for ever to the grave!
> How silent did his old companions tread,
> By midnight lamps, the mansions of the dead,
> Through breathing statues, then unheeded things,
> Through rows of warriors, and through walks of kings!
> What awe did the slow solemn knell inspire;
> The pealing organ, and the pausing choir;
> The duties by the lawn-rob'd prelate pay'd;
> And the last words, that dust to dust convey'd!
> While speechless o'er thy closing grave we bend,
> Accept these tears, thou dear departed friend,
> Oh gone for ever, take this long adieu;
> And sleep in peace, next thy lov'd Montagu!
> . . . . [44 lines] . . . .
> That awful form (which, so ye heavens decree,
> Must still be lov'd and still deplor'd by me)
> In nightly visions seldom fails to rise,
> Or, rous'd by fancy, meets my waking eyes.
> If business calls, or crowded courts invite,
> Th' unblemish'd statesman seems to strike my sight;
> If in the stage I seek to soothe my care,
> I meet his soul, which breathes in Cato there;
> If pensive to the rural shades I rove,
> His shape o'ertakes me in the lonely grove:
> 'Twas there of Just and Good he reason'd strong,
> Clear'd some great truth, or rais'd some serious song;
> There patient show'd us the wise course to steer,
> A candid censor, and a friend severe;
> There taught us how to live; and (oh! too high
> The price for knowledge) taught us how to die.

XII

A LIFE AFTER DEATH

WRITING an imaginary history supposed to be compiled in the reign of King George the Twentieth, but which was published in the year 1719, Thomas Gordon recorded of his own period: 'Then also flourished the immortal Mr. Addison, whose fame is in every mouth, and his works in every hand . . .',[1] thus making it clear not only that Addison was thought of in his own time as universally admired, but also that he was expected to achieve immortal fame. 'To Addison . . . we are bound by a sentiment as much like affection as any sentiment can be, which is inspired by one who has been sleeping a hundred and twenty years in Westminster Abbey': thus wrote Macaulay of the character and personality of Addison; and his words would have been true at any time until the end of the nineteenth century.

Johnson had already declared of his prose style that: 'Whoever wishes to attain an English style, familiar, but not coarse, and elegant, but not ostentatious, must give his days and nights to the volumes of Addison.' At the end of the nineteenth century Saintsbury found of this opinion that 'abating its exclusiveness a little, it remains true still'.[2]

Writing in our century Mr. C. S. Lewis remarked of Addison: 'If he is not at present the most hated of our writers, that can only be because he is so little read';[3] and lecturing in the United States in 1933, Mr. T. S. Eliot told his audience that 'Addison is a writer towards whom I feel something very like antipathy'.[4]

Of the chorus of praise which followed Addison's death

[1] T. G., *A dedication to a great Man concerning dedications*, 6th edn., 1719, p. 22.
[2] *A Short History of English Literature*, p. 539.
[3] *Essays on the 18th century presented to D. Nichol Smith*: 'Addison', p. 13.
[4] *The Use of Poetry and the Use of Criticism*, 1933, p. 59.

the evidence is everywhere to be found surviving. The
Weekly Medley, for example, felt

bound to lament the death of a great and more than that, a good
Man, and excellent poet, Mr. Addison: I own him to have been in
some things, almost all indeed, excepting his gentlemanly moderation, a person of different party from myself. Be it therefore his
peculiar desert that by the excellence of his vast genius he provok't
my praise while living, and that his death extorts my tears.[1]

The *Post Boy*, also a political opponent, observed that 'his
knowledge of ancient and modern literature well entitled
him to the censorship of Great Britain; so did his success in
all kinds of Poesy gain him the Immortal name of the English
Maro'.[2] At the Oxford funeral of Dr. Fayrer, who had been
Bursar and Vice-President of Magdalen in Addison's time,
the preacher, Thomas Collins, 'dilated on his being a means
of discovering Mr. Addison's genius'.[3] The spell of his
influence continued to bind his companions. Steele's later
life was full of reminiscence of his friend:

he was above all men in that Talent we call Humour, and enjoyed
it in such Perfection, that I have often reflected, after a Night
spent with him apart from all the World, that I had had the pleasure
of conversing with an intimate Acquaintance of Terence or Catul-
lus, who had all their Wit and Nature heighten'd with Humour,
more exquisite and delightful than any other Man ever possessed.

Blackmore wrote of 'that great and good man'.[4] Tickell,
who had a distinguished career both as public servant and
minor poet, caused it to be inscribed on his monument after
his death that 'his highest honour was that of having been
the friend of Addison', whom he thought 'the first man of
the age'.[5] Budgell, who commited suicide by jumping into the Thames with his pockets full of pebbles, left a note
in which he recorded his opinion that 'What Cato did, and
Addison approved, cannot be wrong . . .'. In his own
generation nobody doubted Addison's pre-eminence.

[1] *Weekly Medley*, xviii.
[2] *Post Boy*, 4665.
[3] R. E. Tickell, *Tickell*, letter Young–Tickell, 1/3/1720; also Hearne.
[4] Sir R. Blackmore, *Compleat Key to the Dunciad*, 1728.
[5] Addison's *Works*, 1721, Preface.

In the generation of Johnson and Horace Walpole there was some reaction against the adulation which Addison had received during his lifetime and after his death. The school of criticism which propounded that 'Everything that is one, should have a beginning, a middle, and an end' began to analyse Addison's works and, with ample apologies, to discover that they contained imperfections.[1] But Johnson never questioned Addison's stature. Horace Walpole had read so much of his work that he echoes and quotes almost subconsciously, though enjoying a piece of cynicism at Addison's expense whenever opportunity offers. Gibbon was advised to study Addison and Swift to recover the correctness of the English tongue,[2] and Chesterfield remembered his proudest moment as a meeting with Addison and Steele in youth.[3] Beattie, whose influence upon the education of the young was considerable, thought that:

if writing be good, in proportion as it is useful; and if its noblest use be, to improve the heart, refine the taste, and sweeten the temper, Addison is of all uninspired authors, at least in prose, the best, and the most delightful.[4]

This was the consensus of opinion in the latter part of the century, epitomized in a note from William Pitt the elder to his nephew: 'Spectators, especially Mr. Addison's papers, to be read very frequently at broken times in your room.'[5] In this universal admiration several different elements played their part. As a poet Addison was generally esteemed; as a playwright, *Cato* had earned him a distinction not enjoyed by any predecessor on the strength of a single play; as a writer of periodical papers he was acknowledged, not as the foremost, but as unchallenged master of the field; as a critic he was thought to be more original and penetrating than was perhaps the case because he had made criticism popular; as a writer of travel literature, his was the book which had become the standard of polite composition. But

---

[1] Blair, *Lectures*, many refs.   [2] Low, *Life of Edward Gibbon*, p. 96.
[3] Chesterfield, *Letters*, ed. Dobrée, i. 39.
[4] *Dissertations Moral and Critical*, 1783, p. 198.
[5] Cf.*Spectator* 135: 'For my own part I look upon it as a peculiar Blessing that I was Born an *Englishman*.' King George III, speech from the throne, 1760: 'Born and educated in this country, I glory in the name of Briton.'

H h

it was Addison's reforming influence which impressed contemporaries more than any other of his achievements; and in this it was as much his personal example as his writings which won commendation. A synthesis of what was most admirable in cavalier and puritan, it was felt that he had wrought a powerful revolution in the taste, and hence in the conduct, of the age. As Tickell expressed it: 'If Mr. Addison's example and precepts be the occasion that there now begins to be a great demand for correctness, we may justly attribute it to his being first fashioned by ancient models, and familiarized to propriety of thought and chastity of style.'[1] Blackmore gave it as his opinion that 'all his fine Raillery and Satire, tho admirable in their kind, never reclaim'd one vicious Man, or made one Fool depart from his Folly';[2] but it was the purpose and effect of Addison's example and teaching, not to reclaim the vicious and foolish, but to prevent the mass of mankind from following their example; and a correspondent of the *Spectator* testified:[3]

That your Writings have made Learning a more necessary Part of good Breeding than it was before you appear'd: That Modesty is become fashionable, and Impudence stands in need of some Wit, since you have put them both in their proper Lights. Profaneness, Lewdness, and Debauchery are not now Qualifications, and a Man may be a very fine Gentleman, tho' he is neither a Keeper nor an Infidel.

In the opening years of the nineteenth century it was correct to say with Chalmers, editing the *Spectator*, that that work was 'one of the first books by which both sexes are initiated in the elegancies of knowledge'.[4] And because it was universally read as a model of correctness in style and elegance in humour, as well as for its sentiments which embodied the genius of the age, its teachings gained a currency denied to any other book except the Bible. As the century progressed, the Addison cult gained the fervour of worship. Reproving the type of critic whom Addison had ridiculed in the *Spectator*, Miss Lucy Aikin thus warned mankind against detractors of his teachings: 'Let every

---

[1] Addison, *Works*, 1721, Preface.
[2] Blackmore, *Epistles upon Several Subjects*, Preface, p. xlviii.
[3] S. 461.   [4] *Spectator*, Chalmers edn., Preface.

reader, jealous of the delicacy of his taste, or anxious not to dry up in himself the sources of the purest and most exalted pleasures, shun as his bane these wretched disenchanters, who blast with their pestiferous breath the very roses of paradise.'[1] It was this sensibility to the 'purest and most exalted pleasures' which was particularly associated with Addison. His philosophy of reason and moderation, his restraint, above all his delicate humour and bold character drawing, combining with an earnest religious and moral purpose, derived from Classical sources but fostered the sentimentalism of the age. Sir Roger de Coverley was one of the most substantial persons of the nineteenth century. Tickell had praised Addison because he began in literature a reformation tending to correctness and away from 'natural wildness'.[2] Warton had objected:

> What are the lays of artful Addison,
> Coldly correct, to Shakespeare's warblings wild?[3]

But Addison's philosophy of life was manly and rational, and commanded an admiration which reached a climax in Macaulay:

Men may easily be named, in whom some particular good disposition has been more conspicuous than in Addison. But the just harmony of qualities, the exact temper between the stern and the humane virtues, the habitual observance of every law, not only of moral rectitude, but of moral grace and dignity, distinguishes him from all men who have been tried by equally strong temptations, and about whose conduct we possess equally full information.

So profound and far-reaching was Addison's influence upon the conduct of mankind by the time that Macaulay wrote that his reforming purpose had been largely achieved:

So effectually, indeed, did he retort on vice the mockery which had recently been diverted against virtue, that, since his time, the open violation of decency has always been considered among us as the mark of a fool. And this revolution, the greatest and most salutary ever effected by any satirist, he accomplished, be it remembered, without writing one personal lampoon.

[1] L. Aikin, *Life of Addison*, ch. x.
[2] Addison, *Works*, 1721, Preface.   [3] J. Warton, *The Enthusiast*.

It is this revolution in its completeness which has caused
Addison's writings to pass from the list of favourite reading
in the present century. So fully did mankind endorse his
teaching that many of his precepts came to be thought trite,
axiomatic, or even presumptuous, and to him was attributed
an undisciplined romanticism which had no part in his
make-up. As Mr. C. S. Lewis expressed it:

> He appears to be (as far as any individual can be) the source of a
> quite astonishing number of mental habits which were still
> prevalent when men now living were born. Almost everything
> which my own generation ignorantly called Victorian seems to
> have been expressed by Addison. It is all there in the Spectator—
> the vague religious sensibility, the insistence upon what came later
> to be called Good Form, the playful condescension towards
> women, the untroubled belief in the beneficence of commerce,
> the comfortable sense of security which far from excluding,
> perhaps renders possible the romantic relish for wildness and
> solitude. . . . Everything the moderns detest, all that they call
> *smugness*, *complacency*, and *bourgeois ideology*, is brought together in
> his work and given its most perfect expression.[1]

But Addison set out to raise the cultural and moral
standards of his own time. His crusade and its phenomenal
success are together evidence of the fact that there were
at that time many people who had both the means and the
desire to become more 'polite'. Readers of the *Spectator*,
relatively few of whom were courtiers, clergy, or scholars,
lived at the close of a century of social upheavals at the
beginning of which most people ate with their fingers, but
which ended with the widespread use of knives and forks.
No doubt Addison's writing, addressed to a receptive
society in his own times, did much to establish the standards
of tolerance, civility, and good sense of a later age. The
influence of his life and writings upon the development of
English society would be a fascinating study, and lies far
beyond the purpose and scope of a biography. The present
writer, from a dozen years of intimacy with materials which
would form a small part of such a project, believes that if
completed it would reveal that no other Englishman has
influenced the social development of his country more power-

---

[1] *Essays on the 18th century presented to D. Nichol Smith*: 'Addison', p. 13.

fully. But for the purpose of this book the deliberate judgement of a contemporary is more authoritative than the consequences, sometimes fortuitous, which flow from a man's
work in the course of centuries. Pope, who had analysed
with cruel precision the latent defects of Addison's character,
also committed his achievement to posterity in lines of
sober majesty:

> Unhappy Dryden!—in all Charles's days,
> Roscommon only boasts unspotted bays;
> And in our own (excuse some courtly stains)
> No whiter page than Addison remains.
> He, from the taste obscene reclaims our youth,
> And sets the passions on the side of truth;
> Forms the soft bosom with the gentlest art,
> And pours each human virtue in the heart.[1]

[1] *Imitations of Horace*: Epistle to Augustus, 1737.

INDEX

Academiae Oxoniensis Gratulatio pro exoptato . . . Regis Gulielmi, verses to William III, 21.

Account of the Greatest English Poets, see below, Joseph Addison, *Minor Works*.

Act of Grace projected (1717), 398.

Act of Settlement (1701), 107.

Adams, William, Fellow of Magdalen, 39, 50, 51.

Addison family: Steele's account of, 8–9.

Addison, Mrs., *see* Warwick, Charlotte, Dowager Countess of.

Addison, Anne, sister of Joseph, 4, 5.

Addison, Charlotte, Joseph's daughter: her birth, 447.

Addison, Dorothy (formerly Danvers), stepmother of Joseph, 88, 257, 454.

Addison, Dorothy, sister of Joseph: m. (1) Revd. James de Sarte; (2) Daniel Combes: born, 4; 45 n., 88, 150, 154, 186, 200, 286; second marriage, 321; 454.

Addison, Captain Edward, 235, 311, 318, 327.

Addison, Gulston, brother of Joseph: his birth, 4; and East India Company, 23, 45 n.; small legacy from his father, 88; prospers in India, 111; in Madras, 149, 150; his death, 185; his will, 185–6; his Indian estate, 205–6, 234, 237, 247–8; and Mrs. Pitt's estate, 206; his legacy, 289–91, 318; his legacy settled, 373.

Addison, Jane, sister of Joseph, dies in infancy, 3.

Addison, Jane (formerly Gulston), mother of Joseph, 3; dies at Lichfield in 1684, 7–8; 88.

ADDISON, JOSEPH (1672–1719):
Chronological Index
1. *A Son of the Church* (1672–87), 1–10: studies at Amesbury and at Salisbury Grammar School, 5; his sensitiveness, 5; studies at Lichfield Grammar School, 6; development of his taste, 7; attitude towards his father, 8–9; and the classics, 9; at the Charterhouse, 9–10; sent to Oxford, 10.

2. *An Oxford Career* (1687–99), 11–44: his tact and restraint, 11; matriculated at The Queen's College, 11; influenced by Gilbert Burnet, 12; supporter of William III, 12; Waynflete scholar, 13; early contemporaries, 13–14; college emoluments, 14; Higden scholar, 14; character and habits of life, 15 sqq.; advocates shadow boxing, 16; contempt for minutiae of scholarship, 17; pupils, 18; on the Royal Society, 18; his classicism, 19, 24; B.A., 19; reads philosophy, 20; arrested by the proctors, 20 n.; M.A., 21; agent for Tonson, 22; in London, 23; residence in Oxford, 23; and Dryden, 21–22, 27; projected translation of Herodotus, 23; interest in music, 24; claims substantial knowledge of Greek, 24; disapproves of Milton's politics, 26; aspires to fame as dramatist, 27; quality of his poetic work, 27; inception in faculty of divinity, 28; and the choice of a career, 28–30, 31, 33; and the sea war, 32; considers himself a poet, 32; political verse, 32–33; foreign travel, 33–34; approaching his patrons, 34; his attractions, 34; his translations, 36–37, 44; probationer Fellow, 37; Latin oration, 37; in residence at Magdalen, 37; and the classics, 37; his Latin verse, 37–41; tutoring, 40–41; proposed Treasury grant for travel, 43, 45; memories of Oxford, 43, 44; dispensed from taking holy orders, 43; leaves Oxford for London, 44.

3. *A Grand Tour* (1699–1703), 45–90: his father's financial help, 45; his fellow travellers, 45–46;

Eusden, Laurence, Poet Laureate, 85, 209, 252, 267, 307, 446.
Examen Poeticum, 22.
Examen Poeticum Duplex, 38, 78.
The Examiner: under Swift's control, 200, 201; 256; review of *Cato*, 272; attacks the Duke of Marlborough, 279; attacked by Steele, 283.

Falaiseau, Monsieur, Hanoverian courtier, 108.
Farrington, Thomas, M.P. for Malmesbury, 194, 256.
Fayrer, James, bursar of Magdalen College, Oxford, 17, 464.
Felton, Henry, critic, 226.
The Female Tatler, 203.
Fenelon, François, author of *Télémaque*, 55.
Finch, Daniel, 6th Earl of Winchilsea, 79, 80, 81.
First State of Muhammedanism (Lancelot Addison), 5.
Fisher, John, Bishop of Rochester, 61.
Fleetwood, Edward, trustee of Gulston Addison's estate, 205, 237.
Fleetwood, John, Consul at Naples, 404.
Fleetwood, William, Bishop of St. Asaph, 214.
Florence, Italy, 69–70, 181.
The Flying Post, and Defoe, 297.
Foedera (Thomas Rymer), 169.
A Fond Husband (Thomas D'Urfey), 280.
Fontenelle, Bernard le Bovier de, *Plurality of Worlds*, 77.
Fonvive, J. de, 103.
Forbes, George, 3rd Earl of Granard, Governor of Minorca, 404.
Forbin, Claude, Comte de, French admiral, 131.
Fort St. George, 149, 150, 185, 205; *see also* India.
Forth, Firth of, 130, 131.
The Fountain Tavern, 251.
Fountaine, Sir Andrew, 189.
France: Addison visits, 47–58; on French opera, 47, 57; art, 48, 57; palaces, 49; language, 52; drama, 57–58; and the invasion of Scotland, 130–1, 175, 300–1; and Addison's *The Drummer*, 354; and colonies, 391; Regent of, 392; relations with England, 397–400.
Franchise, parliamentary, 133–4.
Frederick, grandson of George I, his birth and christening, 413–14.
Frederick I, King of Prussia, 109.
The Free Thinker (Ambrose Philips), 439.
The Freeholder (Joseph Addison), 341–50; *see also* Joseph Addison, *Minor Works*.
Freeport, Sir Andrew, *see* the *Spectator*.
Friend, Dr. John, of Christ Church, Oxford, 39.
Frowde, Philip, poet and pupil of Addison, 18, 40, 49, 129, 135.
Frowde, William, army officer, 49, 135.
Fulham, Addison resides at, 137.
Fuller, Mr., Consul at Leghorn, 404.
The Funeral (Sir Richard Steele), 87.

Gallas, Johann Wenzel, Comte de, 410.
Gallia, Italian actress and singer, 120.
Garth, Sir Samuel, Addison's physician, poet, 53, 191, 192, 194, 200, 238, 243, 264, 333, 345, 372, 412, 416, 447, 458.
Gay, John: on *Whig Examiner*, 193; burlesque on *Cato*, 276; *The Shepherd's Week*, 334; *Trivia*, 334; *The What d'ye Call It*, 204, 205, 264, 287, 292, 334, 459.
The Gazette, see *The London Gazette*.
Genoa, Republic of, 60, 72; relations with Britain, 380; *see also* Henry Davenant.
George I, King of England: Addison on, 110; Regency appointed until his arrival, 293; accession proclaimed, 294–5; political opposition not sufficiently prepared, 295; his emergency escort, 297; House of Commons addresses, 298; and Irish government, 298; and France, 300–1; and Queen Anne's funeral, 301; arrangements for bringing him to England and for the

PRINTED IN GREAT BRITAIN
AT THE UNIVERSITY PRESS, OXFORD
BY VIVIAN RIDLER
PRINTER TO THE UNIVERSITY